D1766734

KEELE
UNIVERSITY

LIBRARY

Please return by the last date or time shown

PRIVATE LIBRARIES IN RENAISSANCE ENGLAND

A Collection and Catalogue of Tudor and Early Stuart Book-Lists

Volume V
PLRE 113–137

MEDIEVAL & RENAISSANCE

TEXTS & STUDIES

VOLUME 189

PRIVATE LIBRARIES IN RENAISSANCE ENGLAND

A Collection and Catalogue of
Tudor and Early Stuart Book-Lists

Volume V
PLRE 113–137

R. J. FEHRENBACH
General Editor

E. S. LEEDHAM-GREEN
Editor in the United Kingdom

MEDIEVAL & RENAISSANCE TEXTS & STUDIES
Tempe, Arizona
1998

*The publication of this volume has been supported
by a grant from the National Endowment for the Humanities,
an independent federal agency.*

Library of Congress Cataloging-in-Publication Data

Private libraries in Renaissance England : a collection and catalogue of Tudor and
early Stuart book-lists / R. J. Fehrenbach, general editor, E. S. Leedham-Green,
editor in the United Kingdom.
    v. 1 — (Medieval & renaissance texts & studies : v. 87, 105, 117, 148, 189)
    Includes bibliographical references and index.
    Contents: v. 1. PLRE 1–4. — v. 2. PLRE 5–66. — v. 3. PLRE 67–86. — v. 4. PLRE
87–112. — v. 5. PLRE 113–137.
    ISBN 0–86698–099–7, v. 1; ISBN 0–86698–151–9, v. 2; ISBN 0–86698–170–5, v. 3;
ISBN 0–86698–188–8, v. 4; ISBN 0–86698–231–0, v. 5.
    1. Private libraries—England—History—1400–1600—Sources. 2. Private libraries—
England—History—17th–18th centuries—Sources. 3. Books and reading—England—
History—16th century—Sources. 4. Books and reading—England—History—17th
century—Sources. 5. Private libraries—England—Catalogs—Bibliography. 6. Book
collecting—England—History—Sources. 7. Library catalogs—England—Bibliography.
I. Series.
Z997.2.G7P75 1998
017.10942—dc20   91–18418
                                                                          CIP

This book is made to last.
It is set in Baskerville, smythe-sewn,
and printed on acid-free paper
to library specifications
Printed in the United States of America

Table of Contents

Table of Annotated Book-lists by PLRE Number

Table of Annotated Book-lists by Owner

Contributing Editors

W. P. GRIFFITH
Senior Lecturer, School of History and Welsh History
University of Wales, Bangor

KATY HOOPER
Special Collections Librarian, Sydney Jones Library
University of Liverpool

E. S. LEEDHAM-GREEN
Deputy Keeper of the Archives
and Fellow of Darwin College, Cambridge

SUSAN MARTIN-JOY
Editorial & Research Assistant, *Private Libraries in Renaissance England*

DAVID C. MCPHERSON
Professor of English, University of New Mexico

ANN R. MEYER
Assistant Professor of Literature, Claremont McKenna College

RIVES NICHOLSON
Assistant Editor, *Private Libraries in Renaissance England*

MARC L. SCHWARZ
Associate Professor of History, University of New Hampshire

JOCELYN SHEPPARD
Project Manager, National Technology Transfer Center

GRADY A. SMITH
Independent Scholar

ELIZABETH M. TILYOU
Reference Librarian, Adelphi University and
the United States Merchant Marine Academy

S. P. WAYLAND
Independent Scholar

LAETITIA YEANDLE
Curator of Manuscripts, the Folger Shakespeare Library

Acknowledgments

This, the fourth and largest volume in the Oxford series of PLRE, has been in preparation longer than any in that group, in great part because of the volume's size, but also because of the simultaneous construction of *EXPLORE*, the CD-ROM form of PLRE (see p. xxiv below). The completion of these two separate but complementary projects could only have been accomplished with the support and contributions of those whom I here wish to acknowledge and thank.

I am deeply grateful for the longtime and indispensable support of the National Endowment for the Humanities, an independent federal agency, which support—and this needs saying—is not only financial but includes the encouragement and assistance always forthcoming from the NEH staff. Now, in addition to that public support, I am greatly pleased to express my gratitude to the Gladys Krieble Delmas Foundation for its generous financial assistance that began in 1997 and to Katherine K. Curtis for her valuable gift in 1995 from the estate of her husband, Mark H. Curtis, one of PLRE's original Advisory Editors. Funds from these sources, along with the financial support from The College of William and Mary, particularly from the offices of the Provost and the Dean of the Faculty of Arts and Sciences, have advanced the work of PLRE in general and have helped make possible both this volume and *EXPLORE*.

My gratitude to those who have given of their time and labor—

both diligent and learned—over the last few years is first and primarily expressed to the Contributing Editors listed elsewhere in these pages. The Consulting Editor to PLRE for its Oxford series, Simon Bailey, Archivist of Oxford University, had more questions than usual put to him as a result of historical sources having garbled the records of three owners of book-lists appearing in this volume (Atkins, Grant, and Seacole). I am grateful to him for digging out the correct information, and I am grateful to Sachiko Kusukawa, Fellow of Trinity College, Cambridge, for calling attention to a scrambled portion of the index in Volume 4 (see *Additions and Corrections*, pp. 335–36 below). Kenneth Wilson, who, with good will and perseverance, developed the program for *EXPLORE*, provided information during its construction that was invaluable in removing from the database a variety of motes and beams that eluded the human eye in earlier proofings. Pete Hoyle and Lance Richardson at William and Mary continued to cast their medicinal eyes on the problems that inevitably infect the several computers employed in producing PLRE. With this volume, Georgianna Ziegler joins PLRE's Advisory Editors, having marked that association by answering questions from her vantage place as Reference Librarian at The Folger Shakespeare Library. And my editorial colleague, Elisabeth Leedham-Green, continued, whenever requested, to address with wit and expertise whatever PLRE matters required addressing.

My thanks to all.

Williamsburg, Virginia   R.J.F.
August, 1998

Common Abbreviations

SOURCES

A&R   A. F. Allison and D. M. Rogers. *A Catalogue of Catholic Books in English Printed Abroad or Secretly in England 1558–1640.* Bognor Regis, 1956 [Reprints 1964 and 1968].

ARCR   A. F. Allison and D. M. Rogers. *The Contemporary Printed Literature of the English Counter-Reformation between 1558 and 1640.* 2 volumes. Aldershot, 1989–1994.

Adams   H. M. Adams. *Catalogue of Books Printed on the Continent of Europe, 1501–1600, in Cambridge Libraries.* 2 volumes. Cambridge, 1967.

Alumni Cantabrigienses — John Venn and John Archibald Venn. *Alumni Cantabrigienses: A Biographical List of All Known Students, Graduates and Holders of Office at the University of Cambridge from the Earliest Times to 1751, Part I.* 4 volumes. Cambridge, 1922–1927 [Reprint 1974].

Alumni Oxonienses — Joseph Foster, compiler. *Alumni Oxonienses: The Members of the University of Oxford, 1500–1714, Their Parentage, Birthplace, and Year of Birth . . .* 4 volumes. Oxford, 1891–1892.

Arber   *A Transcript of the Registers of the Company of Stationers of Lon-*

don, edited by Edward Arber. 5 volumes. London/Birmingham, 1875–1894 [Reprint 1967].

Athenae Cantabrigienses — C. H. Cooper and T. Cooper. *Athenae Cantabrigienses.* 3 volumes. Cambridge and London, 1858–1913 [Reprint 1967].

Athenae Oxonienses — Anthony à Wood, with additions by Philip Bliss. *Athenae Oxonienses: An Exact History of All the Writers and Bishops Who Have Had Their Education in the University of Oxford. To Which Are Added the Fasti, or Annals of the Said University.* 5 volumes. London, 1813–1820.

Aureliensis — *Index Aureliensis: Catalogus librorum sedecimo saeculo impressorum.* Volumes 1–11. Baden-Baden, 1965–1996 [incomplete].

Benzing   Josef Benzing. *Lutherbibliographie Verzeichnis der gedruckten Schriften Martin Luthers bis zu dessen Tod.* Baden-Baden, 1966.

Bezzel   Irmgard Bezzel. *Erasmusdrucke des 16. Jahrhunderts in Bayerischen Bibliotheken.* Stuttgart, 1979.

BCI   E. S. Leedham-Green. *Books in Cambridge Inventories: Booklists from Vice-Chancellor's Court Probate Inventories in the Tudor and Stuart Periods.* 2 volumes. Cambridge, 1986.

BL   *General Catalogue of Books Printed to 1955* [in the British Library].

BN   *Catalogue Général des Livres Imprimés de la Bibliothèque Nationale* [Paris].

Boase   C. W. Boase, ed. *Register of the University of Oxford.* Volume 1 (1449–1463; 1505–1571). Oxford, 1885.

Bodleian   *Catalogus librorum impressorum Bibliothecae Bodleianae in Academia Oxoniensi.* 4 volumes. Oxford, 1843–1851.

BRUC   A. B. Emden. *A Biographical Register of the University of Cambridge to 1500.* Cambridge, 1963.

Brunet   Jacques-Charles Brunet. *Manuel du libraire et de l'amateur de livres.* 6 volumes. Paris, 1860–1865 [Reprint 1922] (Supplements, 2 volumes, 1878–1880).

BRUO   A. B. Emden. *A Biographical Register of the University of Oxford to AD 1500.* 3 volumes. Oxford, 1957–1959.

BRUO2   A. B. Emden. *A Biographical Register of the University of Oxford AD 1501 to 1540.* Oxford, 1974.

BSB   *Bayerische Staatsbibliothek alphabetische Katalog 1501–1840.* 60 volumes. Munich, New York, London, Paris, 1987–1990.

BT   Elly Cockx-Indestege and Geneviève Glorieux. *Belgica Typographica 1541–1600. Catalogus librorum impressorum ab anno*

*MDXLI ad annum MDC in regionibus quae nunc Regni Belga-
rum partes sunt.* Nieuwkoop, 1968.

CBEL   George Watson, editor. *The New Cambridge Bibliography of
English Literature [600–1660].* Volume 1. Cambridge, 1974.

Clark   Andrew Clark, ed. *Register of the University of Oxford.* Volume
2. 4 parts (1571–1622). Oxford, 1887–1889.

Clessius   Joannes Clessius. *Unius seculi; eiusque virorum literatorum
monumentis tum florentissimi, tum fertilissimi, ab anno Dom.
1500 ad 1602. Nundinarum autumnalium inclusive elenchus
consummatissimus librorum.* Frankfurt am Main, 1602.

Cockle   Maurice J. D. Cockle. *A Bibliography of Military Books up to
1642.* Second edition. London, 1957 [Reprint 1978].

Copinger   W. A. Copinger. *Supplement to Hain's Repertorium Bibliographicum* [with supplements]. London, 1895 [–1914] [Reprints
1926 and 1950].

Cranz   F. Edward Cranz. *A Bibliography of Aristotle Editions, 1501–
1600.* Second edition, with addenda and revisions by Charles
B. Schmitt. Baden-Baden, 1984.

CSPD   *Calendar of State Papers: Domestic Series.*

CSPD, *Addenda* – *Calendar of State Papers: Domestic Series, Addenda, 1580–
1625.*

CTC   *Catalogus Translationum et Commentarium: Medieval and
Renaissance Latin Translations and Commentaries.* Eds. Paul
Oskar Kristeller, F. Edward Cranz, and Virginia Brown.
Volumes 1–7. Washington, D.C., 1960–1992 [incomplete].

DM   T. H. Darlow and H. F. Moule. *Historical Catalogue of the
Printed Editions of the Holy Scripture in the Library of the British
and Foreign Bible Society.* [English and Non-English] 2 volumes. London, 1903–1911. [See DMH following.]

DMH   T. H. Darlow and H. F. Moule (with revisions by A. S. Her-
bert). *Historical Catalogue of the Printed Editions of the Holy
Scripture in the Library of the British and Foreign Bible Society.*
[English; Volume 1 of DM revised] London, 1968.

DNB   *Dictionary of National Biography.*

Durling   Richard J. Durling. "A Chronological Census of Renaissance
Editions and Translations of Galen." *Journal of the Warburg
and Courtauld Institutes* (1961), 24:230–305.

EUL   *Catalogue of the Printed Books in the Library of the University of
Edinburgh.* 3 volumes. Edinburgh, 1918–1923.

Gardy   Frédéric Gardy. *Bibliographie des oeuvres théologiques, littéraires,
historiques et juridiques de Théodore de Bèze.* Geneva, 1960.

Goff   F. R. Goff. *Incunabula in American Libraries: A Third Census*
            [with supplements]. New York, 1973 [Revised 1964 edition].
Greg   W. W. Greg. *A Bibliography of the English Printed Drama to the
            Restoration*. 4 volumes. London, 1939–1959 [Reprint 1970].
GW   *Gesamtkatalog der Wiegendrucke*. 9 volumes. Leipzig/Stuttgart,
            1925–1938, 1968–1991 [incomplete].
Hain   L. Hain. *Repertorium Bibliographicum*. 2 volumes. Stuttgart,
            1826–1838, 1891 [Reprints 1948 and 1966].
HC *1509–1558* – S. T. Bindoff, editor. *The House of Commons 1509–1558
            (The History of Parliament)*. 3 volumes. London, 1982.
HC *1558–1603* – P. W. Hasler, editor. *The House of Commons 1558–1603
            (The History of Parliament)*. 3 volumes. London, 1981.
HMC   *Historical Manuscripts Commission.*
IGI   *Indice generale degli incunaboli della biblioteche d'Italia*. 6 vol-
            umes. Rome, 1943–1981 [incomplete].
Jayne   Sears Jayne. *Library Catalogues of the English Renaissance.*
            Reissue with new preface and notes. Godalming, 1983.
Keen   Ralph Keen. *A Checklist of Melanchthon Imprints Through
            1560. Sixteenth Century Bibliography 27*. St. Louis, 1988.
Ker   N. R. Ker. "The Provision of Books," in *The Collegiate Univer-
            sity*, edited by James McConica. Volume 3 of *The History of
            the University of Oxford*, General Editor, T. H. Aston. Oxford,
            1986.
Klaiber   Wilbirgis Klaiber. *Katholische Kontroverstheologen und Reformer
            des 16. Jahrhunderts*. Münster, 1978.
Köhler   W. Köhler. *Bibliographia Brentiana*. Berlin, 1904 [Reprint
            1963].
Labarre   Albert Labarre. *Bibliographie du Dictionarium d'Ambrogio
            Calepino (1502–1779)*. Baden-Baden, 1975.
Madan   Falconer Madan. *Oxford Books: A Bibliography of Printed Works
            Relating to the University and City of Oxford or Printed or Published
            There*. 3 volumes. Oxford, 1895–1931 [Reprint 1964].
McConica   James McConica. "Elizabethan Oxford: The Collegiate Soci-
            ety," in *The Collegiate University*, edited by James McConica.
            Volume 3 of *The History of the University of Oxford*, General
            Editor, T. H. Aston. Oxford, 1986.
NK   Wouter Nijhoff and M. E. Kronenberg. *Nederlandshe Bibliogra-
            phie van 1500 tot 1540*. The Hague, 1923–1966.
NLM6   Richard J. Durling. *A Catalogue of Sixteenth Century Printed
            Books in the National Library of Medicine*. Bethesda, Maryland,
            1967.
NUC   *National Union Catalogue. Pre-1956 Imprints.*

OED   *The Oxford English Dictionary.* 20 volumes. Second edition. Prepared by J. A. Simpson and E. S. C. Weiner. Oxford, 1989.

Oates   J. C. T. Oates. *A Catalogue of the Fifteenth-Century Printed Books in the University Library, Cambridge.* Cambridge, 1954.

Ong   Walter J. Ong, S. J. *Ramus and Talon Inventory. A Short-Title Inventory of the Published Works of Peter Ramus (1515-1572) and of Omer Talon (ca. 1510-1562) in Their Original and in Their Variously Altered Forms.* Cambridge, Massachusetts, 1958.

PCC   *Prerogative Court of Canterbury.*

Pell   M. Pellechet and M. L. Polain. *Catalogue général des incunables des bibliothèques publiques de France.* 26 volumes. Lichtenstein, 1970 [Reprint].

Polain   Marie Louis Polain. *Catalogue de livres imprimés au XVe siècle des bibliothèques de Belgique.* 4 volumes [and supplements]. Brussels, 1931-1978.

Proctor   Robert Proctor. *An Index to the Early Printed Books in the British Museum: From the Invention of Printing to the Year MD.* 2 volumes [and supplements]. London, 1898-1906 [several reprints in the 1920s].

RRstc   James J. Murphy. *Renaissance Rhetoric: A Short-Title Catalogue of Works on Rhetorical Theory from the Beginning of Printing to* A.D. *1700, with Special Attention to the Holdings of the Bodleian Library, Oxford.* New York and London, 1981.

Shaaber   M. A. Shaaber. *Check-list of Works of British Authors Printed Abroad, in Languages Other Than English, to 1641.* New York, 1975.

Staedtke   Joachim Staedtke. *Heinrich Bullinger Bibliographie.* Volume 1. Zürich, 1972.

STC   A. W. Pollard, G. R. Redgrave, W. A. Jackson, F. S. Ferguson, and Katherine F. Pantzer. *A Short-title Catalogue of Books Printed in England, Scotland, and Ireland and of English Books Printed Abroad, 1475-1640.* Second edition. 3 volumes. London, 1976-1991.

Stübler   Eberhard Stübler. *Leonhart Fuchs: Leben und Werk.* Münich, 1928.

VD16   *Verzeichnis der im deutschen Sprachbereich erschienenen Drucke des XVI. Jahrhunderts.* 22 volumes. Stuttgart, 1983-1995.

VHc   Ferdinand Vander Haeghen. *Bibliographie des oeuvres de Josse Clicthove.* Ghent, 1888.

VHe   Ferdinand Vander Haeghen. *Bibliotheca Erasmiana.* Ghent, 1893 [Reprints in 1961, 1972, and 1990].

Wellcome   *A Catalogue of Printed Books in the Wellcome Historical Medical Library.* Volumes 1–2. London, 1962.

Wing   Donald Wing. *Short-title Catalogue of Books Printed in England, Scotland, Ireland, Wales, and British America and of English Books Printed in Other Countries: 1641–1700.* Revised edition. 3 volumes. New York, 1972–1988.

DEGREES

B.A.	Bachelor of Arts
M.A.	Master of Arts
B.C.L.	Bachelor of Civil Law
B.Cn.L.	Bachelor of Canon Law
B.Gram.	Bachelor of Grammar
B.M.	Bachelor of Medicine
B.Th.	Bachelor of Theology
D.C.L.	Doctor of Civil Law
D.Cn.L.	Doctor of Canon Law
D.U.L.	Doctor of Civil and Canon Law (LL.D.)
D.M.	Doctor of Medicine
D.Th.	Doctor of Theology
O.P.	Ordinis Praedicatorum

Introduction

With this volume, PLRE continues publication of 162 book-lists[1] contained in the inventories taken between 1507 and 1653 under the juris-
diction of the Chancellor of Oxford University (exercised by the Vice-
Chancellor), mostly for the purposes of probate. The lists are published
in chronological order (see **Order** under *Methodology and Format* below);
two lists, dating from 1560 and long erroneously thought to have been
inventories compiled in 1580, and twenty-three lists, dating from 1570 to
1579, appear in the present volume to bring the total of Oxford lists
edited in PLRE to 133 (Volume 2 of PLRE [1993] contains sixty-two lists,
Volume 3 [1994] contains twenty, and Volume 4 [1995] contains twenty-
six). The remaining twenty-nine Oxford lists will be published in Volumes
6 and 7. Like all book-lists in this Oxford series, the lists appearing in this
volume (except for the supplement to PLRE 4) are found in manuscripts
in the Oxford University Archives housed in the Bodleian, specifically in
the probate records and the Chancellors's Registers. These records have
been made available on microfilm by Research Publications under the
title *The Social History of Property and Possessions: Part I: Inventories and*

---

[1] This number differs from the total given in Volume 1; in editing, several lists
were identified as printer's stock or as books borrowed from colleges, not personally
owned books.

Wills, Including Renaissance Library Catalogues, from the Bodleian Library, Oxford, 1436–1814 (Reading, England, 1990).

A team of nearly fifty international scholars, working from transcriptions of the manuscripts made by Mr. Walter Mitchell, M.A. (sometime Assistant to the Keeper of the University Archives), has been enlisted to edit the 162 lists. By granting PLRE permission to use his transcriptions, a labor of many years, Mr. Mitchell has immeasurably reduced the time required to make this information available to the scholarly community. This professional generosity places the PLRE project and scholars working in the Tudor and early Stuart periods greatly in Mr. Mitchell's debt.

The purpose and three-part design of PLRE has been described in its first volume, to which the reader is referred for details (PLRE, Volume 1, pp. xvi–xviii). In brief, however, Part 1 of PLRE is the published form of annotated book-lists associated with Tudor and early Stuart men and women; PLRE 113–137 are contained in this volume. Part 2 is in electronic form and is a cumulative and more detailed catalogue of those lists and others (Appended, or APND lists) previously published elsewhere. This electronic form of the entire PLRE database, Volumes 1–5 and all the APND lists (as found under 2, APND LISTS in the Cumulative Catalogue at the end of PLRE volumes), appears as *EXPLORE* on CD-ROM and is available from Pegasus Press (University of North Carolina at Asheville, Asheville, North Carolina 28804). As it is made clear in the detailed descriptions of the published and electronic forms (PLRE, Volume 1, pp. xvi–xvii), *EXPLORE* and the PLRE volumes are different and complementary presentations of the PLRE database. They are not substitutes one for the other. Part 3, the PLRE Cumulative Catalogue, is a series of indices and concordances to the complete PLRE database. This Cumulative Catalogue, which appears near the end of each volume of PLRE, is regularly enlarged and revised to incorporate newly edited book-lists.

Errors and Corrections

Anyone with even a passing acquaintance with early book-lists knows that their fragmentary and too often simply illegible entries make identifying books an extremely difficult task. Further, details of these early books resist uniformity, even when the works are identifiable; yet this information must be uniformly entered into a database to meet the categorical requirements of PLRE's design and purpose. However methodical and careful the labor, providing error-free information under such conditions is more to be wished than realized. Happily, however, the ease with which a database can be corrected promises that any misdirection PLRE may inadvertently provide will be temporary, and will encourage PLRE's users to become part of the scholarly collaboration that has always been central to the project. The editors of PLRE ask, therefore, that errors noted and corrections proposed be forwarded (with supporting evidence for the corrections) to either address found in the Appendix.

Methodology and Format

Identification and Annotation. Identification of items, the annotations, and the bio-bibliographical introductions preceding the book-lists are the work of diverse scholars and reflect their individual research and study. But collaboration, intending to provide a reasonable uniformity, is routine at all editorial stages of the PLRE project. Consistency is necessary to avoid offering confusing information when the results of research conducted by individual scholars are combined; it is also required to meet the practical demands of a searchable database. For example, editorial consultation would discourage identifying a late sixteenth-century manuscript entry of *Elucidarius poeticus* as the school text written by Johann Gast and issued, apparently, in a single edition (1544) to the disregard of the widely published encyclopedic work of the same name by Hermann Torrentinus, appearing as it did in at least a dozen editions before 1600. If, however, a Contributing Editor has good reason to question whether such an entry represents the Torrentinus title, the Gast work, or Robert Estienne's book, another popular work of that same name, the Torrentinus identification would carry one of the standard PLRE qualifying terms, *probable* or *perhaps*. Understandably, annotations to such an item may also vary from one Contributing Editor to another.

Among the most troublesome entries to identify with consistency and uniformity are the appearances, by name only, of various widely published authors such as Virgil, Quintilian, Horace, Terence, Sallust, Lucian, and Homer. On occasion, context and supplementary information (e.g., *cum commento*) will help to identify these entries as *Works*, but generally editors choose to qualify such items with *probable* or *perhaps* if they do not list them as *Unidentified*. Similarly, when an entry consists of the name of an author popularly associated with one particular title, that work is assumed in the absence of a clear connection to one of his less well-known works, with a qualification often attached. Thus, an entry of "Agostino Dati" will usually result in an identification of *Elegantiolae*, and an entry of "Theodorus, *Gaza*" will normally result in an identification of *Institutiones grammaticae*, both usually qualified. Such differences as may appear in identifications and commentary, then, reflect the regard that

PLRE has for reasonable disagreement among scholars, particularly in an area of research where the primary material is so often fragmentary and imprecise.

Order. Within each volume, the book-lists are presented in chronological order by year of the owner's death, or, if the date of death is unknown, by year of an owner's will if extant, and then alphabetically within each year. In some cases, however, the dates of death and a will are unknown; in others, documents and biographical sources disagree about the dates; and in still others, such dates are irrelevant (e.g., an inventory of books may have been compiled for purposes other than evaluating an owner's estate, with the owner dying years later). In these cases, other information, such as the date of the inventory, is used to determine the place of a book-list in PLRE order. An explanation of the determining date is parenthetically appended to each owner's name in the Table of Contents. For more complete information about the owners' dates of deaths, wills, and inventories, readers are directed to the individual introductions and to the PLRE database.

Introduction. Each book-list is preceded by an introductory essay treating biographical and bibliographical matters relating to the owner and the collection. The introduction is not intended to provide a complete analysis of the book-list, and even less a full study of the owner's life. Except where two dates are provided (e.g., 25 February 1587/88), all dates are given in new style.

Names of owners have been regularized according to modern forms with, in many cases, variant spellings provided. Such alternate forms are derived from published sources such as BRUO, BRUO2, and *Alumni Oxonienses*; whenever the form given in BRUO or BRUO2 (the standard authorities on members of Oxford University to 1540) differs from the adopted PLRE form, it is listed first among the variants and identified. The name of the owner at the head of the introduction is followed by: the owner's profession and appropriate academic degrees (if any), the kind of source the list of books is taken from (inventory, receipt, will, etc.), and the date of that book-list.

For nearly all of these Oxford men happening to die in residence at whatever stage of their academic career, PLRE has chosen to use the generic term "scholar" to indicate their presumed avocations at the time of death and to distinguish graduates still at the University from those who had gone out into the world. Most of them would have been at least in minor orders, and a good many of them supported in their studies by the revenue of one or more benefices, but they are not here designated "clerics" except where there is some evidence that they were actively serving a cure. (Similarly, medical graduates are not designated "physician" in the absence of evidence for their actually having practiced as such.) Instead their status is indicated either by the term "student," for those who had not yet graduated, or by their degree or degrees. A Doctor of Theology who had pursued the conventional course would previously have graduated B.A., M.A., and B.Th. The dates, and any other details, of these earlier degrees will, when documented, be found in the introductions to each list, but in the headings the senior degree alone will usually be found. Two degrees are given where neither is significantly senior to the other (as in the case of a Doctor of both Civil and Canon Law), where more than one senior faculty is involved (as in the case of a theologian having also qualified in canon law), or when holding certain degrees together indicates the exercise of an option (it was, for example, possible to proceed to medical degrees either via the arts course or not: where a Bachelor of Medicine had previously graduated M.A., both degrees are shown).

Classmarks and Transcriptions. The Oxford University Archives classmark of the document containing the book-list and the source of any previously published transcriptions of the list are appended to the introduction.

Reference List. Placed between the introduction and the annotated entries and serving both, a reference list provides a bibliography of works cited in each (except for the sources found in the Common Abbreviations). The form used in the reference list is the Author-Date System of the *Chicago Manual of Style*, 13th ed., 1982, 399–435.

The List of Books. The book-list is presented, with clarifying emendations, as it appears in the manuscript. Each entry is preceded by its assigned PLRE Number.

Entries. Each entry is composed of some or all of the following:[2]

---

[2] PLRE has attempted to avoid the use of signs and symbols; this design is most prominently seen in the use of *perhaps* and *probable* (or *probably*) to convey degrees of doubt, and of commonly employed abbreviations, such as *c.* and *et seq.*

> **PLRE Number Book-list entry**
>   Name of author (alternative name of author). *Title of work*. Other con-
> tributors. Place of publication: stationer(s), date or range of dates.
>   STC status. Annotations. Language(s) of book. Cost or appraised value
> and date of same. Current location of the book.[2]

PLRE Number. A PLRE Number is always composed of at least two numbers separated by a period. The number preceding the period identifies
the place of the book-list within the PLRE catalogue, and the number following the period identifies the individual entries within that book-list.
Thus, the forty-seventh item in the third book-list published in PLRE is
assigned *3.47*. A PLRE Number that carries an extension (beginning with
a colon) identifies an entry in the book-list that represents two or more
works. If published separately, the works are assigned numeric extensions
(e.g., *3.48:1* and *3.48:2*); if published together in one volume, they are
assigned letters (e.g., *3.49:A* and *3.49:B*). Entries that contain unidentified
multiple works are assigned an appropriate range extension (e.g., *3.50:1–
4* would be used to identify "four bookes of verse"). If the number of
works listed is unknown, the extension given is "multiple" (e.g., *3.51
multiple* would be used to identify "divers small bookes"). PLRE numbers
in APND lists (see p. xxiv above) are preceded by *Ad*, as in *Ad4.36*.

Book-list entry. Within certain limits, book-lists are transcribed to repro-
duce as faithfully as possible the entries as they appear in the manuscript.
The letters *u/v* and *i/j* are regularized and modernized, and thorn is
transcribed *th*. Readily identifiable contractions and abbreviations are not
altered (e.g., *agt, Mr*, and *wch*), but the less common ones, along with unusual or ambiguous spellings, are followed by an emendation placed in
square brackets (e.g., *The trades inclease* is transcribed as *The trades inclease
[increase]*). Damaged or otherwise illegible portions of the manuscript are
treated similarly (e.g., *fil us* [to represent a hole between the *l* and the *u*
in the manuscript] is transcribed as *fil*us [filius]*). Where an item is
recorded as an object of bequest in a Latin will, its accusative form is
retained.

Name of author (alternative name of author). Names are STC forms; for
names not appearing in the STC, forms are taken from a list of Uniform
Names developed by PLRE. Uniformity, as well as ease of recognition, is
the goal of PLRE in establishing names. But 1) in cases where the established name differs from the form in the entry and may cause confusion
for the user, and 2) in cases where two different forms make virtually

equal claims for recognition among scholars, parenthetical alternative forms are given. Examples: *Nicolas Des Gallars* is followed by *(Nicolaus Salicetus)*, *John Holywood* by *(Joannes Sacrobosco)*, and *Nicolaus Tudeschis* by *(Panormitanus)*.

On occasion, the name of an editor will appear in this place, his role appropriately identified. *Unidentified* is used when the author cannot be identified from the entry (which is different from an identified work having been published anonymously).

Title of work. The title of a work (short title, usually terminating with the first full stop) is entered when known. Often, however, the precise title is impossible to determine from the truncated and abbreviated entries commonly found in early book-lists. Further, the standard bibliographical sources (e.g., BL, Goff, Adams), on which Contributing Editors usually depend for determining titles, frequently modify the actual titles. The main principle here, then, must be to identify the *work* rather than a particular title, especially when a work has gone through several editions with varied titles. As with names, uniformity is essential if titles in the PLRE database are to be selected for analysis. Accordingly, a Uniform Titles list has been developed by PLRE along the following principles: 1) a work that exists in a single edition is identified by its short title; 2) a work that exists in two or more editions that bear only slightly varying titles is identified by one of these titles; 3) a work that exists in several editions with widely varied titles is identified by an artificial title, a) in a construction to reflect one or more of the existing titles, but b) often in a construction designed to describe the work without any attempt to simulate a title. Artificial titles are always enclosed in square brackets. Livy's [*Historiae Romanae decades*] is an example of the first kind of artificial title mentioned above (3a), and [*Aristotle–Ethica: commentary*] by Walter Burley is an example of the latter (3b). *Unidentified* is provided when the precise work represented by the entry cannot be determined.

Other contributors. The names of translators, editors, compilers, and illustrators (their contributions appropriately described) are found here. The forms used follow the same principles described in the section *Name of author* above.

Place of publication. If an entry is identified as a single edition of a single work, the city of publication is provided, regularized and modernized. If the entry represents a work of more than one edition printed in more than one city, one of three general locations is provided: *Britain* (if the identified printing houses were all in the British Isles), *Continent* (if the identified printing houses were all located on the Continent), and *Britain or Continent* (if editions were known to have been issued from different presses located in the British Isles and on the Continent). If a work is completely unidentified, the phrase *Place unknown* is used; where the place of publication of an identified book is unknown, the phrase *Place not given* is used. For non-extant manuscripts, the phrase used is *Provenance unknown* in accordance with the generally less precise geographical origins of most surviving manuscripts. The phrase should not be interpreted as relating to previous ownership.

Stationer(s). When an entry represents a specific, identifiable edition, every stationer involved in the publication of the book (printer, publisher, bookseller) is supplied. But since Contributing Editors generally rely upon bibliographical sources rather than a copy of the identified book for this information, the forms of presentation differ. Accordingly, varied forms will be found, such as: "G. Eld for L. Lisle" and "per Johannem Barbier, expensis Dionisii Roce," but also the non-distinguishing "George Bishop, Ralph Newberie, and Robert Barker"; the same stationer will appear in various constructions: "ap. J. Dayum," but elsewhere "John Day" and "J. Daye." All stationers, however, are accessible by uniform names in the database.

When a work is identified as having been published in a single city, but the precise edition of several possibilities issued by different printing houses cannot be determined, the phrase *different houses* is given. If the place of publication is identified as *Britain, Continent,* or *Britain or Continent*—signifying the impossibility of determining a precise place of publication—the impossibility of determining the stationer obviously follows and this section is left blank. *Stationer unknown* is used when a work is completely unidentified or when the printer, publisher, or bookseller for a known book has not been identified by bibliographers.

Date or range of dates. If a precise date of publication is known, it is provided. If two or more editions of different dates are possibilities, either a range of dates (given as, for example, *1562–1573*) or the phrase *date indeterminable* is provided. NOTE: except for works listed in the STC and in Shaaber (which together offer for English authors a practical comprehensiveness if not absolute inclusiveness) date ranges must be understood to be at best a guide. The range represents the limit known to the Contributing Editor who has consulted a number of bibliographical sources, but the chance that at least one earlier or later edition exists unknown to the Contributing Editor remains a possibility. The same reservation also applies to works presented as a sole edition, and doubts, therefore, must be harbored even when a single date is given. A work, however, that is known to have gone through several editions over several years understandably invites questions about any attempt to assign a date range with certainty (excepting the few authors for whom comprehensive censuses exist). Such uncertainty is particularly a problem with authors who were widely published during this period (Aristotle, Saint Augustine, Cicero, Duns, *Scotus*, Peter Lombard, and Virgil, to name but a few).

STC status. A variety of self-explanatory phrases appear in this section, but the primary purpose of this information is to identify the work represented as an STC (or Wing) book. When a work is *known* to have been published both in England and on the Continent, and the edition cannot be identified, its STC (or Wing) number and its non-STC status are both cited. If, however, an entry is unidentified, nothing can be determined about its place of publication; therefore, the phrase *STC/non-STC status unknown* is used. When a work issued in more than one edition is identified as an STC (or Wing) book, but the precise edition cannot be determined, only the first possible STC (or Wing) number is given, and *et seq.* is appended.

Here also is indicated whether an entry is considered to be something other than a printed book, e.g., a manuscript or a book of blank leaves intended for use as a notebook. An entry is assumed to be a printed book unless clear evidence is provided to the contrary (the use of terms and phrases such as *scriptus, books of parchment, written sermons,* or *a book of clean paper*).

Annotations. Here Contributing Editors furnish whatever information they believe will be useful and instructive in connection with the entry. All citations are abbreviated according to the *Chicago Manual of Style*'s Author-Date System (Chapter 15); full bibliographical sources are found in the Common Abbreviations and in the Reference Lists appended to the individual introductions to book-lists.

Language(s). The language (or languages) of the book is given here. If multiple, the languages are listed, without punctuation, in alphabetical order and in the order of probability. Thus, *English Greek Latin* will be found if all are known to have been employed, but *Latin Greek (probable) English (perhaps)* when doubts of varying degrees exist.

Cost or appraised value and date of same. Either 1) the amount the owner paid for the book represented or 2) its appraised value as estimated by the compiler of the book-list is furnished here; the date when the amount was paid or when the appraisal was made is usually limited to a year, which always precedes the day and month when they are given.

Current location of the book. This information is restricted to the physical book cited in the book-list and should not be misunderstood to identify locations of other copies of the book. Whenever possible, the repositories are cited as they appear in the STC (1:xlix–liii), identified by name, not by symbol.

PRIVATE LIBRARIES IN RENAISSANCE ENGLAND

*A Collection and Catalogue of
Tudor and Early Stuart Book-Lists*

Volume V

PLRE 113–137

Henry Atkins. Scholar (M.A.):
Probate Inventory. 1560

RIVES NICHOLSON

Henry Atkins, fellow of Magdalen College, Oxford, is a more puzzling figure than his small library of sixteen books and his tiny entry in the *Alumni Oxonienses* would at first seem to suggest. One puzzle is the date of the inventory itself, which cannot have taken place on 25 September 1580, the date *Alumni Oxonienses* provides (1:40), the compiler, Henry Crosse, having died in 1578 (*Alumni Oxonienses*, 1:356, and Griffiths 1862, 16). The scrawled date could be taken for 1580, but a closer look suggests that 1560 is what was actually intended, a reading confirmed by Simon Bailey, Archivist, Oxford University. For another badly written "1560" penned by Crosse that has been mistaken for 1580, see the book-list of Philip Grant (PLRE 114). Macray (1897, 2:142–43) also misreads the date, but provides more biographical details than the comparatively mum *Alumni Oxonienses*.

Atkins, who came from Warwickshire, obtained his B.A. degree on 24 January 1554 and proceeded M.A. on 11 July 1560. At some time, he was elected into one of the fellowships at Magdalen assigned to natives of Winchester diocese, oddly, since there were also fellowships at the college assigned by the founder to natives of Warwickshire. On 19 March 1560 he was granted three months' leave of absence "ad instruendum pueros, suae promotionis causa" [to instruct boys because of his promotion] having, presumably, been appointed to a schoolmastership. There is no record of his having served as a master or usher at Magdalen College School. He resigned later that year and died, presumably in September 1560.

The chief peculiarity of Atkins's small collection of books is its high concentration of fervently Roman Catholic, intensely pietistic texts. Strebaeus's commentary on Cicero's *De partitione oratoria* (113.14) is the only worldly interloper in a library in which mystics (St. Catherine, *of Siena*, St. Bridget, Walter Hylton) and patristics (Jerome's *Vitae patrum*, Augustine's *De civitate*

Dei) predominate. There are a couple of biblical commentaries, one by Alanus Varenius (113.3) and the other by Ludolphus, *de Saxonia* (113.5), but they are outnumbered by devotional, contemplative works like Joannes de Burgo's *Pupilla oculi* (113.6) and Petrus Dorlandus's *Viola animae* (113.15).

There is an intriguing contrast between the monkish piety of Atkins's library and the accompanying inventory of his possessions, which all together suggest a more material interest (fur-trimmed frocks, a "hatt of taffeta," a coat appraised at ten shillings, a silk-lined hood, and, most interesting, a "blacke horse"). Atkins apparently saw no contradiction between his worldly and religious sides, possessing a nature in which spiritual ardor coexisted peaceably with a disciplined but hearty appreciation for earthly comfort.

Oxford University Archives, Bodleian Library: Hyp.B.10.

§

Griffiths, John. 1862. *An Index to Wills Proved in the Court of the Chancellor of the University of Oxford.* Oxford: Oxford Univ. Press.

Macray, William Dunn. 1897. *A Register of the Members of St. Mary Magdalen College, Oxford, from the Foundation of the College. New Series. Fellows 1522–1575.* Vol. 2. London: Henry Frowde.

§

113.1	Augustinus de Civitate dei
113.2	Scala perfectionis
113.3	Alanus in cantica canticorum
113.4	Revelaciones brittgitte
113.5	Ludolphus super psalmos
113.6	pupilla oculi
113.7	Jeronimus in vitas patrum
113.8	Theologia naturalis
113.9	the orcherd of sion
113.10	opera fulgentii
113.11	Evangelistarium marulli
113.12	methodus confessionis
113.13	Loci communes de sacris litteris
113.14	Strebeus in particiones oratorias
113.15	viola anime
113.16	a primer in greke

§

113.1 Augustinus de Civitate dei
Augustine, *Saint. De civitate Dei*. Continent: date indeterminable.
Language(s): Latin. Appraised at 6d in 1560.

113.2 Scala perfectionis
Walter Hylton. *Scala perfectionis*. London: (different houses), 1494–1533.
STC 14042 *et seq. Language(s)*: English. Appraised at 4d in 1560.

113.3 Alanus in cantica canticorum
Alanus Varenius. *In Canticum canticorum homiliae quindecim* [and other
works]. Paris: (different houses), 1515–1526.
Language(s): Latin. Appraised at 4d in 1560.

113.4 Revelaciones brittgitte
Bridget, *Saint. Revelationes celestes*. Continent: date indeterminable.
Appears only in collections with works by others in the STC. *Language(s)*:
Latin. Appraised at 2s in 1560.

113.5 Ludolphus super psalmos
Ludolphus, *de Saxonia*. [*Psalms: commentary and text*]. (*Bible–O.T.*). Conti-
nent: date indeterminable.
Language(s): Latin. Appraised at 6d in 1560.

113.6 pupilla oculi
Joannes de Burgo. *Pupilla oculi*. Britain or Continent: 1510–1527.
STC 4115 and non-STC. *Language(s)*: Latin. Appraised at 8d in 1560.

113.7 Jeronimus in vitas patrum
Jerome, *Saint. Vitae patrum*. Continent (probable): date indeterminable.
Probably not an STC book, but see STC 14507. The 1495 English version
(STC 14507) is only a remote possibility, but its title is in Latin. *Language(s)*:
Latin (probable) English (perhaps). Appraised at 2d in 1560.

113.8 Theologia naturalis
Raymundus de Sabunde. *Theologia naturalis*. Continent: date indetermin-
able.
Language(s): Latin. Appraised at 6d in 1560.

113.9 the orcherd of sion
Catherine, *of Siena, Saint. Here begynneth the orcharde of Syon, in the whiche is
conteyned the revelacyons of seynt Katheryne of Sene*. Translated by Dane [i.e.,
dom] James. London: W. de Worde, 1519.
STC 4815. *Language(s)*: English. Appraised at 12d in 1560.

113.10   opera fulgentii
Fulgentius, *Bishop of Ruspa*. [*Works*]. Continent: date indeterminable.
Language(s): Latin. Appraised at 3d in 1560.

113.11   Evangelistarium marulli
Marko Marulic. *Evangelistarium*. Continent: date indeterminable.
Language(s): Latin. Appraised at 6d in 1560.

113.12   methodus confessionis
Unidentified. *Methodus confessionis*. Continent (probable): date indeterminable.

Almost certainly not an STC book. Although the identification of the book represented here cannot be determined, the compiler's entry is retained as the title since various works published before the date of this inventory bore that title, including two issued anonymously (Paris, 1538; Lyon, 1547 [see BCI 2:545]) and one by Claude de Viexmont (Paris, 1549). *Language(s)*: Latin. Appraised at 8d in 1560.

113.13   Loci communes de sacris litteris
Unidentified. [*Loci communes*]. Continent: date indeterminable.

Erasmus Sarcerius's *Loci communes* had gone through several editions by 1560, the date of this inventory; Wolfgang Musculus's *Loci communes* was first published in that year. Andreas Musculus's *loci* did not appear until 1563. *Language(s)*: Latin. Appraised at 6d in 1560.

113.14   Strebeus in particiones oratorias
Jacobus Lodovicus Strebaeus. [*Cicero–De partitione oratoria: commentary and text*]. Continent: date indeterminable.
Language(s): Latin. Appraised at 4d in 1560.

113.15   viola anime
Petrus Dorlandus (Petrus, *Diestensis*). *Viola animae*. Continent: date indeterminable.

Most of this was compiled from works of Raymundus de Sabunde. *Language(s)*: Latin. Appraised at 2d in 1560.

113.16   a primer in greke
Probably [*Liturgies–Greek Rite–Horologion*]. Continent: date indeterminable.

The form of the manuscript entry favors a liturgy over a grammar, but the latter should not be entirely discounted. *Language(s)*: Greek. Appraised at 4d in 1560.

Philip Grant. Scholar (student): Probate Inventory. 1560

WILLIAM M. ABBOTT

Philip Grant (Grawnt, Grawnte) was a scholar of New Inn Hall, Oxford, and died in 1560. Both *Alumni Oxonienses* (2:594) and Griffiths (1862, 25) give the date of the inventory of Grant's goods as 1580, and though the badly scribbled number could be reasonably read as 1580, that date is not possible since the compiler of the inventory, Henry Crosse, died in 1578. Simon Bailey, Archivist, Oxford University, confirms that the date is properly read as 1560. For a similar problem with Crosse's hand, see Henry Atkins's book-list (PLRE 113).

New Inn Hall seems to have been noted for scholars of law (Mallet 1924, 2:302; Wood 1786, 676), and Grant's collection of books reflects that interest. Nine of the twenty-six entries are legal books; at least five are related to Justinian I, canon law is represented by part of Nicolaus Tudeschis's commentary on the *Decretales*, and English law appears in the form of abridgements and statutes. The remaining seventeen entries are largely theological works: collections of sermons, proverbs, and prayers, and two versions of the New Testament. Grant's collection also reflects classical interests typical of his time, with copies of Horace and Virgil, while the sixteenth-century comedy on the prodigal son, *Acolastus*, (probably in an anthology of dramas based on Scripture) combines classical form with sacred themes. In addition to the books listed, the inventory mentions "a cappe case with a rownde blacke boxe full of wrytinges in the same boxe, besydes other wrytinges in the cappe case." None of the "wrytinges" is valued.

Oxford University Archives, Bodleian Library: Hyp.B.13.

§

Griffiths, John. 1862. *An Index to Wills Proved in the Court of the Chancellor of the University of Oxford.* Oxford: Oxford Univ. Press.

Mallet, Charles Edward. 1924–1927. *A History of the University of Oxford.* 3 vols. London: Methuen and Co., Ltd.

Wood, Anthony à. 1786. *The History and Antiquities of the Colleges and Halls in the University of Oxford.* Edited by John Gutch. Oxford: Clarendon Press.

§

114.1	iii partes of Panormiton
114.2	one part of Bartholli
114.3	Codex Justiniani
114.4	de verborum obligacionibus
114.5	sermones Augustini
114.6	Natura Brevium in Frenche
114.7	The Brydgement of the Statutes of Englond
114.8	Flores Poetarum
114.9	Sermones dominicales Pipini
114.10	Acolastus cum aliis
114.11	Vergilius
114.12	Oratius
114.13	Erasmus de conscribendis epistolis
114.14	Digestorum pars tertia
114.15	Enchiridion Militis Christiani
114.16	A primer
114.17	Omilia Jacobi Shepperi
114.18	Proverbia Salamonis
114.19	Modus Orandi Deum
114.20	Institutio Tyophili
114.21	Institutio aleandri
114.22	Novum Testamentum Erasmi
114.23	Novum Testamentum Jeronimi
114.24	doctor Smyth de caelibatu
114.25	apothegmata Johannis Brisserii
114.26	precaciones Erasmi

§

114.1 iii partes of Panormiton
   Nicolaus Tudeschis (Panormitanus). [*Decretales: commentary* (part)]. Continent: date indeterminable.
   Language(s): Latin. Appraised at 2s in 1560.

114.2 one part of Bartholli
Bartolus, *de Saxoferrato*. [*Corpus juris civilis: commentary* (part)]. Continent: date indeterminable.
Language(s): Latin. Appraised at 20d in 1560.

114.3 Codex Justiniani
Justinian I. *Codex*. (*Corpus juris civilis*). Continent: date indeterminable.
Language(s): Latin Greek (perhaps). Appraised at 14d in 1560.

114.4 de verborum obligacionibus
Probably Justinian I. *Institutiones* (part). (*Corpus juris civilis*). Continent: date indeterminable.
The assumption is that *de verborum obligacionibus* ("of verbal obligations") refers to Title XV of Book III of Justinian's *Institutiones*. It is unknown whether this entry represents a complete published work or a fragment; it could also be one of many commentaries on the title. *Language(s)*: Latin. Appraised at 6d in 1560.

114.5 sermones Augustini
Augustine, *Saint*. [*Sermones*]. Continent: date indeterminable.
STC 923 *et seq.* are in English, unlikely possibilities here. *Language(s)*: Latin. Appraised at 15d in 1560.

114.6 Natura Brevium in Frenche
Natura brevium. London: (different houses), 1494–1557.
STC 18385 *et seq. Language(s)*: Law/French. Appraised at 16d in 1560.

114.7 The Brydgement of the Statutes of Englond
[*England–Statutes–Abridgements and Extracts*]. London: (different houses), 1481?–1551.
STC 9513 *et seq.* More likely one of the later abridgements. *Language(s)*: English (probable) Latin (perhaps) Law/French (perhaps). Appraised at 18d in 1560.

114.8 Flores Poetarum
Flores poetarum. Continent: date indeterminable.
Language(s): Latin. Appraised at 4d in 1560.

114.9 Sermones dominicales Pipini
Guillaume Pepin. *Sermones dominicales*. Continent: date indeterminable.
Language(s): Latin. Appraised at 3d in 1560.

114.10 Acolastus cum aliis
Gulielmus Fullonius, editor (Gulielmus Gnapheus). Probably *Comoediae ac tragoediae aliquot ex Novo et Vetere Testamento desumptae*. Basle: per Nicolaum Brylingerum, 1541.

The *cum aliis* in the manuscript entry suggests the anthology of Biblical dramas that leads with Fullonius's *Acolastus*. A single edition of *Acolastus* is possible, the *cum aliis* in that case indicating a work or works bound or appraised with that volume. STC 11470, an English version, would then become a possibility. *Language(s)*: Latin. Appraised at 3d in 1560.

114.11 Vergilius
Publius Virgilius Maro. Probably [*Works*]. Continent: date indeterminable. STC 24787 *et seq.* and non-STC. *Language(s)*: Latin (probable). Appraised at 8d in 1560.

114.12 Oratius
Quintus Horatius Flaccus. Probably [*Works*]. Continent: date indeterminable.
Language(s): Latin. Appraised at 6d in 1560.

114.13 Erasmus de conscribendis epistolis
Desiderius Erasmus. *De conscribendis epistolis*. Britain or Continent: 1521–1558.
STC 10496 and non-STC. Date range from VHe. *Language(s)*: Latin. Appraised at 6d in 1560.

114.14 Digestorum pars tertia
Justinian I. Probably *Digestum novum*. (*Corpus juris civilis*). Continent: date indeterminable.
The *Digestum novum* is sometimes referred to as the third part of the *Digesta*. *Language(s)*: Latin. Appraised at 12d in 1560.

114.15 Enchiridion Militis Christiani
Desiderius Erasmus. *Enchiridion militis Christiani*. Continent: date indeterminable.
Language(s): Latin. Appraised at 3d in 1560.

114.16 A primer
[*Liturgies–Latin Rite–Hours and Primers–Salisbury and Reformed*]. Britain or Continent: date indeterminable.
STC 15867 *et seq.* Less likely, one of the prayer books at STC 20373 *et seq. Language(s)*: English (probable) Latin (perhaps). Appraised at 2d in 1560.

114.17 Omilia Jacobi Shepperi
Jacob Schopper, *the Elder. Concionum*. Dortmund: Albertus Sartorius excudebat, 1557–1560.
Schopper's other collection of sermons, *Conciones in epistolas et evangelia dominicalia*, was not published until 1561, a year after Grant died. *Language(s)*: Latin. Appraised at 4d in 1560.

114.18 Proverbia Salamonis
[*Bible–O.T.–Proverbs*]. Continent (probable): date indeterminable.
Probably not an STC book, but see STC 2752 *et seq. Language(s)*: Latin (probable). Appraised at 4d in 1560.

114.19 Modus Orandi Deum
Desiderius Erasmus. *Modus orandi Deum.* Continent: 1523–1553.
Date range is from VHe. *Language(s)*: Latin. Appraised at 2d in 1560.

114.20 Institutio Tyophili
Justinian I. *Institutiones.* (*Corpus juris civilis*). Translated into Greek by Theophilus, *Antecessor.* Continent: date indeterminable.
The *editio princeps* of Theophilus's translation of the *Institutes* into Greek is that of Froben (Basle, 1534); others appeared in Paris in the same year and in Louvain in 1536. The work was subsequently translated into Latin by Jacobus Curtius (Lyon, 1545), and a Latin edition is perhaps likelier here. *Language(s)*: Latin (probable) Greek (perhaps). Appraised at 12d in 1560.

114.21 Institutio aleandri
Justinian I. *Institutiones.* (*Corpus juris civilis*). Translated and edited by Gregorius Haloander. Continent: date indeterminable.
Language(s): Latin. Appraised at 8d in 1560.

114.22 Novum Testamentum Erasmi
[*Bible–N.T.*]. Translated by Desiderius Erasmus. Continent: date indeterminable.
Language(s): Greek Latin. Appraised at 8d in 1560.

114.23 Novum Testamentum Jeronimi
[*Bible–N.T.*]. Continent: date indeterminable.
Language(s): Latin. Appraised at 22s in 1560.

114.24 doctor Smyth de caelibatu
Richard Smith, *Dean. De coelibatu sacerdotum liber unus. De votis monasticis liber alter.* Louvain: apud Joannem Waen (excudebat Hugo Cornwels), 1550.
Shaaber S256–257. Given the manuscript entry, the revised 1550 (1551) Paris edition (Shaaber S258) with its leading title, *Defensio sacri episcoporum et sacerdotum coelibatis* is less likely, but it remains a possibility. *Language(s)*: Latin. Appraised at 2d in 1560.

114.25 apothegmata Johannis Brisserii
Unidentified. Place unknown: stationer unknown, date indeterminable.
STC/non-STC status unknown. Conceivably the compiler picked up the name of an editor of one of the many *Apophthegmata*, including titles by Erasmus, Conrad Lycosthenes (Conrad Wolffhart), and Plutarch, but nothing

matching the manuscript entry has been found. *Language(s)*: Latin. Appraised at 3d in 1560.

114.26   precaciones Erasmi
   Desiderius Erasmus. *Precationes*. Continent: 1535–1557.
   Date range is from VHe. *Language(s)*: Latin. Appraised at 2d in 1560.

John Badger. Scholar (M.A.):
Probate Inventory. 1577

WILLIAM M. ABBOTT

John Badger (Bager) matriculated in 1550 from Christ Church, received the B.A. degree in December 1553 and the M.A. degree in May 1555, and later became superior bedel of divinity at Oxford (*Alumni Oxonienses*, 1:54). His will is dated 15 July 1577, and the inventory of his possessions is dated 7 August 1577.

As a superior bedel, Badger occupied a venerable and privileged post (Cobban 1988, 90–91). During the later Middle Ages and the early modern period, bedels collected fees and fines, kept legal records, read out proclamations and publicized various university events, served summonses and citations, and in some cases acted as agents for colleges in the purchase and sale of property (Cobban 1988, 91).

Badger's book-list is notably strong in history, and otherwise presents a variety of standard texts ranging from Peter Lombard to Ramus, and from elementary dialectic texts to Theophylact. The appearance of seven books by Ramus, nearly ten percent of Badger's collection, is by far the strongest showing of Ramus in this series of Oxford book-lists thus far. The range of the collection is so wide as to furnish grounds for suspicion that Badger was, in a small way, trading in secondhand books, a trade for which his occupation, reflected by the presence of a "boke of appraising," would have afforded many opportunities.

Oxford University Archives, Bodleian Library: Hyp.B.11.

§

Cobban, Alan B. 1988. *The Medieval English Universities: Oxford and Cambridge to c. 1500*. Berkeley and Los Angeles: Univ. of California Press.

§

115.1	phrosardes cronacle
115.2	a old callepyne
115.3	a old wast paper boke
115.4	Josephus
115.5	a olid englyshe boke
115.6	Jacobus de valentia
115.7	a boke of wast paper
115.8	postilla lyre
115.9	elegantie valle
115.10	a pece of mr barber cronacle
115.11	a boke of appraising
115.12	Salust in englyshe
115.13	Sledani commentaria
115.14	quintilianus
115.15	erythimius super logicam
115.16	logica perronii
115.17	petrus martir contra Smythe
115.18	gardanus
115.19	Melength loci communes
115.20	testamentum grec
115.21	Comedia plauti
115.22	Apothegmata erasmi
115.23	confutatio hossii
115.24	Rabanus in genesim
115.25	Erasmi para' in duobus
115.26	theophilac' in evng in 2bus
115.27	barbarus in rethoricam
115.28	pars testamenti
115.29	Columella de re rustica
115.30	Rethorica Tullii
115.31	ethica artistotelis grece
115.32	adrianus
115.33	erodianus
115.34	pandacte scripture
115.35	orogen in matteum
115.36	lucianus
115.37	Institutionis Calvini
115.38	testamentum 16
115.39	testamentum Jheronimi
115.40	therentius
115.41	Sutonius
115.42	cronica Carionis
115.43	epistole loncolli

115.44	copia verborum
115.45	grammatica Ceporini greca
115.46	Justinus
115.47	diodorus siculus
115.48	Cesar dialectica
115.49	testamentum Castalionis
115.50	problemata aristotelis
115.51	epithomi Sententiarum
115.52	gram pitridici [?]
115.53	Wyderius de prestig
115.54	dialectica sturmii
115.55	Ramus
115.56	Slyther pars
115.57	fabule esopii
115.58	de potestate ecclesiastica
115.59	dialectica Rami
115.60	Calvinus contra con tri
115.61	Ramus de cesaris malitia
115.62	armethica gemi p
115.63	dionisius de collacione verborum
115.64	Ramus de liberalibus artibus
115.65	nowall contra dorman
115.66	patricus de republica gallii
115.67	osorius de nobilitate
115.68	Cathek' nowell
115.69	Westfalius
115.70	anditotarius
115.71	erasmus de racione vere theologie
115.72	Hortensius
115.73	Ramus in gramma
115.74	oraciones aliquot tulii
115.75	arithmetica Ramii
115.76	iiia pars Carionis
115.77	Ramus de Retho
115.78:1:1–2	ii old paper bokes with other od bokes besides in nomber xxti by estimacion
115.78:2:1–20	[See 115.78:1]

§

115.1 phrosardes cronacle

Jean Froissart. *Chroniques*. Britain or Continent: date indeterminable.
STC 11396 *et seq.* and non-STC. The entry suggests the English translation,

but other languages cannot be ruled out. *Language(s)*: English (perhaps) French (perhaps) Latin (perhaps). Appraised at 8s in 1577.

115.2 a old callepyne

Ambrogio Calepino. *Dictionarium*. Continent: date indeterminable.

Some editions contained vernacular languages by the date of this inventory. *Language(s)*: Greek Latin. Appraised at 3s 4d in 1577.

115.3 a old wast paper boke

Unidentified. Provenance unknown: date indeterminable.

Manuscript. Perhaps a notebook. Another at 115.7. *Language(s)*: Unknown. Appraised at 4d in 1577.

115.4 Josephus

Flavius Josephus. Unidentified. Continent: date indeterminable.

Language(s): Latin (probable) Greek (perhaps). Appraised at 16d in 1577.

115.5 a olid englyshe boke

Unidentified. Britain (probable): date indeterminable.

Unidentifiable in the STC. *Language(s)*: English. Appraised at 6d in 1577.

115.6 Jacobus de valentia

Jacobus Perez de Valentia, *Bishop*. Unidentified. Continent (probable): date indeterminable.

Probably not an STC book, but see STC 19627. Among other works, Perez de Valentia wrote commentaries on the Psalms and on the Song of Solomon. The one work of his published in England, in 1481, is not likely represented here. *Language(s)*: Latin. Appraised at 12d in 1577.

115.7 a boke of wast paper

Unidentified. Provenance unknown: date indeterminable.

Manuscript. Perhaps a notebook. Another at 115.3. *Language(s)*: Unknown. Appraised at 2d in 1577.

115.8 postilla lyre

Nicolaus de Lyra. [*Postilla* (part)]. Continent: date indeterminable.

At this valuation, only a part. *Language(s)*: Latin. Appraised at 2d in 1577.

115.9 elegantie valle

Laurentius Valla. *Elegantiae*. Continent: date indeterminable.

Language(s): Latin. Appraised at 4d in 1577.

115.10 a pece of mr barber cronacle

John Barbour. *The acts and life of Robert Bruce* (part). Edinburgh (probable):

[R. Lekpreuik, at the expense of H. Charteris?], 1571 (probable).
STC 1377.5. *Language(s)*: Scots. Appraised at 6d in 1577.

115.11   a boke of appraising
Unidentified. Provenance unknown: date indeterminable.

Manuscript. Perhaps Badger's; he may have conducted appraisals as part of his duties as superior bedel of divinity at Oxford. *Language(s)*: English (probable). Appraised at 4d in 1577.

115.12   Salust in englyshe
Caius Sallustius Crispus. *Here begynneth the famous cronycle of the warre, which the romayns had agaynst Jugurth.* Translated by Alexander Barclay. London: R. Pynson, 1520?–1525?

STC 21626 *et seq. Language(s)*: English Latin. Appraised at 6d in 1577.

115.13   Sledani commentaria
Joannes Philippson, *Sleidanus. De statu religionis et reipublicae, Carolo Quinto, Caesare, commentarii.* Continent (probable): date indeterminable.

Probably not an STC book, but see STC 19848 *et seq.* See 115.56. *Language(s)*: Latin (probable). Appraised at 10d in 1577.

115.14   quintilianus
Marcus Fabius Quintilianus. Unidentified. Continent: date indeterminable.

Either the *Declamationes* or, perhaps more likely, the *Institutiones oratoriae*, but the complete works is possible. *Language(s)*: Latin. Appraised at 12d in 1577.

115.15   erythimius super logicam
Valentinus Erythraeus. [*Tabulae in dialectica Sturmii*]. Strassburg: (different houses), 1541–1565.

Language(s): Latin. Appraised at 12d in 1577.

115.16   logica perronii
Joachim Perion. Probably *De dialectica*. Continent: 1544–1554.

Conceivably his commentary on Porphyry's *Institutiones* and Aristotle's *Organon. Language(s)*: Latin. Appraised at 6d in 1577.

115.17   petrus martir contra Smythe
Pietro Martire Vermigli (Peter Martyr). *Defensio ad Riccardi Smythaei Angli duos libellos de caelibatu sacerdotum, et votis monasticis.* Basle: apud Petrum Pernam, 1559–1570.

The compiler first wrote and then struck out *de votis*. See the entry at PLRE 1.98. *Language(s)*: Latin. Appraised at 6d in 1577.

115.18 gardanus
Girolamo Cardano. Unidentified. Continent (probable): date indeterminable.
Almost certainly not an STC book, but see STC 4607 *et seq. Language(s)*: Latin (probable). Appraised at 10d in 1577.

115.19 Melength loci communes
Philipp Melanchthon. [*Loci communes theologici*]. Continent: date indeterminable.
Language(s): Latin. Appraised at 10d in 1577.

115.20 testamentum grec
[*Bible–N.T.*]. Continent: date indeterminable.
Language(s): Greek. Appraised at 8d in 1577.

115.21 Comedia plauti
Titus Maccius Plautus. *Comoediae*. Continent: date indeterminable.
Language(s): Latin. Appraised at 8d in 1577.

115.22 Apothegmata erasmi
Desiderius Erasmus. *Apophthegmata*. Continent: 1531–1577.
Language(s): Latin. Appraised at 8d in 1577.

115.23 confutatio hossii
Stanislaus Hozyusz, *Cardinal. Confutatio prolegomenon Brentii*. Continent: date indeterminable.
Language(s): Latin. Appraised at 6d in 1577.

115.24 Rabanus in genesim
Rabanus Maurus. *Commentaria in Genesim libri III. Exodum libri IIII.* (*The Bible*). Cologne: Joannes Prael excudebat, 1532.
Language(s): Latin. Appraised at 8d in 1577.

115.25 Erasmi para' in duobus
Desiderius Erasmus. [*New Testament: paraphrase*]. (*The Bible*). Continent (probable): date indeterminable.
Probably not an STC book, but see STC 2854 *et seq.* Perhaps only part. *Language(s)*: Latin (probable) English (perhaps). Appraised at 20d in 1577.

115.26 theophilac' in evng in 2bus
Theophylact, *Archbishop of Achrida*. [*Gospels: commentary and text*]. (*Bible–N.T.*). Continent: date indeterminable.
Language(s): Latin. Appraised at 16d in 1577.

115.27 barbarus in rethoricam

Daniel Barbarus. [*Aristotle–Rhetorica: commentary*]. Translation of Aristotle's text by Hermolaus Barbarus. Continent: 1540–1558.

Language(s): Latin. Appraised at 8d in 1577.

115.28 pars testamenti

[*Bible–N.T.* (part)]. Place unknown: stationer unknown, date indeterminable.

STC/non-STC status unknown. *Language(s)*: Latin. Appraised at 2d in 1577.

115.29 Columella de re rustica

Lucius Junius Moderatus Columella. *De re rustica*. Continent: date indeterminable.

Perhaps a solo edition; perhaps the popular compilation of this title that contained texts of Varro and Cato. *Language(s)*: Latin. Appraised at 12d in 1577.

115.30 Rethorica Tullii

Marcus Tullius Cicero. Probably [*Selected works–Rhetorica*]. Continent (probable): date indeterminable.

If not one of the several collections of Cicero's rhetorical works, conceivably the widely published *Rhetorica ad Herennium*, then believed to be Cicero's, which had been printed in England by the date of this inventory (STC 5323.5). *Language(s)*: Latin. Appraised at 10d in 1577.

115.31 ethica artistotelis grece

Aristotle. *Ethica*. Continent: date indeterminable.

Language(s): Greek. Appraised at 10d in 1577.

115.32 adrianus

Probably Hadrianus Castellensis, *Cardinal*. Unidentified. Continent: date indeterminable.

Other less likely possibilities include Adrian Junius and Hadrian Amerotius. *Language(s)*: Latin. Appraised at 6d in 1577.

115.33 erodianus

Herodian. [*Historiae*]. Continent: date indeterminable.

In two other entries (Sallust and Theophylact), the compilers of this booklist make note of English translations; hence it is probable that this work is in Latin or Greek. *Language(s)*: Latin (probable) Greek (perhaps). Appraised at 8d in 1577.

115.34 pandacte scripture

Probably Otto Brunfels. Probably *Pandectae scripturarum*. Continent: date indeterminable.

The *Pandectes scripturae* of Antiochus, *Monk of Laura St. Saba*, is another but less likely possibility. *Language(s)*: Latin. Appraised at 6d in 1577.

115.35   orogen in matteum
Origen. [*Works* (part)]. Continent: date indeterminable.
STC/non-STC status unknown. No solo edition of this commentary has been found in the standard sources. *Language(s)*: Latin. Appraised at 4d in 1577.

115.36   lucianus
Lucian, *of Samosata*. Unidentified. Place unknown: stationer unknown, date indeterminable.
STC/non-STC status unknown. What arrangement of the *Dialogues* (whether collected or selected) cannot be determined. *Language(s)*: Latin (probable). Appraised at 3d in 1577.

115.37   Institutionis Calvini
Jean Calvin. *Institutio Christianae religionis*. Continent: date indeterminable.
STC 4414 and non-STC. *Language(s)*: Latin. Appraised at 12d in 1577.

115.38   testamentum 16
[*Bible–N.T.*]. Britain or Continent: date indeterminable.
STC 2800 *et seq.* and non-STC. *Language(s)*: Latin. Appraised at 6d in 1577.

115.39   testamentum Jheronimi
[*Bible–N.T.*]. Britain or Continent: date indeterminable.
STC 2816 *et seq.* and non-STC. If not a separately issued New Testament, many other editions are possible. *Language(s)*: Latin. Appraised at 6d in 1577.

115.40   therentius
Publius Terentius, *Afer*. [*Works*]. Britain or Continent: date indeterminable.
STC 23885 *et seq.* and non-STC. *Language(s)*: Latin. Appraised at 8d in 1577.

115.41   Sutonius
Caius Suetonius Tranquillus. *De vita Caesarum*. Continent: date indeterminable.
The *De grammaticis* is a remote possibility. *Language(s)*: Latin. Appraised at 6d in 1577.

115.42   cronica Carionis
Johann Carion. *Chronica*. Continent: date indeterminable.
See also 115.76. *Language(s)*: Latin. Appraised at 6d in 1577.

115.43 epistole loncolli
Christophorus Longolius. [*Epistolae*]. Continent: date indeterminable.
Language(s): Latin. Appraised at 4d in 1577.

115.44 copia verborum
Probably Desiderius Erasmus. *De duplici copia verborum ac rerum*. Britain or Continent: date indeterminable.
STC 10471.4 *et seq.* and non-STC. Others with the short title of the entry are possible, but the Erasmus work was much more widely known. *Language(s)*: Latin. Appraised at 2d in 1577.

115.45 grammatica Ceporini greca
Jacobus Ceporinus. *Compendium grammaticae graecae*. Continent: date indeterminable.
Language(s): Greek Latin. Appraised at 3d in 1577.

115.46 Justinus
Trogus Pompeius and Justinus, *the Historian*. [*Epitomae in Trogi Pompeii historias*]. Britain or Continent: date indeterminable.
STC 24287 *et seq.* and non-STC. Conceivably Justinus, *Martyr*, but the valuation and context argue for the *Epitomae*. *Language(s)*: Latin. Appraised at 3d in 1577.

115.47 diodorus siculus
Diodorus, *Siculus*. *Bibliotheca historia*. Continent: date indeterminable.
Language(s): Latin. Appraised at 4d in 1577.

115.48 Cesar dialectica
Joannes Caesarius, *Juliacensis*. *Dialectica*. Continent: date indeterminable.
Joannes Murmellius's commentary on Aristotle's *Categoriae* was issued with most Renaissance editions of the *Dialectica*. *Language(s)*: Latin. Appraised at 3d in 1577.

115.49 testamentum Castalionis
[*Bible–N.T.*]. Translated by Sebastian Castalio. Continent: date indeterminable.
The New Testament portion of Castalio's translation of the Bible was sometimes issued separately. *Language(s)*: Latin. Appraised at 6d in 1577.

115.50 problemata aristotelis
Aristotle (spurious). *Problemata*. Continent: date indeterminable.
Language(s): Latin Greek (probable). Appraised at 4d in 1577.

115.51 epithomi Sententiarum
Unidentified. Continent (probable): date indeterminable.

Almost certainly not an STC book. Probably something along the lines of Nicolaus de Orbellis's *Super Sententias compendium* or Gulielmus Gorns's *Scotus pauperum*. *Language(s)*: Latin. Appraised at 2d in 1577.

115.52   gram pitridici [?]
Unidentified. Place unknown: stationer unknown, date indeterminable.
STC/non-STC status unknown. *Language(s)*: Latin (probable). Appraised at 2d in 1577.

115.53   Wyderius de prestig
Johann Wier. *De praestigiis daemonum*. Basle: (different houses), 1563–1577.
Joannes Oporinus or his successors were the printers. *Language(s)*: Latin. Appraised at 8d in 1577.

115.54   dialectica sturmii
Joannes Sturmius. [*Dialectica*]. Continent: date indeterminable.
Language(s): Latin. Appraised at 6d in 1577.

115.55   Ramus
Pierre de La Ramée. Unidentified. Place unknown: stationer unknown, date indeterminable.
STC/non-STC status unknown. *Language(s)*: Latin (probable). Appraised at 6d in 1577.

115.56   Slyther pars
Unidentified. Place unknown: stationer unknown, date indeterminable.
STC/non-STC status unknown. Part of something by Joannes Philippson, *Sleidanus*. See 115.13. *Language(s)*: Unknown. Appraised at 4d in 1577.

115.57   fabule esopii
Aesop. *Fabulae*. Britain or Continent: date indeterminable.
STC 168 *et seq.* and non-STC. *Language(s)*: Latin (probable) Greek (perhaps). Appraised at 4d in 1577.

115.58   de potestate ecclesiastica
Unidentified. Continent: date indeterminable.
Works by Augustinus, *de Ancona*, Aegidius, *Romanus*, and Joannes Antonius Delphinus, among others, could be so identified. *Language(s)*: Latin. Appraised at 3d in 1577.

115.59   dialectica Rami
Pierre de La Ramée. [*Dialectica*]. Britain or Continent: date indeterminable. 1555–1577.

STC 15241.7 *et seq.* and non-STC. *Language(s)*: Latin. Appraised at 3d in 1577.

115.60 Calvinus contra con tri
Jean Calvin. *Acta synodi Tridentinae cum antidoto.* (*Councils–Trent*). Geneva: (stationer unknown), 1547. *Language(s)*: Latin. Appraised at 3d in 1577.

115.61 Ramus de cesaris malitia
Pierre de La Ramée. *Liber de Caesaris militia.* Continent: 1559–1574. Ong nos. 506–07. *Language(s)*: Latin. Appraised at 2d in 1577.

115.62 armethica gemi p
Probably Reiner Gemma, *Frisius. Arithmetica practicae methodus facilis.* Continent: date indeterminable. *Language(s)*: Latin. Appraised at 2d in 1577.

115.63 dionisius de collacione verborum
Dionysius, *of Halicarnassus. De compositione verborum.* Continent: date indeterminable. *Language(s)*: Greek Latin. Appraised at 2d in 1577.

115.64 Ramus de liberalibus artibus
Pierre de La Ramée. Unidentified. Basle: (different houses), date indeterminable.

Either the *Professio regia, hoc est, septem artes liberales in regia cathedra, per ipsum Parisiis propositae* (1576) or the *Scholae in liberales artes* (1569). See Ong nos. 651 and 695 (Adams R115 and R123). *Language(s)*: Latin. Appraised at 2d in 1577.

115.65 nowall contra dorman
Alexander Nowell. *A reproufe of a booke entituled, A proufe of certayne articles.* London: Henry Wykes, 1564–1567.

STC 18740 *et seq.* The 1566 enlarged edition carries a slightly different title. *A confutation, as wel of M. Dormans last boke as also of D. Sander* (STC 18739) is possible but less likely. *Language(s)*: English (probable). Appraised at 4d in 1577.

115.66 patricus de republica gallii
Francesco Patrizi, *Bishop.* [*De institutione reipublicae libri novem*]. Continent: date indeterminable.

The French titles of this work vary. *Language(s)*: French. Appraised at 3d in 1577.

115.67 osorius de nobilitate
Jeronimo Osorio da Fonseca, *Bishop. De nobilitate civili libri II. De nobilitate*

christiana libri III. Continent: date indeterminable.
Language(s): Latin. Appraised at 6d in 1577.

115.68　Cathek' nowell

Alexander Nowell. *Catechismus.* London: (different houses), 1570–1577.
STC 18701 *et seq.* Whether larger, middle, or shorter cannot be determined. *Language(s)*: Latin (probable) English (perhaps) Greek (perhaps). Appraised at 3d in 1577.

115.69　Westfalius

Probably Joachim Westphal. Unidentified. Continent: date indeterminable.
Language(s): Latin. Appraised at 3d in 1577.

115.70　anditotarius

Perhaps Nicolas Des Gallars (Nicolaus Salicetus). *Antidotarius animae.* Continent: date indeterminable.
The context strongly suggests this work rather than any of the many medical works that might be so entered, including Johann Jacob Wecker, *Antidotarium generale*, and the often reprinted title at STC 675.3 *et seq.*
Language(s): Latin. Appraised at 2d in 1577.

115.71　erasmus de racione vere theologie

Desiderius Erasmus. *Methodus: Ratio verae theologiae.* Continent: date indeterminable.
Language(s): Latin. Appraised at 2d in 1577.

115.72　Hortensius

Lambertus Hortensius. Unidentified. Continent: date indeterminable.
Language(s): Latin. Appraised at 3d in 1577.

115.73　Ramus in gramma

Pierre de La Ramée. [*Grammatica*]. Continent: date indeterminable.
Language(s): Greek (perhaps) Latin (perhaps). Appraised at 4d in 1577.

115.74　oraciones aliquot tulii

Marcus Tullius Cicero. [*Selected works–Orations*]. Continent: date indeterminable.
Language(s): Latin. Appraised at 3d in 1577.

115.75　arithmetica Ramii

Pierre de La Ramée. *Arithmetica.* Continent: 1555–1577.
Language(s): Latin. Appraised at 3d in 1577.

115.76　iiia pars Carionis

Johann Carion. *Chronica* (part 3). Continent: date indeterminable.

See Adams C710. Another Carion at 115.42. *Language(s)*: Latin. Appraised at 3d in 1577.

115.77 Ramus de Retho

Audomarus Talaeus (Omer Talon). *Rhetorica*. Continent: 1548–1577.

Ramus had a major role in its composition. *Language(s)*: Latin. Appraised at 2d in 1577.

115.78:1:1–2 ii old paper bokes with other od bokes besides in nomber xxti by estimacion

Provenances unknown: dates indeterminable.

Manuscripts. *Language(s)*: Unknown. Appraised as a group, with the following, at 2s in 1577.

115.78:2:1–20 [See 115.78:1]

Unidentified. Places unknown: stationers unknown, dates indeterminable.

STC/non-STC status unknown. *Language(s)*: Unknown. Appraised as a group, with the preceding, at 2s in 1577.

Thomas Carpenter. Scholar (M.A.): Probate Inventory. 1577

KATHRYN A. BARBOUR

Little is known of the life of Thomas Carpenter, owner of the books listed below. Foster identifies him as a fellow of All Souls' College from 1569, who received the B.A. degree on 1 February 1572, and the M.A. degree on 25 November 1575. His will was proved at Oxford on 16 August 1577 (*Alumni Oxonienses*, 1:240), with an inventory of his goods, including the books, taken the day before. 1577 was a year of contagion in Oxford, perhaps the plague, probably typhus (see Ker, 473 and McConica, 648), and Carpenter was likely one of the many scholars who succumbed during that epidemic. He is sometimes confused with another Thomas Carpenter, who, admitted for the B.A. on 12 November 1534, was named canon of Hereford in 1548, rector of Byford, Herefordshire in 1550, and rector of Kinnersley, Herefordshire in 1567 (*Alumni Oxonienses*, 1:240).

The library of the All Souls' Carpenter was about average in size for men who had recently earned the M.A. Reasonably varied, it contained, along with books of theological controversy (Vermigli and Osorio, for example) and Biblical works (including a French New Testament), standard works by Aristotle, Seneca, and Cicero. About a fifth of the collection, however, consisted of medical books, ranging from Galen, Hippocrates, and Dioscorides in Latin or Greek, to more recent works, including a book on surgery, in English, by Thomas Gale. N.R. Ker (1971, pp. 103 and 157) cites two books currently in the All Souls' College Library bequeathed to the library by Carpenter: Hanss Jacob Wecker's *Syntaxes utriusque medicinae* (see 116.4) and the *Epitome operum Galeni* (116.5).

In addition to his books, the inventory of Carpenter's goods lists the following items: a coffer of fir with lock and key, five pairs of old sheets, two cloth gowns and one mockado gown, ten shirts, a gold ring, a pair of tongs, a pair of bellows, and a pewter chamber pot, which together were valued at five pounds, six shillings.

Oxford University Archives, Bodleian Library: Hyp.B.11.

§

Ker, N.R., ed. 1971. *Records of All Souls College Library 1437–1600. Oxford Bibliographical Society Publications, New Series, no. 16.* London: Published for the Oxford Bibliographical Society by Oxford Univ. Press.

§

116.1	Coperi dixionar
116.2	biblia lat
116.3	Antidoterium Wickeri spec
116.4	Tabula Wickeri
116.5	Epithom Galeni
116.6	Aristotle de animalibus
116.7	Reanus in Phisicam Arisotelis 2 bus
116.8	opera farnelii in 2 bus
116.9	Boemus
116.10	Eustratius in Ethicam Aristotelis
116.11	Ethica Aristotelis
116.12	Politica Aristotelis
116.13	Rethorica Tullii
116.14	Epistole Tullii
116.15	Epistole ad Athicum
116.16	Tullii 1a pars philo
116.17	Mattheolus
116.18	novum test grece
116.19	Johannis Zacharii de urinis
116.20	Logica Aristotelis
116.21	Physica Velcurii
116.22	Tragica Senece
116.23	Leminus de miraculis
116.24	Epigrammata Martialis
116.25	Physica Aristotelis
116.26	Palengenius
116.27	Diescorides Ruellius
116.28	Psalterium Hesii
116.29	Psalterium Bucanani
116.30	Scola Salerni
116.31	Isocrates grece et latine
116.32	Com Ces
116.33	Oratius cum commento
116.34	Flores Biblie

116.35	Baleus
116.36	a French testament
116.37	Demostenes contra Heskines
116.38:A	Juvenall et Percius
116.38:B	[See 116.38:A]
116.39	Osorius de gloria et nobilitate
116.40	Osorius contra Haddonum
116.41	Instituciones Calvini
116.42	Fucsius de curandis morbis
116.43	Macrobedius de conscribendis epistolis
116.44	Actuarius de compo medicamentorum
116.45	Apothegmata Litostenes
116.46	Instituciones Fuccii
116.47	Erodianus
116.48	Montanus
116.49	Budeus
116.50	Varro de re rustica
116.51	Flores Senece
116.52	Epithomi Plutharki
116.53	Fuccius
116.54	Polidorus de inventione rerum
116.55	Erasmus in Mattheum
116.56	Monster de horolog
116.57	Valerius Maximus
116.58	Grammatica Cleonardi
116.59	Wickerus de generali
116.60	Erasmus
116.61	Va*daranus
116.62	Erasmus in Johannem
116.63	Dimostenis Olnithiaci
116.64	Mathisius
116.65	Vasseus
116.66	Confessio Helvetica
116.67	Aphorismi Hypocratis
116.68	Patricius
116.69	Oppianus
116.70	Kyrugia galei
116.71	Dasipodius
116.72	Tabula Hunteri
116.73	Arithmetica Gemi
116.74	Senesius grece
116.75	Johannes de Sacrobosco
116.76	Laurentius Valla
116.77	Happelius
116.78	Le**ius

116.79   Petrus Martir de eucharistia
116.80   Hadrianus
116.81   Georgius Agricola
116.82   Buritanus
116.83:1–16   certain other bokes in nomber xvi

§

116.1 Coperi dixionar

Thomas Cooper, *Bishop*. *Thesaurus linguae Romanae et Britannicae*. London: (different houses), 1565–1573.

STC 5686 *et seq*. *Language(s)*: English Latin. Appraised at 18s in 1577.

116.2 biblia lat

The Bible. Britain or Continent: date indeterminable.

STC 2055 *et seq*. and non-STC. *Language(s)*: Latin. Appraised at 10s in 1577.

116.3 Antidoterium Wickeri spec

Hanss Jacob Wecker. *Antidotarium speciale*. Basle: per Eusebium Episcopium et Nicolai fr. haered., 1574–1577.

See 116.59. *Language(s)*: Latin. Appraised at 3s in 1577.

116.4 Tabula Wickeri

Hanss Jacob Wecker. Probably [*Medicinae utriusque syntaxes*]. Continent: 1562–1583.

The work consists almost entirely of tables. A copy was bequeathed to the All Souls' College Library by Carpenter according to N.R. Ker (1971, p. 103). *Language(s)*: Latin. Appraised at 8s in 1577.

116.5 Epithom Galeni

Galen. [*Works–Epitome*]. Epitomized by Andres de Laguna. Continent: date indeterminable.

According to N.R. Ker (1971, p. 157), a copy of this work was bequeathed to the All Souls' College Library by Carpenter. *Language(s)*: Latin. Appraised at 7s in 1577.

116.6 Aristotle de animalibus

Aristotle. *Historia animalium*. Continent: date indeterminable.

The title is sometimes given as *De animalibus historia*. *Language(s)*: Latin. Appraised at 18d in 1577.

116.7 Reanus in Phisicam Arisotelis 2 bus

Hermannus Rayanus, *Welsdalius*. *Primus (secundus) tomus librorum omnium naturalis philosophiae* [and other works]. Cologne: apud haeredes A. Birck-manni, 1568.

Contains a work by Plato in the second volume. *Language(s)*: Latin. Appraised at 4s in 1577.

116.8 opera farnelii in 2 bus

Joannes Fernelius. *Universa medicina*. Continent: date indeterminable.

His smaller *Medicina*, sometimes confused with the later *Universa Medicina*, also appeared in at least one two-volume edition. *Language(s)*: Latin. Appraised at 5s in 1577.

116.9 Boemus

Joannes Boemus. [*Omnium gentium mores, leges et ritus*]. Continent (probable): date indeterminable.

Probably not an STC book, but see STC 3196.5 *et seq*. An English translation of part of this work appeared in 1554 and another in 1555. *Language(s)*: Latin (probable) English (perhaps). Appraised at 6d in 1577.

116.10 Eustratius in Ethicam Aristotelis

Eustratius, *Archbishop of Nicaea*. [*Aristotle–Ethica: commentary and text*]. Continent: date indeterminable.

Language(s): Latin (probable) Greek (perhaps). Appraised at 2s in 1577.

116.11 Ethica Aristotelis

Aristotle. *Ethica*. Britain or Continent: date indeterminable.

STC 752 and non-STC. *Language(s)*: Latin (probable) Greek (perhaps). Appraised at 18d in 1577.

116.12 Politica Aristotelis

Aristotle. *Politica*. Continent: date indeterminable.

Language(s): Latin (probable) Greek (perhaps). Appraised at 12d in 1577.

116.13 Rethorica Tullii

Marcus Tullius Cicero. [*Selected works–Rhetorica*]. Continent: date indeterminable.

The popular *Rhetorica ad Herennium*, falsely ascribed to Cicero, is a possibility. *Language(s)*: Latin. Appraised at 14d in 1577.

116.14 Epistole Tullii

Marcus Tullius Cicero. [*Selected works–Epistolae*]. Continent: date indeterminable.

Language(s): Latin. Appraised at 12d in 1577.

116.15 Epistole ad Athicum

Marcus Tullius Cicero. *Epistolae ad Atticum*. Continent: date indeterminable.

Language(s): Latin. Appraised at 12d in 1577.

116.16 Tullii 1a pars philo
Marcus Tullius Cicero. [*Selected works–Philosophica* (part)]. Continent: date indeterminable.
Language(s): Latin. Appraised at 12d in 1577.

116.17 Mattheolus
Pietro Andrea Mattioli. Unidentified. Continent: date indeterminable.
Language(s): Latin. Appraised at 14d in 1577.

116.18 novum test grece
[*Bible–N.T.*]. Continent: date indeterminable.
Language(s): Greek. Appraised at 16d in 1577.

116.19 Johannis Zacharii de urinis
Joannes Zacharias. *De urinis*. Continent: date indeterminable.
After appearing as *Tractatus de urinarum judiciis* under the name of Bartholomeus Montagnana (Padua, 1487), it was published only in the *Hortus sanitatis* and assigned to Zacharias. *Language(s)*: Latin. Appraised at 10d in 1577.

116.20 Logica Aristotelis
Aristotle. [*Selected works–Logica*]. Continent: date indeterminable.
Language(s): Latin (probable) Greek (perhaps). Appraised at 3s in 1577.

116.21 Physica Velcurii
Joannes Velcurio. [*Aristotle–Physica: commentary*]. Continent: date indeterminable.
Language(s): Latin (probable) Greek (perhaps). Appraised at 10d in 1577.

116.22 Tragica Senece
Lucius Annaeus Seneca. *Tragoediae*. Continent: date indeterminable.
Language(s): Latin. Appraised at 6d in 1577.

116.23 Leminus de miraculis
Levinus Lemnius. *De miraculis occultis naturae libri IIII*. Continent: date indeterminable.
Language(s): Latin. Appraised at 16d in 1577.

116.24 Epigrammata Martialis
Marcus Valerius Martialis. *Epigrammata*. Continent: date indeterminable.
Language(s): Latin. Appraised at 8d in 1577.

116.25 Physica Aristotelis
Aristotle. *Physica*. Continent: date indeterminable.
Language(s): Latin (probable) Greek (perhaps). Appraised at 14d in 1577.

116.26 Palengenius
Marcellus Palingenius (Pietro Angelo Manzolli [Stellatus]). *Zodiacus vitae.* Britain or Continent: date indeterminable.
STC 19138.5 *et seq.* and non-STC. *Language(s)*: Latin. Appraised at 6d in 1577.

116.27 Diescorides Ruellius
Dioscorides. *De medica materia.* Translated by Joannes Ruellius. Continent: date indeterminable.
A few editions of the Ruellius translation also carried the Greek text. *Language(s)*: Latin Greek (perhaps). Appraised at 6d in 1577.

116.28 Psalterium Hesii
[*Bible–O.T.–Psalms*]. Translated by Helius Eobanus, *Hessus.* Britain or Continent: 1537–1575.
STC 2356 and non-STC. See Adams B1415 and B1429. *Language(s)*: Latin. Appraised at 6d in 1577.

116.29 Psalterium Bucanani
George Buchanan. [*Psalms: paraphrase*]. (*Bible–O.T.*). Continent: 1565–1576.
See Shaaber B759–772 and Adams B1465. *Language(s)*: Latin. Appraised at 8d in 1577.

116.30 Scola Salerni
[*Regimen sanitatis Salernitatum*]. Britain or Continent: date indeterminable.
STC 21596 *et seq.* and non-STC. *Language(s)*: Latin English (perhaps). Appraised at 8d in 1577.

116.31 Isocrates grece et latine
Isocrates. Unidentified. Continent (probable): date indeterminable.
Probably not an STC book. Either *Orationes* or *Epistolae* or both. *Language(s)*: Greek Latin. Appraised at 2s 4d in 1577.

116.32 Com Ces
Caius Julius Caesar. *Commentarii.* Continent: date indeterminable.
Language(s): Latin. Appraised at 2s in 1577.

116.33 Oratius cum commento
Quintus Horatius Flaccus. Probably [*Works*]. Continent: date indeterminable.
Language(s): Latin. Appraised at 6d in 1577.

116.34 Flores Biblie
Flores Bibliae. (Bible–Selections). Compiled by Thomas, *Hibernicus*. Continent: 1555–1574.
Language(s): Latin. Appraised at 12d in 1577.

116.35 Baleus
John Bale, *Bishop*. Unidentified. Place unknown: stationer unknown, date indeterminable.
STC/non-STC status unknown. *Language(s)*: Latin (probable) English (perhaps). Appraised at 6d in 1577.

116.36 a French testament
[*Bible–N.T.*]. Britain or Continent: date indeterminable.
STC 2957.6 *et seq.* and non-STC. *Language(s)*: French. Appraised at 8d in 1577.

116.37 Demostenes contra Heskines
Aeschines and Demosthenes. [*Selected works–Orations*]. Continent: date indeterminable.
Language(s): Latin Greek (probable). Appraised at 4d in 1577.

116.38:A Juvenall et Percius
Decimus Junius Juvenalis. [*Works*]. Continent: date indeterminable (composite publication).
Language(s): Latin. Appraised [a composite volume] at 3d in 1577.

116.38:B [See 116.38:A]
Aulus Persius Flaccus. [*Works*]. [Composite publication].
Language(s): Latin. Appraised [a composite volume] at 3d in 1577.

116.39 Osorius de gloria et nobilitate
Jeronimo Osorio da Fonseca, *Bishop*. [*Selected works*]. Continent: 1571–1576.
An oft-printed collection of his *De gloria* and *De nobilitate civili et Christiani*. *Language(s)*: Latin. Appraised at 12d in 1577.

116.40 Osorius contra Haddonum
Jeronimo Osorio da Fonseca, *Bishop*. *In Gualterum Haddonum magistrum libellorum supplicum libri tres*. Continent (probable): 1567–1576.
Probably not an STC book, but see STC 18889. An English version of Osorio's reply was published in Louvain. *Language(s)*: Latin (probable). Appraised at 8d in 1577.

116.41 Instituciones Calvini
Jean Calvin. *Institutio Christianae religionis*. Britain or Continent: date indeterminable.
STC 4414 and non-STC. *Language(s)*: Latin. Appraised at 2s 8d in 1577.

116.42 Fucsius de curandis morbis
Leonard Fuchs. *De medendi methodo*. Continent: date indeterminable.
Language(s): Latin. Appraised at 14d in 1577.

116.43 Macrobedius de conscribendis epistolis
Georgius Macropedius. *Methodus de conscribendis epistolis*. Britain or Continent: date indeterminable.
STC 17175.7 and non-STC. *Language(s)*: Latin. Appraised at 4d in 1577.

116.44 Actuarius de compo medicamentorum
Joannes Actuarius. *De medicamentorum compositione*. Continent: 1539–1546.
Language(s): Latin. Appraised at 4d in 1577.

116.45 Apothegmata Litostenes
Conrad Lycosthenes (Conrad Wolffhart). *Apophthegmata*. Continent: date indeterminable.
Language(s): Latin. Appraised at 2s in 1577.

116.46 Instituciones Fuccii
Leonard Fuchs. *Institutiones medicinae*. Continent: 1555–1572.
See Adams F1113–1117. *Language(s)*: Latin. Appraised at 14d in 1577.

116.47 Erodianus
Herodian. [*Historiae*]. Continent: date indeterminable.
Given the context, Erotianus's *Vocum, quae apud Hippocratem sunt, collectio* must be considered a possibility, but it was issued in only one edition compared to the wide appearance of Herodian, and it appears in no other collection in the Oxford or the Cambridge book-lists (see BCI). *Language(s)*: Latin. Appraised at 6d in 1577.

116.48 Montanus
Probably Joannes Baptista Montanus. Unidentified. Continent: date indeterminable.
Language(s): Latin. Appraised at 6d in 1577.

116.49 Budeus
Gulielmus Budaeus. Unidentified. Continent: date indeterminable.
Language(s): Latin. Appraised at 4d in 1577.

116.50 Varro de re rustica
Marcus Terentius Varro. *De re rustica*. Continent: date indeterminable.
Frequently published in a collection with works by Cato and Columella.
Language(s): Latin. Appraised at 10d in 1577.

116.51 Flores Senece
Lucius Annaeus Seneca. [*Selections–Flores selecti*]. Continent: date indeterminable.
Language(s): Latin. Appraised at 6d in 1577.

116.52 Epithomi Plutharki
Plutarch. [*Vitae parallelae–Epitome*]. Continent: date indeterminable.
Language(s): Latin. Appraised at 8d in 1577.

116.53 Fuccius
Leonard Fuchs. Unidentified. Continent: date indeterminable.
The one STC book (STC 11408) is highly unlikely. *Language(s)*: Latin. Appraised at 16d in 1577.

116.54 Polidorus de inventione rerum
Polydorus Vergilius. *De inventoribus rerum*. Continent: date indeterminable.
Language(s): Latin. Appraised at 12d in 1577.

116.55 Erasmus in Mattheum
Desiderius Erasmus. [*Matthew: paraphrase*]. (*Bible–N.T.*). Continent: 1520–1557.
Date range from VHe. *Language(s)*: Latin. Appraised at 4d in 1577.

116.56 Monster de horolog
Sebastian Muenster. [*Horologiographia*]. Basle: excudebat Henricus Petrus, 1531–1533.
Language(s): Latin. Appraised at 12d in 1577.

116.57 Valerius Maximus
Valerius Maximus. *Facta et dicta memorabilia*. Continent: date indeterminable.
Language(s): Latin. Appraised at 12d in 1577.

116.58 Grammatica Cleonardi
Nicolaus Clenardus. Probably *Institutiones linguae graecae*. Continent: date indeterminable.
There is no evidence of Hebrew in Carpenter's library, making Clenard's *Tabula in grammaticen Hebraeam* very unlikely here. *Language(s)*: Greek Latin. Appraised at 16d in 1577.

116.59 Wickerus de generali
Hanss Jacob Wecker. *Antidotarium generale*. Basle: per Eusebium Episco-
pium, et Nicolai fr. haeredes, 1576.
See 116.3. *Language(s)*: Latin. Appraised at 10d in 1577.

116.60 Erasmus
Desiderius Erasmus. Unidentified. Place unknown: stationer unknown,
date indeterminable.
STC/non-STC status unknown. *Language(s)*: Latin (probable). Appraised
at 3d in 1577.

116.61 Va*daranus
Unidentified. Place unknown: stationer unknown, date indeterminable.
STC/non-STC status unknown. *Language(s)*: Unknown. Appraised at 3d in
1577.

116.62 Erasmus in Johannem
Desiderius Erasmus. [*John: paraphrase*]. (*Bible–N.T.*). Continent: 1523–
1557.
Date range from VHe. *Language(s)*: Latin. Appraised at 3d in 1577.

116.63 Dimostenis Olnithiaci
Demosthenes. *Olynthiacae orationes tres*. Continent (probable): date indeterminable.
Probably not an STC book. Conceivably STC 6577, *Selected works*, with this
title leading. *Language(s)*: Greek Latin. Appraised at 4d in 1577.

116.64 Mathisius
Unidentified. Continent (probable): date indeterminable.
Probably not an STC book. Possibilities include Johann Mathesius; Gerard
Matthisius, *Geldrensis*; Joannes Mahusius; and Corneille Mathys. The first and
the last wrote on medicine, which subject is represented in about a fifth of
Carpenter's books. *Language(s)*: Latin (probable). Appraised at 4d in 1577.

116.65 Vasseus
Unidentified. Continent (probable): date indeterminable.
Almost certainly not an STC book. Whether Lodovicus Vassaeus or Jo-
annes Vasseus, whose *De judiciis urinarum* was translated into English in 1553
(STC 24595), cannot be determined. *Language(s)*: Latin (probable). Appraised
at 6d in 1577.

116.66 Confessio Helvetica
Confessio et expositio simplex orthodoxae fidei [Helveticae]. (*Switzerland–Reformed
Church*). Zürich: Christoph Froschouer, 1566–1568.
See Staedtke, nos. 433–435. *Language(s)*: Latin. Appraised at 3d in 1577.

116.67 Aphorismi Hypocratis
Hippocrates. *Aphorismi.* Continent: date indeterminable.
Language(s): Latin Greek (probable). Appraised at 10d in 1577.

116.68 Patricius
Probably Francesco Patrizi, *Bishop.* Unidentified. Continent (probable): date indeterminable.
Almost certainly not an STC book, but see STC 19475. Conceivably, Francesco Patrizi, the philosophical writer, but much of his work was published too late for Carpenter to acquire it, and the Bishop's works, one of which was abridged in English in 1576, were very popular. *Language(s)*: Latin. Appraised at 2d in 1577.

116.69 Oppianus
Oppianus. [*Alieuticon*]. Continent: date indeterminable.
Language(s): Latin Greek (perhaps). Appraised at 14d in 1577.

116.70 Kyrugia galei
Thomas Gale. *Certaine workes of chirurgerie, newly compiled.* London: R. Hall (for T. Gale), 1563.
STC 11529. *Language(s)*: English. Appraised at 16d in 1577.

116.71 Dasipodius
Probably Conradus Dasypodius. Unidentified. Continent: date indeterminable.
The context, and less so the valuation, argue for one of the mathematical or astronomical works of Conradus Dasypodius rather than the Latin-German dictionary of Petrus Dasypodius. *Language(s)*: Latin. Appraised at 4d in 1577.

116.72 Tabula Hunteri
Joannes Honterus. [*Rudimenta cosmographica*]. Continent: date indeterminable.
Language(s): Latin. Appraised at 4d in 1577.

116.73 Arithmetica Gemi
Reiner Gemma, *Frisius. Arithmetica practicae methodus facilis.* Continent: 1540–1576.
Language(s): Latin. Appraised at 4d in 1577.

116.74 Senesius grece
Synesius, *Bishop.* Unidentified. Continent: date indeterminable.
Language(s): Greek. Appraised at 6d in 1577.

116.75 Johannes de Sacrobosco
John Holywood (Joannes Sacrobosco). *Sphaera mundi.* Continent: date

indeterminable.
Language(s): Latin. Appraised at 4d in 1577.

116.76 Laurentius Valla
Laurentius Valla. Unidentified. Continent: date indeterminable.
May very well be the *Elegantiae*, but other works possible. *Language(s)*:
Latin. Appraised at 4d in 1577.

116.77 Happelius
Wigandus Happellius. Unidentified. Continent: date indeterminable.
Language(s): Latin. Appraised at 6d in 1577.

116.78 Le**ius
Unidentified. Place unknown: stationer unknown, date indeterminable.
STC/non-STC status unknown. An illegible manuscript that could represent Livy, Levinus Lemnius, Simon Levinus, and doubtless others. Carpenter's interest in medicine might suggest Lemnius as the strongest candidate.
Language(s): Unknown. Appraised at 6d in 1577.

116.79 Petrus Martir de eucharistia
Pietro Martire Vermigli (Peter Martyr). Unidentified. Place unknown: stationer unknown, date indeterminable.
STC/non-STC status unknown. Vermigli was the author of several tracts touching the sacraments. *Language(s)*: Latin. Appraised at 6d in 1577.

116.80 Hadrianus
Perhaps Hadrianus Castellensis, *Cardinal*. Unidentified. Continent: date indeterminable.
Other Adrians or Hadrians are possible. *Language(s)*: Latin. Appraised at 6d in 1577.

116.81 Georgius Agricola
Georgius Agricola. Unidentified. Continent: date indeterminable.
Language(s): Latin. Appraised at 12d in 1577.

116.82 Buritanus
Joannes Buridanus. [*Aristotle–Unidentified: commentary*]. Paris: (different houses), date indeterminable.
Language(s): Latin. Appraised at 12d in 1577.

116.83:1–16 certain other bokes in number xvi
Unidentified. Place unknown: stationer unknown, date indeterminable.
STC/non-STC status unknown. *Language(s)*: Unknown. Appraised as a group at 2s in 1577.

Roger Charnock. Scholar (M.A.): Inventory. 1577

DAVID C. MCPHERSON

Roger Charnock (Charnocke, Charnoke), from Lancashire, was admitted as a scholar at Corpus Christi College on 24 December 1563 at the age of four-teen (Fowler 1893, 389); he became a fellow in 1566. He was granted the Bachelor of Arts degree on 14 October 1568 and the Master of Arts degree on 14 June 1572. On 18 February 1577, an inventory of his "goodes and debtes" was made (*Alumni Oxonienses*, 1:264), the purpose of which is not known; the compiler gives no reason for the inventory and only ambiguously refers to Charnock as "late fellow" of Corpus Christi, which does not neces-sarily mean that Charnock had died. Charnock was likely of a staunchly Roman Catholic family of Charnock and Astley, Lancashire, with one brother, John, executed for his part in the Babington plot (Gillow 1885–1902, 1:472). Roman Catholic sympathies, however, are not particularly reflected in Charnock's books, which, indeed, number among them several items of a Cal-vinist bent (see 117.3, 117.4:1–2, 117.5, 117.13, 117.61, and 117.78; see also 117.8:1–2).

Charnock's library is a standard academic collection, containing works of the expected kind on logic, rhetoric (especially Cicero), as well as the Greco-Roman classics of history and literature. The collection is unusual, as one of the larger Oxford academic book-lists of this period, not to contain, apparent-ly, one work by Erasmus.

The inventory exists in two manuscripts: the original (A) and a fair copy (B). Manuscript A has been adopted as the copy-text except where manuscript B clearly presents a preferred reading. Significant variants are noted in the annotations.

Oxford University Archives, Bodleian Library: Hyp.B.11.

§

Fowler, Thomas. 1893. *The History of Corpus Christi College, With Lists of Its Members*. Oxford: For the Oxford Historical Society at the Clarendon Press.

Gillow, Joseph. 1885–1902. *A Literary and Biographical History or Bibliographical Dictionary of the English Catholics from the Breach with Rome, in 1534, to the Present Time*. 5 vols. London and New York: Burns & Oates.

§

117.1	Opera Tullii
117.2	Loci Communes Musculi
117.3	Calvini Epistole
117.4:1	Calvinus super 4 evangelistis et Actis
117.4:2	[See 117.4:1]
117.5	Calvini super Epist. pauli
117.6	in Proverbia, Ecclesiast' et Cantica Canticorum
117.7	Opera Gregorii
117.8:1	In Genesis et Psalmos
117.8:2	[See 117.8:1]
117.9	Concordantie Biblie
117.10	Quintilianus
117.11	Historia Polidori Virgilii
117.12	Cronica Pantolionis
117.13	Testamentum Besae
117.14	Alexander ab Alexandro
117.15	Lichosthenes, Apothegmes
117.16	Meander's Sentenses
117.17	Haymer's Iliades
117.18	Gwalterus super Actis
117.19	testamente
117.20	Comedie Plauti
117.21	Cronica Sleidani
117.22	Psalterium grec'
117.23	Sententia Ciceronis
117.24	Herodotus
117.25	Flores Poetarum
117.26	Valerius Maximus
117.27	Mardus super Tullio
117.28	Eutropii Historie
117.29	Hunei Logica
117.30	Officia Tullii
117.31:A	Licosthenes, Similitudines
117.31:B	[See 117.31:A]

117.32	Manutius de legibus
117.33	Virgilius
117.34	Guntheri Rethorica
117.35	Hesiodorus grece et latine
117.36	Plutharke de montibus et fluminibus
117.37	Radolphi Logica
117.38	Cires, Grammatica
117.39	Eliarus de varia historia
117.40	Brandolinus de conscribendis epistolis
117.41	Opera Prudentii
117.42	Logica Sturmi
117.43	Virgilius
117.44	Disciplina Ecclesie Anglicane
117.45	Ringilberdus
117.46	Melancton
117.47	Foxius
117.48	Regule Vite
117.49	Partitiones Tullii
117.50	Instituciones Ciri ex Xenophonte
117.51	Nassobenius
117.52	Strabeus
117.53	Biblia
117.54	Flores Rethorici
117.55	Mathisius de rerum principiis
117.56	Sturmius de periodis
117.57	Fridericus
117.58	Psalterium cum Psalmis
117.59	Fenestella de magistratibus
117.60	Dialogi Luciani
117.61	Calvinus, Cathakisme
117.62	Rethorica ad Herenium
117.63	Boetius, Historia
117.64	Vergilius cum commento
117.65	Lyra super 4 evangelistis
117.66	Frithreus, Tables
117.67	3 part' of Garsenes Worke
117.68	Quintus Curtius
117.69	Tropezantius, Rethorica
117.70	Robertollus de artificio dicendi
117.71	Boetius cum commento
117.72	Hemmingius de methodis
117.73	The forme of prayers
117.74	Horatius
117.75	Sententiae Ciceronis
117.76	Epistole Ovidii

117.77   Palengenius
117.78   Beza de predestinacione
117.79:1-2   ii paper bookes
117.80 multiple   certen other paper bookes

§

117.1 Opera Tullii

Marcus Tullius Cicero. [*Works*]. Continent (probable): date indeterminable.

Probably not an STC book, but see STC 5265.7 *et seq.* STC 5265.7 does not contain anything like the entire corpus. *Language(s)*: Latin. Appraised at 20s in 1577.

117.2 Loci Communes Musculi

Wolfgang Musculus. *Loci communes*. Continent: date indeterminable.

Conceivably Andreas Musculus's *Loci communes sacri*. *Language(s)*: Latin. Appraised at 5s in 1577.

117.3 Calvini Epistole

Jean Calvin. [*Epistolae*]. Continent: date indeterminable.

At this valuation, probably a folio edition of the *Epistolae et responsa*, first published in 1575, but the 1537 *Epistolae duae de rebus hoc saeculo cognitu necessariis* must remain a possibility. *Language(s)*: Latin. Appraised at 4s in 1577.

117.4:1 Calvinus super 4 evangelistis et Actis

Jean Calvin. *Harmonia*. Continent: 1555-1572.

This and the commentary on Acts were printed separately. This entry must, therefore, refer to two different books. The inventory exists in two manuscripts, the original (A) and a fair copy (B); manuscript A has been adopted as the copy-text. Manuscript B omits *Actis* in this entry. *Language(s)*: Latin. Appraised with one other at 6s 8d in 1577.

117.4:2 [See 117.4:1]

Jean Calvin. [*Acts: commentary*]. Continent: 1552-1573.

Perhaps bound with the preceding. *Language(s)*: Latin. Appraised with one other at 6s 8d in 1577.

117.5 Calvini super Epist. pauli

Jean Calvin. [*Epistles–Paul: commentary*]. Continent: 1548-1572.

This entry occurs only in manuscript B. *Language(s)*: Latin. Appraised at 5s in 1577.

117.6 in Proverbia, Ecclesiast' et Cantica Canticorum

Unidentified. [*Hagiographa: commentary*]. Continent (probable): date indeterminable.

Probably not an STC book. The manuscript entry is located just after Calvin's commentaries on the Gospels and Acts, but Calvin does not seem to have published commentaries on any of the three books of the Bible named here. Manuscript B omits *et Cantica Canticorum*. *Language(s)*: Latin (probable). Appraised at 5s in 1577.

117.7 Opera Gregorii

Perhaps Gregory I, *Saint, Pope*. [*Works*]. Continent: date indeterminable.

Others are possible, including Gregory, *of Nazianzus* and Gregory, *of Nyssa*. *Language(s)*: Latin. Appraised at 4s in 1577.

117.8:1 In Genesis et Psalmos

Probably Jean Calvin. [*Genesis: commentary*]. Continent: date indeterminable.

Manuscript A reads *Genesis et Psalmos*, an unusual combination. Manuscript B prefaces the entry with *In* as above. Since Calvin wrote on both (unlike Gregory, whose work precedes this) and since Calvin is represented in entries at 117.4 and 117.5, one can reasonably conjecture that this entry represents those two commentaries bound together. *Language(s)*: Latin. Appraised with one other at 6s in 1577.

117.8:2 [See 117.8:1]

Probably Jean Calvin. [*Psalms: commentary and text*]. (*Bible–O.T.*). Continent: date indeterminable.

See the annotations to the preceding. *Language(s)*: Latin. Appraised with one other at 6s in 1577.

117.9 Concordantie Biblie

Unidentified [Biblical concordance]. Continent: date indeterminable. *Language(s)*: Latin. Appraised at 2s 6d in 1577.

117.10 Quintilianus

Marcus Fabius Quintilianus. Unidentified. Continent: date indeterminable.

Probably Quintilian's *Institutiones oratoriae*, but possibly the whole works or the *Declamationes*. *Language(s)*: Latin. Appraised at 13d in 1577.

117.11 Historia Polidori Virgilii

Polydorus Vergilius. *Anglica historia*. Continent: date indeterminable.

Manuscript B reads: *Historici pollidori*. *Language(s)*: Latin. Appraised at 2s 6d in 1577.

117.12 Cronica Pantolionis
Heinrich Pantaleon. *Chronographia ecclesiae christianae*. Continent: date indeterminable.
Language(s): Latin. Appraised at 12d in 1577.

117.13 Testamentum Besae
[*Bible–N.T.*]. Translated and edited by Théodore de Bèze. Britain or Continent: date indeterminable.
STC 2802 *et seq.* and non-STC. *Language(s)*: Latin Greek (perhaps). Appraised at 2s in 1577.

117.14 Alexander ab Alexandro
Alexander ab Alexandro. *Geniales dies*. Continent: date indeterminable.
Language(s): Latin. Appraised at 2s in 1577.

117.15 Lichosthenes, Apothegmes
Conrad Lycosthenes (Conrad Wolffhart). *Apophthegmata*. Continent: date indeterminable.
Language(s): Latin. Appraised at 2s in 1577.

117.16 Meander's Sentenses
Menander. *Sententiae*. Continent: date indeterminable.
This seems not to have been published separately by the date of this inventory, but it appears in several varied collections (see, e.g., Adams P1692). *Language(s)*: Latin Greek (perhaps). Appraised at 12d in 1577.

117.17 Haymer's Iliades
Homer. *Iliad*. Continent: date indeterminable.
Language(s): Latin (probable) Greek (perhaps). Appraised at 6d in 1577.

117.18 Gwalterus super Actis
Rudolph Walther. [*Acts: commentary and text*]. (*Bible–N.T.*). Continent: date indeterminable.
Language(s): Latin. Appraised at 16d in 1577.

117.19 testamente
[*Bible–N.T.*]. Probably edited and translated by Rudolph Walther. Continent: date indeterminable.
Since the manuscript entry is indented under *Gwalterus*, a presumption is created that it, like the previous entry, refers to Walther. Since Walther did in fact edit and translate the New Testament, the identification becomes almost certain. Manuscript B reads: *testamentum*. *Language(s)*: Latin. Appraised at 20d in 1577.

117.20 Comedie Plauti

Titus Maccius Plautus. *Comoediae*. Continent: date indeterminable. *Language(s)*: Latin. Appraised at 6d in 1577.

117.21 Cronica Sleidani

Joannes Philippson, *Sleidanus*. Unidentified. Continent: date indeterminable.

The author published two popular chronicles, one about the reign of his contemporary, the Emperor Charles V, and the other about the principal empires of Biblical times. *Language(s)*: Latin. Appraised at 16d in 1577.

117.22 Psalterium grec'

[*Bible–O.T.–Psalms*]. Continent: date indeterminable.

Conceivably a liturgical form. *Language(s)*: Greek. Appraised at 6d in 1577.

117.23 Sententia Ciceronis

Marcus Tullius Cicero. [*Selections*]. Continent (probable): date indeterminable.

Probably not an STC book, but see STC 5318.3. The entry is from manuscript B; manuscript A reads *Comedie*. Charnock owned another copy of Cicero's *sententiae*; see 117.75. STC 5318.3 contains selections from Demosthenes and Terence as well, but the title page begins with the words *Sententiae Ciceronis*, thus creating the possibility that this entry refers to that book. See Adams C2012 *et seq. Language(s)*: Latin. Appraised at 6d in 1577.

117.24 Herodotus

Herodotus. [*Historiae*]. Continent: date indeterminable.

Language(s): Greek (probable) Latin (probable). Appraised at 8d in 1577.

117.25 Flores Poetarum

Flores poetarum. Continent: date indeterminable.

An anthology with editions dating from 1480. *Language(s)*: Latin. Appraised at 6d in 1577.

117.26 Valerius Maximus

Valerius Maximus. *Facta et dicta memorabilia*. Continent: date indeterminable.

Language(s): Latin. Appraised at 6d in 1577.

117.27 Mardus super Tullio

Petrus Marsus. [*Cicero–De officiis: commentary*]. Continent: date indeterminable.

Appears most frequently in collections with other works by Cicero and

other commentators. The entry is from manuscript B; manuscript A reads
Nardus for *Mardus*. *Language(s)*: Latin. Appraised at 6d in 1577.

117.28 Eutropii Historie
Flavius Eutropius. [*Historia Romana*]. Continent: date indeterminable.
Language(s): Latin. Appraised at 4d in 1577.

117.29 Hunei Logica
Augustinus Hunnaeus. *Logices fundamentum*. Continent: date indetermin-
able.
The entry is from manuscript B; manuscript A reads *Logica Hyrdi*.
Language(s): Latin. Appraised at 5d in 1577.

117.30 Officia Tullii
Marcus Tullius Cicero. *De officiis*. Continent: date indeterminable.
Probably not an STC book, but see STC 5281.8 *et seq.* STC 5281.8 *et seq.*
contain both Latin and English, but a Continental edition, Latin only, seems
more likely. Collections often lead with *De officiis*. *Language(s)*: Latin English
(perhaps). Appraised at 3d in 1577.

117.31:A   Licosthenes, Similitudines
Conrad Lycosthenes (Conrad Wolffhart). *Similium loci communes*. Basle: per
E. Episcopium et Nicolai fr. haeredes, 1575 (composite publication).
Language(s): Latin. Appraised [a composite volume] at 6d in 1577.

117.31:B   [See 117.31:A]
Theodor Zwinger. *Similitudinem methodo*. [Composite publication].
Language(s): Latin. Appraised [a composite volume] at 6d in 1577.

117.32 Manutius de legibus
Paolo Manuzio. *Antiquitatum Romanarum liber de legibus*. Continent: date
indeterminable.
Language(s): Latin. Appraised at 6d in 1577.

117.33 Virgilius
Publius Virgilius Maro. Probably [*Works*]. Britain or Continent: date indeterminable.
STC 24787 and non-STC. The appraisal value is low, but not impossible for
the *opera*; perhaps only part. See 117.64 appraised at 5s. Nor is Polydore Ver-
gil likely, entered as "Polidori" in 117.11. See also 117.43. *Language(s)*: Latin.
Appraised at 4d in 1577.

117.34 Guntheri Rethorica
Petrus Guntherus. *De arte rhetorica libri duo*. Continent: 1521–1568.
One edition in each of these years, with the 1568 edition carrying a com-

mentary by Valentinus Erythraeus. *Language(s)*: Latin. Appraised at 4d in 1577.

117.35 Hesiodorus grece et latine
Perhaps Hesiod. [*Works*]. Continent: date indeterminable.

Both manuscripts read *Hesiodorus*, a most unusual form for Hesiod. B omits *grec et latine*. Perhaps Heliodorus (the *Historica Aethiopica*) was intended, but if so, no Greek-Latin edition seems to have been published by this date, although the Greek edition of 1534 bears the titles in both Greek and Latin. *Language(s)*: Greek Latin. Appraised at 6d in 1577.

117.36 Plutharke de montibus et fluminibus
Plutarch (spurious). *De fluviorum et montium nominibus*. Continent: date indeterminable.

This does not seem to have been published separately by the date of this inventory. Two collections in which it did appear are found at Adams A2014 (under Flavius Arrianus) and C2430 (under Natalis Comes). *Language(s)*: Latin (probable) Greek (perhaps). Appraised at 6d in 1577.

117.37 Radolphi Logica
Unidentified. Continent: date indeterminable.

Manuscript B reads *Ridolphi*. Either Rodolphus Agricola or Caspar Rhodolphus, both of whom wrote on logic. *Language(s)*: Latin. Appraised at 2d in 1577.

117.38 Cires, Grammatica
Unidentified. Continent (probable): date indeterminable.

Probably not an STC book. Martin Crusius? Joannes Sartoris? Jacobus Ceporinus? Manuscript B gives *Grammatica* only; perhaps the copier was puzzled also. *Language(s)*: Latin (probable). Appraised at 4d in 1577.

117.39 Eliarus de varia historia
Claudius Aelianus. *Varia historia*. Continent: date indeterminable.

Both manuscripts read *Eliarus*. *Language(s)*: Latin (probable) Greek (perhaps). Appraised at 4d in 1577.

117.40 Brandolinus de conscribendis epistolis
Aurelius Brandolinus (Lippus). *De ratione scribendi*. Britain or Continent: 1549–1573.

STC 3542 and non-STC. Editions usually include other works. *Language(s)*: Latin. Appraised at 6d in 1577.

117.41 Opera Prudentii
Aurelius Prudentius Clemens. [*Works*]. Continent: date indeterminable. *Language(s)*: Latin. Appraised at 4d in 1577.

117.42 Logica Sturmi

Joannes Sturmius. [*Dialectica*]. Continent: date indeterminable. *Language(s)*: Latin. Appraised at 6d in 1577.

117.43 Virgilius

Publius Virgilius Maro. Unidentified. Place unknown: stationer unknown, date indeterminable.

STC/non-STC status unknown. Perhaps a single work, as 117.33 may be. See 117.64. *Language(s)*: Latin. Appraised at 2d in 1577.

117.44 Disciplina Ecclesie Anglicane

Walter Travers. *Ecclesiastica disciplina*. Heidelberg: Michael Schirat, 1574. Manuscript B reads *Ecclesiastica Angel*. Shaaber T110. *Language(s)*: Latin. Appraised at 2d in 1577.

117.45 Ringilberdus

Joachimus Fortius Ringelbergius. Unidentified. Continent: date indeterminable.

A rather low valuation for his popular encyclopedic *opera*, but that work could be intended. *Language(s)*: Latin. Appraised at 2d in 1577.

117.46 Melancton

Philipp Melanchthon. Unidentified. Continent (probable): date indeterminable.

Probably not an STC book. Several of Melanchthon's treatises had been translated into English before 1577, but a Continental Latin volume is much more likely. *Language(s)*: Latin (probable). Appraised at 2d in 1577.

117.47 Foxius

Unidentified. Place unknown: stationer unknown, date indeterminable.

STC/non-STC status unknown. John Foxe, Sebastiano Fox Morzillo, and Edward Fox, *Bishop* are all reasonable possibilities. *Language(s)*: Latin. Appraised at 3d in 1577.

117.48 Regule Vite

Unidentified. Continent (probable): date indeterminable.

Probably not an STC book. Georg Walther's *Regulae vitae christianae* (1572) and the much more popular *Regulae vitae* by David Chytraeus (from 1555) are among the possibilities of manuals for Christian life that this entry almost certainly represents. Manuscript B reads *Regula*. *Language(s)*: Latin. Appraised at 4d in 1577.

117.49 Partitiones Tullii

Marcus Tullius Cicero. *De partitione oratoria*. Continent: date indeterminable.

Language(s): Latin. Appraised at 4d in 1577.

117.50 Instituciones Ciri ex Xenophonte
Xenophon. *Cyropaedia*. Continent: date indeterminable.
Language(s): Latin. Appraised at 6d in 1577.

117.51 Nassobenius
Nascimbaenus Nascimbaenius. [*Cicero–De inventione: commentary*]. Venice: apud Bologninum Zalterium, 1563–1564.
Language(s): Latin. Appraised at 6d in 1577.

117.52 Strabeus
Jacobus Lodovicus Strebaeus. Unidentified. Continent: date indeterminable.

Manuscript B reads *Strebeus*. Strebaeus wrote at least three works on rhetoric, two of them commentaries on rhetorical works by Cicero, one a commentary on the *De partitione*, for which see 117.49. *Language(s)*: Latin. Appraised at 2d in 1577.

117.53 Biblia
The Bible. Britain or Continent: date indeterminable.
STC 2055 and non-STC. *Language(s)*: Latin. Appraised at 6d in 1577.

117.54 Flores Rethorici
Unidentified. Place unknown: stationer unknown, date indeterminable.
STC/non-STC status unknown. *Language(s)*: Latin. Appraised at 4d in 1577.

117.55 Mathisius de rerum principiis
Gerardus Matthisius (Geldrensis). [*Aristotle–Selected works–Philosophia naturalis–Epitome: commentary*]. Continent: 1556–1570.
Language(s): Latin. Appraised at 3d in 1577.

117.56 Sturmius de periodis
Joannes Sturmius. *De periodis*. Strassburg: (different houses), 1550–1567.
Language(s): Latin Greek (perhaps). Appraised at 6d in 1577.

117.57 Fridericus
Unidentified. Continent (probable): date indeterminable.
Probably not an STC book. Manuscript B reads *Friderius*, which would allow for Joannes Freder as a possibility. *Language(s)*: Latin (probable). Appraised at 6d in 1577.

117.58 Psalterium cum Psalmis
[*Bible–O.T.–Psalms*]. Britain or Continent: date indeterminable.

STC 2368 *et seq.* and non-STC. A book containing two versions of the Psalms, perhaps one liturgical and the other not, or one metrical and one prose, or even a diglot. There were English as well as numerous Latin editions containing, opposite the liturgical text, either a verse paraphrase or a text derived from one of the new scholarly editions. *Language(s)*: Latin (probable) English (perhaps). Appraised at 8d in 1577.

117.59 Fenestella de magistratibus
Andreas Dominicus Floccus (Lucius Fenestella). *De magistratibus sacerdotiisque Romanorum.* Continent: date indeterminable.
Language(s): Latin. Appraised at 2d in 1577.

117.60 Dialogi Luciani
Lucian, *of Samosata.* Unidentified. Place unknown: stationer unknown, date indeterminable.
STC/non-STC status unknown. What arrangement of the *Dialogues* cannot be determined. *Language(s)*: Latin (probable) Greek (perhaps). Appraised at 4d in 1577.

117.61 Calvinus, Cathakisme
Jean Calvin. [*Catechism*]. Britain or Continent: date indeterminable.
STC 4375 *et seq.* and non-STC. *Language(s)*: Latin. Appraised at 1d in 1577.

117.62 Rethorica ad Herenium
Marcus Tullius Cicero (spurious). *Rhetorica ad Herennium.* Britain or Continent: date indeterminable.
STC 5323.5 and non-STC. *Language(s)*: Latin. Appraised at 12d in 1577.

117.63 Boetius, Historia
Hector Boethius (Boece). *Scotorum historiae.* Britain or Continent: 1526–1575.
STC 3203 and non-STC. The entry is from manuscript B; manuscript A reads *Boeteus, Histories,* which may indicate that the book was the English translation. *Language(s)*: Latin (probable) English (perhaps). Appraised at 8d in 1577.

117.64 Vergilius cum commento
Publius Virgilius Maro. [*Works*]. Britain or Continent: date indeterminable.
STC 24788 and non-STC. Charnock owned two less expensive works by Virgil; see 117.33 and 117.43. *Language(s)*: Latin. Appraised at 5s in 1577.

117.65 Lyra super 4 evangelistis
Nicolaus de Lyra. [*Postilla* (part)]. Continent: date indeterminable.
Language(s): Latin. Appraised at 12d in 1577.

117.66 Frithreus, Tables

Probably Valentinus Erythraeus. Unidentified. Continent: date indeterminable.

Almost certainly a slip of the pen for Erithreus—a common spelling of Erythraeus, who published at least three different works on logic or rhetoric that contain the Latin word *tabulae* in a prominent place in the title. *Language(s)*: Latin. Appraised at 8d in 1577.

117.67 3 part' of Garsenes Worke

Perhaps Joannes Gerson (Jean Charlier de Gerson). [*Works* (part)]. Continent: date indeterminable.

The entry is from manuscript B; manuscript A reads *Garsies workes*. *Language(s)*: Latin. Appraised at 21d in 1577.

117.68 Quintus Curtius

Quintus Curtius Rufus. *De rebus gestis Alexandri Magni*. Continent: date indeterminable.

Manuscript B reads: *Quintus Muveius*. *Language(s)*: Latin. Appraised at 4d in 1577.

117.69 Tropezantius, Rethorica

Georgius Trapezuntius. [*Rhetorica*]. Continent: date indeterminable. *Language(s)*: Latin. Appraised at 6d in 1577.

117.70 Robertollus de artificio dicendi

Franciscus Robortellus. *De artificio dicendi*. Bologna: typis Alexandri Benatii, 1567.
Language(s): Latin. Appraised at 10d in 1577.

117.71 Boetius cum commento

Anicius M.T.S. Boethius. *De consolatione philosophiae*. Continent: date indeterminable.
Language(s): Latin. Appraised at 6d in 1577.

117.72 Hemmingius de methodis

Niels Hemmingsen. *De methodis*. Continent: date indeterminable.
Language(s): Latin. Appraised at 4d in 1577.

117.73 The forme of prayers

Unidentified. Britain (probable): date indeterminable.

Unidentifiable in the STC. Manuscript B reads *Prayer*. Possibilities include: STC 16479 *et seq.*, STC 16505 *et seq.*, as well as STC 20188.3 and 20188.7. *Language(s)*: English. Appraised at 4d in 1577.

117.74 Horatius
Quintus Horatius Flaccus. Probably [*Works*]. Britain or Continent: date indeterminable.
STC 13784 and non-STC. *Language(s)*: Latin. Appraised at 2d in 1577.

117.75 Sententiae Ciceronis
Marcus Tullius Cicero. [*Selections*]. Britain or Continent: date indeterminable.
Probably not an STC book, but see STC 5318.3. See 117.23 for another copy. STC 5318.3 contains selections from Demosthenes and Terence as well, but the title page begins with the words *Sententiae Ciceronis*, thus creating the possibility that this entry refers to that book. *Language(s)*: Latin. Appraised at 4d in 1577.

117.76 Epistole Ovidii
Publius Ovidius Naso. *Heroides*. Continent: date indeterminable.
Language(s): Latin. Appraised at 2d in 1577.

117.77 Palengenius
Marcellus Palingenius (Pietro Angelo Manzolli [Stellatus]). *Zodiacus vitae*. Britain or Continent: date indeterminable.
STC 19138.5 *et seq.* and non-STC, and see also STC 19148 *et seq.* Latin editions from England from 1569; English versions from 1560. Manuscript B omits this entry. *Language(s)*: Latin (probable) English (perhaps). Appraised at 6d in 1577.

117.78 Beza de predestinacione
Théodore de Bèze. *Ad sycophantarum quorundam responsio*. Geneva (probable): excudebat Conradus Badius, 1558–1559.
Bèze's *De praedestinationes doctrina et vero* ... did not appear until 1582, five years after the date of this inventory. The phrase *Dei Praedestionationem* appears in the long title of this work. Gardy nos. 93–94. *Language(s)*: Latin. Appraised at 4d in 1577.

117.79:1–2   ii paper bookes
Unidentified. Provenances unknown: dates indeterminable.
Manuscripts. Taken to be notebooks, not blank books. *Language(s)*: Unknown. Appraised at 8d in 1577.

117.80 multiple   certen other paper bookes
Unidentified. Provenances unknown: dates indeterminable.
Manuscripts. Manuscript B omits this entry. *Language(s)*: Unknown. Appraised at 2s in 1577.

Cliffley. Probably Cleric: Inventory. 1577

ELIZABETH M. TILYOU

When the inventory of the goods of "Sir" Cliffley (Clyffley, Clyfly, Clifley) was compiled on 26 June 1577, he apparently was, or recently had been, a resident at Broadgates Hall (now Pembroke College), which was also the annex for commoners of Christ Church (McConica 1986, 40). Nothing is known of Cliffley, including his given name; the term "Sir" was in general use as a term of respect, and in academic circles it usually meant B.A. The wording of the inventory, "minister in Brored Yates," (rather than "of"), as well as the absence of Cliffley's name in *Alumni Oxonienses* and in the *Register of the University of Oxford* (Clark 2.ii) suggests that Cliffley was renting rooms (a "chamber and Studie") in Broadgates and was not a graduate. Whether he was a cleric or a servant, another meaning of the word "minister," cannot be determined, but his collection of books does display an interest in theology and gives evidence of an interest, of a Puritan bent, in contemporary religious issues. Taken in the presence of Broadgates' principal, one "Master Somaster," probably George Sommastre or Summaster (*Alumni Oxonienses*, 4:1388), the inventory carries no appraisals and provides no reason for its purpose.

His books include a seven-volume Hebrew (perhaps polyglot) Bible and Muenster's *Grammatica hebraica*, revealing an aspiration to Hebrew. The collection contains works of theology, the classics (both Latin and Greek), and materials traditionally used in the liberal arts curriculum. Of the classics, two works by Cicero, two works by Demosthenes, and one work each by Ovid and Marcus Aurelius are listed. Also represented are works on logic, including Aristotle's *Organon* and probably Cornelius Valerius's *Tabula totius dialectices*.

Of the twenty named titles in the collection, more than a third are theological, including both scriptural and contemporary religious works. Thus, it might be conjectured that Cliffley's library was used in part for his ministry. Along with the books found in his chambers Cliffley also had many "other goodes," which may indicate that he had been residing at Broadgates for some time.

Oxford University Archives, Bodleian Library: Hyp.B.11

§

McConica, James. 1986. "The Rise of the Undergraduate College," in *The Collegiate University*, ed. James McConica. Volume 3 of *The History of the University of Oxford*, gen. ed., T.H. Aston. Oxford: Oxford Univ. Press, pp. 1–68.

§

118.1   Erasmi Colloquium
118.2   Clenardi Grammatica
118.3   Novum testamentum
118.4   A Legendarie of the cardinal of Lorran
118.5   Muenster's grammar
118.6   Mr Kyngesmylle's treateis of affliction
118.7   a Latten grammar
118.8:1–7   7 smale volumes of the ebrue bible
118.9   Tulli's Epistelles
118.10   Calven's Institucons
118.11   Ovide's Episteles
118.12   Psalmes in Latten
118.13   Tully's Office
118.14   Marcus Aurelius
118.15   Cleanarde's Grammer
118.16   Mr Norb**oke
118.17   Valerius Tables
118.18:1–3   iii paper bokes
118.19   Demostenes Pro Corona
118.20   Demosthenes Pro Megapolitis
118.21   Aristoteles, Organum
118.22:1–2   ii lytell paper bokes

§

118.1 Erasmi Colloquium
    Desiderius Erasmus. *Colloquia*. Britain or Continent: date indeterminable.
    STC 10450.6 *et seq.* and non-STC. *Language(s)*: Latin.

118.2 Clenardi Grammatica

Nicolaus Clenardus. Probably [*Institutiones linguae graecae*]. Continent: date indeterminable.

See 118.15. *Language(s)*: Greek Latin.

118.3 Novum testamentum

[*Bible–N.T.*]. Britain or Continent: date indeterminable.

STC 2799 *et seq.* and non-STC. *Language(s)*: Latin (probable) English (perhaps) Greek (perhaps).

118.4 A Legendarie of the cardinal of Lorran

Louis Regnier de la Planche (François de L'Isle, *pseudonym*). *A legendarie, conteining an ample discourse of the life of Charles cardinal of Lorraine.* London (probable): (stationer unknown), 1577.

STC 20855. *Language(s)*: English.

118.5 Muenster's grammar

Sebastian Muenster. Probably [*Grammatica hebraica*]. Continent: date indeterminable.

See 118.15. There is a remote possibility that this represents Muenster's *Chaldaica grammatica*. *Language(s)*: Hebrew Latin.

118.6 Mr Kyngesmylle's treateis of affliction

Andrew Kingsmill. *A most excellent and comfortable treatise, for all such as are troubled in minde. And also a conference betwixt a Christian & an afflicted conscience.* Edited by Francis Mills. London: C. Barkar, 1577.

STC 15000. If Cliffley did not acquire the work in the last year of his life, when it was first printed, he may have had access to a circulating copy of a manuscript. *Language(s)*: English.

118.7 a Latten grammar

Unidentified. Place unknown: stationer unknown, date indeterminable.

STC/non-STC status unknown. *Language(s)*: Latin.

118.8:1–7 7 smale volumes of the ebrue bible

[*Bible–O.T.*]. Continent: date indeterminable.

A portion or all of the thirteen-part Robert Stephanus edition (1544–1546) is most likely (see Adams B1224). The later Plantin edition (Adams B1228 *et seq.*) is also a possibility. Both editions are sextodecimo. *Language(s)*: Hebrew.

118.9 Tulli's Epistelles

Marcus Tullius Cicero. Probably [*Selected works–Epistolae*]. Continent: date indeterminable.

Conceivably the popular *Epistolae ad familiares*. *Language(s)*: Latin.

118.10 Calven's Institucons

Jean Calvin. *Institutio Christianae religionis*. Britain or Continent: date indeterminable.

STC 4414 *et seq.* and non-STC. The entry suggests the possibility of an English edition. *Language(s)*: Latin (probable) English (perhaps).

118.11 Ovide's Episteles

Publius Ovidius Naso. *Heroides*. Continent: date indeterminable.
Language(s): Latin.

118.12 Psalmes in Latten

[*Bible–O.T.–Psalms*]. Britain or Continent: date indeterminable.
STC 2354 *et seq.* and non-STC. *Language(s)*: Latin.

118.13 Tully's Office

Marcus Tullius Cicero. *De officiis*. Continent (probable): date indeterminable.

Probably not an STC book, but see STC 5278 *et seq.* Conceivably this entry
represents one of the many editions of Cicero's *Works* with *De officiis* leading.
The English wording of the entry also suggests the possibility of one of the
English-Latin editions. *Language(s)*: Latin (probable) English (perhaps).

118.14 Marcus Aurelius

Probably Marcus Aurelius Antoninus. [*De vita sua*]. Continent: date indeterminable.

Antonio de Guevara's fictional romantic biography, *The golden boke of Marcus Aurelius*, is not something Cliffley is likely to have had in his library,
though it cannot be rejected as a possibility. *Language(s)*: Latin (probable)
Greek (perhaps).

118.15 Cleanarde's Grammer

Nicolaus Clenardus. Perhaps *Tabula in grammaticen hebraeam*. Continent:
date indeterminable.

Since there are two grammars of Clenard's in Cliffley's inventory, it seems
likely that one is Greek and one is Hebrew. This is particularly feasible
because the list contains seven volumes of the Hebrew Bible. Both entries
(118.2 and this) may, however, represent copies of Clenard's much more
popular Greek grammar, especially since a Hebrew grammar is likely represented by 118.5. *Language(s)*: Hebrew Latin.

118.16 Mr Norb**oke

John Northbrooke. Unidentified. London: (different houses), date indeterminable.

See STC 18663, 18644.5, and 18670 *et seq.* Of Northbrook's three different works, all with titles beginning *Spiritus est vicarius Christi in terra*, the most likely are STC 18663, *Spiritus est . . . A breefe and pithie summe of the Chritian faith*, and STC 18644.5, *Spiritus est . . . The poore mans Garden*, both first published in 1571. STC 18670, *Spiritus est . . . A treatise wherein dicing, daunting, Vaine playes or Enterluds with other idle pastimes . . . are reproved by the Authoritie of the word of God and auntient writers*, did not appear until 1577, the date of this inventory. *Language(s)*: English.

118.17 Valerius Tables
Cornelius Valerius. Probably *Tabulae totius dialectices*. Continent: 1548–1575.

Valerius's *In universam bene dicendi rationem tabula* is a less likely possibility. *Language(s)*: Latin.

118.18:1–3 iii paper bokes
Unidentified. Provenances unknown: dates indeterminable. Manuscripts. *Language(s)*: Unknown.

118.19 Demostenes Pro Corona
Demosthenes. *De corona*. Continent: 1555–1570.

The date range represents solo editions. The entry, however, may, with the following item, come from a collection of Demosthenes' orations. *Language(s)*: Greek (probable) Latin (perhaps).

118.20 Demosthenes Pro Megapolitis
Demosthenes. *Pro Megalopolitis*. Continent: date indeterminable.

Not published alone prior to the date of this inventory, but leads in a Greek collection of Demosthenes (Louvain, 1546). See the annotation to the preceding item. *Language(s)*: Greek (probable) Latin (perhaps).

118.21 Aristoteles, Organum
Aristotle. *Organon*. Continent: date indeterminable.
Language(s): Latin (probable) Greek (perhaps).

118.22:1–2 ii lytell paper bokes
Unidentified. Provenances unknown: dates indeterminable. Manuscripts. Perhaps personal notebooks. *Language(s)*: Unknown.

William Dawson. Scholar (M.A.):
Probate Inventory. 1577

JOCELYN SHEPPARD

William Dawson graduated B.A. on 13 December 1570 and proceeded M.A. on 1 July 1573. He was elected fellow of Queen's College in 1575 and died intestate in 1577 (*Alumni Oxonienses*, 1:387). Along with a number of other Oxford scholars that year, Dawson may have fallen victim to the plague (Ker, 473), or an epidemic of typhus (McConica, 648).

The book-list below is taken from an inventory of his goods dated 25 October 1577. In light of Queen's College's emphasis on the study of theology (Green 1974, 10 and McConica 1986, 59, 62), it is not surprising that Dawson's collection should consist primarily of religious works. Indeed, over eighty percent of the books named by the compilers are concerned with theology or church history (forty-six unnamed "prented bokes and paper bokes" are curiously and frustratingly lumped together at the end of the list). In addition, the many reformist writers represented (Bèze, Bucer, Bullinger, Calvin, Hemmingsen, Mainardi, and Veron, among others) probably reflect Dawson's theological sympathies, which would be in keeping with Jennifer Loach's description of Queen's as being "especially noted for [its] radical atmosphere" (Loach 1986, 391). Dawson apparently had undertaken to learn Hebrew as the appearance of a Hebrew grammar shows (119.12); no other books in that language, however, are listed. He owned one book in Greek and Latin (119.19), but his library, apart from the forty-six unnamed titles, consists mainly of Latin texts, although an unusually large portion of books, nearly a third, are in English. Given his apparent reformist leanings, presses in German-speaking Europe, not surprisingly, account for about a third of the books listed.

Oxford University Archives, Bodleian Library: Hyp.B.12.

§

Green, V.H.H. 1974. *A History of Oxford University*. London: B.T. Batsford.

Loach, Jennifer. 1986. "Reformation Controversies," in *The Collegiate University*, ed., James K. McConica. Volume 3 of *The History of the University of Oxford*, gen. ed., T.H. Aston. Oxford: Clarendon Press, pp. 363–96.

McConica, James K. 1986. "The Rise of the Undergraduate College," in *The Collegiate University*, ed., James K. McConica. Volume 3 of *The History of the University of Oxford*, gen. ed., T.H. Aston. Oxford: Clarendon Press, pp. 1–68.

§

119.1	Theatrum Humane Vite in v volum
119.2	gulater in Johannem
119.3	loci communes Marloreti
119.4	Musculus in mattheum
119.5	pars eras paraph:
119.6	buserus in epist pauli ad ro:
119.7	musculus super psal:
119.8	nichola blones
119.9	Institu: Calvini anglice
119.10	Calvinus in Galathos anglice
119.11	Calvinus ad ephesios
119.12	gram: Civeleri
119.13	Selneccerr in epist: petri
119.14	pedegogea selnec:
119.15	Epist Martirum in Englyshe
119.16	Epist: Bese
119.17	pericope evangeliorum
119.18	vita christiani hemingii
119.19	Capita Religionis
119.20	anotami of the masse
119.21	Cathakysmus Canisii
119.22	flores barnardi
119.23	Enchiridion hemingii
119.24	Novum testa: besi latin:
119.25	novum test: anglice
119.26	Christian Prayers
119.27	Epist: barnardi
119.28	Ethica abetsii

119.29   harmonus Episcop:
119.30   Hipperius
119.31   Confessio besi anglic
119.32   Major in Thest
119.33   Consiones funebres
119.34   de jure magestratuum
119.35   Veron de predestinacione
119.36   Sheperdes callender
119.37:1–46   prented bokes and paper bokes in nomber lxvi

§

119.1 Theatrum Humane Vite in v volum

Conrad Lycosthenes (Conrad Wolffhart) and Theodor Zwinger. *Theatrum vitae humanae.* Continent: 1565–1572.

Work was begun by Lycosthenes. This entry is likely to be five volumes of a larger set, or, perhaps, a larger set bound in five volumes. *Language(s)*: Latin. Appraised at 13s 4d in 1577.

119.2 gulater in Johannem

Rudolph Walther. [*John: commentary and text*]. (*Bible–N.T.*). Continent: date indeterminable.

Language(s): Latin. Appraised at 5s in 1577.

119.3 loci communes Marloreti

Augustine Marlorat. [*Thesaurus sacrae scripturae*]. Britain or Continent: 1574–1575.

STC 17409 and non-STC. *Language(s)*: Latin. Appraised at 5s in 1577.

119.4 Musculus in mattheum

Wolfgang Musculus. [*Matthew: commentary and text*]. (*Bible–N.T.*). Basle: Joannes Hervagius (with other houses), 1544–1567.

Language(s): Latin. Appraised at 16d in 1577.

119.5 pars eras paraph:

Desiderius Erasmus. [*New Testament: paraphrase* (part)]. (*Bible–N.T.*). Continent: date indeterminable.

Language(s): Latin. Appraised at 12d in 1577.

119.6 buserus in epist pauli ad ro:

Martin Bucer. *Metaphrasis et enarratio in epistolam ad Romanos.* (*Bible–N.T.*). Basle: apud Petrum Pernam, 1562.

Language(s): Latin. Appraised at 3s in 1577.

119.7 musculus super psal:
Wolfgang Musculus. [*Psalms: commentary and text*]. (*Bible–O.T.*). Basle: Joannes Hervagius, 1551–1573.
Eusebius Episcopius joined Hervagius in the publication of the 1573 edition. *Language(s)*: Latin. Appraised at 6s 8d in 1577.

119.8 nichola blones
Nicolaus, *de Blony* (Nicolaus, *de Plove*). Unidentified. Continent: date indeterminable.
Language(s): Latin. Appraised at 2s in 1577.

119.9 Institu: Calvini anglice
Jean Calvin. *The institution of christian religion*. Translated by Thomas Norton. London: R. Harison, 1561–1562.
STC 4415 *et seq*. A third edition, issued in quarto in 1574, is probably not represented here at this valuation, an appraisal more appropriate for one of the two folio editions cited. Reyner Wolfe collaborated with Harrison on the 1561 edition. *Language(s)*: English. Appraised at 4s 6d in 1577.

119.10 Calvinus in Galathos anglice
Jean Calvin. *Sermons upon the epistle to the Galathians*. Translated by Arthur Golding. London: H. Bynneman for L. Harison and G. Byshop, 1574.
STC 4449. The English version of Calvin's commentary on Galatians was not published until 1581. *Language(s)*: English. Appraised at 2s 6d in 1577.

119.11 Calvinus ad ephesios
Jean Calvin. *The sermons of M. John Calvin, upon the epistle too the Ephesians*. (*Bible–N.T.*). Translated by Arthur Golding. London: [Thomas Dawson] for L. Harison and G. Byshop, 1577.
STC 4448. Only French and English versions of this work had appeared by the time of this inventory, and Dawson's collection gives no evidence of his reading French. *Language(s)*: English. Appraised at 20d in 1577.

119.12 gram: Civeleri
Antonius Rodolphus Cevallerius. *Rudimenta hebraicae linguae*. Continent: 1560–1574.
Language(s): Hebrew Latin. Appraised at 12d in 1577.

119.13 Selneccerr in epist: petri
Nicolaus Selneccer. *In D. Petri apostoli epistolas carmen paraphrasticum et homiliae*. (*Bible–N.T.*). Jena: excudebat Thomas Rebart, 1567.
Language(s): Latin. Appraised at 6d in 1577.

119.14 pedegogea selnec:
Nicolaus Selneccer. *Pedagogia Christiana*. Frankfurt am Main: (different houses), 1565–1577.
Language(s): Latin. Appraised at 20d in 1577.

119.15 Epist Martirum in Englyshe
Certain most godly, fruitful, and comfortable letters of such true saintes and holy martyrs as in the late bloodye persecution gave their lyves. Edited by Miles Coverdale, *Bishop*. London: J. Daye, 1564.
STC 5886. *Language(s)*: English. Appraised at 4d in 1577.

119.16 Epist: Bese
Théodore de Bèze. *Epistolarum theologicarum liber unus*. Geneva: Eustathius Vignon, 1573–1575.
On the Reformed Church. Gardy nos. 296–97. *Language(s)*: Latin. Appraised at 8d in 1577.

119.17 pericope evangeliorum
Johann Brentz, *the Elder*. [*Gospels (liturgical): commentary*]. Continent: 1556–1572.
Language(s): Latin. Appraised at 4d in 1577.

119.18 vita christiani hemingii
Niels Hemmingsen. *Via vitae*. Leipzig: excudebat Andrea Schneider in officina Vogeliana, 1574.
Language(s): Latin. Appraised at 3d in 1577.

119.19 Capita Religionis
Probably Joachim Camerarius, *the Elder*. *Capita pietas et religionis christianae*. Leipzig: (different houses), 1545–1576.
Language(s): Greek Latin. Appraised at 3d in 1577.

119.20 anotami of the masse
Agostino Mainardi (Anthoni de Adamo, *pseudonym*). *An anatomi, that is to say a parting in peeces of the mass*. Strassburg: Heirs of W. Köpfel, 1556.
STC 17200. *Language(s)*: English. Appraised at 2d in 1577.

119.21 Cathakysmus Canisii
Petrus Canisius, *Saint*. [*Summa doctrinae christianae*]. Continent: date indeterminable.
Language(s): Latin. Appraised at 2d in 1577.

119.22 flores barnardi
Bernard, *Saint. Flores*. Continent: date indeterminable.
Language(s): Latin. Appraised at 8d in 1577.

119.23 Enchiridion hemingii
Niels Hemmingsen. *Enchiridion theologicum.* Britain or Continent: 1557–1577.
STC 13056.5 and non-STC. The 1577 edition was published in London. *Language(s)*: Latin. Appraised at 2d in 1577.

119.24 Novum testa: besi latin:
[*Bible–N.T.*]. Edited and translated by Théodore de Bèze. Britain or Continent: date indeterminable.
STC 2802 *et seq.* and non-STC. *Language(s)*: Latin. Appraised at 12d in 1577.

119.25 novum test: anglice
[*Bible–N.T.*]. Britain or Continent: 1525–1577.
STC 2823 *et seq. Language(s)*: English. Appraised at 8d in 1577.

119.26 Christian Prayers
Probably Henry Bull. *Christian prayers and holy meditations.* London: Henry Middleton, 1568–1576?
STC 4028 *et seq.* Thomas East printed the 1568 edition for Middleton. *Language(s)*: English. Appraised at 4d in 1577.

119.27 Epist: barnardi
Bernard, *Saint.* [*Epistolae*]. Continent: date indeterminable.
Language(s): Latin. Appraised at 6d in 1577.

119.28 Ethica abetsii
Unidentified. Place unknown: stationer unknown, date indeterminable.
STC/non-STC status unknown. The second word in the entry may read *betsii*, but what that or *abetsii* might be has not been determined. This is likely either a commentary on or an edition of Aristotle's *Ethica. Language(s)*: Latin (probable). Appraised at 8d in 1577.

119.29 harmonus Episcop:
Haymo, *Bishop of Halberstadt.* Unidentified. Continent: date indeterminable.
Language(s): Latin. Appraised at 3d in 1577.

119.30 Hipperius
Andreas Gerardus, *Hyperius.* Unidentified. Continent: date indeterminable.
The compiler usually noted if an item was in English, making a translation here remote. *Language(s)*: Latin. Appraised at 2d in 1577.

119.31   Confessio besi anglic
Théodore de Bèze. *A briefe and piththie summe of the christian faith.*
Translated by Robert Filles. London: (different houses), 1563–1572.
STC 2006.7 *et seq. Language(s)*: English. Appraised at 2d in 1577.

119.32   Major in Thest
Georg Meier, *Professor at Wittenberg. Enarratio duarum Epistolarum Pauli ad
Thessalonicenses.* Wittenberg: Joannis Lufft, 1563.
Language(s): Latin. Appraised at 2d in 1577.

119.33   Consiones funebres
Unidentified. Place unknown: stationer unknown, date indeterminable.
STC/non-STC status unknown. Among the possibilities are Fridericus
Nausea, *Concio funebris* (1539); Edmund Grindal, *Concio funebris in obitum* . . .
Ferdinandi caesaris (1564), STC 12378; and Johann Brandmueller, *Conciones fu-
nebres* (1572). *Language(s)*: Latin. Appraised at 2d in 1577.

119.34   de jure magestratuum
Théodore de Bèze. *De jure magistratuum in subditos.* Lyon: apud Joannem
Mareschallum, 1576.
    Published anonymously. Gardy no. 303. *Language(s)*: Latin. Appraised at
2d in 1577.

119.35   Veron de predestinacione
Jean Veron. *A frutefull treatise of predestination.* London: J. Tisdale, 1557–
1563.
    STC 24680 *et seq.* See 119.11 for another English title entered in Latin by
the compiler. *Language(s)*: English. Appraised at 2d in 1577.

119.36   Sheperdes callender
Shepherds' Kalendar. London: (different houses), 1506–1570?
    STC 22408 *et seq.* All but a 1503 Scottish edition (STC 22407) were pub-
lished in London. Spenser's work was first published in 1579, two years after
the date of this inventory. *Language(s)*: English. Appraised at 2d in 1577.

119.37:1–46   prented bokes and paper bokes in number lxvi
Unidentified. Places unknown: stationers unknown, date indeterminable.
STC/non-STC status unknown. *Language(s)*: Unknown. Appraised as a
group at 2s in 1577.

William Dayrell. Scholar (B.A.):
Probate Inventory. 1577

ANN R. MEYER

William Dayrell (Darrell), of Buckinghamshire, matriculated from Magdalen Hall in 1572, received a B.A. on 29 March 1576, and was elected a fellow of Magdalen on 29 July 1576. He died 28 July 1577 (Macray 1901, 3:61), perhaps of the plague, or perhaps of some other contagion that visited Oxford that year (see Ker, 473 and McConica, 648). An inventory of his goods was made nearly two months later, on 20 September 1577. One brother, Francis, also matriculated with William from Magdalen Hall in 1572, and another, Walter, followed him to Oxford, matriculating from St. Mary Hall in 1579 (*Alumni Oxonienses*, 1:388–89). The name "Dayrell" is one of a group found inscribed at the end of several theological books, mostly of a reformist character, that came to Magdalen Library in the second half of the sixteenth century, a number from the library of Bishop John Jewel (Gunther 1923, 1:483–84). Whether this is William of Magdalen or a George Dayrell, with no known association with Magdalen, but mentioned by Neil Ker (1977, 264) as a possibility, cannot be determined.

Dayrell's small library consisted primarily of works of theology, philosophy, logic, and literature, with a Geneva Bible, a collection of sermons by Bernard of Clairvaux, commentaries on Aristotle, and works by Erasmus and by Cicero among his books. Most, predictably, were in Latin published on the Continent. In addition to the standard academic fare, he had on his shelves Sir Thomas Elyot's *Governour* and a first edition of Roger Ascham's *Letters* [1576]. Several items in the inventory were not appraised, and these carry marginal notations indicating that they were either the books of others, borrowed, one hopes, by Dayrell, or that Dayrell had left directions to give the books to the persons mentioned, most of whom can be identified as Magdalen fellows. See 120.3, 120.13, 120.14, 120.19, and 120.30.

Oxford University Archives, Bodleian Library: Hyp.B.12.

§

Gunther, R.T. 1923. "The Circulating Library of a Brotherhood of Reformers of the Sixteenth Century, at Magdalen College, Oxford," *Notes & Queries,* 13th series. 1:483–84.

Ker, Neil. 1977. "The Library of John Jewel," *The Bodleian Library Record.* 9:256–65.

Macray, William Dunn. 1901. *A Register of the Members of St. Mary Magdalen College, Oxford, from the Foundation of the College. New Series. Fellows: 15761648.* Vol. 3. London: Henry Frowde.

§

120.1	a Englesh Geneva Bible
120.2	Schola Lovaniensis
120.3	ii volumes of Berosus
120.4	Velcurio
120.5	Thesaurus lingue lat
120.6	Aristotelis Logica
120.7	Colloquiun Erasmi
120.8	Sydoracratis Geographia
120.9	Melancthon de anima
120.10	Dialectica Setoni
120.11	liber cartasius
120.12	compendium Titilmani
120.13	Plutharchi opera moralia
120.14	Theatrum vite humane
120.15	Historia Plinii
120.16	Faber in Phisica Aristotelis
120.17	Victorius in Ciceronem
120.18	Eliotts Governer
120.19	Novum Testamente lat Erasmo interprete
120.20	Rodolphus
120.21	Similitudines Erasmi
120.22	liber cartasius
120.23	Epistole fam. Ciceronis
120.24	Gwalterus de quantitate sillabarum
120.25	duo volumina Livii
120.26	Melanthonis Rethorica

120.27 Epistole hascami
120.28 Sermones Barnardi
120.29 Margarita Theologica
120.30 Tusculani questiones

§

120.1 a Englesh Geneva Bible

The Bible. Britain or Continent: 1560–1577.
STC 2093 *et seq. Language(s)*: English. Appraised at 12s in 1577.

120.2 Schola Lovaniensis

Commentaria in Isagogen Porphyrii et in omnes libros Aristotelis de dialectica. (*Louvain University*). Louvain: [probably] Servatius Sassenus, 1535–1568.

See BCI 2:505. Sassenus published the 1535 and 1568 editions; bibliographical sources do not name the publisher of the 1547 and 1553 editions. *Language(s)*: Latin Greek (probable). Appraised at 5s in 1577.

120.3 ii volumes of Berosus

Berosus, *the Chaldean* and Giovanni Nanni (Joannes Annius). Probably [*De antiquitatibus*]. Continent: date indeterminable.

It is possible that two separate works are represented. Not appraised, presumably because it was owned by or perhaps given to a "Mr Hunt" cited in the margin, probably George Hunt, fellow of Magdalen, 1575–1583. *Language(s)*: Latin.

120.4 Velcurio

Joannes Velcurio. Perhaps [*Aristotle–Physica: commentary*]. Continent: date indeterminable.

Velcurio's main work. *Language(s)*: Latin. Appraised at 8d in 1577.

120.5 Thesaurus lingue lat

Probably Robert Estienne, *the Elder. Thesaurus linguae latinae*. Continent: date indeterminable.

Conceivably Thomas Cooper's *Thesaurus linguae Romanae et Britannicae. Language(s)*: Latin. Appraised at 20d in 1577.

120.6 Aristotelis Logica

Aristotle. [*Selected works–Logica*]. Continent: date indeterminable. *Language(s)*: Latin. Appraised at 18d in 1577.

120.7 Colloquiun Erasmi

Desiderius Erasmus. *Colloquia*. Britain or Continent: date indeterminable. STC 10450.6 *et seq.* and non-STC. *Language(s)*: Latin. Appraised at 2d in 1577.

120.8 Sydoracratis Geographia
Samuel Siderocrates (Samuel Eisenmenger). *Libellus geographicus.* Tübingen: apud vidua Ulrici Morhardi, 1562.
Language(s): Latin. Appraised at 8d in 1577.

120.9 Melancthon de anima
Philipp Melanchthon. [*Liber de anima*]. Continent: 1540–1576.
Language(s): Latin. Appraised at 6d in 1577.

120.10 Dialectica Setoni
John Seton. *Dialectica.* London: (different houses), 1545–1577.
STC 22250 *et seq. Language(s)*: Latin. Appraised at 8d in 1577.

120.11 liber cartasius
Unidentified. Place unknown: stationer unknown, date indeterminable.
Manuscript. See also 120.22. *Language(s)*: Latin (probable). Appraised at 4d in 1577.

120.12 compendium Titilmani
Franz Titelmann. Unidentified. Continent: date unknown.
Either Titelmann's *Compendium physice ad libros Aristotelis de naturali philosophia* or his *Compendium dialecticae ad libros logicorum Aristotelis utile ac necessarium. Language(s)*: Latin. Appraised at 12d in 1577.

120.13 Plutharchi opera moralia
Plutarch. *Moralia.* Continent: date indeterminable.
Not appraised, presumably because it was owned by or perhaps given to a "Mr Breodbrant" cited in the margin, probably Laurence Broadbrent, demy at Magdalen College, 1575–1580 (*Alumni Oxonienses*, 1:184). *Language(s)*: Latin Greek (perhaps).

120.14 Theatrum vite humane
Conrad Lycosthenes (Conrad Wolffhart) and Theodor Zwinger. *Theatrum vitae humanae.* Continent: 1565–1572.
Not appraised, presumably because it was owned by or perhaps given to a "Mr Bradbrant" cited in the margin, probably Laurence Broadbrent, demy at Magdalen College, 1575–1580 (*Alumni Oxonienses*, 1:184). *Language(s)*: Latin.

120.15 Historia Plinii
Pliny, *the Elder. Historia naturalis.* Continent: date indeterminable.
Language(s): Latin. Appraised at 6s in 1577.

120.16 Faber in Phisica Aristotelis
Jacobus Faber, *Stapulensis.* [*Aristotle–Physica: commentary and paraphrase*].

Continent: date indeterminable.
Language(s): Latin. Appraised at 2s in 1577.

120.17 Victorius in Ciceronem
Petrus Victorius, *the Elder*. Unidentified. Continent: date indeterminable. Either the *Castigationes in M. T. Ciceronis Epistolas* or the *Explicationes suarum in Ciceronem castigationum*. *Language(s)*: Latin. Appraised at 12d in 1577.

120.18 Eliotts Governer
Sir Thomas Elyot. *The boke named the governour*. London: (different houses), 1531–1565.
STC 7635 *et seq. Language(s)*: English. Appraised at 8d in 1577.

120.19 Novum Testamente lat Erasmo interprete
Desiderius Erasmus. [*New Testament: commentary*]. Continent: date indeterminable.
Not appraised, presumably because it was owned by or perhaps given to a "Deves" or "Dewes" cited in the margin. Perhaps Thomas Dawes, "of Magdalen Hall, in or before 1572" (*Alumni Oxonienses*, 1:386) may be intended. *Language(s)*: Latin.

120.20 Rodolphus
Unidentified. Continent (probable): date indeterminable.
Probably not an STC book. Rodolphus Agricola, Caspar Rhodolphus, and Rudolph Walther (see 120.24) are possibilities. *Language(s)*: Latin. Appraised at 8d in 1577.

120.21 Similitudines Erasmi
Desiderius Erasmus. *Parabolae sive similia*. Continent: date indeterminable.
Language(s): Latin. Appraised at 6d in 1577.

120.22 liber cartasius
Unidentified. Place unknown: stationer unknown, date indeterminable.
Manuscript. See also 120.11. *Language(s)*: Latin (probable). Appraised at 4d in 1577.

120.23 Epistole fam. Ciceronis
Marcus Tullius Cicero. *Epistolae ad familiares*. Britain or Continent: date indeterminable.
STC 5295 *et seq.* and non-STC. *Language(s)*: Latin. Appraised at 4d in 1577.

120.24 Gwalterus de quantitate sillabarum
Rudolph Walther. *De syllabarum et carminum libri duo*. Britain or Continent: date indeterminable.
STC 25011 and non-STC. *Language(s)*: Latin. Appraised at 3d in 1577.

120.25   duo volumina Livii

Titus Livius. [*Historiae Romanae decades*]. Continent: date indeterminable. Two volumes might comprise all, or only some, of the surviving *decades*. *Language(s)*: Latin. Appraised at 2s in 1577.

120.26   Melanthonis Rethorica

Philipp Melanchthon. [*Rhetorica*]. Continent: date indeterminable. *Language(s)*: Latin. Appraised at 1d in 1577.

120.27   Epistole hascami

Roger Ascham. *Familiarium epistolarum libri tres*. Edited by Edward Grant. London: [H. Middleton], imp. F. Coldocki, 1576 (probable). STC 826. *Language(s)*: Latin. Appraised at 8d in 1577.

120.28   Sermones Barnardi

Bernard, *Saint*. [*Sermones*]. Continent: date indeterminable. *Language(s)*: Latin. Appraised at 1d in 1577.

120.29   Margarita Theologica

Johann Spangenberg. *Margarita theologica*. Britain or Continent: date indeterminable. STC 23001 *et seq.* and non-STC. *Language(s)*: Latin. Appraised at 1d in 1577.

120.30   Tusculani questiones

Marcus Tullius Cicero. *Quaestiones Tusculanae*. Britain or Continent: date indeterminable. STC 5314.5 *et seq.* and non-STC. Not appraised, presumably because it was owned by or perhaps given to a "Mr Lord," cited in the margin as "per lord," probably Edward Lorde, fellow of Magdalen College, 1575–1586 (*Alumni Oxonienses*, 3:938). *Language(s)*: Latin.

Giles Dewhurst. Scholar (M.A.):
Probate Inventory. 1577

RIVES NICHOLSON

The life of Giles Dewhurst of Christ Church is as poorly documented as those of most of his contemporaries at Oxford. A slim entry in the *Alumni Oxonienses* (1:400) reveals only that he was awarded his B.A. degree on 26 January 1571 and proceeded M.A. 9 March 1574. The inventory of his goods and possessions, evidently taken at his death, is dated 15 October 1577, a year notable for an outbreak of plague or typhus that claimed many of Dewhurst's Oxford colleagues that year (see Ker, 473 and McConica, 648) and perhaps Dewhurst's own.

With few exceptions Dewhurst's library is a standard one, made up predominantly of volumes of classical poetry and drama, mainly in Latin, and dictionaries and grammars, including two copies of Calepino's *Dictionarium* (121.2,3). The remainder of the library is comprised mainly of Aristotle texts and popular commentaries on Aristotle of the period by Niphus (121.6), Faber (121.26), and Acciaiolus (121.27)—staples of the M.A. course—although the Buridanus (121.10) is more characteristic of a late medieval library. Rather specialized medical texts by Triverius and Actuarius (121.14,15) seem slightly out of place given the strongly literary character of the collection, unless Dewhurst had embarked on medical studies. The theological texts one might expect in the collection of an intending B.D. are notably absent. The collection's chief puzzlement is found at 121.41, where the manuscript entry tantalizingly suggests the Italian revenge tragedy of Gregorio Corraro, *Progne*, but which more likely is another medical book, one on prognostics, perhaps an edition of or a commentary on Hippocrates' *Prognostica*.

Oxford University Archives, Bodleian Library: Hyp.B.12.

§

121.1	Minsingerus super Institutis
121.2	Calepinus
121.3	Calepinus
121.4	Opuscula Augustini
121.5	Arborius in Novum Testamentum
121.6	Niphus in Topic Aristotelis
121.7	Tomas Aquinus in Phisic Aristotelis
121.8	Cornucopia
121.9	Boetius
121.10	Buridanus in Ethic Aristotelis
121.11	a old Vergell
121.12	Aristophanes, Commed
121.13	Groperus de eucharistia
121.14	Brackelius de sanguinbis missione
121.15	Actuarius de urinis
121.16	Phisica Aristotelis
121.17	Psalterium
121.18	Calfeye contra Marshall
121.19	Euripidis Repus
121.20	Issocrates grece et latine
121.21	Danneus de heresibus
121.22	Euripid Tragedie
121.23	Ectica Arist'
121.24	Omerus grece
121.25	Ectica per Donatum
121.26	Philosophia Vatabli
121.27	Donatus in Politica
121.28	Vergilii opera
121.29	Dixionarium Poeticum
121.30	Garsonus
121.31	Psalterium Vatabli
121.32	Tragedie Senece
121.33	Quintus Cursius
121.34	Grammatica Greca
121.35	Novum Testamentum Erasmi
121.36	Theorica Planetarum
121.37	Oratius
121.38	Toxites ad herenium
121.39	Ovius, Meta
121.40	Fuccii Practica
121.41	Progne
121.42	2o volumina Oracionis Ciceronis
121.43:1–2	ii paper bokes

121.44   2a pars Operum Zenophontis
121.45:1–40 xlti old bokes

§

121.1 Minsingerus super Institutis
Joachim Mynsinger. *Apotelesma.* (*Corpus juris civilis*). Continent: date indeterminable.
Language(s): Latin. Appraised at 3s 6d in 1577.

121.2 Calepinus
Ambrogio Calepino. *Dictionarium.* Continent: date indeterminable.
Published in numerous editions from 1502 with an increasing number of vernacular languages. Another copy at 121.3. *Language(s)*: Greek Latin. Appraised at 12d in 1577.

121.3 Calepinus
Ambrogio Calepino. *Dictionarium.* Continent: date indeterminable.
See annotation to 121.2 where there is another copy. The valuation suggests that this might be the older edition of the two or one with fewer languages. *Language(s)*: Greek Latin. Appraised at 4d in 1577.

121.4 Opuscula Augustini
Augustine, *Saint.* [*Selected works–Opuscula*]. Continent: date indeterminable.
Language(s): Latin. Appraised at 16d in 1577.

121.5 Arborius in Novum Testamentum
Joannes Arboreus. Perhaps *Commentarii in quatuor Domini Evangelistas.* (*Bible–N.T.*). Paris: apud (aere ac sumptu) Joannem Roigny, 1551.
Arboreus is not known to have written on the entire New Testament. His *Theosophia* (1540, 1553) might have been descriptively entered in this way as well. *Language(s)*: Latin. Appraised at 4s in 1577.

121.6 Niphus in Topic Aristotelis
Augustinus Niphus. [*Aristotle–Topica: commentary*]. Continent: 1535–1569.
Language(s): Latin Greek (probable). Appraised at 20d in 1577.

121.7 Tomas Aquinus in Phisic Aristotelis
Thomas Aquinas, *Saint.* [*Aristotle–Physica: commentary*]. Continent: date indeterminable.
Language(s): Latin. Appraised at 2s in 1577.

121.8 Cornucopia
Probably Nicolaus Perottus. *Cornucopia.* Continent: date indeterminable.
Other possibilities include Eustathius, *Bishop of Thessalonica*, and Joannes

Ravisius, *Textor. Language(s)*: Latin Greek (perhaps). Appraised at 8d in 1577.

121.9 Boetius
Anicius M.T.S. Boethius. Probably *De consolatione philosophiae*. Britain or Continent: date indeterminable.
STC 3199 *et seq.* Some early editions printed in England bore the Latin title and were published in both Latin and English. *Language(s)*: Latin (probable) English (perhaps). Appraised at 8d in 1577.

121.10 Buridanus in Ethic Aristotelis
Joannes Buridanus. [*Aristotle–Ethica: commentary*]. Continent: 1489–1518. *Language(s)*: Latin. Appraised at 12d in 1577.

121.11 a old Vergell
Publius Virgilius Maro. Probably [*Works*]. Britain or Continent: date indeterminable.
STC 24787 *et seq.* and non-STC. See also 121.28 for an entry definitely the *opera. Language(s)*: Latin. Appraised at 8d in 1577.

121.12 Aristophanes, Commed
Aristophanes. [*Works*]. Continent: date indeterminable.
Language(s): Latin (probable) Greek (perhaps). Appraised at 16d in 1577.

121.13 Groperus de eucharistia
Johann Groepper. *De veritate corporis et sanguinis Christi in eucharistia*. Continent: 1559–1560.
Language(s): Latin. Appraised at 20d in 1577.

121.14 Brackelius de sanguinbis missione
Hieremias Triverius (Brachelius). *De missione sanguinis in pleuritide deceptatio. Commentarius de victu ab arthriticis morbis vindicante*. Louvain: ex off. Rutgeri Rescii, sumpt. eiusdem ac Bartholomaei Gravii, 1532.
Language(s): Latin. Appraised at 12d in 1577.

121.15 Actuarius de urinis
Joannes Actuarius. *De urinis*. Continent: 1522–1563.
Language(s): Latin. Appraised at 4d in 1577.

121.16 Phisica Aristotelis
Aristotle. *Physica*. Continent: date indeterminable.
Language(s): Latin (probable) Greek (perhaps). Appraised at 2s in 1577.

121.17 Psalterium
[*Bible–O.T.–Psalms*]. Britain or Continent: date indeterminable.
STC 2354 *et seq.* and non-STC. A liturgical psalter is possible. *Language(s)*: Latin. Appraised at 8d in 1577.

121.18 Calfeye contra Marshall

James Calfhill. *An aunswere to the Treatise of the crosse*. London: H. Denham for L. Harryson, 1565.

STC 4368. Answers STC 17496. *Language(s)*: English. Appraised at 12d in 1577.

121.19 Euripidis Repus

Euripides (attributed). *Rhesus*. Continent: date indeterminable.

No separate editions of the *Rhesus* appear to be recorded for this period, but see BCI l:xxiii, n. 28, offering an explanation for its repeated appearance in BCI book-lists despite the absence of recorded editions. See PLRE 67.122 (a 1558 list) for another edition of the drama, apparently solo. *Language(s)*: Greek (probable) Latin (perhaps). Appraised at 4d in 1577.

121.20 Issocrates grece et latine

Isocrates. Probably [*Works*]. Continent: date indeterminable.

Language(s): Greek Latin. Appraised at 20d in 1577.

121.21 Danneus de heresibus

Augustine, *Saint*. Perhaps *De haeresibus*. Edited by Lambert Daneau. Geneva: apud Eustathium Vignon, 1576.

Daneau's own *Elenchi haereticorum* is also similarly possible. *Language(s)*: Latin. Appraised at 20d in 1577.

121.22 Euripid Tragedie

Euripides. [*Works*]. Continent: date indeterminable.

Language(s): Latin (probable) Greek (perhaps). Appraised at 10d in 1577.

121.23 Ectica Arist'

Aristotle. *Ethica*. Britain or Continent: date indeterminable.

STC 752 and non-STC. *Language(s)*: Latin. Appraised at 6d in 1577.

121.24 Omerus grece

Homer. Probably [*Works*]. Continent: date indeterminable.

Language(s): Greek. Appraised at 8d in 1577.

121.25 Ectica per Donatum

Donatus Acciaiolus. [*Aristotle–Ethica: commentary*]. Continent: 1504–1566.

Language(s): Latin. Appraised at 18d in 1577.

121.26 Philosophia Vatabli

Jacobus Faber, *Stapulensis*. [*Aristotle–Selected works–Philosophia naturalis: paraphrase*]. Edited by Franciscus Vatablus. Continent: 1528–1540.

Several editions include commentary by Jodocus Clichtoveus. *Language(s)*: Latin. Appraised at 10d in 1577.

121.27 Donatus in Politica
Donatus Acciaiolus. [*Aristotle–Politica: commentary*]. Continent: date indeterminable.
Language(s): Latin. Appraised at 20d in 1577.

121.28 Vergilii opera
Publius Virgilius Maro. [*Works*]. Britain or Continent: date indeterminable.
STC 24787 *et seq.* and non-STC. See also 121.11. *Language(s)*: Latin. Appraised at 6d in 1577.

121.29 Dixionarium Poeticum
Hermann Torrentinus. Probably [*Elucidarius carminum*]. Continent: date indeterminable.

This widely published work is difficult to distinguish from Robert Estienne's *Dictionarium historicum ac poeticum*. *Language(s)*: Latin. Appraised at 6d in 1577.

121.30 Garsonus
Joannes Gerson (Jean Charlier de Gerson). Probably [*Works*]. Continent: date indeterminable.
Language(s): Latin. Appraised at 16d in 1577.

121.31 Psalterium Vatabli
Franciscus Vatablus. Perhaps *Liber Psalmorum Davidis: Annotationes in eosdem ex Hebraeorum commentariis*. (*Bible–O.T.*). Paris: ex officina Rob. Stephani typographi Regii, 1546.

This is a separate edition of the Psalms issued as the first part of another edition of the 1545 Stephanus Bible, but nothing more appeared. The entry conceivably describes a separated part of several Bibles that carried Vatablus's notes to the Psalms. *Language(s)*: Latin. Appraised at 3d in 1577.

121.32 Tragedie Senece
Lucius Annaeus Seneca. *Tragoediae*. Continent: date indeterminable.
Language(s): Latin. Appraised at 2d in 1577.

121.33 Quintus Cursius
Quintus Curtius Rufus. *De rebus gestis Alexandri Magni*. Continent (probable): date indeterminable.
Probably not an STC book, but see STC 6141.5 *et seq. Language(s)*: Latin. Appraised at 3d in 1577.

121.34 Grammatica Greca
Unidentified. Place unknown: stationer unknown, date indeterminable.
STC/non-STC status unknown. Numerous possibilities include grammars of Clenardus, Ceporinus, and Melanchthon. Also, a Greek grammar was pub-

lished in England in 1575 (STC 12188). *Language(s)*: Greek Latin. Appraised at 2d in 1577.

121.35 Novum Testamentum Erasmi
[*Bible–N.T.*]. Edited by Desiderius Erasmus. Britain or Continent: date indeterminable.
STC 2800 and non-STC. Less likely, his *Annotationes* or *Paraphrases*. *Language(s)*: Latin Greek (perhaps). Appraised at 4d in 1577.

121.36 Theorica Planetarum
Unidentified. Continent: date indeterminable.
Georg Purbach's *Novae thoricae planetarum*, which saw numerous editions in the sixteenth century, is a strong candidate for this entry, as is the *Theorica planetarum* of Gerardus, *Cremonensis, the Younger* (Sablonetanus), which often appeared with John Holywood's (Sacrobosco) widely published *Sphaera mundi* but also in solo editions as early as 1472. BL alone attributes the work to Gerardus, *Cremonensis, the Elder*. *Language(s)*: Latin. Appraised at 12d in 1577.

121.37 Oratius
Quintus Horatius Flaccus. Probably [*Works*]. Britain or Continent: date indeterminable.
STC 13784 and non-STC. *Language(s)*: Latin. Appraised at 3d in 1577.

121.38 Toxites ad herenium
Michael Toxites. [*Cicero (spurious)–Rhetorica ad Herennium: commentary and text*]. Basle: Joannes Oporinus, 1556–1568.
The 1568 edition was a collaborative printing. *Language(s)*: Latin. Appraised at 9d in 1577.

121.39 Ovius, Meta
Publius Ovidius Naso. *Metamorphoses*. Continent: date indeterminable.
Language(s): Latin. Appraised at 2d in 1577.

121.40 Fuccii Practica
Leonard Fuchs. *A worthy practise of the moste learned phisition L. Fuchsius, necessary in this tyme of our visitation*. London: R. Hall for M. Lobley, 1563.
STC 11408. Evidence of the compiler entering an English title in Latin. *Language(s)*: English (probable). Appraised at 6d in 1577.

121.41 Progne
Unidentified. Place unknown: stationer unknown, date indeterminable.
STC/non-STC status unknown. It is tempting to take the manuscript entry at face value and identify this item as Gregorio Corraro's gory Italian revenge tragedy *Progne*, but even if one allowed it to be the play's Latin translation (1558), such a work would be greatly out of place in Dewhurst's library. It is more likely either an edition or a commentary on a work on prognostics,

perhaps Hippocrates' *Prognostica*, especially given that the book apparently rested next to Fuchs's medical work in Dewhurst's collection (see 121.40). Then again, the truncated manuscript entry could also represent a book of prognostications, such as Leonard Digges's (STC 435.35 *et seq.*), or even, perhaps, a separated piece of Ovid's *Metamorphoses*. *Language(s)*: Latin (probable). Appraised at 2d in 1577.

121.42 2o volumina Oracionis Ciceronis
Marcus Tullius Cicero. [*Selected works–Orations*]. Continent: date indeterminable.

Whether Dewhurst's two volumes contained all or only some of the *Orationes* cannot be determined. *Language(s)*: Latin. Appraised at 12d in 1577.

121.43:1–2 ii paper bokes
Unidentified. Provenances unknown: dates indeterminable.
Manuscripts. *Language(s)*: Unknown. Appraised at 12d in 1577.

121.44 2a pars Operum Zenophontis
Xenophon. [*Works* (part)]. Continent: date indeterminable.
Language(s): Latin (probable) Greek (perhaps). Appraised at 8d in 1577.

121.45:1–40 xlti old bokes
Unidentified. Places unknown: stationers unknown, date indeterminable.
STC/non-STC status unknown. *Language(s)*: Unknown. Appraised as a group at 2s 6d in 1577.

Tristram Faringdon. Scholar (student): Probate Inventory. 1577

SUSAN MARTIN-JOY

The inventory of "all and singuler the bokes and other goodes" belonging to Tristram Faringdon (Farringdon, Farryngdon) was made on 3 September 1577. This document describes Faringdon as a "gentelman, late student in Exeter Colledge." Faringdon is not listed among other matriculants of Exeter in the Exeter College register (Boase 1879, 185–86; Boase 1894, xcvi–xcvii), although such records are incomplete for the 1570s (McConica 1986, 49–50). Apart from a notice of Faringdon's will being proved on 6 September, three days after the probate inventory was drawn up (*Alumni Oxonienses*, 2:483), no other evidence documenting Faringdon's student days in Oxford appears to exist. Faringdon may have been a victim of an epidemic of typhus that appeared in the summer of 1577. Associated with one Roland Jenkes, a bookseller and "the most notorious recusant of Elizabethan Oxford" (Hammer 1986, 77), it claimed the lives of hundreds in Oxford, including "an hundred scholars" (Boase 1887, 130; McConica, 648).

Faringdon may have come from Devon or Cornwall, counties long associated with Exeter and "whence so many of the members of the college came" (Boase 1894, lxxx), and he may have been Roman Catholic. In the year of his death, a "religious census" revealed Exeter to be one of four Oxford colleges (together with All Souls', Balliol, and Queen's) in which Catholics were found to reside. As Penry Williams points out, "Exeter was the least conformist of the colleges" (Williams 1986, 413). Writing in 1579, one commentator observed that in the previous year at Exeter "of eighty were found but four obedient subjects, all the rest secret or open Roman affectionaries . . . These were chiefly such as came out of the western parts, where popery greatly prevailed and the gentry bred up in that religion" (quoted in Boase 1894, lxxx; Williams 1986, 411).

His collection of books, as listed in the inventory, does not, however, give particular evidence of the old faith; indeed one item (122.10) may be a work by the reformer Bernardino Ochino. Predictably the lion's share was printed on the Continent. Only one has been definitely identified as being published in England: John Cheke's translation of Chrysostom's *Homiliae duae* (122.9), the first book to have been printed in England in Greek characters. Nearly all of the books identified by author on Faringdon's inventory (twelve out of a total of fourteen) are by Greek authors, and most of these are in both Greek and Latin or exclusively in Greek. Notably devoted to the arts, Faringdon's collection includes works of history, rhetoric, philosophy, and literature, while theology is also modestly represented.

Two items of Faringdon's apparel stand out among his "other goodes" as reminders of his social status: a "cloke faced with velvett" and a "goulde rynge with ix small turkeis" ("turkey" or turquoise stones). Each of these items was valued at fifty shillings, ten times the value of Faringdon's most highly appraised book.

Oxford University Archives, Bodleian Library: Hyp.B.12.

§

Boase, C.W. 1879. *Register for the Rectors and Fellows, Scholars, Exhibitioners and Bible Clerks of Exeter College*. Oxford: [Rector and Fellows of Exeter College].

—— 1887. *Oxford*. London: Longmans, Green, and Co.

—— 1894. *Register of the Rectors, Fellows, and Other Members on the Foundation of Exeter College, Oxford*. Oxford: Printed for the Oxford Historical Society at the Clarendon Press.

Hammer, Carl I., Jr. 1986. "Oxford Town and Oxford University," in *The Collegiate University*, ed. James McConica. Volume 3 of *The History of the University of Oxford*, gen. ed., T.H. Aston. Oxford: Oxford Univ. Press.

McConica, James. 1986. "The Rise of the Undergraduate College," in *The Collegiate University*, ed. James McConica. Volume 3 of *The History of the University of Oxford*, gen. ed., T.H. Aston. Oxford: Oxford Univ. Press.

Williams, Penry. 1986. "Elizabethan Oxford: State, Church and University," in *The Collegiate University*, ed. James McConica. Volume 3 of *The History of the University of Oxford*, gen. ed., T.H. Aston. Oxford: Oxford Univ. Press.

§

122.1   Thucydides grece
122.2   Philo Judeus grece
122.3   Harmogenes grece et latine
122.4   Epictetus grece et latine
122.5   Johannes Grammaticus grece
122.6   Dionisius Areopagita latine
122.7:1 Willelmus misoorius
122.7:2 De situ orbis
122.8   Adanasius grece et latine
122.9   due homelie Chrisostomi grece et latine
122.10   okins, apollo
122.11   Dimosthenis Oraciones Olnitheace
122.12   aeedem [eadem] grece et latine
122.13   Epicteti Enchiridion grece et latine
122.14   due oraciones Dimosthenis grece et latine
122.15   Dialogi Luciani grece et latine
122.16   Iamblichus latine
122.17   a wryten paper boke

§

122.1 Thucydides grece

Thucydides. *De bello peloponnesiaco*. Continent: date indeterminable.

The compiler struck out *et latine*. *Language(s)*: Greek. Appraised at 4s in 1577.

122.2 Philo Judeus grece

Philo, *Judaeus. In libros Mosis, de mundi opificio, historicos, de legibus*. Paris: ex officina Adriani Turnebi, 1552.

This is the only Greek edition of a work by Philo in folio—a size consistent with the valuation—issued by the date of this inventory. *Language(s)*: Greek. Appraised at 5s in 1577.

122.3 Harmogenes grece et latine

Hermogenes. [*Rhetorica*]. Continent: date indeterminable.

The valuation suggests an assemblage of works, perhaps with those of others. *Language(s)*: Greek Latin. Appraised at 2s in 1577.

122.4 Epictetus grece et latine

Epictetus. Probably [*Works*]. Continent: date indeterminable.

A copy of Epictetus' *Enchiridion* at 122.13 and the higher valuation of this item suggest the collection here rather than the *Enchiridion* alone. Works of other writers seem generally to be included. *Language(s)*: Greek Latin. Appraised at 12d in 1577.

122.5 Johannes Grammaticus grece
Joannes Philoponus, *Grammaticus*. Unidentified. Continent: date indeterminable.

Probably one of the many commentaries written by Philoponus on works of Aristotle. *Language(s)*: Greek. Appraised at 8d in 1577.

122.6 Dionisius Areopagita latine
Dionysius *Areopagita*. Probably [*Works*]. Continent: date indeterminable.

The compiler struck through *grece et*, which preceded *latine*, with part of the line striking *latine* as well. *Language(s)*: Latin. Appraised at 8d in 1577.

122.7:1 Willelmus misoorius
Unidentified. Continent (probable): date indeterminable.

Almost certainly not an STC book. Entered on a line separate from the next but sharing with it an appraised value. Perhaps a volume from the printing house of Gulielmus Morelius, though *Willelmus misoorius* is a very unlikely misheard or miscopied form of that name. Morelius did, however, publish *De situ orbis* of Dionysius, *Periegetes* (see next entry). *Language(s)*: Latin (probable). Appraised with one other at 6d in 1577.

122.7:2 De situ orbis
Unidentified. Place unknown: stationer unknown, date indeterminable.

STC/non-STC status unknown. Entered on a line separate from the preceding but sharing with it an appraised value. Perhaps the *De situ orbis* of Dionysius, *Periegetes* (see previous entry) or of Pomponius Mela. *Language(s)*: Latin (probable) Greek (perhaps). Appraised with one other at 6d in 1577.

122.8 Adanasius grece et latine
Athanasius, *Saint*. Unidentified. Continent: date indeterminable.

Language(s): Greek Latin. Appraised at 8d in 1577.

122.9 due homelie Chrisostomi grece et latine
John, *Chrysostom, Saint. Homiliae duae*. Translated by Sir John Cheke. London: apud Reynerum Wolfium in Coemiterio Divi Pauli ad signum aenei serpentis, 1543.

STC 14634. This work is the first to be printed in England using Greek characters. *Language(s)*: Greek Latin. Appraised at 4d in 1577.

122.10 okins, apollo
Probably Bernardino Ochino. Continent (probable): date indeterminable.

Probably not an STC book. If Ochino, perhaps his *Apologi*, but the only editions found are in Continental vernaculars. *Language(s)*: Unknown. Appraised at 4d in 1577.

122.11 Dimosthenis Oraciones Olnitheace
Demosthenes. *Olynthiacae orationes tres*. Continent: date indeterminable. *Language(s)*: Latin. Appraised at 6d in 1577.

122.12 aeedem [eadem] grece et latine
Demosthenes. *Olynthiacae orationes tres*. Continent: date indeterminable. *Language(s)*: Greek Latin. Appraised at 6d in 1577.

122.13 Epicteti Enchiridion grece et latine
Epictetus. *Enchiridion*. Continent: date indeterminable.
See 122.4 for another Epictetus. *Language(s)*: Greek Latin. Appraised at 4d in 1577.

122.14 due oraciones Dimosthenis grece et latine
Demosthenes. [*Selected works–Orations*]. Continent: date indeterminable. *Language(s)*: Greek Latin. Appraised at 4d in 1577.

122.15 Dialogi Luciani grece et latine
Lucian, *of Samosata*. Unidentified. Continent: date indeterminable.
What arrangement of the *Dialogues* (whether collected or selected) cannot be determined. *Language(s)*: Greek Latin. Appraised at 4d in 1577.

122.16 Iamblichus latine
Iamblichus. *De mysteriis Aegyptiorum, Chaldaeorum, Assyriorum*. Continent: date indeterminable.
Language(s): Latin. Appraised at 6d in 1577.

122.17 a wryten paper boke
Unidentified. Provenance unknown: date indeterminable.
Manuscript. Perhaps a personal notebook. *Language(s)*: Unknown. Appraised at 6d in 1577.

Richard Ferne. Scholar (M.A.):
Probate Inventory. 1577

RUDOLPH P. ALMASY

Richard Ferne (Fearne), a member of University College, Oxford, was granted a B.A. on 27 January 1573 and an M.A. on 5 June 1576 (*Alumni Oxonienses*, 2:493). He was probably born in the early 1550s and died in 1577. An inventory of all his "goodes and debite" was made on 10 November 1577.

Ferne was comfortable with Greek, and a majority of his books were theological and exegetical, revealing, perhaps, a Calvinist bias. It is worth noting the appearance of *The Courtier* in English (123.20) in what otherwise is a library made up almost entirely of classical and theological texts.

Oxford University Archives, Bodleian Library: Hyp.B.12.

§

123.1   Theosophia Harborei
123.2   Loci Communes Musculi
123.3   Lexicon Grecum Crispini
123.4   Sermones Augustini
123.5   Instituciones Calvini
123.6   biblia gallica
123.7   Aristologia Euripidea
123.8   Chetreus, Postilla
123.9   Postilla Hemmingei
123.10   Aristophanes grece
123.11   Loci Communes Hipperii
123.12   Chitreus in Deutronomiam
123.13   Chetreus in Apocalypsin

123.14   Toxotes ad Serenissimum
123.15   Confessio Besa
123.16   Ethica Donati
123.17   Osorius de justicia
123.18   biblia Jheronimi
123.19   Erasmus in Lucam
123.20   The Courtier
123.21   Billic contra Buserum
123.22   The Images of Bothe Churches
123.23   Cathekismus Calvini
123.24   Enchiridion Hemmingii
123.25   Ethica Aristotelis grece
123.26   Augustinus de spiritu et littera
123.27   Ethica Perionii
123.28   Commentarium anglice Pauli Epistolarum
123.29   Regule Chitrei
123.30   Luterus ad Galathas
123.31   Novum Testamentum Besa
123.32   Oraciones Dimostonis Olnithiace
123.33   Opera Xenophontis in 3bus
123.34   Orationes Isocratis graece
123.35   Loci Communes Sarcerii
123.36   Grammatica Clenardi
123.37   Enchiridion Erasmi
123.38   Assertio
123.39   Edmundus Alen, Cathahisme
123.40   Genesis Liber
123.41   2a pars Phylosophic' Ciceronis
123.42   Psalterium Hesii
123.43   Novum Testamentum Erasmi
123.44   Testamentum grecum
123.45   Calvini Cathakysmus
123.46   Flores Poetarum
123.47   Epistole ad Atticum
123.48   Rethorica Ciceronis
123.49   Ovidius de fastis
123.50:1–8   viii bokes band in parchment
123.51:1–16   xvi paper and note bokes

§

123.1 Theosophia Harborei
    Joannes Arboreus. *Theosophia*. Paris: (different houses), 1540–1555.
    Language(s): Latin. Appraised at 4s in 1577.

123.2 Loci Communes Musculi

Probably Wolfgang Musculus. *Loci communes*. Continent: date indeterminable.

The less widely published *Loci communes sacri* of Andreas Musculus is possible. *Language(s)*: Latin. Appraised at 5s in 1577.

123.3 Lexicon Grecum Crispini

Jean Crespin. *Lexicon graecolatinum*. Continent: 1566–1568.

Gulielmus Budaeus's lexicon, with two editions published by Crespin, is also a possibility. *Language(s)*: Greek Latin. Appraised at 16s in 1577.

123.4 Sermones Augustini

Augustine, *Saint*. *Sermones*. Continent: date indeterminable.

Language(s): Latin. Appraised at 2s 6d in 1577.

123.5 Instituciones Calvini

Jean Calvin. *Institutio christianae religionis*. Britain or Continent: date indeterminable.

STC 4414 and non-STC. *Language(s)*: Latin. Appraised at 3s 4d in 1577.

123.6 biblia gallica

The Bible. Continent: date indeterminable.

Language(s): French. Appraised at 2s 4d in 1577.

123.7 Aristologia Euripidea

Euripides. *Aristologia Euripidea graecolatina*. Edited by Michael Neander. Basle: per Joannem Oporinum, 1559 (probable).

Adams E1061. *Language(s)*: Greek Latin. Appraised at 10d in 1577.

123.8 Chetreus, Postilla

David Chytraeus. Unidentified. Continent (probable): date indeterminable.

Probably not an STC book, but see STC 5263. Arthur Golding's translation of Chytraeus's *Dispositiones epistolarum, A postil, or orderly disposing of certeine epistles*, was printed in 1570 and 1577, but this entry is more likely to represent any one of Chytraeus's many commentaries on various books of the Bible, all published on the Continent. *Language(s)*: Latin. Appraised at 12d in 1577.

123.9 Postilla Hemmingei

Niels Hemmingsen. Perhaps [*Gospels (liturgical): commentary*]. Continent (probable): 1562–1569.

Probably not an STC book, but see STC 13061. Or, if the entry is descriptive, one of his other Biblical commentaries. *Language(s)*: Latin. Appraised at 16d in 1577.

123.10   Aristophanes grece
Aristophanes. [*Works*]. Continent: date indeterminable.
Language(s): Greek. Appraised at 8d in 1577.

123.11   Loci Communes Hipperii
Andreas Gerardus, *Hyperius*. [*Methodus theologiae sive loci communes*]. Basle:
Joannes Oporinus, 1567–1574.
Language(s): Latin. Appraised at 3s 4d in 1577.

123.12   Chitreus in Deutronomiam
David Chytraeus. *In Deuteronomium Mosis enarratio*. Wittenberg: excusa a
Clemens Schleich et Antonio Schöne, 1575.
Language(s): Latin. Appraised at 16d in 1577.

123.13   Chetreus in Apocalypsin
David Chytraeus. [*Revelation: commentary and text*]. Wittenberg: Johann
Crato (with different houses), 1563–1575.
Language(s): Latin. Appraised at 14d in 1577.

123.14   Toxotes ad Serenissimum
Michael Toxites. [*Cicero (spurious)–Rhetorica ad Herennium: commentary and
text*]. Basle: (different houses), 1556–1568.
Language(s): Latin. Appraised at 10d in 1577.

123.15   Confessio Besa
Théodore de Bèze. *Confessio christianae fidei*. Britain or Continent: 1560–
1577.
STC 2006 and non-STC. Gardy nos. 114–119. *Language(s)*: Latin. Appraised at 12d in 1577.

123.16   Ethica Donati
Donatus Acciaiolus. [*Aristotle–Ethica: commentary*]. Continent: date indeterminable.
This could be one of his editions with commentary. *Language(s)*: Latin. Appraised at 18d in 1577.

123.17   Osorius de justicia
Jeronimo Osorio da Fonseca, *Bishop*. *De justitia*. Continent: 1564–1574.
Language(s): Latin. Appraised at 8d in 1577.

123.18   biblia Jheronimi
The Bible. Translated by Jerome, *Saint*. Britain or Continent: date indeter-
minable.
STC 2055 and non-STC. *Language(s)*: Latin. Appraised at 20d in 1577.

123.19 Erasmus in Lucam
Desiderius Erasmus. [*Luke: paraphrase*]. Continent: date indeterminable.
Language(s): Latin. Appraised at 6d in 1577.

123.20 The Courtier
Baldassare Castiglione, *Count. The Courtyer*. Translated by Sir Thomas
Hoby. London: (different houses), 1561–1577.
STC 4778. *Language(s)*: English. Appraised at 20d in 1577.

123.21 Billic contra Buserum
Everhard Billick. *Judicii Universitatis et cleri Coloniensis, adversus calumnias
Philippi Melanthonis, Martini Buceri, Oldendorpii, et eorum asseclarum defensio.*
Continent: 1543–1545.
Language(s): Latin. Appraised at 8d in 1577.

123.22 The Images of Bothe Churches
John Bale, *Bishop. The image of both churches, after the revelacion of saynt
Johan the evangelyst*. Britain or Continent: 1545 (probable)–c.1570 (probable).
STC 1296.5 *et seq. Language(s)*: English. Appraised at 16d in 1577.

123.23 Cathekismus Calvini
Jean Calvin. [*Cathechism*]. Britain or Continent: 1538–1575.
STC 4375 and non-STC. *Language(s)*: Latin. Appraised at 12d in 1577.

123.24 Enchiridion Hemmingii
Niels Hemmingsen. *Enchiridion theologicum*. Continent: 1557–1577.
Language(s): Latin. Appraised at 12d in 1577.

123.25 Ethica Aristotelis grece
Aristotle. *Ethica*. Continent: date indeterminable.
Language(s): Greek. Appraised at 12d in 1577.

123.26 Augustinus de spiritu et littera
Augustine, *Saint. De spiritu et littera*. Continent: 1530–1557.
Language(s): Latin. Appraised at 8d in 1577.

123.27 Ethica Perionii
Aristotle. *Ethica*. Translated by Joachim Perion. Continent: date indeterminable.
A less likely possibility is Perion's commentary, *De optimo genere interpretandi in Aristotelis X libros Ethicorum. Language(s)*: Latin. Appraised at 4d in 1577.

123.28 Commentarium anglice Pauli Epistolarum
Unidentified. [*Epistles–Paul: commentary*]. Britain: date indeterminable.
Unidentifiable in the STC. *Language(s)*: English. Appraised at 8d in 1577.

123.29 Regule Chitrei
David Chytraeus. *Regulae vitae*. Continent: 1555–1573.
Language(s): Latin. Appraised at 12d in 1577.

123.30 Luterus ad Galathas
Martin Luther. [*Galatians: commentary*]. Continent: date indeterminable.
Language(s): Latin. Appraised at 12d in 1577.

123.31 Novum Testamentum Besa
[*Bible–N.T.*]. Translated and edited by Théodore de Bèze. Britain or Continent: date indeterminable.
STC 2802 *et seq.* and non-STC. The editions from England were in Latin only. *Language(s)*: Latin Greek (probable). Appraised at 18d in 1577.

123.32 Oraciones Dimostonis Olnithiace
Demosthenes. *Olynthiacae orationes tres*. Continent (probable): date indeterminable.
Probably not an STC book, but see STC 6577. The 1571 London edition of Demosthenes' selected orations leads with this title. *Language(s)*: Latin (probable) Greek (perhaps). Appraised at 10d in 1577.

123.33 Opera Xenophontis in 3bus
Xenophon. [*Works*]. Continent: date indeterminable.
Perhaps the three-volume Greek edition issued in Halle in 1540. *Language(s)*: Latin (probable) Greek (perhaps). Appraised at 2s in 1577.

123.34 Orationes Isocratis graece
Isocrates. Probably [*Selected works–Orations*]. Continent: date indeterminable.
Language(s): Greek. Appraised at 16d in 1577.

123.35 Loci Communes Sarcerii
Erasmus Sarcerius. [*Loci communes*]. Continent: date indeterminable.
A number of English printings from 1538 to 1577, but the compiler does not specify English as he did at 123.28 (*anglice*). *Language(s)*: Latin. Appraised at 10d in 1577.

123.36 Grammatica Clenardi
Nicolaus Clenardus. [*Institutiones linguae graecae*]. Continent: date indeterminable.
Language(s): Greek Latin. Appraised at 6d in 1577.

123.37 Enchiridion Erasmi
Desiderius Erasmus. *Enchiridion militis Christiani.* Continent: date indeterminable.
The 1533 English edition does not seem likely. *Language(s)*: Latin. Appraised at 4d in 1577.

123.38 Assertio
Unidentified. Place unknown: stationer unknown, date indeterminable.
STC/non-STC status unknown. *Language(s)*: Latin (probable). Appraised at 8d in 1577.

123.39 Edmundus Alen, Cathahisme
Edmond Allen. *A catechism.* Britain or Continent: 1548–1562.
STC 358.5 *et seq.* The *shorte catechisme* was printed in Zürich with a London imprint. *Language(s)*: English. Appraised at 2d in 1577.

123.40 Genesis Liber
[*Bible–O.T.–Genesis*]. Continent: date indeterminable.
Perhaps the *Pentateuch*. *Language(s)*: Latin. Appraised at 2d in 1577.

123.41 2a pars Phylosophic' Ciceronis
Marcus Tullius Cicero. [*Selected works–Philosophica* (part)]. Continent: date indeterminable.
Several two-volume editions of this work appeared on the Continent between 1523 and 1574. *Language(s)*: Latin. Appraised at 2d in 1577.

123.42 Psalterium Hesii
[*Bible–O.T.–Psalms*]. Translated by Helius Eobanus, *Hessus.* Britain or Continent: 1537–1575.
STC 2356 and non-STC. *Language(s)*: Latin. Appraised at 4d in 1577.

123.43 Novum Testamentum Erasmi
[*Bible–N.T.*]. Edited by Desiderius Erasmus. Britain or Continent: date indeterminable.
STC 2800 and non-STC. The entry might also refer to either his *Annotationes* or *Paraphrases*. *Language(s)*: Latin Greek (perhaps). Appraised at 6d in 1577.

123.44 Testamentum grecum
[*Bible–N.T.*]. Continent: date indeterminable.
Language(s): Greek. Appraised at 10d in 1577.

123.45 Calvini Cathakysmus
Jean Calvin. [*Catechism*]. Britain or Continent: 1538–1575.
STC 4375 and non-STC. *Language(s)*: Latin Greek (perhaps). Appraised at 8d in 1577.

123.46 Flores Poetarum

Flores poetarum. Continent: date indeterminable.
Language(s): Latin. Appraised at 9d in 1577.

123.47 Epistole ad Atticum

Marcus Tullius Cicero. *Epistolae ad Atticum.* Continent: date indeterminable.
Language(s): Latin. Appraised at 6d in 1577.

123.48 Rethorica Ciceronis

Marcus Tullius Cicero. [*Selected works–Rhetorica*]. Continent: date indeterminable.
At this valuation, perhaps the widely printed *Rhetorica ad Herennium*. *Language(s)*: Latin. Appraised at 8d in 1577.

123.49 Ovidius de fastis

Publius Ovidius Naso. *Fasti.* Britain or Continent: date indeterminable.
STC 18947.5 and non-STC. *Language(s)*: Latin. Appraised at 6d in 1577.

123.50:1–8 viii bokes band in parchment

Unidentified. Places unknown: stationers unknown, dates indeterminable.
STC/non-STC status unknown. *Language(s)*: Unknown. Appraised at 2s in 1577.

123.51:1–16 xvi paper and note bokes

Unidentified. Provenances unknown: dates indeterminable.
Manuscripts. *Language(s)*: Unknown. Appraised at 12d in 1577.

Thomas Foster. Profession unknown: Probate Inventory. 1577

R. J. FEHRENBACH and E. S. LEEDHAM-GREEN

The identity and standing of Thomas Foster, the owner of these few books, most of them compilations of English statutes, is obscure. The heading of his inventory describes him as "of thuniuersitie of oxon," rather than as of any college, and indeed it is clear that he cannot have been a fellow or student of any college as he was a married man living in the town. Administration of his estate was granted, he having died intestate, to his widow Elizabeth on 9 September 1577. He is not designated a graduate, and indeed the surviving lists show no Thomas Foster as having graduated at Oxford within a possible time scale.

There was a Thomas Foster described by Anthony à Wood in his *Survey of the Antiquities of the City of Oxford* as having been in 1524 the common carrier from Oxford to London (Clark 1899, 28), and it is just barely possible that this might be the man. A Thomas Foster also appealed to the university Congregation in 22 March 1574 in respect to a law suit with one Squier (Clark 2:105), and it is not unlikely that that this was the man who died in 1577. Unfortunately his profession and status are not given; Clark indexes him as possibly a citizen of the town.

The inventory reveals that Foster lived in a house comprising a hall and a parlor, both with chambers over them, a kitchen, a servant's (or servants') chamber, and a pewter buttery. His pewter was worth a good deal more than his books, and his furnishings were substantial but, with the exception of a bedstead of walnut, at two pounds worth twice as much as anything else in the house, not luxurious. He did, however, boast a chess set.

His domestic circumstances are somewhat at odds with his books. Collections of statutes are most often found in the libraries of those likely to be called on to act as magistrates, and both his modest quarters and his absence from the records argue against Foster being of that standing. They also occur, if less frequently, in the libraries of lawyers, but then only among other legal texts of interest to either working or academic lawyers. There is no Thomas Foster of the appropriate dates listed in any of the registers of the Inns of Court.

Only surmise remains: Foster may have been a retainer to a magistrate in the town courts, or may have come by the books more by accident than design as, for example, pledges against a debt.

Oxford University Archives, Bodleian Library: Hyp.B.12.

§

Clark, Andrew, ed. 1899. *Wood's History of the City of Oxford.* Vol. 3. Oxford: Printed for the Oxford Historical at the Clarendon Press.

§

124.1	the statutes of kyng henrie the third to kyng henry the viiith
124.2	the hole statutes of kyng henrie the viiith
124.3	the brydgment of the statutes
124.4	dixionarium a freinche
124.5	Aster uppon the lawe
124.6	les prese de corun
124.7	Edward the third
124.8	Registrum omnium brevium
124.9:1–6	vi old bokes

§

124.1 the statutes of kyng henrie the third to kyng henry the viiith

In this volume are conteined the statutes from Henry the thirde, unto the fyrste yere of Henry the .viii. (England–Statutes–General Collections). London: (different houses), 1543–1577.

STC 9301. *Language(s)*: English Latin Law/French. Appraised at 3s in 1577.

124.2 the hole statutes of kyng henrie the viiith

The second volume conteyninge those statutes, made in the tyme of Henry the eyght. (England–Statutes–General Collections). London: (different houses), 1543–1575.

STC 9303.4 *et seq. Language(s)*: English Latin Law/French. Appraised at 3s in 1577.

124.3 the brydgment of the statutes

Probably [*Abbreviamentum statutorum*]. (*England–Statutes–Abridgements and Extracts*). London: (different houses), 1481?–1551.

STC 9513 *et seq.* The valuation does not suggest an abridgement of an individual year (STC 9533.2 *et seq.*), though it could conceivably refer to STC 9306 *et seq.*, Rastell's abridgement. *Language(s)*: English Latin Law/French. Appraised at 2s in 1577.

124.4 dixionarium a freinche

Unidentified [dictionary]. Place unknown: stationer unknown, date indeterminable.

STC/non-STC status unknown. At least one French dictionary published in England (STC 6832) may be intended, and a Law French dictionary (see, e.g., STC 20701 *et seq.*) cannot be ruled out, but see the following. *Language(s)*: French English (perhaps) Latin (perhaps) Law/French (perhaps). Appraised at 12d in 1577.

124.5 Aster uppon the lawe

Unidentified. Britain (probable): date indeterminable.

Unidentifiable in the STC, but almost certainly published in England. The entry's *Aster* could conceivably be a misheard "Rastell" for either William or John, and given that the preceding is a dictionary, John Rastell's Law French *Expositiones terminorum legum anglorum*, STC 20701 *et seq.*, would be an appropriate companion volume. Another, perhaps more imaginative conjecture is that *Aster* is a partially heard "Mulcaster," for STC 11194 (*A learned commendation of the politique lawes of Englande*), Robert Mulcaster's translation of Sir John Fortescue's *De politica administratione* (STC 1193). *Language(s)*: English (probable). Appraised at 6d in 1577.

124.6 les prese de corun

Probably Sir William Stanford. *Les plees del coron: divisees in plusiours titles.* London: in aed. R. Tottelli, 1557–1574.

STC 23219 *et seq.* Other possibilities, less likely than the popular Stanford work, include STC 9599–9600. See the annotations to 124.7. *Language(s)*: Law/French. Appraised at 4d in 1577.

124.7 Edward the third

Probably [*England–Yearbooks–Edward III*]. London: (different houses), 1511?–c.1565.

STC 9551 *et seq.* The identification excludes items at STC 9599–9605, which should, nonetheless, be considered remote possibilities. See the annotations to 124.6. *Language(s)*: Latin Law/French (perhaps). Appraised at 8d in 1577.

124.8 Registrum omnium brevium

Registrum omnium brevium tam originalium quam judicialium. Edited by William Rastell. London: by W. Rastell and it is to sell at the house of the sayde Wyllyam, or of R. Redman, 1531.

STC 20836 *et seq.* One edition, with a variant printing, by the date of this inventory. *Language(s)*: Latin. Appraised at 8d in 1577.

124.9:1–6 vi old bokes

Unidentified. Places unknown: stationers unknown, dates indeterminable.

STC/non-STC status unknown. *Language(s)*: Unknown. Appraised as a group at 12d in 1577.

John Gray. Scholar (student): Probate Inventory. 1577

S. P. WAYLAND

John Gray was registered as a Dudley Exhibitioner of Oriel College, Oxford, in October 1574. His will was made on 24 July 1577 and proved in the Chancellor's Court on 17 December 1577 (Chancellor's Court Register GG [Hyp.A.5] fol. 232v). Both the date of the making of the will and the date of probate seem uncomplicated, but Shadwell's edition of the *Registrum Orielense* (1893, 45) suggests rather that Gray died in December 1576 when his exhibition is noted to have passed to his successor on account of Gray's death. Gray's successor in the exhibition, Robert Walker, was also the residuary legatee and chief beneficiary of his will (Shadwell 1893, 47). It is, perhaps, just conceivable that for the period of Gray's last sickness the exhibition was effectively shared by the two scholars, and that this might account for the scribe of the register backdating Gray's death.

The core of identifiable works in Gray's library consists of fairly standard student materials, primarily in Latin, on rhetorical, logical, ethical, and theological subjects.

Oxford University Archives, Bodleian Library: Hyp.B.13.

§

Shadwell, Charles Lancelot. 1893. *The Commensales, Commoners and Battellers Admitted During the Years 1500–1700.* Vol. 1 of *Registrum Orielense: An Account of the Members of Oriel College, Oxford.* London: Henry Frowde.

§

125.1   Stanhurst uppon Purphirii
125.2   testamentum anglice
125.3   Hunius super logica
125.4   organum aristotelis
125.5   valerius max
125.6   Hystrie biblie
125.7   tulii officia
125.8   copia verborum
125.9   titillmanus
125.10   vergilius
125.11   Jeraldus
125.12   phrases manucii
125.13   logica valerii
125.14   fabulae Isopi grece et lat
125.15   melangthone
125.16:1–2   ii pap bokes
125.17   valerius max
125.18:1–21 xxi litell old bokes

§

125.1 Stanhurst uppon Purphirii
Richard Stanyhurst. *Harmonia seu catena dialectica, in Porphyrianas institutiones.* London: apud R. Wolfium, 1570.
STC 23229. *Language(s)*: Latin. Appraised at 20d in 1577.

125.2 testamentum anglice
[*Bible–N.T.*]. Britain or Continent: 1525–1577.
STC 2823 *et seq.* Perhaps, however, the New Testament of a complete Bible. *Language(s)*: English. Appraised at 2s in 1577.

125.3 Hunius super logica
Augustinus Hunnaeus. Unidentified. Continent: date indeterminable.
Either his *Dialectica, seu generalis logices praecepta* or his *Logices fundamentum. Language(s)*: Latin. Appraised at 6d in 1577.

125.4 organum aristotelis
Aristotle. *Organon.* Continent: date indeterminable.
Language(s): Latin (probable) Greek (perhaps). Appraised at 6d in 1577.

125.5 valerius max
Valerius Maximus. *Facta et dicta memorabilia.* Continent: date indeterminable.

Another copy at 125.17. *Language(s)*: Latin. Appraised at 2d in 1577.

125.6 Hystrie biblie
Perhaps Hans Sebald Beham. *Biblicae historiae*. Frankfurt am Main: Christianus Egenolphus excudebat, 1537–1539.
The title of Beham's collection of woodcuts bears a close verbal resemblance to this entry, though other works with less similar titles cannot be completely ruled out. The 1537 edition of the *Biblicae historiae* is also in German, and the 1539 edition, in Latin only, carries commentary by Georgius Aemelius. *Language(s)*: Latin German (perhaps). Appraised at 6d in 1577.

125.7 tulii officia
Marcus Tullius Cicero. *De officiis*. Britain or Continent: date indeterminable.
STC 5278 *et seq.* and non-STC. Two bilingual versions printed in England are among the possibilities: see STC 5278 *et seq.* and 5281.8 *et seq. Language(s)*: Latin English (perhaps). Appraised at 2d in 1577.

125.8 copia verborum
Probably Desiderius Erasmus. *De duplici copia verborum ac rerum*. Britain or Continent: date indeterminable.
STC 10471.4 *et seq.* and non-STC. Erasmus's popular handbook is most likely, but other works are possible, such as Johannes Oldendorp's *De copia verborum & rerum in jure civili. Language(s)*: Latin. Appraised at 2d in 1577.

125.9 titillmanus
Franz Titelmann. Unidentified. Continent: date indeterminable.
Language(s): Latin. Appraised at 2d in 1577.

125.10 vergilius
Publius Virgilius Maro. Probably [*Works*]. Britain or Continent: date indeterminable.
STC 24787 *et seq.* and non-STC. Polydorus Vergilius is also possible, but he is less likely referred to as *Vergilius* alone. *Language(s)*: Latin. Appraised at 2d in 1577.

125.11 Jeraldus
Unidentified. Place unknown: stationer unknown, date indeterminable.
STC/non-STC status unknown. This entry resists identification. Possible authors include Geraldus, *de Solo*; Geraldus, *Cambrensis*; and Lilius Gregorius Giraldus. *Language(s)*: Unknown. Appraised at 4d in 1577.

125.12 phrases manucii
Aldo Manuzio, *the Younger. Purae, elegantes et copiosae latinae linguae phrases*.

Britain or Continent: date indeterminable.

STC 17278.8 *et seq.* and non-STC. *Language(s)*: Latin. Appraised at 2d in 1577.

125.13 logica valerii

Probably Cornelius Valerius. *Tabulae totius dialectices.* Continent: date indeterminable.

Language(s): Latin. Appraised at 3d in 1577.

125.14 fabulae Isopi grece et lat

Aesop. *Fabulae.* Continent: date indeterminable.

Language(s): Greek Latin. Appraised at 3d in 1577.

125.15 melangthone

Philipp Melanchthon. Unidentified. Place unknown: stationer unknown, date indeterminable.

STC/non-STC status unknown. *Language(s)*: Latin (probable) English (perhaps). Appraised at 2d in 1577.

125.16:1–2 ii pap bokes

Unidentified. Provenances unknown: dates indeterminable.

Manuscripts. Perhaps notebooks. *Language(s)*: Unknown. Appraised at 6d, the pair in 1577.

125.17 valerius max

Valerius Maximus. *Facta et dicta memorabilia.* Continent: date indeterminable.

Another copy at 125.5. *Language(s)*: Latin. Appraised at 2d in 1577.

125.18:1–21 xxi litell old bokes

Unidentified. Places unknown: stationers unknown, dates indeterminable.

STC/non-STC status unknown. *Language(s)*: Unknown. Appraised as a group at 12d in 1577.

John Marshall. Scholar (M.A.): Probate Inventory. 1577

DOUGLAS BRUSTER

John Marshall was a student of St. Alban Hall in or before 1572; he graduated B.A. 30 June 1575, and incepted M.A. 6 July 1577. He must have died soon thereafter, as the following inventory was compiled at Oxford on 6 November 1577 (*Alumni Oxonienses*, 3:974).

No other information about Marshall has been located. His modest collection consists largely of texts appropriate to the M.A. course, with some items remaining from the B.A. course. There is, however, a marked emphasis on rhetoric; see 126.7, 126.8, 126.15, 126.16, and 126.22, the last two of which are relatively uncommon items.

Oxford University Archives, Bodleian Library: Hyp.B.16

§

126.1	a Cooper's Dictionary of the thirde edicion
126.2	one Byble of Geneva in Englishe
126.3	Schola Loveniensis
126.4	Opera Raiani
126.5	Livii v volumen in oct [octavo]
126.6	Tregidii Euripides
126.7	Ortioni Ciceronis in oct [octavo], iii vol.
126.8	Orationis Isocratis grece
126.9	moral: plutharc: iii vol.
126.10	Orgenum Arist:
126.11	dialect: Radolphi
126.12	Justine
126.13	Tully's Office

126.14   Homer's worckes
126.15   Apthonius
126.16   Demetrius Vallerius
126.17   Cronica Charionis
126.18   Cleonardes grammer in greeke
126.19   Tullyes epistells
126.20   Phisica Petri Erami
126.21   Cornelius Agrippa de occulta philosophia
126.22   Orationis Muriti
126.23   Velcuri
126.24   Tittelman's Logique
126.25   Epistole Manutii
126.26   Historia Ariani
126.27   Cesar's Commentaryes
126.28   Ozorius de gloria
126.29   Aristotell's Ethickes in Greeke
126.30:1-6   six paper bookes

§

126.1 a Cooper's Dictionary of the thirde edicion

Sir Thomas Elyot and Thomas Cooper, *Bishop. Bibliotheca Eliotae Eliotis librarie. The third tyme corrected and enriched by T. Cooper.* London: in aed. nuper T. Bertheleti, 1562–1563 (single edition).

STC 7663. The description, *of the thirde edicion*, drives the identification of this item; the title page not only carries that designation but bears Cooper's name as well. The third edition of Cooper's *Thesaurus*, which is not so described on the title page, is too late for this inventory. *Language(s)*: English Latin. Appraised at 10s in 1577.

126.2 one Byble of Geneva in Englishe

The Bible. Britain or Continent: 1560–1577.

STC 2093 *et seq. Language(s)*: English. Appraised at 12s in 1577.

126.3 Schola Loveniensis

Commentaria in Isagogen Porphyrii et in omnes libros Aristotelis de dialectica. (*Louvain University*). Louvain: [probably] Servatius Sassenus, 1535–1568.

Sassenus published the 1535 and 1568 editions; bibliographical sources do not name the publisher of the 1547 and 1553 editions. *Language(s)*: Latin Greek (probable). Appraised at 4s in 1577.

126.4 Opera Raiani

Hermannus Rayanus, *Welsdalius.* Unidentified. Continent: date indeterminable.

The only work associated with Rayanus (as editor and commentator) that seems to have been published in a form larger than octavo and that might have justified the 5s valuation is the 1568 two-volume quarto edition of various works of Aristotle and Plato (Cranz 108.540). The two volumes might also explain the compiler's loosely employed *Opera*. *Language(s)*: Latin. Appraised at 5s in 1577.

126.5 Livii v volumen in oct [octavo]

Titus Livius. [*Historiae Romanae decades*]. Continent: date indeterminable.

The compiler struck out *iiiior*, substituting *v* on finding the item that he started to enter between 126.10 and 126.11 and then deleted: "one other worcke of lyvy." This, taken with the valuation, confirms that the entry should have read "v volumnia" [five volumes] rather than "vta volumen" [fifth volume] or *v volumen* as it stands. The Aldine octavo edition of Livy (1518–1533) is in five volumes, but the entry here could represent a collection of various octavo volumes. *Language(s)*: Latin. Appraised at 6s in 1577.

126.6 Tregidii Euripides

Euripides. Probably [*Works*]. Continent: date indeterminable.

The compiler appears to have noted when a book is in Greek; this could be a Greek-Latin edition, conceivably *Selected works*. *Language(s)*: Latin (probable) Greek (perhaps). Appraised at 20d in 1577.

126.7 Ortioni Ciceronis in oct [octavo], iii vol.

Marcus Tullius Cicero. [*Selected works–Orations*]. Continent: date indeterminable.

Language(s): Latin. Appraised at 3s in 1577.

126.8 Orationis Isocratis grece

Isocrates. [*Selected works–Orations*]. Continent: date indeterminable.
Language(s): Greek. Appraised at 18d in 1577.

126.9 moral: plutharc: iii vol.

Plutarch. *Moralia*. Continent: date indeterminable.

Compiler orginally wrote: *iiii vol*. Without the compiler's customary Greek identification when the item is in that language, a Latin edition is probably intended. *Language(s)*: Latin (probable) Greek (perhaps). Appraised at 5s in 1577.

126.10 Orgenum Arist:

Aristotle. *Organon*. Continent: date indeterminable.

Struck out: *one other* following the appraisal. *Language(s)*: Latin (probable) Greek (perhaps). Appraised at 12d in 1577.

126.11 dialect: Radolphi
Rodolphus Agricola. *De inventione dialectica*. Continent: date indeterminable.
Language(s): Latin. Appraised at 8d in 1577.

126.12 Justine
Probably Trogus Pompeius and Justinus, *the Historian*. [*Epitomae in Trogi Pompeii historias*]. Britain or Continent: date indeterminable.
STC 24287 *et seq.* and non-STC. *Language(s)*: Latin. Appraised at 10d in 1577.

126.13 Tully's Office
Marcus Tullius Cicero. [*De officiis*]. Britain or Continent: date indeterminable.
STC 5278 *et seq.* and non-STC. Although editions of Cicero's works often begin with *De officiis*, the latter thus providing the collection's title, the comparatively low appraisal of this book suggests the single work. The entry suggests either an English or an English-Latin edition. *Language(s)*: English (probable) Latin (perhaps). Appraised at 8d in 1577.

126.14 Homer's worckes
Homer. [*Works*]. Continent: date indeterminable.
Illiaddes deleted. Customarily the *Iliad* was the leading title in the *Works*. Not appraised, but 12*d* struck out; perhaps not Marshall's book. Here the compiler entered either a Latin or a Greek edition in English. *Language(s)*: Latin (probable) Greek (perhaps).

126.15 Apthonius
Aphthonius, *Sophista*. *Progymnasmata*. Britain or Continent: date indeterminable.
STC 699 *et seq.* and non-STC. *Language(s)*: Latin (probable) Greek (perhaps). Appraised at 6d in 1577.

126.16 Demetrius Vallerius
Demetrius, *Phalereus*. Unidentified. Continent: date indeterminable.
The *De elocutione* was Phalereus's most widely published work. *Language(s)*: Latin (probable) Greek (perhaps). Appraised at 8d in 1577.

126.17 Cronica Charionis
Johann Carion. *Chronica*. Continent (probable): date indeterminable.
Probably not an STC book, but see STC 4626. Very unlikely that the English translation would be so entered, but the compiler's habits of entering are not consistent. *Language(s)*: Latin. Appraised at 16d in 1577.

126.18   Cleonardes grammer in greeke
   Nicolaus Clenardus. [*Institutiones linguae graecae*]. Continent: date indeterminable.
   Language(s): Greek Latin. Appraised at 16d in 1577.

126.19   Tullyes epistells
   Marcus Tullius Cicero. [*Selected works–Epistolae*]. Continent: date indeterminable.
   The popular *Epistolae ad familiares*, which had been printed in England by the date of this inventory, may be intended. *Language(s)*: Latin. Appraised at 10d in 1577.

126.20   Phisica Petri Erami
   Pierre de La Ramée. *Scholarum physicarum libri octo, in totidem acroamaticos libros Aristotelis*. Paris: apud Andream Wechelum, 1565.
   Ong no. 592. *Language(s)*: Latin. Appraised at 8d in 1577.

126.21   Cornelius Agrippa de occulta philosophia
   Henricus Cornelius Agrippa. *De occulta philosophia*. Continent: 1531–1567.
   Language(s): Latin. Appraised at 12d in 1577.

126.22   Orationis Muriti
   Marcus Antonius Muretus. [*Selected works–Orations*]. Continent: date indeterminable.
   Language(s): Latin. Appraised at 10d in 1577.

126.23   Velcuri
   Joannes Velcurio. Perhaps [*Aristotle–Physica: commentary*]. Continent: 1537–1575.
   With the set of Livy at 126.5, Velcurio's commentary on that author is also a possibility, but the proximity of this item to Ramus's commentary on the *Physica* at 126.20 makes the qualified identification of the commentary on the *Physica* somewhat more likely. *Language(s)*: Latin. Appraised at 8d in 1577.

126.24   Tittelman's Logique
   Franz Titelmann. [*Dialectica*]. Continent: date indeterminable.
   Language(s): Latin. Appraised at 8d in 1577.

126.25   Epistole Manutii
   Paolo Manuzio. [*Epistolae*]. Britain or Continent: date indeterminable.
   STC 17286 *et seq.* and non-STC. A remote possibility is Manuzio's commentary on Cicero's epistles. *Language(s)*: Latin. Appraised at 4d in 1577.

126.26   Historia Ariani
   Flavius Arrianus. *Expeditio Alexandri*. Continent: date indeterminable.

Language(s): Latin (probable) Greek (perhaps). Appraised at 6d in 1577.

126.27 Cesar's Commentaryes

Caius Julius Caesar. [*Commentarii*]. London: 1530 (probable)–1565.
STC 4335 *et seq*. Given the valuation, probably Arthur Golding's octavo 1530 translation rather than the 1530 folio English-Latin edition. Conceivably a Latin edition entered in English as the compiler did at 126.14. *Language(s)*: English Latin (perhaps). Appraised at 4d in 1577.

126.28 Ozorius de gloria

Jeronimo Osorio da Fonseca, *Bishop*. *De gloria*. Continent: date indeterminable.

Whether this is the single solo edition (Florence, 1552) or Osorio's widely published *Selected works*, commonly referred to by the leading *De gloria*, cannot be determined. *Language(s)*: Latin. Appraised at 4d in 1577.

126.29 Aristotell's Ethickes in Greeke

Aristotle. *Ethica*. Continent: date indeterminable.
Language(s): Greek. Appraised at 6d in 1577.

126.30:1–6   six paper bookes

Unidentified. Provenances unknown: dates indeterminable.
Manuscripts. At this valuation, presumably substantial items, and perhaps Marshall's own work. *Language(s)*: Unknown. Appraised at 3s in 1577.

James Reynolds. Scholar (M.A.):
Probate Inventory. 1577

R. J. FEHRENBACH and MORDECHAI FEINGOLD

James Reynolds (Rainolds, Raynolds), born in Pinhoe, Devonshire, was the youngest member of the Rainolds dynasty, six of whose members became Oxford dons. He was brother of Jerome (PLRE 96), but no relation to John (PLRE 97). James was elected fellow of Exeter College in 1566, graduated B.A. 29 November 1569, and received his M.A. on 20 June 1573 (*Alumni Oxonienses*, 3:1247). In June 1577 he was appointed College Lecturer in the Humanities—"qui nostrae iuventuti praelegeret et eam instrueret vel historiarum cognitione vel poetarum, vel aliarum disciplinarum preceptis ut leges nostrae postulant imbueret." His tenure was cut short by his death the following October (Boase 1894, 75).

Reynolds's library was larger than the number of entries (229) indicate. For example, 127.228 is a group appraisal of "a hundreth parchment old bookes" (valued at 26s 8d), while 127.229 consists of thirty "Englyshe bokes" (13s 4d), and 127.183 seven "smale poetes in parchment"—totalling over 360 books. The collection was valued at a little more than £14.

As befitting a young don, and a College Lecturer in the Humanities, a significant portion of Reynolds's library was composed of common humanistic texts: rhetoric, history, literary works, and moral philosophy account for nearly two-thirds of the identifiable titles. In addition, some thirty-five of the known titles are religious works, while a smaller collection of fourteen titles are related to medicine. A handful of natural philosophy textbooks and a half dozen logical texts lead us to conclude that Reynolds's interest in these subjects went no further than what he was required to study as a student. In contrast, Reynolds was a lover of music, and among his possessions we find "a payre of virginalles" (valued at 20s) and a lute (valued at 8s) (Caldwell 1986, 208, n.5).

Oxford University Archives, Bodleian Library: Hyp.B.18.

§

Boase, Charles W. 1894. *Registrum Collegii Exoniensis*. Oxford: at the Clarendon Press for the Oxford Historical Society.

Caldwell, John. 1986. "Music in the Faculty of Arts," in *The Collegiate University*, ed., James K. McConica. Volume 3 of *The History of the University of Oxford*, gen. ed. T.H. Aston. Oxford: the Clarendon Press, pp. 202–12.

§

127.1	Bibliotheca Gesnerii
127.2	Dixionarium Cowperi
127.3	Nisorius
127.4	Appianus Alexandrinus
127.5	Virgilius cum comment
127.6	Lactantius
127.7	Lucanus cum comment
127.8	Speculum Vincentii
127.9	Lucius Florus
127.10	Franciscus Florus
127.11	Salustius cum comment
127.12	Lucanus cum comment
127.13	Sallenger
127.14	Cornucopia
127.15	Quintilianus
127.16	Nicholaus Garbelius
127.17	Monsterus de horologiis
127.18	Fabule Hyginii
127.19	Oratius
127.20	Opus Regale
127.21	A Frenche story
127.22	Eustratius in Ethica
127.23	Brickott in Phisica
127.24	Burleus in Phisica
127.25	Thomas Aquinus
127.26	Athanatii opera
127.27	Eusebii opera
127.28	Basilii opera
127.29	Fasiculus Rerum
127.30	Omelia Nasei
127.31:1	Erasmus in novum test in mattheum
127.31:2	[See 127.31:1]
127.32	Plutharcus

127.33	Epiphanius
127.34	Sermones Taulleri
127.35	Hyllarius
127.36	Sermones Lanspergii
127.37	Antidodum contra Hereses
127.38	Polianthea
127.39	Dionisius de coelestis hererc
127.40	Onus Ecclesie
127.41	The Fall of Prences
127.42	Brunus de legacionibus
127.43	Herbarium Turneri
127.44	Juvenallus
127.45	Boetius de consolacione cum comment
127.46	Martialis
127.47	Policraticus
127.48	Tolletus in Phisica
127.49	Questiones Tusculani
127.50	Cardanus de sapientia
127.51	Cardanus de somniis
127.52	Politica Aristotelis
127.53	Oration Amasei
127.54	Cleonardi Gramatica
127.55	Omeri opera
127.56	Partitiones Ciceronis
127.57	Cicero de oratore
127.58	Herdesius de oratore
127.59	Diogenes latius
127.60	Historia Pandulphi
127.61	Ycones Imperatorum
127.62	Origenes in Johannem
127.63	Doceus de eterna generacione
127.64	Novum Testamentum grec
127.65	Rofensis contra Lutherum
127.66	Pontanii opera
127.67	Ecclesiastes Erasmi
127.68	Rivius de stulticia
127.69	Evangelistarium Marilli
127.70	Isiodorus
127.71	Confessio Caroli Quinti
127.72	Contarenus
127.73	Garretius
127.74	Homolia Hamonis
127.75	Laurentius Humferedus
127.76	Vives de institucione femine
127.77	Vives de dissiplinis

127.78	Osorius de gloria
127.79	Wierius de prestigiis
127.80	Alexandro ab Alexandro
127.81	Arithmetica Tonstalli
127.82	Dialectica Hunei
127.83	Clitoveus
127.84	Tunstallus in Ethica
127.85	Ligica [Logica] Javelli
127.86	Epitomi Wildenburgii
127.87	Epitom Matisii
127.88	Philosophia Foccii
127.89	Ciceronianus Fregii
127.90	Agrippa de occluta [occulta] philosophia
127.91	Athaneus
127.92	Vives de anima
127.93	Officia Ciceronis
127.94	Velcurio
127.95	Philosophia Titilmanni
127.96	Valerii opera
127.97	Mathisii Phisica
127.98	Franciscus Vatables
127.99	Donatus in Politica
127.100	Epitomi Leibleri
127.101	Arithmetica Scheubelii
127.102	Copia Verborum
127.103	Rethorica Sturmii
127.104:A	Similia Licostenis
127.104:B	[See 127.104:A]
127.105	Theonis Sophiste
127.106	Omphalius
127.107	Sambucus de imitacione
127.108	Rethorica Cruseii
127.109	Selius Secundus
127.110	Sturmii Particiones
127.111	Cicero de oratore
127.112	Epigrammata Martialis
127.113	Dares Frigius
127.114	Prudentius
127.115	Stroceus
127.116	Hatman
127.117	Picta Poesis
127.118	Isiodus
127.119	Aristophanis commedi
127.120	Spinili opera
127.121	Sinthei Epigrammata

127.122   Tragedie Senece
127.123   Pontanii opera
127.124   Oratius
127.125   Vergilius
127.126   Catullus
127.127   Fragmenta Poetarum
127.128   Epiteta Textoris
127.129   Historia Giraldi
127.130   Lucretius
127.131   Ovidii Epistol
127.132   Historia Poetarum
127.133   Vergilius
127.134   Gwalterus de quantitate etc.
127.135   Grammatica regia
127.136   Opera Ringibargii
127.137   Sermones Maximi Tirii
127.138   Epstole [Epistole] Manusii
127.139   Facetie Bebellii
127.140   Luciani Dialogi
127.141   Cato de re rustica
127.142   Columella de re rustica
127.143   Predium Rusticum
127.144   Harasbackius de re rustica
127.145   Theophrastus
127.146   De vita Buseri
127.147   Commentaria Cesaris
127.148   Amianus Masselinus
127.149   Lucius Florus
127.150   Ipographia Antique Romane
127.151   Exempla Sabellisi
127.152   Olaus Magnus
127.153   Cronicon Melangtonis
127.154   Zenophon
127.155   Abdias Babilonicus
127.156   Aule Tursice
127.157   Descriptio Affrice
127.158   Newbrigenses
127.159   Valerius Maximus
127.160   Olimpius
127.161   Valerius Maximus
127.162   Epithome Vadiani
127.163   Ciprinum Bellum
127.164   Bodinus
127.165   Chitreus de lectione historiarum

127.166 Quintus Cursius
127.167 Suetonius
127.168 Salustius
127.169 Apothegmata Licostenis
127.170 Patricius in 2bus
127.171 Epigrammata Johannis Secundi
127.172 Catullus
127.173 Ovidius de fastis
127.174 Flores Epigrammatum in 2bus
127.175 Dialigi Textoris
127.176 Jheronimi Vita
127.177 Ovidii Methamorphoses
127.178 Ausonius
127.179 Palengenius
127.180 Prudentius
127.181 Epigrammata Stephani
127.182 Claudianus
127.183:1–7 vii smale poetes in parchment
127.184 Apianus Alexadrinus
127.185 Salustius
127.186 Lucius Florus
127.187 Quintus Cursus
127.188 Diodorus Siculus
127.189 Justinus
127.190 Dionisius Halicarniseus
127.191 Cornelius Tacitus
127.192 Julius Solinus
127.193 Quintus Cursius
127.194 Epitom Plutharchi
127.195 Compendium Patricii
127.196 Extremum Judicium
127.197 Rethorica Ciceronis
127.198 Colloquium Erasmi
127.199 Problemata Aristotelis
127.200 Apothegmata Erasmi
127.201 Compendium Theologicum
127.202 Colloquium Erasmi
127.203 Epiteta Textoris
127.204 Misaldus
127.205 Petrus Crinicus
127.206 Orationes Mureti
127.207 Problemata Aristotelis
127.208 Sententia Aristotelis
127.209 Testamentum Benedicti

127.210   Exempla Virtutum
127.211   Hossius de expresso Dei verbo
127.212   Precaciones Erasmi
127.213   Fabulae Isopi
127.214   Galenus de diebus decretoriis
127.215   Epistol' Medicinalis
127.216   Fuccius
127.217   Fernelius
127.218   Hypocrates
127.219   Diescorides
127.220   Macer de metari
127.221   Dessenius de compositione
127.222   Epistol Medicinales
127.223   Methodus Fuctii
127.224   Epidemie Galleni
127.225   Tituli Juris Canonici
127.226   Harbarium Dodanei
127.227   Marianus
127.228:1–100   a hundreth parchment old bokes
127.229:1–30   xxxti Englyshe bokes

§

127.1 Bibliotheca Gesnerii

Conrad Gesner. Unidentified. Continent: date indeterminable.

Either the *Bibliotheca universalis, sive Catalogus omnium scriptorum* or the *Bibliotheca instituta*, both of which were published in folio editions that would justify the high valuation. *Language(s)*: Latin. Appraised at 6s in 1577.

127.2 Dixionarium Cowperi

Thomas Cooper, *Bishop*. *Thesaurus linguae Romanae et Britannicae*. London: (different houses), 1565–1573.

STC 5686 *et seq.* Cooper had been the reviser of a number of the later editions of Sir Thomas Elyot's dictionary, but the work issued in Cooper's own name is clearly intended here. *Language(s)*: English Latin. Appraised at 16s in 1577.

127.3 Nisorius

Marius Nizolius. [*Observationes*]. Continent: date indeterminable. *Language(s)*: Latin. Appraised at 5s in 1577.

127.4 Appianus Alexandrinus

Appian, *of Alexandria*. [*Historia Romana*]. Continent: date indeterminable. *Language(s)*: Latin. Appraised at 3s 4d in 1577.

127.5 Virgilius cum comment

Publius Virgilius Maro. Probably [*Works*]. Britain or Continent: date indeterminable.

STC 24788 *et seq.* and non-STC. STC 24787 does not carry commentary. *Language(s)*: Latin. Appraised at 3s in 1577.

127.6 Lactantius

Lucius Coelius Lactantius. Probably [*Works*]. Continent: date indeterminable.

Not identified as an STC book, but see STC 15118. STC 15118 is an edition of *Selected works*, which could be intended here. *Language(s)*: Latin. Appraised at 2s 4d in 1577.

127.7 Lucanus cum comment

Marcus Annaeus Lucanus. *Pharsalia*. Continent: date indeterminable. Another copy at 127.12. *Language(s)*: Latin. Appraised at 16d in 1577.

127.8 Speculum Vincentii

Vincentius, *Bellovacensis* (Vincent, *de Beauvais*). *Speculum major*. Continent: date indeterminable.

Language(s): Latin. Appraised at 8d in 1577.

127.9 Lucius Florus

Lucius Annaeus Florus. [*Epitomae de Tito Livio bellorum omnium annorum*]. Continent: date indeterminable.

See 127.149 and 127.186. Not appraised. *Language(s)*: Latin.

127.10 Franciscus Florus

Franciscus Floridus, *Sabinus*. Perhaps *Apologia in M.A. Plauti calumniatores*. Continent: 1537–1540.

Language(s): Latin. Appraised at 12d in 1577.

127.11 Salustius cum comment

Caius Sallustius Crispus. Probably [*Works*]. Britain or Continent: date indeterminable.

STC 21622.2 *et seq.* and non-STC. See 127.168 and 127.185. *Language(s)*: Latin. Appraised at 4s in 1577.

127.12 Lucanus cum comment

Marcus Annaeus Lucanus. *Pharsalia*. Continent: date indeterminable. Another copy at 127.7. *Language(s)*: Latin. Appraised at 8d in 1577.

127.13 Sallenger

Unidentified. Place unknown: stationer unknown, date indeterminable. STC/non-STC status unknown. If one of the Scaligers, Julius Caesar Scaliger marginally more likely since more of his works had been published by this date and in sizes that would be more commensurate with the valuation. *Language(s)*: Unknown. Appraised at 3s in 1577.

127.14 Cornucopia

Probably Nicolaus Perottus. *Cornucopia*. Continent: date indeterminable. *Language(s)*: Latin Greek (perhaps). Appraised at 3s in 1577.

127.15 Quintilianus

Marcus Fabius Quintilianus. Unidentified. Continent: date indeterminable.

Could be the *Declamationes, Institutiones oratoriae*, or the *Works*. *Language(s)*: Latin. Appraised at 12d in 1577.

127.16 Nicholaus Garbelius

Nicolaus Gerbelius. Unidentified. Continent: date indeterminable. *Language(s)*: Latin. Appraised at 6d in 1577.

127.17 Monsterus de horologiis

Sebastian Muenster. [*Horologiographia*]. Basle: excudebat Henricus Petrus, 1531–1533.

Language(s): Latin. Appraised at 16d in 1577.

127.18 Fabule Hyginii

Hyginus, *Mythographer*. *Fabularum liber. Poeticon astronomicon* [and other works]. Continent: 1535–1570.

Often wrongly attributed to Caius Julius Hyginus, none of whose works survive. *Language(s)*: Latin. Appraised at 18d in 1577.

127.19 Oratius

Quintus Horatius Flaccus. Probably [*Works*]. Britain or Continent: date indeterminable.

STC 13784 and non-STC. *Language(s)*: Latin. Appraised at 4d in 1577.

127.20 Opus Regale

Joannes Lodovicus Vivaldus. *Opus regale*. Continent: 1507–1512. *Language(s)*: Latin. Appraised at 4d in 1577.

127.21 A Frenche story

Unidentified. Place unknown: stationer unknown, date indeterminable. STC/non-STC status unknown. *Language(s)*: French. Appraised at 8d in 1577.

127.22 Eustratius in Ethica

Eustratius, *Archbishop of Nicaea*. [*Aristotle–Ethica: commentary and text*].

Continent: date indeterminable.
Language(s): Latin (probable) Greek (perhaps). Appraised at 20d in 1577.

127.23 Brickott in Phisica

Thomas Bricot. [*Aristotle–Phisica: commentary*]. Continent: date indeterminable.
Language(s): Latin. Appraised at 12d in 1577.

127.24 Burleus in Phisica

Walter Burley. [*Aristotle–Physica: commentary*]. Continent: date indeterminable.
Language(s): Latin. Appraised at 12d in 1577.

127.25 Thomas Aquinus

Thomas Aquinas, *Saint*. Unidentified. Continent: date indeterminable.
Language(s): Latin. Appraised at 4d in 1577.

127.26 Athanatii opera

Athanasius, *Saint*. [*Works*]. Continent: date indeterminable.
Language(s): Latin Greek (perhaps). Appraised at 5s in 1577.

127.27 Eusebii opera

Eusebius, *Pamphili, Bishop*. [*Works*]. Continent: date indeterminable.
Language(s): Latin. Appraised at 4s in 1577.

127.28 Basilii opera

Basil, *Saint, the Great*. [*Works*]. Continent: date indeterminable.
Language(s): Latin. Appraised at 5s in 1577.

127.29 Fasiculus Rerum

Fasciculus rerum expetendarum ac fugiendarum. Edited by Ortuinus Gratius.
Cologne: [Petrus Quentel?], 1535.
Language(s): Latin. Appraised at 3s 4d in 1577.

127.30 Omelia Nasei

Fridericus Nausea, *Bishop*. *Evangelicae veritatis homiliarum centuriae*.
Continent: date indeterminable.
Language(s): Latin. Appraised at 3s 4d in 1577.

127.31:1 Erasmus in novum test in mattheum

Desiderius Erasmus. [*New Testament: commentary*]. Continent: date indeterminable.

The phrase *in mattheum* is inserted at the end of the next line of the manuscript with *Plutharchus* (127.32), an author with whom it is hardly intended to be associated. There is no space in the manuscript between *Erasmus in novum test* and its appraisal, doubtless the reason the compiler wrote *in mattheum* on the next line. This item could represent an edition of some form of Erasmus's *Paraphrases in novum testamentum* rather than his commentary on the New Testament, with a separate edition of the paraphrase of Matthew. *Language(s)*: Latin. Appraised with one other at 2s 6d in 1577.

127.31:2   [See 127.31:1]
Desiderius Erasmus. [*Matthew: paraphrase*]. (*Bible–N.T.*). Continent: date indeterminable.

See the annotation to 127.31:1. *Language(s)*: Latin. Appraised with one other at 2s 6d in 1577.

127.32 Plutharcus
Plutarch. Unidentified. Continent: date indeterminable.

The valuation indicates a large volume, probably the *Works*, the *Vitae parallelae*, or the *Moralia*, none of which was published in England at the time of this inventory except for an English translation of the *Moralia*. *Language(s)*: Latin (probable) Greek (perhaps). Appraised at 2s in 1577.

127.33 Epiphanius
Epiphanius, *Bishop of Constantia*. Perhaps *Contra octoginta haereses*. Continent: date indeterminable.

Language(s): Latin. Appraised at 2s in 1577.

127.34 Sermones Taulleri
Johann Tauler. [*Sermones*]. Continent: date indeterminable.

Conceivably his *Works*, which long title begins: *Homiliae, seu Sermones. Language(s)*: Latin. Appraised at 12d in 1577.

127.35 Hyllarius
Hilary, *Saint, Bishop of Poitiers*. Unidentified. Continent: date indeterminable.

Either *Works* or *Lucubrationes*. *Language(s)*: Latin. Appraised at 20d in 1577.

127.36 Sermones Lanspergii
Johann Justus, *Landsberger* (Lanspergius). [*Sermones*]. Continent: date indeterminable.

Language(s): Latin. Appraised at 2s 6d in 1577.

127.37 Antidodum contra Hereses
Antidotum contra diversas omnium fere seculorum haereses. Edited by Joannes Sichardus. Basle: excud. Henricus Petrus, 1528.

Language(s): Latin. Appraised at 2s 6d in 1577.

127.38 Polianthea
Dominicus Nannus, *Mirabellius. Polyanthea.* Continent: date indeterminable.
Language(s): Greek Latin. Appraised at 6d in 1577.

127.39 Dionisius de coelestis hererc
Dionysius *Areopagita.* [*Works*]. Continent: date indeterminable.
Usually begins with *De caelestis heirarchia. Language(s)*: Latin (probable)
Greek (perhaps). Appraised at 2s in 1577.

127.40 Onus Ecclesie
Joannes Ebser. *Onus ecclesiae.* Continent: date indeterminable.
Language(s): Latin. Appraised at 8d in 1577.

127.41 The Fall of Prences
Giovanni Boccaccio. *Here begynnethe the boke calledde John bochas descrivinge the falle of princis.* Translated by John Lydgate. London: (different houses), 1494–1554.
STC 3175 *et seq. Language(s)*: English. Appraised at 16d in 1577.

127.42 Brunus de legacionibus
Conrad Brunus. *Opera tria: De legationibus libri quinque. De caeremoniis libri sex. De imaginibus liber unus.* Mainz: apud S. Victorem, ex off. (excud.) Francisci Behem, 1548.
Language(s): Latin. Appraised at 2s in 1577.

127.43 Herbarium Turneri
William Turner. *A new herball, wherin are conteyned the names of herbes.* Britain or Continent: 1551–1568.
STC 24365 *et seq. Language(s)*: English. Appraised at 4s in 1577.

127.44 Juvenallus
Decimus Junius Juvenalis. Probably [*Works*]. Continent: date indeterminable.
Language(s): Latin. Appraised at 4d in 1577.

127.45 Boetius de consolacione cum comment
Anicius M.T.S. Boethius. *De consolatione philosophiae.* Continent (probable): date indeterminable.
Probably not an STC book, but see STC 3199. The 1478 edition published in England carries an English translation along with the Latin. *Language(s)*: Latin English (perhaps). Appraised at 4d in 1577.

127.46 Martialis
Marcus Valerius Martialis. *Epigrammata.* Continent: date indeterminable.
Language(s): Latin. Appraised at 8d in 1577.

127.47 Policraticus

John, *of Salisbury, Bishop of Chartres. Policraticus de nugis curialium.* Continent: c.1480–1513.
Language(s): Latin. Appraised at 6d in 1577.

127.48 Tolletus in Phisica

Franciscus Toletus, *Cardinal.* [*Aristotle–Physica: commentary*]. Continent: 1574–1577.
Language(s): Latin. Appraised at 2s 6d in 1577.

127.49 Questiones Tusculani

Marcus Tullius Cicero. *Quaestiones Tusculanae.* Britain or Continent: date indeterminable.
STC 5314.5 *et seq.* and non-STC. *Language(s)*: Latin. Appraised at 2d in 1577.

127.50 Cardanus de sapientia

Girolamo Cardano. *De sapientia* [and other works]. Nuremberg: apud J. Petreium, 1544.
Language(s): Latin. Appraised at 10d in 1577.

127.51 Cardanus de somniis

Girolamo Cardano. *Somniorum Synesiorum, omnis generis insomnia explicantes* [and other works]. Basle: (different houses), 1562–1575.
Language(s): Latin. Appraised at 18d in 1577.

127.52 Politica Aristotelis

Aristotle. *Politica.* Continent: date indeterminable.
Language(s): Latin (probable) Greek (perhaps). Appraised at 12d in 1577.

127.53 Oration Amasei

Romulus Amasaeus. *Orationes.* Bologna: impressit Joannes Rubrius, 1564.
Adams A911. *Language(s)*: Latin. Appraised at 8d in 1577.

127.54 Cleonardi Gramatica

Nicolaus Clenardus. [*Institutiones linguae graecae*]. Continent: date indeterminable.
Language(s): Greek Latin. Appraised at 2s 6d in 1577.

127.55 Omeri opera

Homer. [*Works*]. Continent: date indeterminable.
Language(s): Greek (probable) Latin (probable). Appraised at 3s in 1577.

127.56 Partitiones Ciceronis

Marcus Tullius Cicero. *De partitione oratoria.* Continent: date indeterminable.
Language(s): Latin. Appraised at 12d in 1577.

127.57 Cicero de oratore
Marcus Tullius Cicero. *De oratore.* Britain or Continent: date indeterminable.
STC 5290 and non-STC. *Language(s)*: Latin. Appraised at 20d in 1577.

127.58 Herdesius de oratore
Perhaps Joannes Herbetius. *De oratore libri quinque.* Paris: apud Joannem Ruellium, 1574.
Less possibly, Gabriel Harvey's *Rhetor, vel duorum dierum oratio* (STC 12904). Harvey's name was commonly latinized as Hervesius or Harvesius. *Language(s)*: Latin. Appraised at 14d in 1577.

127.59 Diogenes latius
Diogenes Laertius. [*De vita et moribus philosophorum*]. Continent: date indeterminable.
Language(s): Latin. Appraised at 6d in 1577.

127.60 Historia Pandulphi
Pandolpho Collenucio. *Historiae Neapolitanae libri vi.* Translated by J. N. Stupanus. Basle: apud Petrum Pernam, 1572.
Language(s): Latin. Appraised at 10d in 1577.

127.61 Ycones Imperatorum
Jacobus de Strada. *Epitome thesauri antiquitatum, hoc est, imperatorum romanorum icones.* Continent: 1553–1557.
Language(s): Latin. Appraised at 16d in 1577.

127.62 Origenes in Johannem
Origen. *In evangelium Joannis explanationum, tomi XXXII.* Venice: Andream et Jacobum Spinellos, 1551.
Language(s): Latin. Appraised at 18d in 1577.

127.63 Doceus de eterna generacione
Joannes Docaeus. *De aeterna generatione Filii Dei.* Paris: apud Carolum Perier, 1554.
Language(s): Latin. Appraised at 16d in 1577.

127.64 Novum Testamentum grec
[*Bible–N.T.*]. Continent: date indeterminable.
Language(s): Greek. Appraised at 2s in 1577.

127.65 Rofensis contra Lutherum
John Fisher, *Saint and Cardinal.* Probably *Assertionis Lutheranae confutatio.* Continent: 1523–1564.
Perhaps, however, *Sacri sacerdotii defensio contra Lutheram* (five editions between 1525 and 1562; Shaaber F95–99), but the *Confutatio* was much more

widely published with at least fifteen Latin editions and several German editions; see Shaaber F42–64. Some editions contain Luther's *Assertio*. A book in the 1571 probate inventory of Reynolds's brother, Jerome, is entered as James's book here; see PLRE 96.94; see also 127.201. *Language(s)*: Latin. Appraised at 6d in 1577.

127.66 Pontanii opera

Joannes Jovianus Pontanus. Probably [*Works*]. Continent: date indeterminable.

Of the various Pontanuses, he seems to have been the only one whose works were collected in an *opera*, of which there were many editions. The manuscript entry could, however, represent a group, bound together or loose, of the works of another Pontanus. See 127.123. *Language(s)*: Latin. Appraised at 8d in 1577.

127.67 Ecclesiastes Erasmi

Desiderius Erasmus. *Ecclesiastes, sive de ratione concionandi*. Continent: 1535–1554.
Language(s): Latin. Appraised at 6d in 1577.

127.68 Rivius de stulticia

Joannes Rivius. *De stultitia mortalium, in procrastinanda correctione vitae, liber*. Basle: [Joannes Oporinus], 1547.
Language(s): Latin. Appraised at 8d in 1577.

127.69 Evangelistarium Marilli

Marko Marulic. *Evangelistarium*. Continent: date indeterminable.
Language(s): Latin. Appraised at 6d in 1577.

127.70 Isiodorus

Isidore, *Saint, Bishop of Seville*. Unidentified. Continent (probable): date indeterminable.
Probably not an STC book, but see STC 14270. *Language(s)*: Latin (probable). Appraised at 6d in 1577.

127.71 Confessio Caroli Quinti

[*Confessio fidei exhibita Augustae*]. (*Augsburg Confession*). Continent: date indeterminable.
First published in 1530. *Language(s)*: Latin. Appraised at 8d in 1577.

127.72 Contarenus

Probably Gasparo Contarini, *Cardinal*. Unidentified. Continent: date indeterminable.
There were several other Contarini who might be represented here, but Gasparo was the more widely published. *Language(s)*: Latin. Appraised at 8d in 1577.

127.73 Garretius
Joannes Garetius. Unidentified. Continent: date indeterminable.
Language(s): Latin. Appraised at 8d in 1577.

127.74 Homolia Hamonis
Haymo, *Bishop of Halberstadt*. [*Homiliae*]. Continent: date indeterminable.
Language(s): Latin. Appraised at 6d in 1577.

127.75 Laurentius Humferedus
Laurence Humphrey. Unidentified. Place unknown: stationer unknown, date indeterminable.
STC/non-STC status unknown. Only one of his numerous works appeared in English (STC 13964) by the date of this inventory. *Language(s)*: Latin (probable). Appraised at 12d in 1577.

127.76 Vives de institucione femine
Joannes Ludovicus Vives. *De institutione foeminae christianae*. Continent: date indeterminable.
Editions after 1538 seem always to appear with other works. *Language(s)*: Latin. Appraised at 8d in 1577.

127.77 Vives de dissiplinis
Joannes Ludovicus Vives. *De disciplinis libri xx*. Continent: date indeterminable.
An appraisal of 17*d* is struck out. *Language(s)*: Latin. Appraised at 16d in 1577.

127.78 Osorius de gloria
Jeronimo Osorio da Fonseca, *Bishop*. *De gloria*. Florence: apud Laurentium Torrentinum, 1552.
His frequently published selected works with *De gloria* leading is also possible. *Language(s)*: Latin. Appraised at 16d in 1577.

127.79 Wierius de prestigiis
Johann Wier. *De praestigiis daemonum*. Continent: 1563–1577.
Language(s): Latin. Appraised at 16d in 1577.

127.80 Alexandro ab Alexandro
Alexander ab Alexandro. *Geniales dies*. Continent: date indeterminable.
Language(s): Latin. Appraised at 20d in 1577.

127.81 Arithmetica Tonstalli
Cuthbert Tunstall, *Bishop*. *De arte supputandi libri quattuor*. Britain or Continent: 1522–1551.
STC 24319 and non-STC. Shaaber T155–159. *Language(s)*: Latin. Appraised at 6d in 1577.

127.82 Dialectica Hunei
Augustinus Hunnaeus. [*Aristotle–Organon: commentary*]. Continent: 1550–1575.
Language(s): Latin. Appraised at 16d in 1577.

127.83 Clitoveus
Jodocus Clichtoveus. Unidentified. Continent: date indeterminable.
His theological works are not as likely here as something on logic, given the philosophical and logical works in this section. *Language(s)*: Latin. Appraised at 2d in 1577.

127.84 Tunstallus in Ethica
Cuthbert Tunstall, *Bishop. Compendium et synopsis in decem libros ethicorum Aristotelis*. Paris: ex officina Michaëlis Vascosani, 1554.
Language(s): Latin. Appraised at 8d in 1577.

127.85 Ligica [Logica] Javelli
Chrysostomus Javellus. [*Aristotle–Selected works–Logica: commentary*]. Continent: date indeterminable.
The epitome is also possible. *Language(s)*: Latin. Appraised at 10d in 1577.

127.86 Epitomi Wildenburgii
Hieronymus Wildenbergius. [*Aristotle–Selected works–Philosophia naturalis–Epitome*]. Continent: 1544–1554.
Language(s): Latin. Appraised at 8d in 1577.

127.87 Epitom Matisii
Gerardus Matthisius (Geldrensis). Perhaps *Epitoma Aristoteleae logicae graecolatina*. Cologne: [see annotation], 1569.
The stationer is not provided by the bibliographical sources that list this now rare work. Matthisius's commentary on the *Philosophia naturalis* is certainly possible, but it is found as 127.97. Both logic and natural philosophy are found in this section. *Language(s)*: Latin. Appraised at 6d in 1577.

127.88 Philosophia Foccii
Sebastiano Fox Morzillo. *De naturae philosophia, seu de Platonis et Aristotelis consensione*. Continent: 1551–1560.
Language(s): Latin. Appraised at 10d in 1577.

127.89 Ciceronianus Fregii
Joannes Thomas Freigius. *Ciceronianus*. Basle: per ex officina Sebastianum Henricpetri, 1575.
Freig's edition of Ramus's *Ciceronianus* must be considered also. *Language(s)*: Latin. Appraised at 10d in 1577.

127.90 Agrippa de occluta [occulta] philosophia
Henricus Cornelius Agrippa. *De occulta philosophia*. Continent: 1531–1567.
Language(s): Latin. Appraised at 18d in 1577.

127.91 Athaneus
Athenaeus. *Deipnosophistae*. Continent: date indeterminable.
Language(s): Latin (probable) Greek (perhaps). Appraised at 16d in 1577.

127.92 Vives de anima
Joannes Ludovicus Vives. *Exercitationes animi in Deum*. Continent: date
indeterminable.
Language(s): Latin. Appraised at 6d in 1577.

127.93 Officia Ciceronis
Marcus Tullius Cicero. *De officiis*. Continent: date indeterminable.
An appraisal of 2*d* is struck out. *Language(s)*: Latin. Appraised at 12d in
1577.

127.94 Velcurio
Joannes Velcurio. [*Aristotle–Physica: commentary*]. Continent: 1537–1575.
His commentaries on Livy and Erasmus are less likely in this context. *Language(s)*: Latin. Appraised at 10d in 1577.

127.95 Philosophia Titilmanni
Franz Titelmann. [*Aristotle–Selected works–Philosophia naturalis: commentary*].
Continent: 1530–1574.
Language(s): Latin. Appraised at 12d in 1577.

127.96 Valerii opera
Unidentified. Place unknown: stationer unknown, date indeterminable.
STC/non-STC status unknown. Perhaps Valerius Maximus's *Facta et dicta
memorabilia*, perhaps the works of Cornelius Valerius bound together. See
127.159 and 127.161. *Language(s)*: Latin (probable). Appraised at 16d in 1577.

127.97 Mathisii Phisica
Gerardus Matthisius (Geldrensis). [*Aristotle–Selected works–Philosophia naturalis–Epitome: commentary*]. Cologne: 1556–1570.
The stationers are not provided by the bibliographical sources that list this
work. See 127.87. *Language(s)*: Latin. Appraised at 8d in 1577.

127.98 Franciscus Vatables
Jacobus Faber, *Stapulensis*. [*Aristotle–Selected works–Philosophia naturalis:
paraphrase*]. Revised and edited by Franciscus Vatablus. Continent: 1528–
1540.
Language(s): Latin. Appraised at 4d in 1577.

127.99 Donatus in Politica
Donatus Acciaiolus. [*Aristotle–Politica: commentary*]. Venice: (different houses), 1504–1566.

More likely the 1566 edition than the 1504. *Language(s)*: Latin. Appraised at 16d in 1577.

127.100 Epitomi Leibleri
Georg Liebler. [*Aristotle–Selected works–Philosophia naturalis–Epitome*]. Continent: 1561–1573.

Language(s): Latin. Appraised at 6d in 1577.

127.101 Arithmetica Scheubelii
Joannes Scheubelius. *Compendium arithmeticae artis*. Basle: Jacobus Parcus and Joannes Oporinus, 1549–1560.

Language(s): Latin. Appraised at 12d in 1577.

127.102 Copia Verborum
Probably Desiderius Erasmus. *De duplici copia verborum ac rerum*. Britain or Continent: date indeterminable.

STC 10471.4 *et seq.* and non-STC. *Language(s)*: Latin. Appraised at 6d in 1577.

127.103 Rethorica Sturmii
Joannes Sturmius. Unidentified. Continent: date indeterminable.

At least four of his works could be described as *rhetorica*. *Language(s)*: Latin. Appraised at 8d in 1577.

127.104:A Similia Licostenis
Conrad Lycosthenes (Conrad Wolffhart). *Similium loci communes*. Basle: per E. Episcopium et Nicolai fr. haeredes, 1575 (composite publication).

Language(s): Latin. Appraised [a composite volume] at 10d in 1577.

127.104:B [See 127.104:A]
Theodor Zwinger. *Similitudinem methodo*. [Composite publication].

Language(s): Latin. Appraised [a composite volume] at 10d in 1577.

127.105 Theonis Sophiste
Aelius Theon (Sophista). *Progymnasmata*. Continent: 1520–1541.

Language(s): Greek Latin (perhaps). Appraised at 8d in 1577.

127.106 Omphalius
Jacobus Omphalius. Perhaps *De elocutionis imitatione ac apparatu*. Continent: date indeterminable.

The conjecture is based on the context and the popularity of this work. *Language(s)*: Latin. Appraised at 3d in 1577.

127.107 Sambucus de imitacione
Joannes Sambucus. *Tres dialogi de imitatione Ciceroniana*. Continent: 1561–1568.
Each edition contains at least one other work. *Language(s)*: Latin. Appraised at 8d in 1577.

127.108 Rethorica Cruseii
Probably Philipp Melanchthon. [*Rhetorica*]. Edited by Martin Crusius. Continent: date indeterminable.
See BCI 2:540. *Language(s)*: Latin. Appraised at 12d in 1577.

127.109 Selius Secundus
Caelius Secundus Curio. Unidentified. Continent: date indeterminable.
Language(s): Latin. Appraised at 10d in 1577.

127.110 Sturmii Particiones
Joannes Sturmius. *In partitiones oratorias Ciceronis dialogi*. Continent: 1539–1565.
Context makes this much more likely than his *Partitionum dialecticarum libri quatuor*. *Language(s)*: Latin. Appraised at 10d in 1577.

127.111 Cicero de oratore
Marcus Tullius Cicero. *De oratore*. Britain or Continent: date indeterminable.
STC 5290 and non-STC. *Language(s)*: Latin. Appraised at 8d in 1577.

127.112 Epigrammata Martialis
Marcus Valerius Martialis. *Epigrammata*. Continent: date indeterminable.
Language(s): Latin. Appraised at 8d in 1577.

127.113 Dares Frigius
Dares, *the Phrygian*. *De excidio Troiae historia*. Continent: date indeterminable.
The work is often associated with Dictys, *Cretensis*. *Language(s)*: Latin. Appraised at 10d in 1577.

127.114 Prudentius
Aurelius Prudentius Clemens. Probably [*Works*]. Continent: date indeterminable.
See also 127.180. *Language(s)*: Latin. Appraised at 6d in 1577.

127.115 Stroceus
Unidentified. Continent (probable): date indeterminable.
Probably not an STC book. Perhaps one of the Strozzi, or, less probably, Ibrahim Strotschius, or even Strebaeus. *Language(s)*: Latin (probable). Appraised at 8d in 1577.

127.116 Hatman
 Probably François Hotman. Unidentified. Place unknown: stationer unknown, date indeterminable.
 STC/non-STC status unknown. If Hotman, more likely in this context, his commentary on Cicero's orations than his historical or legal works. *Language(s)*: Latin (probable). Appraised at 6d in 1577.

127.117 Picta Poesis
 Unidentified. Continent: date indeterminable.
 For possibilities, see Adams P1162–1163 (the latter listed as R414 also) and an earlier version of P1162 in Brunet 4:634. *Language(s)*: Latin. Appraised at 4d in 1577.

127.118 Isiodus
 Hesiod. Probably [*Works*]. Continent: date indeterminable.
 Language(s): Greek (perhaps) Latin (perhaps). Appraised at 6d in 1577.

127.119 Aristophanis commedi
 Aristophanes. [*Works*]. Continent: date indeterminable.
 Language(s): Latin (probable) Greek (perhaps). Appraised at 6d in 1577.

127.120 Spinili opera
 Probably Alessandro Spinello. Unidentified. Continent: date indeterminable.
 If Spinello, perhaps the compiler's use of *opera* is descriptive, there being nothing published of his, apparently, except *Cleopatra. Tragedia* (1550). *Language(s)*: Latin. Appraised at 8d in 1577.

127.121 Sinthei Epigrammata
 Giovanni Battista Giraldi Cinthio. Unidentified. Continent: date indeterminable.
 His epigrams seem not to have been published separately by the date of this inventory. They do, however, appear in a 1537 collection as "Epigrammaton libri duo," and in the *Poematia* (1540 and 1544). Either the compiler was reading from a running head in one of those collections, or the epigrams had become detached from one of those volumes. *Language(s)*: Latin. Appraised at 6d in 1577.

127.122 Tragedie Senece
 Lucius Annaeus Seneca. *Tragoediae*. Continent: date indeterminable.
 Language(s): Latin. Appraised at 8d in 1577.

127.123 Pontanii opera
 Joannes Jovianus Pontanus. Probably [*Works*]. Continent: date indeterminable.

See the annotations to 127.66. *Language(s)*: Latin. Appraised at 4d in 1577.

127.124   Oratius
Quintus Horatius Flaccus. Probably [*Works*]. Britain or Continent: date indeterminable.
STC 13784 and non-STC. *Language(s)*: Latin. Appraised at 8d in 1577.

127.125   Vergilius
Publius Virgilius Maro. Probably [*Works*]. Britain or Continent: date indeterminable.
STC 24787 *et seq.* and non-STC. *Language(s)*: Latin. Appraised at 10d in 1577.

127.126   Catullus
Probably Caius Valerius Catullus, Albius Tibullus, and Sextus Propertius. Probably [*Works*]. Continent: date indeterminable.
Conceivably, of course, Catullus separated, unlikely the apparently sole single edition of 1473 (see Goff C324). Another copy at 127.172. *Language(s)*: Latin. Appraised at 8d in 1577.

127.127   Fragmenta Poetarum
Fragmenta poetarum veterum latinorum. Compiled by Robert Estienne, *the Elder* and edited by Henri Estienne, *the Younger*. Geneva (probable): Henricus Stephanus [II], H. Fuggeri typog., 1564.
BL gives [Paris?] as the supplied place of publication, but Geneva is the consensus of the rest of the bibliographical sources. *Language(s)*: Latin. Appraised at 10d in 1577.

127.128   Epiteta Textoris
Joannes Ravisius (Textor). *Epitheta*. Continent: date indeterminable.
See also 127.203. *Language(s)*: Latin. Appraised at 16d in 1577.

127.129   Historia Giraldi
Perhaps Lilius Gregorius Giraldus. *De Deis gentium varia et multiplex historia*. Continent: 1548–1565.
See 127.132 for another of Giraldus's works. *L'histoire de France*, by Bernard de Gerard, *Seigneur du Haillan*, is a remote possibility here. *Language(s)*: Latin. Appraised at 8d in 1577.

127.130   Lucretius
Titus Lucretius Carus. *De rerum natura*. Continent: date indeterminable.
Language(s): Latin. Appraised at 10d in 1577.

127.131 Ovidii Epistol
Publius Ovidius Naso. *Heroides.* Continent: date indeterminable.
Language(s): Latin. Appraised at 4d in 1577.

127.132 Historia Poetarum
Lilius Gregorius Giraldus. *Historiae poetarum tam graecorum quam latinorum.*
Basle: [Michael Isingrinius], 1545.
See 127.129. *Language(s)*: Latin. Appraised at 6d in 1577.

127.133 Vergilius
Publius Virgilius Maro. Probably [*Works*]. Britain or Continent: date indeterminable.
STC 24787 *et seq.* and non-STC. *Language(s)*: Latin. Appraised at 4d in 1577.

127.134 Gwalterus de quantitate etc.
Rudolph Walther. *De syllabarum et carminum libri duo.* Continent: date indeterminable.
Language(s): Greek Latin. Appraised at 4d in 1577.

127.135 Grammatica regia
William Lily. *Institutio compendiaria totius grammaticae.* Britain or Continent:
1540–1577.
STC 15610.5 *et seq. Language(s)*: Latin English (perhaps). Appraised at 10d
in 1577.

127.136 Opera Ringibargii
Joachimus Fortius Ringelbergius. [*Works*]. Continent: 1531–1556.
Language(s): Latin. Appraised at 10d in 1577.

127.137 Sermones Maximi Tirii
Maximus, *of Tyre. Sermones.* Continent: date indeterminable.
Language(s): Latin (probable) Greek (perhaps). Appraised at 12d in 1577.

127.138 Epstole [Epistole] Manusii
Paolo Manuzio. [*Epistolae*]. Britain or Continent: date indeterminable.
STC 17286 *et seq.* and non-STC. *Language(s)*: Latin. Appraised at 16d in
1577.

127.139 Facetie Bebellii
Heinrich Bebel. *Facetiae.* Continent: date indeterminable.
Language(s): Latin. Appraised at 8d in 1577.

127.140 Luciani Dialogi
Lucian, *of Samosata.* Probably [*Works*]. Continent: date indeterminable.

Probably not an STC book. If *Selected dialogues*, London would be a possible place of publication. *Language(s)*: Latin (probable) Greek (perhaps). Appraised at 8d in 1577.

127.141 Cato de re rustica
Marcus Portius Cato. *De re rustica*. Continent: date indeterminable.
Often published with Columella and Varro, but see the next entry. Perhaps these are separated items from a single volume. *Language(s)*: Latin. Appraised at 12d in 1577.

127.142 Columella de re rustica
Lucius Junius Moderatus Columella. *De re rustica*. Continent: date indeterminable.
See the annotations to the preceding entry. *Language(s)*: Latin. Appraised at 16d in 1577.

127.143 Predium Rusticum
Charles Estienne. *Praedium rusticum*. Paris: apud Carolum Stephanum, 1554.
Language(s): Latin. Appraised at 12d in 1577.

127.144 Harasbackius de re rustica
Conrad Heresbach. *Rei rusticae libri iv*. Continent: 1570–1573.
Language(s): Latin. Appraised at 12d in 1577.

127.145 Theophrastus
Theophrastus. Unidentified. Continent: date indeterminable.
Language(s): Latin. Appraised at 10d in 1577.

127.146 De vita Buseri
Sir John Cheke and Nicholas Carr. *De obitu doctissimi et sanctissimi theologi doctoris M. Buceri, epistolae duae*. London: in officina R. Wolfii, 1551.
STC 5108. The first letter is by Cheke to Pietro Martire Vermigli (Peter Martyr); the second is by Carr to Cheke. *Language(s)*: Latin. Appraised at 6d in 1577.

127.147 Commentaria Cesaris
Caius Julius Caesar. *Commentarii*. Continent: date indeterminable.
Language(s): Latin. Appraised at 18d in 1577.

127.148 Amianus Masselinus
Marcellinus Ammianus. [*Res gestae*]. Continent: date indeterminable.
Language(s): Latin. Appraised at 12d in 1577.

127.149 Lucius Florus
Lucius Annaeus Florus. [*Epitomae de Tito Livio bellorum omnium annorum*].

Continent: date indeterminable.
   See 127.9 and 127.186. *Language(s)*: Latin. Appraised at 10d in 1577.

127.150   Ipographia Antique Romane
Unidentified. Continent (probable): date indeterminable.
   Probably not an STC book. Perhaps the manuscript entry "Ipographia" is
an attempt at "Epigraphia," or inscriptions. But a search of the bibliographical
sources has not turned up a work on ancient Romans with an approximate
title. *Language(s)*: Latin (probable). Appraised at 6d in 1577.

127.151   Exempla Sabellisi
Marcus Antonius Sabellicus (Marcus Antonius Coccius, *Sabellicus*). *Exemplo-
rum libri decem*. Continent: date indeterminable.
   Language(s): Latin. Appraised at 6d in 1577.

127.152   Olaus Magnus
Olaus Magnus. Probably *Historia de gentibus septentrionalibus*. Continent:
date indeterminable.
   Conceivably, the epitome. *Language(s)*: Latin. Appraised at 8d in 1577.

127.153   Cronicon Melangtonis
Philipp Melanchthon. [*Chronica*]. Continent: date indeterminable.
   Language(s): Latin. Appraised at 16d in 1577.

127.154   Zenophon
Xenophon. Unidentified. Continent (probable): date indeterminable.
   Probably not an STC book. The context does not suggest an English version, excluding, therefore, any of Xenophon's works published in England at
the date of this inventory. *Language(s)*: Latin (probable) Greek (perhaps). Appraised at 8d in 1577.

127.155   Abdias Babilonicus
Abdias, *Bishop of Babylon*. Unidentified. Continent: date indeterminable.
   Language(s): Latin. Appraised at 6d in 1577.

127.156   Aule Tursice
Antoine Geuffroy. *Aulae turcicae*. Basle: per Sebastianum Henricpetri,
1573–1577.
   This is less likely the collection of several works on Turkish history by
Geuffroy, Petrus Bizzarus, and Nicolaus Hoeniger than the first part of that
collection by Geuffroy, which gives its title, *Aulae turcicae*, to the whole. The
Bizzarus contribution, part two of the collection, is found at 127.163, and
since it is not known to have been issued solo, must appear in this inventory
separated, like the Geuffroy work, from the whole. The lower appraisal of the
Aulae turcicae listed here, compared with the separated Bizzarus at 127.163,

gives further evidence that it is the first part only, not the whole collection. *Language(s)*: Latin. Appraised at 8d in 1577.

127.157 Descriptio Affrice

Joannes Leo Africanus. *De totius Africae descriptione libri IX.* Continent: 1556–1559.

Language(s): Latin. Appraised at 8d in 1577.

127.158 Newbrigenses

William, *of Newburgh. Rerum Anglicarum libri quinque.* Antwerp: ex officina Gulielmi Silvii, 1567.

Language(s): Latin. Appraised at 10d in 1577.

127.159 Valerius Maximus

Valerius Maximus. *Facta et dicta memorabilia.* Continent: date indeterminable.

Another copy at 127.161. *Language(s)*: Latin. Appraised at 10d in 1577.

127.160 Olimpius

Unidentified. Continent (probable): date indeterminable.

Probably not an STC book. The *Bucolica* of Marcus Aurelius Olympius Nemesianus seems not to have been published before 1590. Remote possibilities include: Pindar's Olympian odes, something of Olympia Fulvia Morata, and a miswriting of Olympiodorus. *Language(s)*: Latin (probable). Appraised at 10d in 1577.

127.161 Valerius Maximus

Valerius Maximus. *Facta et dicta memorabilia.* Continent: date indeterminable.

Another copy at 127.159. *Language(s)*: Latin. Appraised at 10d in 1577.

127.162 Epithome Vadiani

Joachim Vadianus. [*Epitome trium terrae partium*]. Continent: 1534–1548.

Language(s): Latin. Appraised at 6d in 1577.

127.163 Ciprinum Bellum

Petrus Bizzarus. *Cyprium bellum.* Basle: per Sebastianum Henricpetri, 1573–1577.

See the annotations to 127.156. *Language(s)*: Latin. Appraised at 12d in 1577.

127.164 Bodinus

Jean Bodin, *Bishop. Methodus ad facilem historiarum cognitionem.* Continent: date indeterminable.

Language(s): Latin. Appraised at 12d in 1577.

127.165   Chitreus de lectione historiarum
David Chytraeus. *De lectione historiarum*. Continent: 1563–1565.
Language(s): Latin. Appraised at 6d in 1577.

127.166   Quintus Cursius
Quintus Curtius Rufus. *De rebus gestis Alexandri Magni*. Continent (probable): date indeterminable.
Probably not an STC book, but see STC 6141.5 *et seq.* Since there are three copies in Reynolds's collection (see 127.187 and 127.193), one might very well be an English version. *Language(s)*: Latin (probable) English (perhaps). Appraised at 6d in 1577.

127.167   Suetonius
Caius Suetonius Tranquillus. *De vita Caesarum*. Continent: date indeterminable.
Language(s): Latin. Appraised at 2d in 1577.

127.168   Salustius
Caius Sallustius Crispus. Unidentified. Place unknown: stationer unknown, date indeterminable.
STC/non-STC status unknown. If the complete works, it could be one of the Latin editions printed in London from 1569, and it could also be the English translation of *De bello Jugurthino*. See 127.11 and 127.185. *Language(s)*: Latin. Appraised at 2d in 1577.

127.169   Apothegmata Licostenis
Conrad Lycosthenes (Conrad Wolffhart). *Apophthegmata*. Continent: date indeterminable.
Language(s): Latin. Appraised at 16d in 1577.

127.170   Patricius in 2bus
Probably Francesco Patrizi, *Bishop*. Unidentified. Continent: date indeterminable.
Much more likely multiple volumes, whether two copies or two different works of this Patrizi, who is also more likely than the Patrizi known as the *Philosophical writer*. See also 127.195. *Language(s)*: Latin. Appraised at 2s in 1577.

127.171   Epigrammata Johannis Secundi
Joannes Nicolaus Secundus. Perhaps [*Works*]. Continent: 1541–1561.
Secundus's epigrams seem not to have been published alone by the date of this inventory. Conceivably, a separated section of Secundus's *Works* is intended here, or, alternatively, the compiler was reading from a running head instead of the title page of the collection. Secundus's epigrams were fre-

quently published with the epigrams of Michael Marullus Tarchaniota, but according to the standard bibliographical sources, the earliest combined printing of their verses postdates this inventory. *Language(s)*: Latin. Appraised at 4d in 1577.

127.172 Catullus
Probably Caius Valerius Catullus, Albius Tibullus, and Sextus Propertius. Probably [*Works*]. Continent: date indeterminable.
See the annotations to 127.126. *Language(s)*: Latin. Appraised at 4d in 1577.

127.173 Ovidius de fastis
Publius Ovidius Naso. *Fasti*. Britain or Continent: date indeterminable. STC 18947.5 and non-STC. *Language(s)*: Latin. Appraised at 12d in 1577.

127.174 Flores Epigrammatum in 2bus
Perhaps *Anthologia graeca*. Continent: date indeterminable.
It could, however, be the *Epigrammata graeca* or some other collection. See 127.181. *Language(s)*: Greek Latin. Appraised at 16d in 1577.

127.175 Dialigi Textoris
Joannes Ravisius (Textor). *Dialogi. Epigrammata*. Continent: date indeterminable.
Language(s): Latin. Appraised at 6d in 1577.

127.176 Jheronimi Vita
Perhaps Jerome, *Saint. Vitae patrum*. Continent: date indeterminable.
But the manuscript entry reads "a life of Jerome," and one of several may be intended here. *Language(s)*: Latin. Appraised at 8d in 1577.

127.177 Ovidii Methamorphoses
Publius Ovidius Naso. *Metamorphoses*. Continent: date indeterminable.
Language(s): Latin. Appraised at 3d in 1577.

127.178 Ausonius
Decimus Magnus Ausonius. Perhaps [*Works*]. Continent: date indeterminable.
Language(s): Latin Greek (perhaps). Appraised at 8d in 1577.

127.179 Palengenius
Marcellus Palingenius (Pietro Angelo Manzolli [Stellatus]). *Zodiacus vitae*. Britain or Continent: date indeterminable.
STC/non-STC status unknown. *Language(s)*: Latin (probable) English (perhaps). Appraised at 6d in 1577.

127.180 Prudentius
Aurelius Prudentius Clemens. Probably [*Works*]. Continent: date indeterminable.
See 127.114. *Language(s)*: Latin. Appraised at 6d in 1577.

127.181 Epigrammata Stephani
Perhaps *Epigrammata graeca*. Edited by Henricus Stephanus, *the Elder*. Geneva: Henricus Stephanus, *the Elder*, date indeterminable.
This could just as well be the *Anthologia graeca*, which Stephanus also published. See Adams E246 for the Stephanus *Epigrammata* and A1187 for the Stephanus *Anthologia*. See 127.174. *Language(s)*: Greek Latin. Appraised at 8d in 1577.

127.182 Claudianus
Claudius Claudianus. Probably [*Works*]. Continent: date indeterminable. *Language(s)*: Latin. Appraised at 8d in 1577.

127.183:1–7 vii smale poetes in parchment
Unidentified. Places unknown: stationers unknown, dates indeterminable.
STC/non-STC status unknown. Bound in vellum. *Language(s)*: Unknown. Appraised as a group at 2s 6d in 1577.

127.184 Apianus Alexadrinus
Appian, *of Alexandria*. [*Historia Romana*]. Continent: date indeterminable. *Language(s)*: Latin. Appraised at 12d in 1577.

127.185 Salustius
Caius Sallustius Crispus. Unidentified. Place unknown: stationer unknown, date indeterminable.
STC/non-STC status unknown. Perhaps [*Works*], or alternatively *De bello Jugurthino* or *De conjuratione Catilinae*. If *De bello Jugurthino*, an English translation is possible. See 127.11 and 127.168. *Language(s)*: Latin (probable). Appraised at 6d in 1577.

127.186 Lucius Florus
Lucius Annaeus Florus. [*Epitomae de Tito Livio bellorum omnium annorum*]. Continent: date indeterminable.
See 127.9 and 127.149. *Language(s)*: Latin. Appraised at 6d in 1577.

127.187 Quintus Cursus
Quintus Curtius Rufus. *De rebus gestis Alexandri Magni*. Continent (probable): date indeterminable.
Probably not an STC book, but see STC 6141.5 *et seq.* Other copies or editions at 127.166 and 127.193; see the annotations to 127.166. *Language(s)*: Latin (probable) English (perhaps). Appraised at 8d in 1577.

127.188   Diodorus Siculus
Diodorus, *Siculus. Bibliotheca historica*. Continent: date indeterminable.
There is no reason to believe that this entry represents the English selection printed in 1569. *Language(s)*: Latin. Appraised at 12d in 1577.

127.189   Justinus
Trogus Pompeius and Justinus, *the Historian*. [*Epitomae in Trogi Pompeii historias*]. Britain or Continent: date indeterminable.
STC 24287 *et seq.* and non-STC. *Language(s)*: Latin. Appraised at 8d in 1577.

127.190   Dionisius Halicarniseus
Dionysius, *of Halicarnassus. Antiquitates sive origines Romanae*. Continent: date indeterminable.
Language(s): Latin. Appraised at 12d in 1577.

127.191   Cornelius Tacitus
Publius Cornelius Tacitus. Unidentified. Continent: date indeterminable.
The *Annales* and the *Historiae* are the most likely possibilities. *Language(s)*: Latin. Appraised at 10d in 1577.

127.192   Julius Solinus
Caius Julius Solinus. *Polyhistor*. Continent: date indeterminable.
Language(s): Latin. Appraised at 10d in 1577.

127.193   Quintus Cursius
Quintus Curtius Rufus. *De rebus gestis Alexandri Magni*. Continent (probable): date indeterminable.
Probably not an STC book, but see STC 6141.5 *et seq.* Other copies or editions at 127.166 and 127.187; see the annotations to 127.166. *Language(s)*: Latin (probable) English (perhaps). Appraised at 8d in 1577.

127.194   Epitom Plutharchi
Plutarch. [*Vitae parallelae–Epitome*]. Continent: date indeterminable.
Language(s): Latin (probable) Greek (perhaps). Appraised at 8d in 1577.

127.195   Compendium Patricii
Francesco Patrizi, *Bishop. Compendiosa rerum memorandarum descriptio*. Continent: date indeterminable.
See 127.170. *Language(s)*: Latin. Appraised at 8d in 1577.

127.196   Extremum Judicium
Joannes Fredericus Lumnius. [*De extremo Dei judicio*]. Continent: 1567–1569.
Adams L1715. *Language(s)*: Latin. Appraised at 4d in 1577.

127.197   Rethorica Ciceronis

Marcus Tullius Cicero. [*Selected works–Rhetorica*]. Continent: date indeterminable.

Conceivably the popular, and falsely ascribed, *Rhetorica ad Herennium*, with many Continental editions and one (STC 5323.5) by the date of this inventory. *Language(s)*: Latin. Appraised at 12d in 1577.

127.198   Colloquium Erasmi

Desiderius Erasmus. *Colloquia*. Britain or Continent: date indeterminable. STC 10450.6 *et seq.* and non-STC. Another copy at 127.202. *Language(s)*: Latin. Appraised at 6d in 1577.

127.199   Problemata Aristotelis

Aristotle (spurious). *Problemata*. Continent: date indeterminable. Another copy at 127.207. *Language(s)*: Latin. Appraised at 6d in 1577.

127.200   Apothegmata Erasmi

Desiderius Erasmus. *Apophthegmata*. Continent: 1531–1573. The date range is from VHe. *Language(s)*: Latin. Appraised at 8d in 1577.

127.201   Compendium Theologicum

Probably Desiderius Erasmus. *Methodus: Ratio verae theologiae*. Continent: date indeterminable.

The context argues for this being Erasmus's work. The title also appears in the 1571 probate inventory of Reynolds's brother, Jerome (PLRE 96.103). *Language(s)*: Latin. Appraised at 8d in 1577.

127.202   Colloquium Erasmi

Desiderius Erasmus. *Colloquia*. Britain or Continent: date indeterminable. Possibly 10450.6 *et seq.* and non-STC. Another copy at 127.198. *Language(s)*: Latin. Appraised at 6d in 1577.

127.203   Epiteta Textoris

Joannes Ravisius (Textor). *Epitheta*. Continent: date indeterminable. See also 127.128. *Language(s)*: Latin. Appraised at 6d in 1577.

127.204   Misaldus

Antoine Mizauld. Unidentified. Continent: date indeterminable. *Language(s)*: Latin. Appraised at 8d in 1577.

127.205   Petrus Crinicus

Petrus Crinitus. Probably *De honesta disciplina* [and other works]. Continent: date indeterminable.

Repeatedly published from 1504. *Language(s)*: Latin. Appraised at 12d in 1577.

127.206   Orationes Mureti
Marcus Antonius Muretus. [*Selected works–Orations*]. Continent: date indeterminable.
Language(s): Latin. Appraised at 6d in 1577.

127.207   Problemata Aristotelis
Aristotle (spurious). *Problemata*. Continent: date indeterminable.
Another copy at 127.199. *Language(s)*: Latin. Appraised at 4d in 1577.

127.208   Sententia Aristotelis
Aristotle. [*Selections*]. Continent: date indeterminable.
Language(s): Latin. Appraised at 4d in 1577.

127.209   Testamentum Benedicti
[*Bible–N.T.*]. Edited by Joannes Benedictus, *Biblical commentator*. Continent: date indeterminable.
Language(s): Latin. Appraised at 10d in 1577.

127.210   Exempla Virtutum
Nicolaus Hanapus. *Exempla sacrae scripturae*. (*The Bible*). Continent (probable): date indeterminable.
Probably not an STC book, but see STC 2993. Hanapus's authorship unlikely. *Language(s)*: Latin. Appraised at 4d in 1577.

127.211   Hossius de expresso Dei verbo
Stanislaus Hozyusz, *Cardinal*. *De expresso Dei verbo*. Continent: date indeterminable.
Language(s): Latin. Appraised at 4d in 1577.

127.212   Precaciones Erasmi
Desiderius Erasmus. *Precationes*. Continent: date indeterminable.
Language(s): Latin. Appraised at 2d in 1577.

127.213   Fabulae Isopi
Aesop. *Fabulae*. Britain or Continent: date indeterminable.
STC 168 *et seq.* and non-STC. *Language(s)*: Latin Greek (perhaps). Appraised at 4d in 1577.

127.214   Galenus de diebus decretoriis
Galen. *De diebus decretoriis*. Lyon: apud Guillaume Rouillium, 1550–1559.
In collections, leading, from 1529. *Language(s)*: Latin. Appraised at 12d in 1577.

127.215   Epistol' Medicinalis
Unidentified. Continent: date indeterminable.

There are several books with this title, including the anthology *Epistolae medicinales diversorum authorum* and works by Joannes Manardus and by Aloysius Mundella. The manuscript entry was altered from *Medicinales*. See 127.222. *Language(s)*: Latin. Appraised at 4d in 1577.

127.216   Fuccius

Probably Leonard Fuchs. Unidentified. Place unknown: stationer unknown, date indeterminable.

STC/non-STC status unknown. Remaclus Fuchs (Fusch), also a writer of medical works, is less likely than the widely published Leonard. See 127.223 for a work definitely by Leonard Fuchs. *Language(s)*: Latin (probable). Appraised at 4d in 1577.

127.217   Fernelius

Joannes Fernelius. Unidentified. Continent: date indeterminable. *Language(s)*: Latin. Appraised at 10d in 1577.

127.218   Hypocrates

Hippocrates. Unidentified. Continent: date indeterminable.

Almost certainly not an STC book. Very little of Hippocrates was published in England by the date of this inventory. *Language(s)*: Latin (probable) Greek (perhaps). Appraised at 10d in 1577.

127.219   Diescorides

Dioscorides. *De medica materia*. Continent: date indeterminable. *Language(s)*: Latin Greek (perhaps). Appraised at 10d in 1577.

127.220   Macer de metari

Odo, *Magdunensis*. *De viribus herbarum*. Continent: date indeterminable.

The long title of a Frankfurt am Main edition (1540) begins with a reference to Aemilius Macer, *Floridus* to whom this work was attributed: *Macri De materia medica....* That edition may very well be represented here. *Language(s)*: Latin. Appraised at 2d in 1577.

127.221   Dessenius de compositione

Bernardus Dessenius. *De compositione medicamentorum*. Continent: 1555–1556.

Language(s): Latin. Appraised at 16d in 1577.

127.222   Epistol Medicinales

Unidentified. Continent: date indeterminable.

See the annotations to 127.215. *Language(s)*: Latin. Appraised at 6d in 1577.

127.223 Methodus Fuctii
Leonard Fuchs. [*Methodus seu ratio compendiaria perveniendi ad medicinam*]. Continent: 1531–1550.
See 127.216. *Language(s)*: Latin. Appraised at 10d in 1577.

127.224 Epidemie Galleni
Galen. Probably [*Works–Epitome*]. Edited by Andres de Laguna. Continent: date indeterminable.
There is no record of a Galen *Epidemia*. *Language(s)*: Latin. Appraised at 6d in 1577.

127.225 Tituli Juris Canonici
Unidentified. Continent: date indeterminable.
Parts of the *Corpus juris canonici* are most likely, and, at this valuation, probably only fragments. *Language(s)*: Latin. Appraised at 6d in 1577.

127.226 Harbarium Dodanei
Rembert Dodoens. Unidentified. Continent: date indeterminable.
Which of his several herbals cannot be determined; indeed, it could be one of his botanical titles. *Language(s)*: Latin. Appraised at 12d in 1577.

127.227 Marianus
Unidentified. Continent (probable): date indeterminable.
Almost certainly not an STC book. Marianus Scotus and Marianus Socinus, both *the Elder* and *the Younger*, are all possibilities. *Language(s)*: Latin (probable). Appraised at 8d in 1577.

127.228:1–100 a hundreth parchment old bokes
Unidentified. Places unknown: stationers unknown, dates indeterminable. STC/non-STC status unknown. May include manuscripts. Appraisal reads: *by estimacion worth*, and the *hundreth* itself is surely an estimate also. *Language(s)*: Unknown. Appraised as a group at 26s 8d in 1577.

127.229:1–30 xxxti Englyshe bokes
Unidentified. Britain (probable): dates indeterminable.
STC identification impossible. Appraisal reads: *warth by estimacion*. *Language(s)*: English. Appraised as a group at 13s 4d in 1577.

Richard Seacole. Scholar (B.A.):
Probate Inventory. 1577

JOCELYN SHEPPARD

Richard Seacole (Seacoll, Secoll), a scholar at New College in 1570, was granted the B.A. on 24 May 1574; he died on 26 July 1577 at the age of twenty-six, perhaps of the plague or typhus that ravaged Oxford collegiate society that year (see Ker, 463 and McConica, 648). For some unaccountable reason, *Alumni Oxonienses* (4:1329) erroneously gives the year of his death as 1567 and his age at that time as seventy. A fellow of New College, he was buried in the college chapel (*Alumni Oxonienses*, 4:1329) where a monumental inscription contains the above information about his age and the date of death (Wood 1786, 1:220). A list of about 130 books is found in an inventory taken of his goods two months later on 25 September 1577.

Seacole arrived at New College—long "one of the most learned and devout centres of catholic humanism" according to Penry Williams (1986, 407)—after it had undergone purges in the 1560s to rid it of members who had refused to subscribe to the Elizabethan settlement. By the time of Seacole's death, the college seems to have reached conformity in religion (Williams 1986, 408). The atmosphere of New College during that period may, then, help to account for the eclectic character of the theological works in Seacole's library, including a moderate conformist strain. Early Christian writers (Ignatius, Chrysostom, and John, *of Damascus*, among them) are mixed with reformers (Luther and Calvin, the two most notable), while the contemporary polemic on matters theological is represented by several English conformist writers— specifically, by Thomas Cooper, *Bishop of Lincoln*, by an unidentified "Awnsur to Fecknam" at 128.119 ("Fecknam" being John Feckenham, the Abbot of Westminster, who objected to the Oath of Supremacy), and by several of John Jewel's works. An unidentified work of Cranmer's is also listed (128.102). Approximately a fourth of the collection is literature and history, the standard classics of each solidly represented. The occasional distinctive, though hardly unique item, however, catches the eye: a Greek Aristophanes (128.4)–along with the more common Seneca, Euripides, and Sophocles–and the one non-classical history: Froissart. There is very little English (a Bible and the items of religious controversy), a good deal of Greek–at least a dozen books, perhaps as many as two dozen–and, with Sebastian Muenster's Hebrew dictionary (128.19) and a Hebrew and Aramaic grammar (128.2), evidence that Seacole had undertaken a study of Hebrew, though there is no item explicitly identified as being in Hebrew other than these grammatical works. Muenster's dictionary may in fact have been a very recent purchase (see the next paragraph).

In an account dated 22 November 1577 (Oxford University Archives, Hyp.B.20., fo 36v), prepared by the administrator of Seacole's estate, William Seacole, seven of the books listed in Seacole's inventory are challenged as having been borrowed or, in one case, apparently unpaid for. The appraisal amounts mentioned in the account coincide exactly with the appraisals for the comparable items in the inventory. In the case of one (128.112), the work, given only by the author's name in the inventory, is identified in the account (Eusebius's *Chronicon*). According to "mr Aylworth subwarden," almost certainly Anthony Aylworth, fellow of New College and later Regius Professor of Medicine and physician to Queen Elizabeth (*Alumni Oxonienses*, 1:48), that book and three others (128.5, 128.6, and 128.10) were the property of New College. One unidentified book was challenged by "Mr *ayne of the same house," presumably Richard Payne, scholar at New College in 1568 and B.C.L. in 1576 (*Alumni Oxonienses*, 3:1129), and another (128.52) by "Gregorie scholler of the same colledge," probably Richard Gregory, who is listed in *Alumni Oxonienses* as a scholar at New College in 1576 (2:603). A Hebrew dictionary, surely Muenster's dictionary at 128.19 (appraised for 8*d* in both lists, though called a "grammar" in the account listing; Corneille Bertram's comparative Aramaic and Hebrew grammar is appraised for 2*s* in the inventory), was challenged by Richard Garbrand, the Oxford bookseller, indicating that the book probably was only recently acquired by Seacole and not paid for at the time of his death. I wish to express special thanks to Simon Bailey, Archivist of Oxford University, for forwarding me a transcript of the administrator's account.

Oxford University Archives, Bodleian Library: Hyp.B.18.

§

Williams, Penry. 1986. "Elizabethan Oxford: State, Church and University," in *The Collegiate University*, ed., James K. McConica. Volume 3 of *The History of the University of Oxford*, gen. ed., T.H. Aston. Oxford: Clarendon Press, pp. 397–440.

Wood, Anthony à. 1786. *The History and Antiquities of the Colleges and Halls in the University of Oxford.* Edited by John Gutch. 2 Vols. Oxford: Clarendon Press.

§

128.1:1	petrus hispanus et tartaretus
128.1:2	[See 128.1:1]
128.2	Gramatica Bartrammi
128.3	Loci communes Musculi
128.4	Aristophanes grece
128.5	Annotaciones glawriani in Livium
128.6	Cornelius Tasitis
128.7	Omilia Chrisostomi
128.8	Faber in Aristotelem
128.9	Ilias Homeri grece
128.10	Boetius
128.11	Nicholaus Hannappe
128.12	Loci communes Sarcerii
128.13	Euripides grece
128.14	Luther ad Galathos
128.15	Cleonardi Gramatica
128.16	Buridanus in Ethicam
128.17	Harbartus de oratore
128.18	Ysocrates grece et latine
128.19	dixionarium hebraicum Monsteri
128.20	Phisica Titillmanni
128.21	Biblia Hieronimi
128.22	Psalterium Opicii
128.23	Moria Erasmi
128.24	Sphera Procli
128.25	Gemma Platonis
128.26	Albertus Magnus
128.27	Epistole ad Atticum
128.28	Foctius, Phylosophia
128.29	Epistole Familiares
128.30	Frosord
128.31	Pyndarus
128.32	Calvini cathakismi
128.33	Dialectica Radulphi
128.34	2 et 3 volumina Oracionis Tullii
128.35	Juell contra Harden'
128.36	Apollogie contra Harden'
128.37	One of the veteres
128.38	Dialogi Luciani

128.39	Oraciones Themistii grece
128.40	Paratitla upon the law
128.41	Dammassenus grece
128.42	Elementa Euclitis grece
128.43	pewcerus de circulis
128.44	Hyroditis
128.45	Toletus de anima
128.46	Luciani opera
128.47	Ethica Aristotelis
128.48	Problemata Aristotelis
128.49	Omnium gentium mores
128.50	Cronica Carionis
128.51	Vita Plutharchi
128.52	Paulus Jovius in 2bus
128.53	Testamentum vesei grece et latine
128.54	Diodorus Siculus
128.55	Rethorica Valerii
128.56	Posselli Evangelii Epist'
128.57	Quintus Curtius
128.58	Salustius
128.59	Sturmii epistole
128.60	Herodianus
128.61	Sententie Ciceronis
128.62	Suetonius
128.63	Tragediae Senice
128.64	Titus Livius
128.65	Commentarii Cesaris
128.66	Lexicon graecum
128.67	Aristo' grece
128.68	Plinius
128.69	Budei Commentarii
128.70	Biblia anglice
128.71	Zenophon grece et latine
128.72	Problemata Theologica
128.73:A	Similia a Licosthene
128.73:B	[See 128.73:A]
128.74	Institucio Calvini
128.75	Marter in Epistolas
128.76	Repertorium Byel in Sententias
128.77	Compendium Bunderii
128.78	Conciliaciones Aultemeri
128.79	Phrases Schori
128.80	Horatius
128.81	Sintaxis Mirabil'
128.82	Lemnius de astrologia

128.83   Lucanus
128.84   Valerius Maximus
128.85   Hesiodus grece
128.86   Hapothegmata Licostenis
128.87   Officia Textoris
128.88   Tabulae Frigii
128.89   Sturmius de imitatione
128.90   Sophocles grece
128.91   Phrases Manucii
128.92   Rhetorica Cicero[nis]
128.93   Instituciones Fuccii
128.94   Facetii Brisonii
128.95   Ozei prophete
128.96   Chetreus
128.97   Sphera Marcatori[s]
128.98   A sermon of Thomas Couper, bishoppe Lyncoll'
128.99   Officia Ciceronis
128.100   Pluthar[cus] de placitis philosorum grece et latine
128.101   Questiones Frigii
128.102   Cranmerus
128.103   Lucius Florus
128.104   Apologia Anglicana
128.105   Rethorica Hormognis
128.106   Enchiridion Epicteti
128.107   Philosophia Segei
128.108   Vita Romanorum Roberti Baronis
128.109   Jure Magistratuum
128.110   Arithmetica Missilli
128.111   Psalterium Davidis
128.112   Eusebius
128.113   Gesta Romanorum
128.114   Osorius de gloria
128.115   Epistole Ignacii grece
128.116   Conciones Livii
128.117   Theocretus grece
128.118   Erasmus de conscribendis
128.119   Awnsur to Fecknam
128.120   Arithmetica Gemme
128.121   multiple   Divers small bookes
128.122   Tullii Philosophia
128.123   Vergilius

§

128.1:1 petrus hispanus et tartaretus

John XXI, *Pope* (Petrus, *Hispanus*). [*Summulae logicales*]. Continent: date indeterminable.

The manuscript entry presents *petrus hispanus* on a line above *et tartaretus* with a bracket connecting the two to the single appraisal, which form indicates two works. Conceivably, however, the entry represents only Tartaretus's work. *Language(s)*: Latin. Appraised with one other at 22d in 1577.

128.1:2 [See 128.1:1]

Petrus Tartaretus. *Expositio in summulas Petri Hispani*. Continent: date indeterminable.

See the annotations to 128.1:1. *Language(s)*: Latin. Appraised with one other at 22d in 1577.

128.2 Gramatica Bartrammi

Bonaventure Corneille Bertram. *Comparitio grammaticae hebraicae et aramicae*. Geneva: apud Eustathium Vignon, 1574.

Language(s): Aramaic Hebrew Latin. Appraised at 2s in 1577.

128.3 Loci communes Musculi

Probably Wolfgang Musculus. *Loci communes*. Continent: date indeterminable.

The less frequently published *Loci communes sacri* of Andreas Musculus remains a possibility. *Language(s)*: Latin. Appraised at 20d in 1577.

128.4 Aristophanes grece

Aristophanes. Unidentified. Continent: date indeterminable.

Probably a single play at this valuation. *Language(s)*: Greek. Appraised at 2d in 1577.

128.5 Annotaciones glawriani in Livium

Henricus Loritus Glareanus. [*Livius–Historiae Romanae decades: commentary*]. Continent: date indeterminable.

Challenged by "mr Aylworth subwarden" of New College (probably Anthony Aylworth, *Alumni Oxonienses*, 1:48) on behalf of the college in an administrator's account that was submitted two months after the inventory was compiled. *Language(s)*: Latin. Appraised at 4d in 1577.

128.6 Cornelius Tasitis

Publius Cornelius Tacitus. Unidentified. Continent: date indeterminable.

Either a very tattered copy of the *Works* or a single work. This item was challenged by "mr Aylworth subwarden" of New College (probably Anthony Aylworth, *Alumni Oxonienses*, 1:48) on behalf of the college in an administrator's account that was submitted two months after the inventory was compiled. *Language(s)*: Latin. Appraised at 2d in 1577.

128.7 Omilia Chrisostomi
John *Chrysostom, Saint.* [*Homiliae*]. Britain or Continent: date indeterminable.
STC 14634 and non-STC. *Language(s)*: Latin. Appraised at 10d in 1577.

128.8 Faber in Aristotelem
Jacobus Faber, *Stapulensis*. [*Aristotle–Unidentified: commentary*]. Continent: date indeterminable.
Faber produced commentaries on several works of Aristotle. *Language(s)*: Latin. Appraised at 12d in 1577.

128.9 Ilias Homeri grece
Homer. *Iliad*. Continent: date indeterminable.
Language(s): Greek. Appraised at 20d in 1577.

128.10 Boetius
Probably Anicius M.T.S. Boethius. *De consolatione philosophiae*. Continent (probable): date indeterminable.
Probably not an STC book, but see STC 3199. The 1478 London edition is in both English and Latin. This item was challenged by "mr Aylworth subwarden" of New College (probably Anthony Aylworth, *Alumni Oxonienses*, 1:48) on behalf of the college in an administrator's account that was submitted two months after the inventory was compiled. *Language(s)*: Latin. Appraised at 8d in 1577.

128.11 Nicholaus Hannappe
Nicolaus Hanapus. *Exempla sacrae scripturae*. (*The Bible*). Britain or Continent: date indeterminable.
STC 12742 and non-STC. This could well be the English version since he is called Hanape on the title page. *Language(s)*: English (probable) Latin (perhaps). Appraised at 6d in 1577.

128.12 Loci communes Sarcerii
Erasmus Sarcerius. [*Loci communes*]. Continent: date indeterminable.
Language(s): Latin. Appraised at 6d in 1577.

128.13 Euripides grece
Euripides. Probably [*Works*]. Continent: date indeterminable.
Language(s): Greek. Appraised at 8d in 1577.

128.14 Luther ad Galathos
Martin Luther. [*Galatians: commentary*]. Continent: date indeterminable.
Two English editions had been published by the date of this inventory (STC 16965–16966), but the manuscript entry suggests a Latin version. *Language(s)*: Latin. Appraised at 8d in 1577.

128.15   Cleonardi Gramatica
Nicolaus Clenardus. [*Institutiones linguae graecae*]. Continent: date indeterminable.
Language(s): Greek Latin. Appraised at 2d in 1577.

128.16   Buridanus in Ethicam
Joannes Buridanus. [*Aristotle–Ethica: commentary*]. Paris: (different houses), 1489–1518.
Language(s): Latin. Appraised at 4d in 1577.

128.17   Harbartus de oratore
Joannes Herbetius. *De oratore libri quinque*. Paris: apud Joannem Ruellium, 1574.
Language(s): Latin. Appraised at 6d in 1577.

128.18   Ysocrates grece et latine
Isocrates. Probably [*Works*]. Continent: date indeterminable.
The two languages suggest the complete works. *Language(s)*: Greek Latin. Appraised at 20d in 1577.

128.19   dixionarium hebraicum Monsteri
Sebastian Muenster. *Dictionarium hebraicum*. Basle: (different houses), 1523–1564.
Language(s): Hebrew Latin. Appraised at 8d in 1577.

128.20   Phisica Titillmanni
Franz Titelmann. [*Aristotle–Selected works–Philosophia naturalis: commentary*]. Continent: 1530–1574.
Language(s): Latin. Appraised at 8d in 1577.

128.21   Biblia Hieronimi
The Bible. Britain or Continent: date indeterminable.
STC 2055 and non-STC. The Vulgate. *Language(s)*: Latin. Appraised at 2s in 1577.

128.22   Psalterium Opicii
[*Bible–O.T.–Psalms*]. Edited by Hieronymus Opitius, *Junior*. Wittenberg: (different houses), 1566–1576.
Three editions, two in 1566. *Language(s)*: Hebrew Latin. Appraised at 8d in 1577.

128.23   Moria Erasmi
Desiderius Erasmus. *Moriae encomium*. Continent: date indeterminable.
Language(s): Latin. Appraised at 2d in 1577.

128.24   Sphera Procli
Diadochus Proclus. *Sphaera*. Britain or Continent: date indeterminable.
STC 20398.3 *et seq.* and non-STC. *Language(s)*: Latin (probable) Greek (perhaps). Appraised at 6d in 1577.

128.25   Gemma Platonis
Plato. *Gemmae, sive illustriores sententiae*. Continent: date indeterminable.
Language(s): Latin. Appraised at 4d in 1577.

128.26   Albertus Magnus
Albertus Magnus. Unidentified. Place unknown: stationer unknown, date indeterminable.
STC/non-STC status unknown. *Language(s)*: Latin. Appraised at 4d in 1577.

128.27   Epistole ad Atticum
Marcus Tullius Cicero. *Epistolae ad Atticum*. Continent: date indeterminable.
Language(s): Latin. Appraised at 6d in 1577.

128.28   Foctius, Phylosophia
Sebastiano Fox Morzillo. Perhaps *De naturae philosophia, seu de Platonis et Aristotelis consensione*. Continent: date indeterminable.
Marginally more likely than his *Ethices philosophiae compendium*. *Language(s)*: Latin. Appraised at 2d in 1577.

128.29   Epistole Familiares
Marcus Tullius Cicero. *Epistolae ad familiares*. Britain or Continent: date indeterminable.
STC 5295 *et seq.* and non-STC. *Language(s)*: Latin. Appraised at 6d in 1577.

128.30   Frosord
Jean Froissart. [*Chroniques*]. Britain or Continent: date indeterminable.
STC 11396 *et seq.* and non-STC. *Language(s)*: Latin (probable) English (perhaps) French (perhaps). Appraised at 2d in 1577.

128.31   Pyndarus
Pindar. Probably [*Works*]. Continent: date indeterminable.
Language(s): Latin (probable) Greek (perhaps). Appraised at 8d in 1577.

128.32   Calvini cathakismi
Jean Calvin. [*Catechism*]. Britain or Continent: date indeterminable.
STC 4375 *et seq.* and non-STC. *Language(s)*: Latin Greek (perhaps). Appraised at 3d in 1577.

128.33 Dialectica Radulphi
Caspar Rhodolphus. [*Dialectica*]. Continent: date indeterminable.
Rodolphus Agricola's *De inventione dialectica* is another possibility.
Language(s): Latin. Appraised at 4d in 1577.

128.34 2 et 3 volumina Oracionis Tullii
Marcus Tullius Cicero. [*Selected works–Orations*]. Continent: date indeterminable.
Language(s): Latin. Appraised at 16d in 1577.

128.35 Juell contra Harden'
John Jewel, *Bishop. A replie unto M. Hardinges answeare*. London: Henry Wykes, 1565–1566.
STC 14606 *et seq.* Appraisal includes following item. *Language(s)*: English. Appraised with one other at 6s in 1577.

128.36 Apollogie contra Harden'
John Jewel, *Bishop. A defence of the Apologie of the Churche of Englande*. London: H. Wykes, 1567–1571.
STC 14600 *et seq. Language(s)*: English. Appraised with one other at 6s in 1577.

128.37 One of the veteres
Unidentified. Place unknown: stationer unknown, date indeterminable.
STC/non-STC status unknown. The manuscript entry could also be read as *voteres*, but neither reading provides an identification. Perhaps a reference to the "ancients," suggesting one of the church "fathers." Then again, perhaps one of the writers represented in such collections as found at Adams P1685–1686 (*Poetae christiani veteres*). *Language(s)*: Latin (probable). Appraised at 2d in 1577.

128.38 Dialogi Luciani
Lucian, *of Samosata*. Probably [*Dialogues–Selected*]. Britain or Continent: date indeterminable.
STC 16891 *et seq.* and non-STC. A low appraisal for the collected works. *Language(s)*: Latin (probable) Greek (perhaps). Appraised at 4d in 1577.

128.39 Oraciones Themistii grece
Themistius. *Orationes*. Geneva: excudebat Henricus Stephanus, H. Fuggeri typog., 1562.
Announced as a Greek-Latin edition, it does not appear with the Latin. *Language(s)*: Greek. Appraised at 3s in 1577.

128.40 Paratitla upon the law
Jacques Cujas. [*Paratitla*]. Continent: date indeterminable.

Possibilities include Paratitla on the Codex, the Digest, and the Codex and Digest. *Language(s)*: Latin. Appraised at 2d in 1577.

128.41 Dammassenus grece
John, *of Damascus, Saint.* Unidentified. Continent: date indeterminable. *Language(s)*: Greek. Appraised at 8d in 1577.

128.42 Elementa Euclitis grece
Euclid. *Elementa.* Continent: date indeterminable. *Language(s)*: Greek. Appraised at 7d or 8d in 1577.

128.43 pewcerus de circulis
Kaspar Peucer. *Elementa doctrinae de circulis coelestibus.* Wittenberg: (different houses), 1551–1576. *Language(s)*: Latin. Appraised at 6d in 1577.

128.44 Hyroditis
Herodotus. [*Historiae*]. Continent: date indeterminable. *Language(s)*: Latin (probable) Greek (perhaps). Appraised at 8d in 1577.

128.45 Toletus de anima
Franciscus Toletus, *Cardinal.* [*Aristotle–De anima: commentary*]. Continent: 1575–1577.
The colophon of the 1575 edition is dated 1574. *Language(s)*: Latin. Appraised at 10d in 1577.

128.46 Luciani opera
Lucian, *of Samosata.* [*Works*]. Continent: date indeterminable. *Language(s)*: Latin (probable) Greek (perhaps). Appraised at 16d in 1577.

128.47 Ethica Aristotelis
Aristotle. *Ethica.* Britain or Continent: date indeterminable.
STC 752 and non-STC. *Language(s)*: Latin (probable) Greek (perhaps). Appraised at 12d in 1577.

128.48 Problemata Aristotelis
Aristotle (spurious). *Problemata.* Continent: date indeterminable. *Language(s)*: Latin. Appraised at 3d in 1577.

128.49 Omnium gentium mores
Joannes Boemus. [*Omnium gentium mores, leges et ritus*]. Continent: date indeterminable.
Language(s): Latin. Appraised at 6d in 1577.

128.50 Cronica Carionis
Johann Carion. *Chronica*. Continent: date indeterminable.
Language(s): Latin. Appraised at 6d in 1577.

128.51 Vita Plutharchi
Plutarch. *Vitae parallelae*. Continent: date indeterminable.
Language(s): Latin (probable) Greek (perhaps). Appraised at 16d in 1577.

128.52 Paulus Jovius in 2bus
Giovio Paolo, *Bishop*. Unidentified. Continent: date indeterminable.
Language(s): Latin. Appraised at 18d in 1577.

128.53 Testamentum vesei grece et latine
[*Bible–N.T.*]. Continent: date indeterminable.
The puzzling manuscript entry *vesei* may be an attempt at some form of Théodore de Bèze as translator and editor. *Language(s)*: Greek Latin. Appraised at 2s in 1577.

128.54 Diodorus Siculus
Diodorus, *Siculus*. *Bibliotheca historia*. Continent: date indeterminable.
Language(s): Latin (probable) Greek (perhaps). Appraised at 10d in 1577.

128.55 Rethorica Valerii
Cornelius Valerius. *In universam bene dicendi rationem tabula*. Continent: date indeterminable.
Language(s): Latin. Appraised at 4d in 1577.

128.56 Posselli Evangelii Epist'
Joannes Posselius. [*Gospels and Epistles (liturgical): commentary and text*]. (*Bible–N.T.*). Wittenberg: (different houses), 1572.
Language(s): Greek. Appraised at 4d in 1577.

128.57 Quintus Curtius
Quintus Curtius Rufus. *De rebus gestis Alexandri Magni*. Continent: date indeterminable.
Language(s): Latin. Appraised at 8d in 1577.

128.58 Salustius
Caius Sallustius Crispus. Unidentified. Place unknown: stationer unknown, date indeterminable.
STC/non-STC status unknown. *Language(s)*: Latin. Appraised at 6d in 1577.

128.59 Sturmii epistole
Joannes Sturmius. Perhaps *Classicarum epistolarum, libri III*. Strassburg:

excudebat Josias Rihelius, 1565–1573.
Other works of Sturmius could also be entered as *epistole*. *Language(s)*:
Latin. Appraised at 4d in 1577.

128.60 Herodianus
Herodian. [*Historiae*]. Continent: date indeterminable.
Language(s): Latin Greek (perhaps). Appraised at 4d in 1577.

128.61 Sententie Ciceronis
Marcus Tullius Cicero. [*Selections*]. Britain or Continent: date indeterminable.
STC 5318.3 *et seq.* and non-STC. *Language(s)*: Latin. Appraised at 4d in
1577.

128.62 Suetonius
Caius Suetonius Tranquillus. *De vita Caesarum*. Continent: date indeterminable.
Language(s): Latin. Appraised at 3d in 1577.

128.63 Tragediae Senice
Lucius Annaeus Seneca. *Tragoediae*. Continent: date indeterminable.
Language(s): Latin. Appraised at 2d in 1577.

128.64 Titus Livius
Titus Livius. [*Historiae Romanae decades*]. Continent: date indeterminable.
Language(s): Latin. Appraised at 3s in 1577.

128.65 Commentarii Cesaris
Caius Julius Caesar. *Commentarii*. Continent: date indeterminable.
Language(s): Latin. Appraised at 12d in 1577.

128.66 Lexicon graecum
Unidentified [dictionary]. Continent: date indeterminable.
Language(s): Greek Latin. Appraised at 6s 8d in 1577.

128.67 Aristo' grece
Aristotle. Perhaps [*Works*]. Continent: date indeterminable.
Language(s): Greek. Appraised at 8s in 1577.

128.68 Plinius
Pliny, *the Elder*. *Historia naturalis*. Continent: date indeterminable.
The valuation identifies this as the *Historia naturalis* and not the *Epistolae* of
Pliny, *the Younger*. *Language(s)*: Latin. Appraised at 5s in 1577.

128.69   Budei Commentarii
Gulielmus Budaeus. *Commentarii linguae graecae*. Continent: date indeterminable.
Language(s): Greek Latin. Appraised at 2s in 1577.

128.70   Biblia anglice
The Bible. Britain or Continent: date indeterminable.
STC 2063 *et seq*. At this valuation, unless elaborately bound, this is a large, folio edition. *Language(s)*: English. Appraised at 12s in 1577.

128.71   Zenophon grece et latine
Xenophon. Probably [*Works*]. Continent: date indeterminable.
The valuation would indicate the complete works. *Language(s)*: Greek Latin. Appraised at 5s in 1577.

128.72   Problemata Theologica
Probably Benedictus Aretius. [*Problemata theologica*]. Lausanne: Franciscus Le Preux, 1573–1576.
There may be works by others with such a title, but none has been found published before the date of this inventory. *Language(s)*: Latin. Appraised at 3s 4d in 1577.

128.73:A   Similia a Licosthene
Conrad Lycosthenes (Conrad Wolffhart). *Similium loci communes*. Basle: E. Episcopius et Nicolai fr. haeredes, 1575 (composite publication).
Language(s): Latin. Appraised [a composite volume] at 2s in 1577.

128.73:B   [See 128.73:A]
Theodor Zwinger. *Similitudinem methodo*. [Composite publication].
Language(s): Latin. Appraised [a composite volume] at 2s in 1577.

128.74   Institucio Calvini
Jean Calvin. *Institutio Christianae religionis*. Britain or Continent: date indeterminable.
STC 4414 and non-STC. *Language(s)*: Latin. Appraised at 4s in 1577.

128.75   Marter in Epistolas
Pietro Martire Vermigli (Peter Martyr). Unidentified. Continent: date indeterminable.
Whether his commentary on Romans or Corinthians cannot be determined. *Language(s)*: Latin. Appraised at 20d in 1577.

128.76   Repertorium Byel in Sententias
Gabriel Biel. [*Sentences: commentary*]. Continent: date indeterminable.
Language(s): Latin. Appraised at 6d in 1577.

128.77 Compendium Bunderii
Joannes Bunderius. *Compendium concertationis.* Continent: date indeterminable.
Language(s): Latin. Appraised at 6d in 1577.

128.78 Conciliaciones Aultemeri
Andreas Althamer. *Conciliatio locorum scripturae.* Continent: date indeterminable.
Language(s): Latin. Appraised at 6d in 1577.

128.79 Phrases Schori
Antonius Schorus. *Phrases linguae latinae.* Continent: date indeterminable.
Language(s): Latin. Appraised at 8d in 1577.

128.80 Horatius
Quintus Horatius Flaccus. Probably [*Works*]. Britain or Continent: date indeterminable.
STC 13784. *Language(s)*: Latin. Appraised at 2d in 1577.

128.81 Sintaxis Mirabil'
Petrus Gregorius, *Tholosanus. Syntaxis artis mirabilis.* Lyon: apud Antonium Gryphium, 1575–1576.
Language(s): Latin. Appraised at 4d in 1577.

128.82 Lemnius de astrologia
Levinus Lemnius. *Libelli tres* (*De astrologia, De praefixo cuique vitae termino, De honesto animi et corporis oblectamento*). Antwerp: apud Martinum Nutium, 1554.
Language(s): Latin. Appraised at 2d in 1577.

128.83 Lucanus
Marcus Annaeus Lucanus. *Pharsalia.* Continent: date indeterminable.
Language(s): Latin. Appraised at 2d in 1577.

128.84 Valerius Maximus
Valerius Maximus. *Facta et dicta memorabilia.* Continent: date indeterminable.
Language(s): Latin. Appraised at 6d in 1577.

128.85 Hesiodus grece
Hesiod. Probably [*Works*]. Continent: date indeterminable.
Language(s): Greek. Appraised at 10d in 1577.

128.86 Hapothegmata Licostenis
Conrad Lycosthenes (Conrad Wolffhart). *Apophthegmata*. Continent: date indeterminable.
Language(s): Latin. Appraised at 18d in 1577.

128.87 Officia Textoris
Joannes Ravisius (Textor). [*Officina*]. Continent: date indeterminable.
Language(s): Latin. Appraised at 10d in 1577.

128.88 Tabulae Frigii
Joannes Thomas Freigius. Unidentified. Continent: date indeterminable.
Freigius's works on Ovid, Ramus, and Virgil are all possible. *Language(s)*:
Latin. Appraised at 4d in 1577.

128.89 Sturmius de imitatione
Joannes Sturmius. *De imitatione oratoria*. Edited by Valentinus Erythraeus.
Continent: imprim. Bernhardus Jobinus, 1574–1576.
Language(s): Latin. Appraised at 8d in 1577.

128.90 Sophocles grece
Sophocles. Probably [*Works*]. Continent: date indeterminable.
Language(s): Greek. Appraised at 4d in 1577.

128.91 Phrases Manucii
Aldo Manuzio, *the Younger. Purae, elegantes et copiosae latinae linguae phrases.*
Britain or Continent: date indeterminable.
STC 17278.8 and non-STC. The 1573 London edition contained an English
translation. *Language(s)*: Latin English (perhaps). Appraised at 4d in 1577.

128.92 Rhetorica Cicero[nis]
Marcus Tullius Cicero (spurious). *Rhetorica ad Herennium*. Continent: date
indeterminable.
STC 5323.5 and non-STC. *Language(s)*: Latin. Appraised at 8d in 1577.

128.93 Instituciones Fuccii
Leonard Fuchs. *Institutiones medicinae*. Continent: date indeterminable.
Language(s): Latin. Appraised at 10d in 1577.

128.94 Facetii Brisonii
Lucius Domitius Brusonius. *Facetiarum exemplorumque libri VII*. Continent:
date indeterminable.
Language(s): Latin. Appraised at 14d in 1577.

128.95 Ozei prophete

[*Bible–O.T.–Hosea*]. Continent: date indeterminable.
Language(s): Latin. Appraised at 20d in 1577.

128.96 Chetreus

David Chytraeus. Unidentified. Continent: date indeterminable.
The single work of Chytraeus translated into English (STC 5276 *et seq.*) is
not likely here. *Language(s)*: Latin. Appraised at 4d in 1577.

128.97 Sphera Marcatori[s]

Bartholomaeus Mercator. *Breves in sphaeram meditatiunculae*. Cologne: apud
haeredes Arnoldi Birckmanni, 1563.
Language(s): Latin. Appraised at 3d in 1577.

128.98 A sermon of Thomas Couper, bishoppe Lyncoll'

Thomas Cooper, *Bishop. The true and perfect copie of a godly sermon, preached
at Lincolne the .28. of August. 1575*. London: H. Middleton for R. Newberie,
1575 (probable).
STC 5691. *Language(s)*: English. Appraised at 4d in 1577.

128.99 Officia Ciceronis

Marcus Tullius Cicero. *De officiis*. Continent (probable): date indeterminable.
Probably not an STC book, but see STC 5278 *et seq.* Some early English editions contained the Latin text as well. *Language(s)*: Latin. Appraised at 2d in
1577.

128.100 Pluthar[cus] de placitis philosorum grece et latine

Plutarch (spurious). *De placitis philosophorum*. Continent: date indeterminable.
Language(s): Greek Latin. Appraised at 4d in 1577.

128.101 Questiones Frigii

Joannes Thomas Freigius. Unidentified. Continent: date indeterminable.
Freigius produced "Questiones" on a variety of topics. *Language(s)*: Latin
(probable). Appraised at 6d in 1577.

128.102 Cranmerus

Thomas Cranmer, *Archbishop*. Unidentified. Place unknown: stationer unknown, date indeterminable.
STC/non-STC status unknown. *Language(s)*: Latin (probable) English (perhaps). Appraised at 4d in 1577.

128.103 Lucius Florus

Lucius Annaeus Florus. [*Epitomae de Tito Livio bellorum omnium annorum*].

Continent: date indeterminable.
Language(s): Latin. Appraised at 8d in 1577.

128.104 Apologia Anglicana
John Jewel, *Bishop. Apologia ecclesiae anglicanae.* London: apud R. Wolfium, 1562.
STC 14581. *Language(s)*: Latin. Appraised at 8d in 1577.

128.105 Rethorica Hormognis
Hermogenes. *Ars rhetorica.* Continent: date indeterminable.
Language(s): Greek (probable) Latin (probable). Appraised at 6d in 1577.

128.106 Enchiridion Epicteti
Epictetus. *Enchiridion.* Continent: date indeterminable.
Language(s): Greek (probable) Latin (probable). Appraised at 4d in 1577.

128.107 Philosophia Segei
Unidentified. Place unknown: stationer unknown, date indeterminable.
STC/non-STC status unknown. *Language(s)*: Latin. Appraised at 2d in 1577.

128.108 Vita Romanorum Roberti Baronis
Robert Barnes, *Doctor. Vitae romanorum pontificum.* Continent: 1536–1567.
Shaaber B242–244, 246. *Language(s)*: Latin. Appraised at 4d in 1577.

128.109 Jure Magistratuum
Théodore de Bèze. *De jure magistratuum in subditos.* Lyon: apud Joannem Mareschallum, 1576.
Gardy no. 303. *Language(s)*: Latin. Appraised at 1d in 1577.

128.110 Arithmetica Missilli
Jacobus Micyllus, *pseudonym* (Jakob Moltzer). *Arithmetica logistica.* Basle: per (ex. off.) Joannem Oporinum, 1555.
Language(s): Greek Latin. Appraised at 4d in 1577.

128.111 Psalterium Davidis
[*Bible–O.T.–Psalms*]. Britain or Continent: date indeterminable.
STC 2356 *et seq.* and non-STC. *Language(s)*: Latin. Appraised at 1d in 1577.

128.112 Eusebius
Eusebius, *Pamphili, Bishop. Chronicon.* Continent: date indeterminable.
Challenged by "mr Aylworth subwarden" of New College (probably Anthony Aylworth, *Alumni Oxonienses*, 1:48) on behalf of the college in an administrator's account that was submitted two months after the inventory

was compiled. The item is named in the account as "Eusebius chronicle," allowing for a more precise identification than the inventory's more spare entry. *Language(s)*: Latin. Appraised at 2d in 1577.

128.113   Gesta Romanorum

[*Gesta Romanorum*]. Britain or Continent: date indeterminable.

STC 21286.2 *et seq.* and non-STC. A number of collections of tales of Roman history, especially popular during the Middle Ages, appeared under this title. *Language(s)*: Latin. Appraised at 1d in 1577.

128.114   Osorius de gloria

Jeronimo Osorio da Fonseca, *Bishop. De gloria*. Florence: apud Laurentium Torrentinum, 1552.

Between *de* and *gloria*, the compiler inserted *te*. An edition of Osorio's oft-published *Selected works* with this title leading is also possible. *Language(s)*: Latin. Appraised at 8d in 1577.

128.115   Epistole Ignacii grece

Ignatius, *Saint, Bishop of Antioch*. [*Epistolae*]. Continent: date indeterminable.

Language(s): Greek. Appraised at 4d in 1577.

128.116   Conciones Livii

Titus Livius. *Conciones*. Continent: date indeterminable.

Language(s): Latin. Appraised at 4d in 1577.

128.117   Theocretus grece

Theocritus. *Idylls*. Continent: date indeterminable.

Language(s): Greek. Appraised at 6d in 1577.

128.118   Erasmus de conscribendis

Desiderius Erasmus. *De conscribendis epistolis*. Britain or Continent: date indeterminable.

STC 10496 and non-STC. *Language(s)*: Latin. Appraised at 2d in 1577.

128.119   Awnsur to Fecknam

Unidentified. London: (different houses), date indeterminable.

Unidentifiable in the STC. Several writers responded to John Feckenham, the Abbot of Wesminster who refused to take the Oath of Supremacy. They include Robert Horne, *Bishop of Winchester*, and two Puritan ministers, John Gough and Laurence Tomson, all of whose responses contained "answer" in the title. Horne's reply would likely fit in Seacole's library better than the other two. *Language(s)*: English. Appraised at 4d in 1577.

128.120   Arithmetica Gemme
Reiner Gemma, *Frisius. Arithmetica practicae methodus facilis.* Continent: date indeterminable.
Language(s): Latin. Appraised at 3d in 1577.

128.121 multiple   Divers small bookes
Unidentified. Places unknown: stationers unknown, dates indeterminable.
STC/non-STC status unknown. *Language(s)*: Unknown. Appraised at 8s in 1577.

128.122   Tullii Philosophia
Marcus Tullius Cicero. [*Selected works–Philosophica*]. Continent: date indeterminable.
Language(s): Latin. Appraised at 6d in 1577.

128.123   Vergilius
Publius Virgilius Maro. Probably [*Works*]. Britain or Continent: date indeterminable.
STC 24787 *et seq.* and non-STC. *Language(s)*: Latin. Appraised at 3d in 1577.

John Simpson. Scholar (M.A.): Probate Inventory. 1577

MARC L. SCHWARZ

John Simpson (Simson, Sympson, Symson), fellow of Exeter College, graduated B.A. in 1567 and proceeded M.A. in 1570. His will was proved at Oxford on 10 September 1577 (*Alumni Oxonienses*, 4:1358), an inventory of his goods that included one hundred and twenty-nine printed books having been taken on the 30th of August preceding.

The identification of books listed in this inventory is hampered, at times, by a number of especially frustrating entries. Some of these puzzling items might suggest that the compiler of Simpson's list, Henry Crosse, long-time yeoman bedel of divinity, and well into his sixties at the time that Simpson died, may have had some difficulty hearing titles that were called out to him by his partner, the Oxford stationer Henry Milward. For example, "Crucii" (129.15) might in fact be "Clusi" (for Clusius), "Gunelli" (at 129.98) might refer to "Bunel," and "dixionarium caddic," meaningless as it is, could conceivably be a mishearing of "dictionarium medic[um]," a descriptive title that would fit Simpson's collection. Other entries, unidentifiable though legible, like "hoffemianii hermaticus" at 129.61 and "Hulkius" at 129.114, may derive from a similar problem. One item, at 129.7, "hermoniae genationum," though clearly written, resists being made into anything meaningful at all.

About half of Simpson's books consist of works on medicine and botany, although there is no documentary evidence that Simpson either studied or practiced medicine. The scant representation of theology—the *Epistolae* of Erasmus (129.72) being the only work in Simpson's library even marginally theological—is unusual for an Oxford fellow.

While there is no great depth in philosophy and literature, two items do bear notice. One, at 129.60, is the first appearance in this series of Oxford book-lists of *A mirrour for magistrates* and the other, at 129.73, is the first definite appearance in the Oxford libraries thus far edited of Bartholomew

Clerke's Latin translation of Castiglione's *Il cortegiano*.

Oxford University Archives, Bodleian Library: Hyp.B.18.

§

129.1	Ruellius de natura stirpium
129.2	tria volumina Galleni
129.3	Tabulae Wickeri in 2bus
129.4	Silvius de febribus
129.5	harbarium Turneri
129.6	matthes bi herbarium
129.7	hermoniae genationum
129.8	Anthidotarium Wickeri
129.9	Harbarium Paene
129.10	Hesius
129.11	Practica Diversorum
129.12	Commentarium Trusiani
129.13	Randoletus
129.14	Ysorates grece et latine
129.15	Harbarium Crucii
129.16	dixionarium caddic
129.17	Columbus
129.18	Gorgonius de regimine sanitatis
129.19	Brassavalus
129.20	Lacuna
129.21	Fucshius de composicione medicamentorum
129.22	Historia Plantarum
129.23	Botarius
129.24	Fernelii libri 7
129.25	Harbarium Donaii in 2
129.26	Cornarius in Hypocraten in 2 voluminibus
129.27	Manardus
129.28	Ferrerius
129.29	Vicinius
129.30	matthias corrnaci
129.31	foesii pharmacopeia
129.32	Fontanonus
129.33	Ysacus Judeus
129.34	Harbarium Dodonaii vetus
129.35	Instituciones Fucscii
129.36	Varie Lectiones Mercurionis

129.37	Pharnelius in 2bus voluminibus
129.38	Gwinterius de pestilentia
129.39	Ferandus
129.40	Cagitanus de pulsibus
129.41	Galenus grece de facultatibus
129.42	Leonardus Joachinus
129.43	liber theoricarum mediocine
129.44	Problemata Jani Matthei
129.45	Brudus Delucitanus de ratione victus
129.46	Practica Fuccii
129.47	Problemata Aloicii Trissini
129.48	Montanus
129.49	Botallius
129.50	Practica Rulandi
129.51	Enchiridion Chyrurgic
129.52	Galenus de hossibus
129.53	Historia Plantarum
129.54	Practica Cuffeneri
129.55	Cornelius Selsus
129.56	Methodus Medendi Monsii
129.57	Historia Frugum Dodonei
129.58	Jacobus Ruffe
129.59	Jacobus Silvius
129.60	The Myrror of Magistrates
129.61	hoffemianii hermaticus
129.62	Boetius de disciplina
129.63	Gemiphrisius
129.64	Questiones Simonis Simonii
129.65	Cladius Dariotus
129.66	Grammatica Antesignani
129.67	opera Haddoni
129.68	Dificiles Questiones Fuccii
129.69	Logica Valerii
129.70	Opothegmata, Licostenes
129.71	Velcurio
129.72	epistole Erasmi
129.73	Aulecus Clarkii
129.74	Copia Verborum et Rerum
129.75	epistole Cecli Secundi
129.76	Philosophia Titilmanni
129.77	Anthonius Scorus
129.78	Asconius Perianus
129.79	Flores Therentii
129.80	lexicon graecum
129.81	Anthonius Misaldus

129.82	Forliviensis super Avicenna
129.83	Laurentius Valla
129.84	Calepinus
129.85	Avicenna
129.86	Rodulphi Dialectica
129.87	epistole familiares Ciceronis
129.88	Phrasii Minutii
129.89	Ethica Aristotelis
129.90	Wildenbargius
129.91	Corderius
129.92	naturalis philosophia Aristotelis in 2bus voluminibus
129.93	Topica Aristotelis
129.94	Hompharius
129.95	Horatius
129.96	Sadoletus
129.97	Sententie Ciceronis
129.98	epistole Gunelli
129.99	Poselius
129.100	Siprianus Lovicius
129.101	Jacobus Silvius de morbis internis
129.102	Susius de emissione sanguinis
129.103	Lucianus grece
129.104	Baccanellus
129.105	Sigonius de vita Scipionis
129.106	Nobilis Socius de purgibus
129.107	Problemata Aristotelis
129.108	Carmina Proverbialia
129.109	Dodoneus de frumentis
129.110	Aphorismi Hipocratis grece
129.111	opera Ciceronis in tribus voluminibus
129.112	Thomas Aquinus in Politica
129.113	Quintilianus
129.114	Hulkius
129.115	Conclusiones Fabri
129.116	Brigot
129.117	Faber
129.118	Erasmus de conscribendis epistolis
129.119	Justinus
129.120	Lippus Brandolinus
129.121	Author ad Herenium
129.122	poemata Pithacorum
129.123	Rethorica Valerii
129.124	Epithata Ciceronis
129.125	Gemma Platonis
129.126	Finistella

129.127   Progimnasmata Verropeia
129.128   Galenus de elementis
129.129   Aphorismi Hypocratis
129.130:1-2   ii paper bookes

§

129.1 Ruellius de natura stirpium

Joannes Ruellius. *De natura stirpium*. Continent: 1536–1543.
Language(s): Latin. Appraised at 5s in 1577.

129.2 tria volumina Galleni

Galen. Unidentified. Continent (probable): date indeterminable.
Probably not STC books. Perhaps three assorted volumes, perhaps three
volumes of a set. At 30*s* almost certainly folio editions and, therefore, not
STC. Entry replaces *iii volumes of Gall*, struck out. *Language(s)*: Latin (probable). Appraised at 30s in 1577.

129.3 Tabulae Wickeri in 2bus

Hanss Jacob Wecker. Unidentified. Continent: date indeterminable.
His *Medicinae utriusque syntaxes* is in table form, but not in two volumes. A
good deal of Wecker's *Antidotarium speciale* is also in tables. Perhaps the *Medicinae utriusque syntaxes*, bound in two volumes, is represented here. The valuation would suggest a folio item, and the *Antidotarium speciale* appeared only
in quarto by the date of this inventory, making a combination of the two titles
unlikely here. See 129.8. *Language(s)*: Latin. Appraised at 8s in 1577.

129.4 Silvius de febribus

Jacques Dubois (Jacobus Sylvius). *De febribus commentarius ex libris aliquot
Hippocratis et Galeni*. Continent: 1554–1561.
A cross is in the margin. *Language(s)*: Latin. Appraised at 3s 4d in 1577.

129.5 harbarium Turneri

William Turner. *A new herball, wherin are conteyned the names of herbes*.
Britain or Continent: 1551–1568.
STC 24365 *et seq*. Entry replaces *Turnerus herball*, struck out. *Language(s)*:
English Greek Latin. Appraised at 4s in 1577.

129.6 matthes bi herbarium

Probably Pietro Andrea Mattioli. *Compendium de plantis*. Continent: date
indeterminable.
The manuscript entry is taken to be a general, descriptive phrase, not unlike the manuscript entry at 129.9. Entry replaces *mattheoli herball*, struck out.
Language(s): Latin. Appraised at 6s 8d in 1577.

129.7 hermoniae genationum
Unidentified. Place unknown: stationer unknown, date indeterminable. STC/non-STC status unknown. *Language(s)*: Latin. Appraised at 3s in 1577.

129.8 Anthidotarium Wickeri
Hanss Jacob Wecker. Unidentified. Continent: date indeterminable.
Whether the *Antidotarium speciale* or the *Antidotarium generale* cannot be determined. See 129.3. *Language(s)*: Latin. Appraised at 4s in 1577.

129.9 Harbarium Paene
Petrus Peña and Matthias de L'Obel. *Stirpium adversaria nova, perfacilis vestigatio*. Britain or Continent: 1570–1576.
STC 19595 *et seq.* The 1576 Antwerp edition is listed in the STC along with the first edition published in London. An edition was issued in 1576 as part two of L'Obel's *Plantarum seu stirpium historia*. *Language(s)*: Latin. Appraised at 3s 4d in 1577.

129.10 Hesius
Probably Helius Eobanus, *Hessus*. [*De tuenda bona valetudine*]. Continent: 1524–1571.
Language(s): Latin. Appraised at 2s 6d in 1577.

129.11 Practica Diversorum
Unidentified. Continent (probable): date indeterminable.
Probably not an STC book. If a descriptive entry, a medical anthology, perhaps the *Articella*, less likely the *Epistolae medicinales diversorum authorum*. *Language(s)*: Latin. Appraised at 4s in 1577.

129.12 Commentarium Trusiani
Turisanus de Turisanis. [*Galen–Ars medica: commentary and text*]. Continent: date indeterminable.
Language(s): Latin. Appraised at 8d in 1577.

129.13 Randoletus
Guillaume Rondelet. Unidentified. Continent: date indeterminable.
His *Methodus curandorum omnium morborum* is Rondelet's most frequently published work, but three shillings is a high valuation for any of the editions, all small. His *Libri de piscibus marinis* appeared in folio, two volumes in one, apparently in only one edition (1554, 1555). *Language(s)*: Latin. Appraised at 3s in 1577.

129.14 Ysorates grece et latine
Isocrates. Probably [*Works*]. Continent: date indeterminable.
Language(s): Greek Latin. Appraised at 3s 6d in 1577.

129.15 Harbarium Crucii
Unidentified. Continent (probable): date indeterminable.
Probably not an STC book. Perhaps a mishearing of "Clucii" for Clusius (Charles de L'Écluse) whose *Rariorum aliquot stirpium* was published in 1576. L'Écluse also edited other books that the compiler might have referred to as an herbal. *Language(s)*: Latin. Appraised at 16d in 1577.

129.16 dixionarium caddic
Unidentified. Continent (probable): date indeterminable.
Probably not an STC book. Perhaps *caddic* is a mishearing of *medic*[um], an appropriate item for this library. *Language(s)*: Latin. Appraised at 2s in 1577.

129.17 Columbus
Realdus Columbus. Probably *De re anatomica*. Continent: 1559–1572. *Language(s)*: Latin. Appraised at 18d in 1577.

129.18 Gorgonius de regimine sanitatis
Bernardus de Gordonio. *Tractatus de conservatione vitae humanae*. Leipzig: imprimebat Joannes Rhamba, curante Ernesto Vogelin, 1570.
Contains only *De regimine sanitatis*; the item could, however, be the fourth part of Gordonio's *Practica* that separated from the volume. *Language(s)*: Latin. Appraised at 6d in 1577.

129.19 Brassavalus
Antonio Musa Brasavola. Unidentified. Continent: date indeterminable. *Language(s)*: Latin. Appraised at 20d in 1577.

129.20 Lacuna
Andres de Laguna. Unidentified. Continent: date indeterminable. *Language(s)*: Latin. Appraised at 12d in 1577.

129.21 Fucshius de composicione medicamentorum
Leonard Fuchs. *De componendorum medicamentorum ratione*. Continent: 1555–1563.
Language(s): Latin. Appraised at 14d in 1577.

129.22 Historia Plantarum
Perhaps Antoine Du Pinet. *Historia plantarum*. Lyon: (different houses), 1561–1567.
See 129.53. *Language(s)*: Latin. Appraised at 10d in 1577.

129.23 Botarius
Perhaps Leonardo Botallo. Unidentified. Continent (probable): date indeterminable.

Probably not an STC book. Again, a possible mishearing. Giovanni Botero's works, except for a rare and slight poem, were all published after the date of this inventory. See 129.49. *Language(s)*: Latin (probable). Appraised at 12d in 1577.

129.24 Fernelii libri 7
Joannes Fernelius. *Therapeutices universalis seu medendi rationis libri septem.* Lyon: 1569–1574.
Language(s): Latin. Appraised at 16d in 1577.

129.25 Harbarium Donaii in 2
Probably Rembert Dodoens. Unidentified. Continent (probable): date indeterminable.
Probably not an STC book. Almost certainly something of Dodoens, but identification is not made easier by the appearance of two possibilities at 129.34 and 129.57. See also 129.109. *Language(s)*: Latin (probable). Appraised at 2s 6d in 1577.

129.26 Cornarius in Hypocraten in 2 voluminibus
Hippocrates. [*Works*]. Edited by Janus Cornarius. Continent: 1546–1575.
At the beginning of the edition, there is a poem by Cornarius in praise of Hippocrates that may account for the form of the manuscript entry. An appraisal of 2*s* is struck out. *Language(s)*: Latin (probable). Appraised at 4s in 1577.

129.27 Manardus
Joannes Manardus. Probably [*Epistolae medicinales*]. Continent: date indeterminable.
Language(s): Latin Greek (perhaps). Appraised at 6d in 1577.

129.28 Ferrerius
Unidentified. Continent: date indeterminable.
Omnibonus Ferrarius, Joannes Ferrarius, *Montanus*, and Joannes Matthaeus Ferrarius, *de Gradi* are among the possibilities. *Language(s)*: Latin. Appraised at 6d in 1577.

129.29 Vicinius
Marsilio Ficino. Unidentified. Continent: date indeterminable.
Likely a medical work. *Language(s)*: Latin. Appraised at 10d in 1577.

129.30 matthias corrnaci
Matthias Cornax. Perhaps *Medicae consultationis apud aegrotos enchiridion.* Basle: per Joannem Oporinum, 1564.
His most widely distributed work. *Language(s)*: Latin. Appraised at 8d in 1577.

129.31　foesii pharmacopeia
Anutius Foesius. *Pharmacopoeia*. Basle: apud Thomam Guermum, 1561. *Language(s)*: Latin. Appraised at 18d in 1577.

129.32　Fontanonus
Denys Fontanon. *De morborum internorum curatione*. Continent: 1549–1574.
His only work. *Language(s)*: Latin. Appraised at 14d in 1577.

129.33　Ysacus Judeus
Isaac Ben Solomon Israeli (Isaac Judaeus). Unidentified. Continent: date indeterminable.
The 1570 octavo edition of his *De diaetis universalibus et particularibus* more likely than the incunable quarto or the early sixteenth-century folio edition of his *Omnia opera*, but the others cannot be discounted. *Language(s)*: Latin. Appraised at 16d in 1577.

129.34　Harbarium Dodonaii vetus
Rembert Dodoens. *Florum et coronaria odoratarumque nonnullarum herbarum historia*. Antwerp: ex officina C. Plantini, 1568–1569.
See also 129.25, 129.57, 129.109. *Language(s)*: Latin. Appraised at 12d in 1577.

129.35　Instituciones Fucscii
Leonard Fuchs. *Institutiones medicinae*. Continent: 1555–1572.
An appraisal of 15*d* is struck out. *Language(s)*: Latin. Appraised at 12d in 1577.

129.36　Varie Lectiones Mercurionis
Hieronymus Mercurialis. *Variarum lectionum libri*. Continent: 1570–1576. *Language(s)*: Latin. Appraised at 12d in 1577.

129.37　Pharnelius in 2bus voluminibus
Joannes Fernelius. Unidentified. Continent: date indeterminable.
Both his *Medicina* and his *Universa medicina* were issued in two volumes, and in folio, which size the valuation would suggest. *Language(s)*: Latin. Appraised at 2s 4d in 1577.

129.38　Gwinterius de pestilentia
Joannes Guinterius (Andernacus). *De pestilentia commentarius*. Strassburg: apud Christianum Mylium, 1565.
Language(s): Latin. Appraised at 6d in 1577.

129.39　Ferandus
Probably Jean Ferrand, *the Elder*. *De nephrisis et lithiasis definitione et*

curatione. Paris: (different houses), 1570.
Language(s): Latin. Appraised at 4d in 1577.

129.40 Cagitanus de pulsibus
Unidentified. Continent (probable): date indeterminable.
Probably not an STC book. *Language(s)*: Latin. Appraised at 12d in 1577.

129.41 Galenus grece de facultatibus
Galen. *De alimentorum facultatibus.* Paris: Gulielmus Morelius, 1557.
The *De naturalibus facultatibus* is also possible, but the sole Greek edition is in folio, not as likely to be assigned a 4*d* valuation as the octavo Greek edition of *De alimentorum facultatibus. Language(s)*: Greek. Appraised at 4d in 1577.

129.42 Leonardus Joachinus
Lionardo Giachini. Unidentified. Continent: date indeterminable.
Language(s): Latin. Appraised at 12d in 1577.

129.43 liber theoricarum mediocine
Probably Walter Hermann Ryff. *Medicinae theoricae et practicae breve enchiridion.* Strassburg: ex officina Knoblochiana, per Georgium Messerschmid, 1542.
Other works with similar titles include those by Damianus and by Jacobus Curio. *Language(s)*: Latin. Appraised at 12d in 1577.

129.44 Problemata Jani Matthei
Janus Matthaeus Durastantes. *Problemata.* Venice: ex officina Jordani Ziletti, 1567.
Language(s): Latin. Appraised at 6d in 1577.

129.45 Brudus Delucitanus de ratione victus
Brudus, *Lusitanus. Liber de ratione victus in singulis febribus secundum Hippocratem.* Venice: (different houses), 1544–1559.
Language(s): Latin. Appraised at 10d in 1577.

129.46 Practica Fuccii
Leonard Fuchs. *A worthy practise of the moste learned phisition L. Fuchsius, necessary in this tyme of our visitation.* London: R. Hall for M. Lobley, 1563.
STC 11408. Evidence of the compiler's entering an English book in Latin. See BCI 2:361 (Hatcher 103). An appraisal of 11*d* is struck out. *Language(s)*: English. Appraised at 6d in 1577.

129.47 Problemata Aloicii Trissini
Aloysius Trissinus. *Problematum medicinalium ex Galeni sententia libri sex.* Basle: per Jacobum Parcum, 1547.
Language(s): Latin. Appraised at 11d in 1577.

129.48 Montanus
Probably Joannes Baptista Montanus. Unidentified. Continent: date indeterminable.
Language(s): Latin. Appraised at 2s 6d in 1577.

129.49 Botallius
Probably Leonardo Botallo. Unidentified. Continent: date indeterminable.
See 129.23. *Language(s)*: Latin. Appraised at 10d in 1577.

129.50 Practica Rulandi
Martin Ruland, *the Elder*. *Medicina practica*. Strassburg: excud. Josias Rihelius, 1564–1567.
Language(s): Latin. Appraised at 8d in 1577.

129.51 Enchiridion Chyrurgic
Perhaps Antonius Chalmeteus. *Enchiridion chirurgicum*. Continent: 1560–1570.
Conceivably a descriptive entry rather than a title. *Language(s)*: Latin. Appraised at 10d in 1577.

129.52 Galenus de hossibus
Galen. *De ossibus ad tyrones*. Translated by Ferdinandus Balamius. Continent: 1535–1555.
Language(s): Latin. Appraised at 6d in 1577.

129.53 Historia Plantarum
Perhaps Antoine Du Pinet. *Historia plantarum*. Lyon: (different houses), 1561–1567.
Like 129.22, this title is closest to the manuscript entry, but if this and the earlier item are only generally described, other works are possible, particularly those by Theophrastus, Ruellius, and Dodoens. *Language(s)*: Latin. Appraised at 7d in 1577.

129.54 Practica Cuffeneri
Perhaps Leonellus de Victoriis (*Faventinus*). *Practica medicinalis*. Edited by Johann Kuefner. Continent: date indeterminable.
Language(s): Latin. Appraised at 10d in 1577.

129.55 Cornelius Selsus
Aulus Cornelius Celsus. Probably [*De re medica*]. Continent: date indeterminable.
Language(s): Latin. Appraised at 10d in 1577.

129.56 Methodus Medendi Monsii
Pamphilius Montius. *Methodus medendi*. Continent: 1540–1545.

The 1545 edition contains other works. An appraisal of 8*d* is struck out. *Language(s)*: Latin. Appraised at 4d in 1577.

129.57 Historia Frugum Dodonei
Rembert Dodoens. *De frugum historia liber unus. Epistolae duae*. Antwerp: ex officina J. Loëi, 1552.
See also 129.25, 129.34, and 129.109. *Language(s)*: Latin. Appraised at 4d in 1577.

129.58 Jacobus Ruffe
Jacob Rueff. Probably *De conceptu et generatione hominis*. Translated by Wolfgang Haller. Zürich: Christophorus Froschouerus excud., 1554.
His most popular work, but it had appeared in only one Latin edition by the date of this inventory. *Language(s)*: Latin. Appraised at 6d in 1577.

129.59 Jacobus Silvius
Jacques Dubois (Jacobus Sylvius). Unidentified. Continent: date indeterminable.
Language(s): Latin. Appraised at 4d in 1577.

129.60 The Myrror of Magistrates
Probably William Baldwin and others. *A myrroure for magistrates*. London: Thomas Marsh, 1559–1575.
STC 1247 *et seq.* The less well-known continuation by John Higgins, *Poet* that first appeared in 1574 (STC 13443 *et seq.*) is possible as well, but much less likely. *Language(s)*: English. Appraised at 14d in 1577.

129.61 hoffemianii hermaticus
Unidentified. Continent (probable): date indeterminable.
Probably not an STC book. An unusually legible manuscript entry that cannot be associated with any Hoffman or with any work on hermetics. *Language(s)*: Latin (probable). Appraised at 6d in 1577.

129.62 Boetius de disciplina
Anicius M.T.S. Boethius. *De disciplina scholarium*. Continent: date indeterminable.
Language(s): Latin. Appraised at 2d in 1577.

129.63 Gemiphrisius
Reiner Gemma, *Frisius*. Unidentified. Continent: date indeterminable.
Probably the *Arithmeticae practicae methodus facilis* or else an astronomical work. *Language(s)*: Latin. Appraised at 10d in 1577.

129.64 Questiones Simonis Simonii
Simon Simonius. *Questionum dialectarum fragmentum*. Basle: per Petrum Pernam, 1573.

Language(s): Latin. Appraised at 2d in 1577.

129.65 Cladius Dariotus
Claude Dariot. *Ad astrorum judicia facilis introductio* [and other works]. Lyon: apud Mauricium Roy, et Ludovicum Pesnot, 1557.

Nothing else of his appears to have been printed in Latin by the date of this inventory. There is no evidence that Simpson read French. *Language(s)*: Latin. Appraised at 8d in 1577.

129.66 Grammatica Antesignani
Nicolaus Clenardus. [*Institutiones linguae graecae*]. Edited by Petrus Antesignanus. Continent: date indeterminable.

Antesignanus's exercises appeared separately in 1572, but at this valuation, the complete edition of Clenard is doubtless represented here. *Language(s)*: Greek Latin. Appraised at 3s in 1577.

129.67 opera Haddoni
Walter Haddon. *Lucubrationes passim collectae, et editae*. Edited by Thomas Hatcher. London: apud G. Seresium, 1567.

STC 12596. *Language(s)*: Latin. Appraised at 12d in 1577.

129.68 Dificiles Questiones Fuccii
Leonard Fuchs. *Libri IIII, difficilium aliquot quaestionum, et hodie passim controversarum explicationes continentes*. Basle: in officina Roberti Winter, 1540.

An enlarged version of Fuchs's *Apologiae tres*, NLM6 no. 1710; Stübler no. 15. *Language(s)*: Latin. Appraised at 8d in 1577.

129.69 Logica Valerii
Cornelius Valerius. *Tabulae totius dialectices*. Continent: 1548–1575. *Language(s)*: Latin. Appraised at 4d in 1577.

129.70 Opothegmata, Licostenes
Conrad Lycosthenes (Conrad Wolffhart). *Apophthegmata*. Continent: date indeterminable.

Language(s): Latin. Appraised at 2s 6d in 1577.

129.71 Velcurio
Joannes Velcurio. Perhaps [*Aristotle–Physica: commentary*]. Continent: 1540–1575.

Language(s): Latin. Appraised at 12d in 1577.

129.72 epistole Erasmi
Desiderius Erasmus. [*Epistolae*]. Continent: date indeterminable. *Language(s)*: Latin. Appraised at 4d in 1577.

129.73 Aulecus Clarkii
Baldassare Castiglione, *Count. De curiali sive aulico libri quatuor ex Italico sermone in Latinum conversi.* Translated by Bartholomew Clerke. London: (different houses), 1571–1577.
STC 4782 *et seq. Language(s)*: Latin. Appraised at 14d in 1577.

129.74 Copia Verborum et Rerum
Desiderius Erasmus. *De duplici copia verborum ac rerum.* Britain or Continent: date indeterminable.
STC 10471.4 *et seq.* and non-STC. *Language(s)*: Latin. Appraised at 6d in 1577.

129.75 epistole Cecli Secundi
Caelius Secundus Curio. *Selectarum epistolarum libri duo. Orationum liber unus.* Basle: per Joannem Oporinum, 1553.
Language(s): Latin. Appraised at 6d in 1577.

129.76 Philosophia Titilmanni
Franz Titelmann. [*Aristotle–Selected works–Philosophia naturalis: commentary*]. Continent: date indeterminable.
Language(s): Latin. Appraised at 4d in 1577.

129.77 Anthonius Scorus
Antonius Schorus. Unidentified. Continent: date indeterminable.
Language(s): Latin Greek (perhaps). Appraised at 8d in 1577.

129.78 Asconius Perianus
Asconius Pedianus, Quintus. [*Cicero–Selected works–Orations: commentary*]. Continent: date indeterminable.
Language(s): Latin. Appraised at 10d in 1577.

129.79 Flores Therentii
Publius Terentius, *Afer.* [*Selections*]. Britain or Continent: date indeterminable.
STC 23899 *et seq.* and non-STC. Several of the editions published in England were diglot. *Language(s)*: Latin English (perhaps). Appraised at 6d in 1577.

129.80 lexicon graecum
Unidentified [dictionary]. Continent: date indeterminable.
Language(s): Greek Latin. Appraised at 9d in 1577.

129.81 Anthonius Misaldus
Antoine Mizauld. Unidentified. Continent: date indeterminable.
Language(s): Latin. Appraised at 10d in 1577.

129.82   Forliviensis super Avicenna
Jacobus, *Forliviensis*. [*Avicenna–Canon medicinae–Book I: commentary and text*]. Continent: date indeterminable.
Language(s): Latin. Appraised at 2s in 1577.

129.83   Laurentius Valla
Laurentius Valla. Unidentified. Continent: date indeterminable.
Language(s): Latin. Appraised at 6d in 1577.

129.84   Calepinus
Ambrogio Calepino. *Dictionarium*. Continent: date indeterminable.
May include one or more vernacular languages and Hebrew. *Language(s)*: Greek Latin. Appraised at 12d in 1577.

129.85   Avicenna
Avicenna. Unidentified. Continent: date indeterminable.
An appraisal of 16*d* is struck out. *Language(s)*: Latin. Appraised at 12d in 1577.

129.86   Rodulphi Dialectica
Probably Caspar Rhodolphus. [*Dialectica*]. Continent: date indeterminable.
Rodolphus Agricola's *De inventione dialectica* is a possibility. *Language(s)*: Latin. Appraised at 6d in 1577.

129.87   epistole familiares Ciceronis
Marcus Tullius Cicero. *Epistolae ad familiares*. Britain or Continent: date indeterminable.
STC 5295 *et seq.* and non-STC. *Language(s)*: Latin. Appraised at 14d in 1577.

129.88   Phrasii Minutii
Aldo Manuzio, *the Younger. Purae, elegantes et copiosae latinae linguae phrases.* Britain or Continent: date indeterminable.
STC 17278.8 and non-STC. The 1573 London edition was in English also. *Language(s)*: Latin English (perhaps). Appraised at 4d in 1577.

129.89   Ethica Aristotelis
Aristotle. *Ethica*. Britain or Continent: date indeterminable.
STC 752 and non-STC. *Language(s)*: Latin. Appraised at 10d in 1577.

129.90   Wildenbargius
Hieronymus Wildenbergius. Unidentified. Continent: date indeterminable.
Very likely a commentary on an Aristotelian work. *Language(s)*: Latin. Appraised at 10d in 1577.

129.91 Corderius
Mathurin Cordier. Unidentified. Continent: date indeterminable.
Probably either *De corrupti sermonis emendatione* or the more elementary handbook of correct diction, *Colloquiorum scholasticorum libri quatuor*. *Language(s)*: Latin. Appraised at 4d in 1577.

129.92 naturalis philosophia Aristotelis in 2bus voluminibus
Aristotle. [*Selected works–Philosophia naturalis*]. Continent: date indeterminable.
Language(s): Latin. Appraised at 2s in 1577.

129.93 Topica Aristotelis
Aristotle. *Topica*. Continent: date indeterminable.
Language(s): Latin. Appraised at 2d in 1577.

129.94 Hompharius
Unidentified. Place unknown: stationer unknown, date indeterminable.
STC/non-STC status unknown. A rhetorical or grammatical work by either Jacobus Omphalius or Laurence Humphrey would fit in this section. *Language(s)*: Latin (probable). Appraised at 6d in 1577.

129.95 Horatius
Quintus Horatius Flaccus. Probably [*Works*]. Britain or Continent: date indeterminable.
STC 13784 and non-STC. *Language(s)*: Latin. Appraised at 4d in 1577.

129.96 Sadoletus
Jacobus Sadoletus. Unidentified. Continent: date indeterminable.
Language(s): Latin. Appraised at 4d in 1577.

129.97 Sententie Ciceronis
Marcus Tullius Cicero. [*Selections*]. Britain or Continent: date indeterminable.
STC 5318.3 and non-STC. *Language(s)*: Latin. Appraised at 3d in 1577.

129.98 epistole Gunelli
Unidentified. Continent (probable): date indeterminable.
Almost certainly not an STC book. Perhaps a mishearing of Pierre Bunel (Petrus Bunellus), whose *Epistolae* went through two editions before the date of this inventory. *Language(s)*: Latin (perhaps). Appraised at 4d in 1577.

129.99 Poselius
Joannes Posselius. Probably *Syntaxis linguae graecae*. Continent: date indeterminable.

His commentary on the liturgical Gospels and Epistles is much less likely. *Language(s)*: Greek Latin. Appraised at 4d in 1577.

129.100   Siprianus Lovicius
Cyprianus von Leowitz. Unidentified. Place unknown: stationer unknown, date indeterminable.
STC/non-STC status unknown. *Language(s)*: Latin. Appraised at 4d in 1577.

129.101   Jacobus Silvius de morbis internis
Jacques Dubois (Jacobus Sylvius). *Morborum internorum prope omnium curatio*. Continent: 1545–1554.
Magister is struck from the entry. *Language(s)*: Latin. Appraised at 6d in 1577.

129.102   Susius de emissione sanguinis
Joannes Baptista Susius, *Mirandulanus*. *Liber de sanguinis mittendi ratione*. Basle: apud Petrum Pernam, 1558–1559.
Language(s): Latin. Appraised at 3d in 1577.

129.103   Lucianus grece
Lucian, *of Samosata*. Unidentified. Continent: date indeterminable.
What arrangement of the dialogues (whether collected or selected) cannot be determined, but at this valuation, the larger collection is not as likely. *Language(s)*: Greek. Appraised at 3d in 1577.

129.104   Baccanellus
Giovanni Battista Baccanelli. Unidentified. Continent: date indeterminable.
Either his *De consensu medicorum in cognoscendis simplicibus liber* or his *De consensu medicorum in curandis morbis* or a composite publication of both, all of which were published by the date of this inventory. *Language(s)*: Latin. Appraised at 12d in 1577.

129.105   Sigonius de vita Scipionis
Carlo Sigonio. *De vita, et rebus gestis P. Scipionis Aemiliani liber*. Bologna: apud Joannem Rossium, 1569.
Language(s): Latin. Appraised at 4d in 1577.

129.106   Nobilis Socius de purgibus
Nobile Socio. *De temporibus et modis purgandi in morbis*. Continent: 1550–1577.
Language(s): Latin. Appraised at 8d in 1577.

129.107 Problemata Aristotelis
Aristotle (spurious). *Problemata.* Continent: date indeterminable.
Language(s): Latin. Appraised at 6d in 1577.

129.108 Carmina Proverbialia
S.A.I. *Carminum proverbialium, ... loci communes, ... selecti.* London: C. Barker, 1577.
STC 14059. Attributed to Hermannus Gembergius. *Language(s)*: Latin. Appraised at 4d in 1577.

129.109 Dodoneus de frumentis
Rembert Dodoens. *De frugum historia liber unus. Epistolae duae.* Antwerp: ex officina J. Loëi, 1552.
See also 129.25, 129.34, and 129.57. *Language(s)*: Latin. Appraised at 4d in 1577.

129.110 Aphorismi Hipocratis grece
Hippocrates. *Aphorismi.* Continent: date indeterminable.
Another copy, in Latin, at 129.129. *Language(s)*: Greek. Appraised at 4d in 1577.

129.111 opera Ciceronis in tribus voluminibus
Marcus Tullius Cicero. [*Works*]. Continent: date indeterminable.
Perhaps a three-volume set or three volumes of a larger set. *Language(s)*: Latin. Appraised at 5s in 1577.

129.112 Thomas Aquinus in Politica
Thomas Aquinas, *Saint.* [*Aristotle–Politica: commentary*]. Continent: date indeterminable.
Completed by Petrus de Alvernia. *Language(s)*: Latin. Appraised at 12d in 1577.

129.113 Quintilianus
Marcus Fabius Quintilianus. Unidentified. Continent: date indeterminable.
Could be the *Declamationes, Institutiones oratoriae,* or the *Works. Language(s)*: Latin. Appraised at 6d in 1577.

129.114 Hulkius
Unidentified. Place unknown: stationer unknown, date indeterminable.
STC/non-STC status unknown. *Language(s)*: Unknown. Appraised at 8d in 1577.

129.115 Conclusiones Fabri
Unidentified. Continent (probable): date indeterminable.

Probably not an STC book. Jacobus Faber, *Stapulensis*; Joannes Fabri, *Jurist*; and Joannes Fabri, *Bishop of Vienna* are all possibilities for the *Fabri* in the manuscript entry, but none can be associated with *Conclusiones*. *Language(s)*: Latin. Appraised at 4d in 1577.

129.116   Brigot
Thomas Bricot. [*Aristotle–Unidentified: commentary*]. Continent: date indeterminable.
One of his works on Aristotelian logic or his commentary on natural philosophy. *Language(s)*: Latin. Appraised at 4d in 1577.

129.117   Faber
Unidentified. Continent (probable): date indeterminable.
Probably not an STC book. See some possible *Faber*s at 129.115. *Language(s)*: Latin. Appraised at 4d in 1577.

129.118   Erasmus de conscribendis epistolis
Desiderius Erasmus. *De conscribendis epistolis*. Britain or Continent: date indeterminable.
STC 10496. *Language(s)*: Latin. Appraised at 4d in 1577.

129.119   Justinus
Trogus Pompeius and Justinus, *the Historian*. [*Epitomae in Trogi Pompeii historias*]. Britain or Continent: date indeterminable.
STC 24287 *et seq.* and non-STC. *Language(s)*: Latin. Appraised at 6d in 1577.

129.120   Lippus Brandolinus
Aurelius Brandolinus (Lippus). Perhaps *De ratione scribendi*. Britain or Continent: 1549–1573.
STC 3542 and non-STC. His *De humanae vitae conditione* is, given the context, less likely. *Language(s)*: Latin. Appraised at 6d in 1577.

129.121   Author ad Herenium
Marcus Tullius Cicero (spurious). *Rhetorica ad Herennium*. Britain or Continent: date indeterminable.
STC 5323.5 and non-STC. An appraisal of 5d is struck out. *Language(s)*: Latin. Appraised at 4d in 1577.

129.122   poemata Pithacorum
Pythagoras. [*Carmina aurea*]. Continent: date indeterminable.
Language(s): Latin Greek (perhaps). Appraised at 2d in 1577.

129.123   Rethorica Valerii
Cornelius Valerius. *In universam bene dicendi rationem tabula*. Continent:

1540–1577.
Language(s): Latin. Appraised at 4d in 1577.

129.124 Epithata Ciceronis
Pedro Juan Nuñez. *Epitheta M.T. Ciceronis*. Continent: 1570–1571.
Language(s): Latin. Appraised at 2d in 1577.

129.125 Gemma Platonis
Plato. *Gemmae, sive illustriores sententiae*. Compiled by Niccolò Liburnio.
Paris: apud Benedictum Prevost, 1556–1557.
Language(s): Latin. Appraised at 2d in 1577.

129.126 Finistella
Andreas Dominicus Floccus (Lucius Fenestella). *De magistratibus sacerdotiisque Romanorum*. Continent: date indeterminable.
Language(s): Latin. Appraised at 3d in 1577.

129.127 Progimnasmata Verropeia
Simon Verepaeus. Unidentified. Continent: date indeterminable.
Language(s): Latin. Appraised at 2d in 1577.

129.128 Galenus de elementis
Galen. *De elementis secundum Hippocratem*. Continent: 1548–1558.
The date range reflects solo editions. The work leads in several editions of
selected works. *Language(s)*: Latin. Appraised at 3d in 1577.

129.129 Aphorismi Hypocratis
Hippocrates. *Aphorismi*. Continent: date indeterminable.
Another copy, in Greek, at 129.110. *Language(s)*: Latin. Appraised at 6d in
1577.

129.130:1–2 ii paper bookes
Unidentified. Provenances unknown: dates indeterminable.
Manuscripts. An appraisal of 6d is struck out. *Language(s)*: Unknown. Appraised as a pair at 4d in 1577.

Robert Singleton. Scholar (M.A.): Probate Inventory. 1577

DALE B. BILLINGSLEY

Robert Singleton (Syngleton, Shingleton) matriculated at Oxford in 1565, took his Bachelor of Arts degree on 1 December 1569, and supplicated for his Master of Arts degree in 1574 (*Alumni Oxonienses*, 4:1359). According to Wood (1674, 2:312), he was born December 1547 in Leicestershire. A fellow of St. John's College, he died there 29 July 1577 and was buried in the college chapel. A monumental brass, mentioned by Wood (1674, 2:312), survives to this day on the wall of the cross-passage of the Baylie chapel, showing Singleton kneeling in gown and hood, with two inscription plates, one of which gives his age at the time of his death as twenty-eight (suggesting a year of birth as 1548 instead of 1547) and his name as "Shingleton." His short career as a fellow was apparently undistinguished, for the usual biographical sources record nothing of his life or activities. Singleton is not to be confused with his namesake, chaplain to Anne Boleyn, hanged in 1544 at Tyburn for his treasonable writings, or with two other earlier Robert Singletons recorded by Emden (BRUO2, 516–17).

Singleton's library, almost all of it in Latin with a few English titles interspersed, is not distinguished by any disciplinary concentration, although works of rhetoric, politics, history, and ethics frequently appear, as well as many theological works and studies of Scripture. His collection includes several works that mark him as inclined toward (or at any rate interested in) Calvinist and evangelical studies.

Oxford University Archives, Bodleian Library: Hyp.B.18.

§

Wood, Anthony à. 1674. *Historia et Antiquitates Universitatis Oxoniensis.* Oxford: e Theatro Sheldoniano.

§

130.1	Problemata Aristotelis cum commento
130.2	The Diall of Princes
130.3	J divi Jronima [Hieronymi] bibliorum
130.4	Foxii Martires latine
130.5	Conciliator
130.6	Epistole Jerenimi
130.7	Oratius cum commento
130.8:A	Juvenall et Pertius cum commento
130.8:B	[See 130.8:A]
130.9	Cornucopia
130.10	Opera Rodolingi
130.11	blia Jenevi
130.12	Biblia Bagnini
130.13	Cagitanus
130.14	Musculi loci communes
130.15	Concordantie Biblie
130.16	Opera Pici Miranduli
130.17	Ethica Maioris
130.18	Logica Aristotelis
130.19	Ethica Aristotelis
130.20	Commentarius in aliquas oraciones Ciceronis
130.21	Gramatica Cleonardi
130.22	Questiones Thome
130.23	Piniderus
130.24	Niphus de anima
130.25	Musculi loci communes
130.26	Calvini Harmonia
130.27	Biblia latinè
130.28	Epicteti Enchiridion
130.29	Strigelius in Novum Testamentum
130.30	Progymnasmata Sylvii
130.31	Horatius cum commento
130.32	Georgica Virgilii cum commento
130.33	Toxites in Herenium
130.34	Pomeranus in psalmos
130.35	Apopthegmata, Lycosthenes
130.36	Ethica Aristotelis
130.37	Hipperius de studio theologiae
130.38	Hipperii loci communes
130.39	Sturmius in Partitiones
130.40	Epistolae Ciceronis
130.41	Olaus Magnus
130.42	Danaeus de haeresibus

130.43   Aristotelis Politica
130.44   Homeri Odyssea
130.45   Vitruvius de architectura
130.46   Danaei Enchiridion
130.47   Polydorus Virgilius
130.48   Hemingii Postilla
130.49   Pigius de controversiis
130.50   Calvini Institutiones
130.51   Ozorius contra Haddonum
130.52   Aristoteles de ortu et interitu
130.53   Moralia Jacobi
130.54   Castigationes Ciceronis
130.55   *agneus in epistolas Pauli
130.56   Suetonius Tranquillus
130.57   Theophilactus in Evangelia
130.58   Cardanus de subtilitate
130.59   Physica Aristotelis
130.60   Sturmii tabulae in Partitiones
130.61   Commentarii Caesaris
130.62   Aneponimus de substantiis physicis
130.63   Bonaventura
130.64   Coningstini concordantiae
130.65   Rodolphi Dialectica
130.66   Artemidorus de insomniis
130.67   Enkius in Aggaeum
130.68   Aristotelis Politica
130.69   Hiperii opuscula duobus voluminibus
130.70   Conciones funebres
130.71   Institutiones Julii Epi: [Episcopi?]
130.72   Physica Aristotelis
130.73   Caelii Secundi Dialectica
130.74   Lactantius
130.75   Aphthonius
130.76   Politica Aristotelis
130.77   Constantinus Caesar de agricultura
130.78   Adagia Erasmi
130.79   Aristotelis Rhetorica
130.80   Isocrates latinè
130.81   Augustini Meditationes
130.82   Calvini epistolae
130.83   Grammatica Clenardi
130.84   The Anatomie of the Masse
130.85   Golden Epistles
130.86   Familiar Epistles
130.87   Whitegiftes Contra Admonitionem

130.88	Ackworth contra Sanderum
130.89	Bunnaei Institutiones
130.90	Senecae tragaediae
130.91	Chronica Melanchthonis
130.92	Foxii Philosophia Naturae
130.93	Longolii epistolae
130.94	Althameri Conciliationes Locorum
130.95	Augustini Confessiones
130.96	Opera Ovidii 3 voluminibus
130.97	Cornelius in psalmos
130.98	Hofmestri loci communes
130.99	Opera Ciceronis
130.100	Avenarii preces
130.101	Terentius
130.102	A service booke
130.103	Novum Testamentum graecè
130.104	Sylva Biblioc' Nominum
130.105	Nowelli catechysmus latinè
130.106	Enchiridion Militis Christiani
130.107	The Ende of the World
130.108	Flores Bibliae
130.109	Picturae Bibl'
130.110	Emblemata Alciati
130.111	Virgilius
130.112	Tragaedy of Tyrantes
130.113	Ceporini Grammatica
130.114	Philo Judeus de mundo
130.115	Ciceronis Epitheta
130.116	Erithraei Elocutio
130.117	Ausonius
130.118	Testamentum latinum
130.119:1–50	50 pamflettes

§

130.1 Problemata Aristotelis cum commento
Aristotle (spurious). *Problemata*. Continent: date indeterminable.
Language(s): Latin. Appraised at 3s 4d in 1577.

130.2 The Diall of Princes
Antonio de Guevara, *Bishop*. *The diall of princes*. Translated by Thomas North. London: (different houses), 1557–1568.
STC 12427 *et seq*. See 130.86. *Language(s)*: English. Appraised at 5s in 1577.

130.3 J divi Jronima [Hieronymi] bibliorum
The Bible. Continent (probable): date indeterminable.

Probably not an STC book, but see STC 2055. The initial *J* is taken to be a false start by the compiler, who then inserted *bibliorum* after completing the entry. Conceivably, the opening strokes represent *In*, which would make this an unidentified commentary on Jerome's Bible. But if the former, at the high valuation, the item is surely not the single edition of the Vulgate issued in England in a quarto format. *Language(s)*: Latin. Appraised at 6s in 1577.

130.4 Foxii Martires latine
John Foxe, *the Martyrologist. Rerum in ecclesia gestarum commentarii.* Continent: 1554–1564.

Shaaber F183–186. *Language(s)*: Latin. Appraised at 2s in 1577.

130.5 Conciliator
Unidentified. Continent (probable): date indeterminable.

Almost certainly not an STC book. Petrus, *de Abano's Conciliator differentiarum philosophorum* and Jacobus Peletarius's *De conciliatione locorum Galeni* are two possibilities among others. *Language(s)*: Latin. Appraised at 2s 6d in 1577.

130.6 Epistole Jerenimi
Jerome, *Saint. Epistolae.* Continent: date indeterminable.
Language(s): Latin. Appraised at 3s 4d in 1577.

130.7 Oratius cum commento
Quintus Horatius Flaccus. Probably [*Works*]. Britain or Continent: date indeterminable.

STC 13784 and non-STC. *Language(s)*: Latin. Appraised at 12d in 1577.

130.8:A Juvenall et Pertius cum commento
Decimus Junius Juvenalis. [*Works*]. Continent: date indeterminable (composite publication).
Language(s): Latin. Appraised [a composite volume] at 3s 4d in 1577.

130.8:B [See 130.8:A]
Aulus Persius Flaccus. [*Works*]. [Composite publication]
Language(s): Latin. Appraised [a composite volume] at 3s 4d in 1577.

130.9 Cornucopia
Probably Nicolaus Perottus. *Cornucopia.* Continent: date indeterminable.

Probably the popular reference (BCI lists twenty-three copies) rather than rarer works of this title by Joannes Ravisius (Textor) or Eustathius, *of Thessalonica. Language(s)*: Latin. Appraised at 20d in 1577.

130.10 Opera Rodolingi
Unidentified. Continent (probable): date indeterminable.
Probably not an STC book. Perhaps a radical mistranscription of "Rhodoginus" or "Rodolphi" (see 130.65). *Language(s)*: Latin (probable). Appraised at 2s in 1577.

130.11 blia Jenevi
The Bible. Britain or Continent: 1560–1577.
STC 2093 *et seq.* A Geneva edition. *Language(s)*: English. Appraised at 10s in 1577.

130.12 Biblia Bagnini
The Bible. Continent: date indeterminable.
The genitive is probably a mistranscription of Sanctes Pagninus, the translator. See 130.11. *Language(s)*: Latin. Appraised at 4s in 1577.

130.13 Cagitanus
Perhaps Thomas de Vio Cajetan, *Cardinal.* Unidentified. Continent: date indeterminable.
Possibly one or several of the works of the prolific Spanish commentator on Aristotle, the *Bible,* and Thomas Aquinas. *Language(s)*: Latin. Appraised at 6d in 1577.

130.14 Musculi loci communes
Wolfgang Musculus. *Loci communes.* Continent: 1560–1573.
The *Loci communes* of the less well known Andreas Musculus is a possibility. Another copy of Andreas's work at 130.25. *Language(s)*: Latin. Appraised at 4s in 1577.

130.15 Concordantie Biblie
Unidentified [Biblical concordance]. Continent: date indeterminable.
Language(s): Latin. Appraised at 2s in 1577.

130.16 Opera Pici Miranduli
Giovanni Pico della Mirandola, *Count.* [*Works*]. Continent: date indeterminable.
Language(s): Latin. Appraised at 3s 4d in 1577.

130.17 Ethica Maioris
Joannes Major. *Ethica Aristotelis peripateticorum principis cum Joannis Majoris commentariis.* Translated (Aristotle's text) by Joannes Argyropoulos. Paris: Vaenundantor cujus impressa sunt Jodoco Badio et in societatem accepto Joannes Parvo, 1530.
Language(s): Latin. Appraised at 8d in 1577.

130.18 Logica Aristotelis
Aristotle. [*Selected works–Logica*]. Continent: date indeterminable.
Language(s): Latin. Appraised at 2d in 1577.

130.19 Ethica Aristotelis
Aristotle. *Ethica*. Britain or Continent: date indeterminable.
STC 752 and non-STC. *Language(s)*: Latin. Appraised at 10d in 1577.

130.20 Commentarius in aliquas oraciones Ciceronis
Unidentified. [*Cicero–Selected works–Orations: commentary*]. Continent: date indeterminable.
Language(s): Latin. Appraised at 10d in 1577.

130.21 Gramatica Cleonardi
Nicolaus Clenardus. [*Institutiones linguae graecae*]. Continent: date indeterminable.
Another copy at 130.83. *Language(s)*: Greek Latin. Appraised at 3d in 1577.

130.22 Questiones Thome
Thomas Aquinas, *Saint*. [*Quaestiones*]. Continent: date indeterminable.
At the low appraisal hardly a complete *Quaestiones disputatae*; nor is a complete *Quaestiones quodlibetales* likely. Doubtless, a part or a selection of one or the other is, however, intended. *Language(s)*: Latin. Appraised at 2d in 1577.

130.23 Piniderus
Perhaps Pindar. Perhaps [*Works*]. Continent: date indeterminable.
The supposition of Pindar, whose works were printed in at least fourteen editions before 1577 (Adams P1218ff.), is the stronger for the absence of any author whose name comes close to this misspelling of the poet's. *Language(s)*: Latin (probable) Greek (perhaps). Appraised at 8d in 1577.

130.24 Niphus de anima
Augustinus Niphus. [*Aristotle–De anima: commentary*]. Continent: date indeterminable.
Language(s): Latin. Appraised at 2d in 1577.

130.25 Musculi loci communes
Wolfgang Musculus. *Loci communes*. Continent: 1560–1573.
See notes to 130.14. *Language(s)*: Latin. Appraised at 4s in 1577.

130.26 Calvini Harmonia
Jean Calvin. *Harmonia*. Geneva: (different houses), 1555–1572.
The work was published twice by Stephanus and once by Crispinianus, all

three editions in a folio format. A 1563 octavo edition is unlikely to be intended here at the valuation assigned. *Language(s)*: Latin. Appraised at 2s 6d in 1577.

130.27 Biblia latinè
The Bible. Britain or Continent: date indeterminable.
STC 2055 and non-STC. *Language(s)*: Latin. Appraised at 20d in 1577.

130.28 Epicteti Enchiridion
Epictetus. *Enchiridion*. Continent: date indeterminable.
Language(s): Latin. Appraised at 20d in 1577.

130.29 Strigelius in Novum Testamentum
Victorinus Strigelius. [*Bible–N.T.: commentary*]. Leipzig: Ernest Voegelin, 1565–c.1566.
Two editions, but bibliographic sources disagree on whether the second is 1565 or 1566. See Adams S1934–1935 and VD16 S9600–9602. *Language(s)*: Latin. Appraised at 20d in 1577.

130.30 Progymnasmata Sylvii
Franciscus Sylvius, *of Amiens. In artem oratoriam progymnasmata*. Paris: (different houses), c.1516–1522.
Language(s): Latin. Appraised at 3d in 1577.

130.31 Horatius cum commento
Quintus Horatius Flaccus. Probably [*Works*]. Britain or Continent: date indeterminable.
STC 13784 and non-STC. *Language(s)*: Latin. Appraised at 3d in 1577.

130.32 Georgica Virgilii cum commento
Publius Virgilius Maro. [*Georgics*]. Continent: date indeterminable.
Language(s): Latin. Appraised at 2d in 1577.

130.33 Toxites in Herenium
Michael Toxites. [*Cicero (spurious)–Rhetorica ad Herennium: commentary and text*]. Basle: ex officina Oporiniana, 1556–1568.
VD16 C3884, C3888, C3891. *Language(s)*: Latin. Appraised at 6d in 1577.

130.34 Pomeranus in psalmos
Johann Bugenhagen (Pomeranus). [*Psalms: commentary*]. Continent: date indeterminable.
Some editions contained the text. *Language(s)*: Latin (probable). Appraised at 4d in 1577.

130.35 Apopthegmata, Lycosthenes
Conrad Lycosthenes (Conrad Wolffhart). *Apophthegmata*. Continent: date indeterminable.
Language(s): Latin. Appraised at 16d in 1577.

130.36 Ethica Aristotelis
Aristotle. *Ethica*. Continent: date indeterminable.
STC 752 and non-STC. *Language(s)*: Latin. Appraised at 3d in 1577.

130.37 Hipperius de studio theologiae
Andreas Gerardus, *Hyperius. De theologo, sive De ratione studii theologici*. Continent: 1559–1572.
Language(s): Latin. Appraised at 12d in 1577.

130.38 Hipperii loci communes
Andreas Gerardus, *Hyperius*. [*Methodus theologiae sive loci communes*]. Basle: Joannes Oporinus, 1567–1574.
Language(s): Latin. Appraised at 14d in 1577.

130.39 Sturmius in Partitiones
Joannes Sturmius. *In partitiones oratorias Ciceronis dialogi*. Continent: date indeterminable.
See also 130.60 and 130.116. Sturm also produced a *Partitionum dialecticarum. Language(s)*: Latin. Appraised at 6d in 1577.

130.40 Epistolae Ciceronis
Marcus Tullius Cicero. [*Selected works–Epistolae*]. Continent: date indeterminable.
The popular *Epistolae ad familiares* is possible; it was published in England from 1571 (STC 5295 *et seq.*). *Language(s)*: Latin. Appraised at 2d in 1577.

130.41 Olaus Magnus
Olaus Magnus. Probably *Historia de gentibus septentrionalibus*. Continent: date indeterminable.
Language(s): Latin. Appraised at 16d in 1577.

130.42 Danaeus de haeresibus
Perhaps Augustine, *Saint. De haeresibus*. Edited by Lambert Daneau. Geneva: Eustathius Vignon, 1576.
See 130.46. Daneau's own *Elenchi haereticorum* is, of course, also a possibility. *Language(s)*: Latin. Appraised at 12d in 1577.

130.43 Aristotelis Politica
Aristotle. *Politica*. Continent: date indeterminable.

Other copies at 130.68 and 130.76. *Language(s)*: Latin (probable) Greek (perhaps). Appraised at 4d in 1577.

130.44 Homeri Odyssea
Homer. *Odyssey*. Continent: date indeterminable.
Language(s): Latin (probable) Greek (perhaps). Appraised at 4d in 1577.

130.45 Vitruvius de architectura
Marcus Vitruvius Pollio. *De architectura*. Continent: date indeterminable.
Many editions included the work of Sextus Julius Frontinus. *Language(s)*: Latin. Appraised at 8d in 1577.

130.46 Danaei Enchiridion
Augustine, *Saint. Enchiridion*. Edited by Lambert Daneau. Geneva: Eustathius Vignon, 1575.
There is a remote possibility that one of Daneau's own works would be described as a handbook, i.e., *Enchiridion*. See 130.42. *Language(s)*: Latin. Appraised at 16d in 1577.

130.47 Polydorus Virgilius
Polydorus Vergilius. Unidentified. Place unknown: stationer unknown, date indeterminable.
STC/non-STC status unknown. Several possibilities. *Language(s)*: Latin (probable) English (perhaps). Appraised at 2d in 1577.

130.48 Hemingii Postilla
Niels Hemmingsen. [*Gospels (liturgical): commentary*]. Continent: date indeterminable.
Language(s): Latin. Appraised at 14d in 1577.

130.49 Pigius de controversiis
Albertus Pighius. *Controversiarum praecipuarum in comitiis Ratisponensibus tractatarum, explicatio*. Continent: date indeterminable.
Language(s): Latin. Appraised at 6d in 1577.

130.50 Calvini Institutiones
Jean Calvin. *Institutio Christianae religionis*. Britain or Continent: date indeterminable.
STC 4414 and non-STC. See 130.89. *Language(s)*: Latin. Appraised at 2s 6d in 1577.

130.51 Ozorius contra Haddonum
Jeronimo Osorio da Fonseca, *Bishop. In Gualterum Haddonum magistrum libellorum supplicum libri tres*. Continent: 1567–1576.
Probably not an STC book, but see STC 18889. STC 18889, the English

version, was printed in Louvain. *Language(s)*: Latin (probable). Appraised at 4d in 1577.

130.52 Aristoteles de ortu et interitu

Aristotle. *De generatione et corruptione*. Translated by Joachim Perion. Continent: 1550–1577.

The entry is the form of the title of Perion's translation. *Language(s)*: Latin. Appraised at 4d in 1577.

130.53 Moralia Jacobi

Probably Jacobus Almain. *Moralia*. Paris: (different houses), 1516–1526.

But also possible is Aristotle's *Ethica (Moralia magna)* in Laurentius Valla's translation with Jacobus Faber, *Stapulensis*'s commentary, or in the translation, with commentary, by Jacobus Lodovicus Strebaeus. *Language(s)*: Latin. Appraised at 1d in 1577.

130.54 Castigationes Ciceronis

Unidentified. Continent (probable): date indeterminable.

Probably not an STC book. Possibilities include Henri Estienne's *In M.T. Ciceronis quamplurimus locos castigationes* and Petrus Victorius's *Castigationes in M. T. Ciceronis Epistolas*, as well as his *Explicationes suarum in Ciceronem castigationum*. *Language(s)*: Latin. Appraised at 12d in 1577.

130.55 *agneus in epistolas Pauli

Probably Joannes Gagneius. [*Epistles–Paul: commentary and text*]. Continent: date indeterminable.

The first letter of the blotted entry is either a "C" or a "G." *Language(s)*: Latin. Appraised at 8d in 1577.

130.56 Suetonius Tranquillus

Caius Suetonius Tranquillus. *De vita Caesarum*. Continent: date indeterminable.

The biographical *De grammaticis et rhetoribus*, available in at least twenty editions between 1473–1567, would probably be identified if intended here, but it must be considered a possibility. *Language(s)*: Latin. Appraised at 6d in 1577.

130.57 Theophilactus in Evangelia

Theophylact, *Archbishop of Achrida*. [*Gospels: commentary and text*]. Continent: date indeterminable.

Language(s): Latin. Appraised at 8d in 1577.

130.58 Cardanus de subtilitate

Girolamo Cardano. *De subtilitate*. Continent: date indeterminable.

Language(s): Latin. Appraised at 10d in 1577.

130.59 Physica Aristotelis

Aristotle. *Physica.* Continent: date indeterminable.

Another copy at 130.72. *Language(s)*: Latin Greek (perhaps). Appraised at 4d in 1577.

130.60 Sturmii tabulae in Partitiones

Probably Valentinus Erythraeus. [*Tabulae in Ciceronem et Sturmium*]. Continent: 1543–1560.

See also 130.39 and 130.116. The form of the entry suggests this work rather than Erythraeus's *Tabulae in dialectica Sturmii*, but the work on logic remains a possibility. *Language(s)*: Latin. Appraised at 3d in 1577.

130.61 Commentarii Caesaris

Caius Julius Caesar. *Commentarii.* Continent: date indeterminable.

Language(s): Latin. Appraised at 6d in 1577.

130.62 Aneponimus de substantiis physicis

Gulielmus, *de Conchis* (Aneponymus). *Dialogus de substantiis physiciis.* Strassburg: excudebat Josias Rihelius, 1567.

Language(s): Latin. Appraised at 4d in 1577.

130.63 Bonaventura

Bonaventura, *Saint.* Unidentified. Place unknown: stationer unknown, date indeterminable.

STC/non-STC status unknown. *Language(s)*: Latin (probable). Appraised at 4d in 1577.

130.64 Coningstini concordantiae

Antonius Broickwy a Konigstein. *Concordantiae breviores ex sacris Bibliorum libris.* Continent: date indeterminable.

Language(s): Latin. Appraised at 6d in 1577.

130.65 Rodolphi Dialectica

Probably Rodolphus Agricola. Probably *De inventione dialectica.* Continent: date indeterminable.

Caspar Rhodolphus's *Dialectica* is possible, as is his commentary on Agricola's work proposed here. *Language(s)*: Latin. Appraised at 3d in 1577.

130.66 Artemidorus de insomniis

Artemidorus, *Daldianus. De somniorum interpretatione.* Continent: 1518–1546.

Language(s): Latin Greek (perhaps). Appraised at 3d in 1577.

130.67 Enkius in Aggaeum
Joannes Eckius. *Super Aggaeo commentarius*. Solingen: J. Soter excudebat, 1538.
Language(s): Greek Hebrew Latin. Appraised at 3d in 1577.

130.68 Aristotelis Politica
Aristotle. *Politica*. Continent: date indeterminable.
Other copies at 130.43 and 130.76. *Language(s)*: Latin (probable) Greek (perhaps). Appraised at 4d in 1577.

130.69 Hiperii opuscula duobus voluminibus
Andreas Gerardus, *Hyperius. Opuscula theologica*. Edited by Hieronymus Vietor. Basle: ex officina Oporiniana, 1570–1571 (single edition).
Language(s): Latin. Appraised at 2s 8d in 1577.

130.70 Conciones funebres
Unidentified. Place unknown: stationer unknown, date indeterminable.
STC/non-STC status unknown. Among the possibilities are Fridericus Nausea, *Bishop, Concio funebris* (1539), and Edmund Grindal, *Archbishop, Concio funebris in obitum . . . Ferdinandi caesaris* (1564), STC 12378. See also PLRE 107.72. *Language(s)*: Latin. Appraised at 12d in 1577.

130.71 Institutiones Julii Epi: [Episcopi?]
Unidentified. Place unknown: stationer unknown, date indeterminable.
STC/non-STC status unknown. Perhaps a collection of papal bulls of Julius II or Julius III, referred to as "bishop" in the Protestant manner; see especially STC 14843 (STC 14077.147). See also, as a work that might be entered as *Institutiones*, Adams J430, *Regulae omnes, ordinationes, et Constitutiones Cancellariae Julii Papae. III. Language(s)*: Latin. Appraised at 3d in 1577.

130.72 Physica Aristotelis
Aristotle. *Physica*. Continent: date indeterminable.
Another copy at 130.59. *Language(s)*: Latin Greek (perhaps). Appraised at 10d in 1577.

130.73 Caelii Secundi Dialectica
Caelius Secundus Curio. Unidentified. Continent: date indeterminable.
Perhaps either Curio's commentary on Joachim Perion's *De dialectica libri tres*, or, given the low valuation, his epitome of Perion. *Language(s)*: Latin. Appraised at 3d in 1577.

130.74 Lactantius
Lucius Coelius Lactantius. Probably [*Works*]. Continent: date indeterminable.

One of the most popular patristic writers whose works were available in various collections and editions from 1465 on. Not likely the smaller collection of *Selected works* published with works by Lily and Erasmus in England about 1522 (STC 15118). *Language(s)*: Latin. Appraised at 12d in 1577.

130.75 Aphthonius
Aphthonius, *Sophista*. *Progymnasmata*. Britain or Continent: date indeterminable.

STC 699 *et seq*. and non-STC. *Language(s)*: Latin. Appraised at 1d in 1577.

130.76 Politica Aristotelis
Aristotle. *Politica*. Continent: date indeterminable.

Other copies at 130.43 and 130.68. *Language(s)*: Latin (probable) Greek (perhaps). Appraised at 4d in 1577.

130.77 Constantinus Caesar de agricultura
[*Geoponica*]. Continent: date indeterminable.

Compiled at the instruction of the Emperor Constantinus VII and sometimes attributed to him. *Language(s)*: Latin. Appraised at 8d in 1577.

130.78 Adagia Erasmi
Desiderius Erasmus. *Adagia*. Continent: date indeterminable.

Language(s): Latin. Appraised at 3d in 1577.

130.79 Aristotelis Rhetorica
Aristotle. *Rhetorica*. Continent: date indeterminable.

Language(s): Latin (probable) Greek (perhaps). Appraised at 8d in 1577.

130.80 Isocrates latinè
Isocrates. Unidentified. Continent: date indeterminable.

Many individual works and collections were published from as early as 1480. *Language(s)*: Latin. Appraised at 4d in 1577.

130.81 Augustini Meditationes
Augustine, *Saint* (spurious). *Meditationes*. Continent: date indeterminable.

Language(s): Latin. Appraised at 10d in 1577.

130.82 Calvini epistolae
Jean Calvin. [*Epistolae*]. Continent: date indeterminable.

Language(s): Latin. Appraised at 16d in 1577.

130.83 Grammatica Clenardi
Nicolaus Clenardus. [*Institutiones linguae graecae*]. Continent: date indeterminable.

Another copy at 130.21. *Language(s)*: Greek Latin. Appraised at 8d in 1577.

130.84 The Anatomie of the Masse
Agostino Mainardi (Anthoni de Adamo, *pseudonym*). *An anatomi, that is to say a parting in peeces of the mass*. Strassburg: Heirs of W. Köpfel, 1556. STC 17200. *Language(s)*: English. Appraised at 10d in 1577.

130.85 Golden Epistles
Sir Geoffrey Fenton. *Golden epistles*. London: H. Middleton for R. Newbery, 1575–1577.
STC 10794 *et seq*. STC notes that this is often bound with the following and considered one book. *Language(s)*: English. Appraised at 14d in 1577.

130.86 Familiar Epistles
Antonio de Guevara, *Bishop*. Probably *The familiar epistles*. Translated by Edward Hellowes. London: (different houses) for R. Newbery, 1574–1577.
STC 12432 *et seq*. See also 130.2 and 130.85, particularly the annotation to the latter. *Language(s)*: English. Appraised at 14d in 1577.

130.87 Whitegiftes Contra Admonitionem
John Whitgift, *Archbishop*. *An answer to a certen libel intituled, An admonition*. London: H. Bynneman for H. Toy, 1572–1573.
STC 25427 *et seq*. Three editions. See also STC 25430–25430.5, *Defense of the Answer* (1574). *Language(s)*: English. Appraised at 6d in 1577.

130.88 Ackworth contra Sanderum
George Acworth. *De visibili Rom'anarchia contra Nich. Sanderi Monarchiam prolegomenon libri duo*. London: ap. J. Dayum, 1573.
STC 99.5. A previous issue, STC 99, appeared the same year, but anonymously. *Language(s)*: Latin. Appraised at 3d in 1577.

130.89 Bunnaei Institutiones
Jean Calvin. [*Institutio Christianae religionis–Epitome*]. Edited by Edmund Bunny. London: impensis G. Bishop et T. Vautrollerii, 1576.
STC 4426.4. Given the valuation, probably the abridgement rather than the complete work, STC 4414 (1576). See 130.50. *Language(s)*: Latin. Appraised at 4d in 1577.

130.90 Senecae tragaediae
Lucius Annaeus Seneca. *Tragoediae*. Continent: date indeterminable. *Language(s)*: Latin. Appraised at 8d in 1577.

130.91 Chronica Melanchthonis
Johann Carion. *Chronica*. Edited by Philipp Melanchthon. Continent: date

indeterminable.
Language(s): Latin. Appraised at 2d in 1577.

130.92 Foxii Philosophia Naturae
Sebastiano Fox Morzillo. *De naturae philosophia, seu de Platonis et Aristotelis consensione.* Continent: 1551–1560.
Language(s): Latin. Appraised at 3d in 1577.

130.93 Longolii epistolae
Christophorus Longolius. [*Epistolae*]. Basle: (different houses), 1533–1570.
Language(s): Latin. Appraised at 4d in 1577.

130.94 Althameri Conciliationes Locorum
Andreas Althamer. *Conciliatio locorum scripturae.* Continent: date indeterminable.
Language(s): Latin. Appraised at 12d in 1577.

130.95 Augustini Confessiones
Augustine, *Saint. Confessiones.* Continent: date indeterminable.
Language(s): Latin. Appraised at 5d in 1577.

130.96 Opera Ovidii 3 voluminibus
Publius Ovidius Naso. [*Works*]. Continent (probable): date indeterminable.
Probably not STC books, but see STC 18926.1 *et seq.* The editions from England are not actually the complete works, although the title page carries the word *opera. Language(s)*: Latin. Appraised at 2s in 1577.

130.97 Cornelius in psalmos
Cornelius Jansenius, *Bishop of Ghent.* [*Psalms: commentary and paraphrase*]. Continent: date indeterminable.
. The only separately issued edition seems to have been Louvain, 1569. Usually published with other Biblical paraphrases and commentaries with this title leading. The entry may represent such a collection. *Language(s)*: Latin. Appraised at 4d in 1577.

130.98 Hofmestri loci communes
Johann Hoffmeister. *Loci communes rerum theologicarum.* Continent: date indeterminable.
Language(s): Latin. Appraised at 6d in 1577.

130.99 Opera Ciceronis
Marcus Tullius Cicero. [*Works*]. Continent: date indeterminable.
Language(s): Latin. Appraised at 5s in 1577.

130.100   Avenarii preces
Johann Habermann (Joannes Avenarius). *Precationes in singulos septimanae dies*. Wittenberg: (different houses), 1576–1577.
No printer is given for the 1576 edition; Clemens Schleich and Anton Schoene collaborated on the 1577 edition. *Language(s)*: Latin. Appraised at 4d in 1577.

130.101   Terentius
Publius Terentius, *Afer*. Probably [*Works*]. Britain or Continent: date indeterminable.
STC 23885 *et seq.* and non-STC. A low appraisal for the *Works*, but not unheard of. *Language(s)*: Latin. Appraised at 2d in 1577.

130.102   A service booke
Unidentified [liturgy]. Place unknown: stationer unknown, date indeterminable.
STC/non-STC status unknown. Possibly the *Book of Common Prayer*. *Language(s)*: Unknown. Appraised at 16d in 1577.

130.103   Novum Testamentum graecè
[*Bible–N.T.*]. Continent: date indeterminable.
The first English printing of the Greek was in 1587 (STC 2793). *Language(s)*: Greek. Appraised at 8d in 1577.

130.104   Sylva Biblioc' Nominum
Andreas Althamer. *Sylva biblicorum nominum*. Continent: 1530–1535.
The 1530 edition was from Nuremberg, the 1535 edition from Basle. *Language(s)*: Latin. Appraised at 3d in 1577.

130.105   Nowelli catechysmus latinè
Alexander Nowell. *Catechismus*. London: (different houses), 1570–1577.
STC 18701 *et seq.* Latin editions appeared almost every year 1570–1577, both in larger and shorter forms. *Language(s)*: Latin. Appraised at 4d in 1577.

130.106   Enchiridion Militis Christiani
Desiderius Erasmus. *Enchiridion militis Christiani*. Continent: date indeterminable.
Language(s): Latin. Appraised at 2d in 1577.

130.107   The Ende of the World
Probably Sheltco à Geveren. Probably *Of the ende of this world, and seconde commyng of Christ*. Translated by Thomas Rogers, *M.A.* London: T. Gardyner and T. Dawson for A. Maunsell, 1577.
STC 11803a.7. Three editions in 1577. See also STC 4070, Heinrich Bullinger's *Of the end of the world*, translated by T. Potter, entered to John Allde 30

September 1577 but stayed until 1580? The Latin original, *De fine saeculi et iudicio venturo Domini nostri Jesu Christi,* appeared in 1577. *Language(s)*: English. Appraised at 3d in 1577.

130.108 Flores Bibliae
Thomas, *Hibernicus.* [*Flores omnium fere doctorum*]. Continent: date indeterminable.
Language(s): Latin. Appraised at 8d in 1577.

130.109 Picturae Bibl'
Unidentified. Place unknown: stationer unknown, date indeterminable.
STC/non-STC status unknown. Perhaps descriptive of an illustrated work, which would suggest something along the lines of the *Biblia pauperum,* Hans Sebald Beham's *Biblicae historiae,* and STC 3043. A lined-through *Ovid* precedes the entry. *Language(s)*: Latin (probable) English (perhaps). Appraised at 10d in 1577.

130.110 Emblemata Alciati
Andrea Alciati. *Emblemata.* Continent: date indeterminable.
Language(s): Latin. Appraised at 8d in 1577.

130.111 Virgilius
Publius Virgilius Maro. Perhaps [*Works*]. Britain or Continent: date indeterminable.
STC 24787 *et seq.* and non-STC. A very low valuation for the complete works. *Language(s)*: Latin. Appraised at 2d in 1577.

130.112 Tragaedy of Tyrantes
Heinrich Bullinger. *The tragedies of tyrantes. Exercised upon the church of God unto 1572.* Translated by Thomas Twine. London: W. How for A. Veale, 1575. STC 4078. Staedtke no. 581. *Language(s)*: English. Appraised at 3d in 1577.

130.113 Ceporini Grammatica
Jacobus Ceporinus. *Compendium grammaticae graecae.* Continent: date indeterminable.
Language(s): Latin. Appraised at 4d in 1577.

130.114 Philo Judeus de mundo
Philo, *Judaeus. De mundo.* Continent: date indeterminable.
Often appears with Aristotle's work. *Language(s)*: Greek. Appraised at 6d in 1577.

130.115 Ciceronis Epitheta
Pedro Juan Nuñez. *Epitheta M.T. Ciceronis.* Continent: 1570–1571.

Language(s): Latin. Appraised at 3d in 1577.

130.116   Erithraei Elocutio
Valentinus Erythraeus. *De elocutione*. Strassburg: excudebat J. Rihelius, 1567.
See also 130.60. *Language(s)*: Latin. Appraised at 4d in 1577.

130.117   Ausonius
Decimus Magnus Ausonius. Perhaps [*Works*]. Continent: date indeterminable.
Language(s): Latin. Appraised at 10d in 1577.

130.118   Testamentum latinum
[*Bible–N.T.*]. Britain or Continent: date indeterminable.
STC 2799 *et seq.* and non-STC. *Language(s)*: Latin. Appraised at 6d in 1577.

130.119:1–50   50 pamflettes
Unidentified. Places unknown: stationers unknown, dates indeterminable.
STC/non-STC status unknown. These ephemera can only tantalize. Knowing their titles and authors would perhaps tell more about Singleton than all the rest of his library. *Language(s)*: Unknown. Appraised at 5d in 1577.

Thomas Stanley. Scholar (B.A.):
Probate Inventory. 1577

R. J. FEHRENBACH and E. S. LEEDHAM-GREEN

Thomas Stanley (Standley) had graduated B.A. from Brasenose College on 25 February 1575, and in the June following was granted leave of absence (*Brasenose College Register* 1909, 1:48), doubtless for a celebratory visit to his home. His inventory suggests that his circumstances were not such as to accommodate the costs of frequent travel. Besides his books his appraised goods consisted only of a scholar's gown, a cloak, a pair of breeches, an old frieze coat, a chest without locks, an old gown, and a silver spoon. The expenses of his final sickness suggest that his death was not sudden, and mention of a bequest of twenty shillings seems to indicate that he did not die intestate, but the will does appear to be extant. His poverty is also acknowledged by the gift of ten shillings "too one Thomas Stanley of Brasyn noose colledge in Oxford" on 6 May 1577 from the monies distributed by Dean Alexander Nowell from the estate of his brother Robert (Grosart 1877, 251).

Stanley's books consist for the most part of texts typical of an aspiring M.A., with a number of texts in natural philosophy, a few in dialectic and rhetoric, doubtless survivors from his undergraduate days, and a few in theology. More unusual are his Hebrew grammar (131.16), and two books, including a grammar, in French (131.17 and 131.32).

Oxford University Archives, Bodleian Library: Hyp.B.18.

§

Brasenose College Register, 1509–1909. 1909. 2 vols. Oxford: B.H. Blackwell.

Grosart, A.B., ed. 1877. *The Spending of the Money of Robert Nowell of Reade Hall, Lancs: brother of Dean Alexander Nowell (The Townley Hall MSS).* Printed for private circulation.

§

131.1	Garseus
131.2	Eobanus Hesius
131.3	Theophilactus in Evangelia
131.4	Seggius in Topica
131.5	Strebeus de oratore
131.6	Toletus de anima
131.7	Phisica Aristotelis
131.8	Instituciones Quintiliani
131.9	philosophia titil**
131.10	philosophia pauli **ventii
131.11	Augustinus in Epistolas
131.12	Talleii opera
131.13	Philosophia Velcurionis
131.14	Dialectica Rodolphi
131.15	Spangibar' in Epistolas
131.16	Grammatica hebreica Schynleri
131.17	Grammatica Piloti
131.18	Paulus ab Eitsone in Ethica
131.19	Ethica Aristotelis
131.20	Venetus in Topica
131.21	Osorius
131.22	Plutarci Vita in 2
131.23	Epistole Familiares Erasmi
131.24	Themistii oraciones
131.25	Questiones Cultmanni
131.26	Themostenes contra Leptinum
131.27	Ramus
131.28	Sintaxis Pactolli
131.29	Ovidius de fastis
131.30	Osorius contra Haddonem
131.31:1–2	ii paper bokes
131.32	psalms in Frenche
131.33	pars Livii
131.34	Philosophia Ciceronis in 2bus
131.35	Epistole Ciceronis
131.36	Rethorica Ciceronis
131.37	Fabricius de re poetie
131.38	Corvinus in Epist

131.39   Palingenius
131.40   Officia Ciceronis

§

131.1 Garseus
Joannes Garcaeus. Unidentified. Continent: date indeterminable.
Language(s): Latin. Appraised at 18d in 1577.

131.2 Eobanus Hesius
Helius Eobanus, *Hessus*. Unidentified. Continent: date indeterminable.
Language(s): Latin. Appraised at 8d in 1577.

131.3 Theophilactus in Evangelia
Theophylact, *Archbishop of Achrida*. [*Gospels: commentary and text*]. (*Bible–N.T.*). Continent: date indeterminable.
Language(s): Latin. Appraised at 10d in 1577.

131.4 Seggius in Topica
Jacob Schegk, *the Elder*. [*Aristotle–Topica: commentary*]. Continent: date indeterminable.
This may be part of Schegk's commentary on the *Organon* (1570 and 1577 editions) or a copy of a single edition that is no longer extant, since the earliest extant edition is 1584. *Language(s)*: Latin. Appraised at 20d in 1577.

131.5 Strebeus de oratore
Marcus Tullius Cicero. *De oratore*. Edited by Jacobus Lodovicus Strebaeus. Continent: date indeterminable.
Less likely because of the form of the manuscript entry, but possible, is Strebaeus's commentary on the *De oratore*. *Language(s)*: Latin. Appraised at 16d in 1577.

131.6 Toletus de anima
Franciscus Toletus, *Cardinal*. [*Aristotle–De anima: commentary*]. Continent: 1575–1577.
Language(s): Latin. Appraised at 16d in 1577.

131.7 Phisica Aristotelis
Aristotle. *Physica*. Continent: date indeterminable.
Language(s): Latin. Appraised at 2s 8d in 1577.

131.8 Instituciones Quintiliani
Marcus Fabius Quintilianus. *Institutiones oratoriae*. Continent: date indeter-

minable.
Language(s): Latin. Appraised at 6d in 1577.

131.9 philosophia titil**
Franz Titelmann. [*Aristotle–Selected works–Philosophia naturalis: commentary*].
Continent: 1530–1574.
Language(s): Latin. Appraised at 14d in 1577.

131.10 philosophia pauli **ventii
Unidentified. Place unknown: stationer unknown, date indeterminable.
STC/non-STC status unknown. The last word in the manuscript entry is
unclear, and the transcription given is not certain. Perhaps it is a smudged
"manutii," making this Paolo Manuzio's commentary on Cicero's *De philosophia*. *Language(s)*: Latin (probable). Appraised at 12d in 1577.

131.11 Augustinus in Epistolas
Augustine, *Saint*. Probably *Expositio in omnes Pauli epistolas*. (*Bible–N.T.*).
Paris: Ulrich Gering and Berthold Rembolt, 1499.
Language(s): Latin. Appraised at 10d in 1577.

131.12 Talleii opera
Audomarus Talaeus (Omer Talon). [*Works*]. Basle: ex officina Petrae Per-
nae, 1575–1576.
Language(s): Latin. Appraised at 2s 8d in 1577.

131.13 Philosophia Velcurionis
Joannes Velcurio. [*Aristotle–Physica: commentary*]. Continent: 1537–1575.
Language(s): Latin. Appraised at 12d in 1577.

131.14 Dialectica Rodolphi
Probably Caspar Rhodolphus. [*Dialectica*]. Continent: date indetermin-
able.
Rodolphus Agricola's *De inventione dialectica* is possible. *Language(s)*: Latin.
Appraised at 10d in 1577.

131.15 Spangibar' in Epistolas
Johann Spangenberg. [*Epistles (liturgical): commentary and text*]. (*Bible–
N.T.*). Continent: date indeterminable.
There are numerous collections of Spangenberg's commentaries on the
Gospels and the Epistles of the lectionary. Whether only the section on the
Epistles is represented here cannot be determined. *Language(s)*: Latin. Ap-
praised at 8d in 1577.

131.16 Grammatica hebreica Schynleri
Valentin Schindler. *Institutionum hebraicarum libri V*. Wittenberg: excud.

Joannes Crato, 1575.
Language(s): Hebrew Latin. Appraised at 14d in 1577.

131.17 Grammatica Piloti
Joannes Pilotus. *Gallicae linguae institutio.* Continent: 1550–1575.
Stanley owned at least one book in French, which helps to identify this item. See 131.32. *Language(s)*: French Latin. Appraised at 7d in 1577.

131.18 Paulus ab Eitsone in Ethica
Paul von Eitzen. *Ethicae doctrinae.* Continent: 1571–1577.
Other works appear in some editions. The date range represents individually published parts. *Language(s)*: Latin. Appraised at 12d in 1577.

131.19 Ethica Aristotelis
Aristotle. *Ethica.* Britain or Continent: date indeterminable.
STC 752 *et seq.* and non-STC. *Language(s)*: Latin. Appraised at 10d in 1577.

131.20 Venetus in Topica
Perhaps *Nova explanatio Topicorum Aristotelis.* (*Academia Veneta*). Venice: Paulus Manutius, 1559.
Language(s): Latin. Appraised at 16d in 1577.

131.21 Osorius
Jeronimo Osorio da Fonseca, *Bishop.* Unidentified. Continent: date indeterminable.
STC/non-STC status unknown. See 131.30. *Language(s)*: Latin. Appraised at 16d in 1577.

131.22 Plutharci Vita in 2
Plutarch. *Vitae parallelae.* Continent: date indeterminable.
An appraisal of "viii" was struck out. *Language(s)*: Latin (probable) Greek (perhaps). Appraised at 3s 4d in 1577.

131.23 Epistole Familiares Erasmi
Desiderius Erasmus. *Epistolae familiares.* Continent: 1538–1552.
Language(s): Latin. Appraised at 6d in 1577.

131.24 Themistii oraciones
Themistius. *Orationes.* Continent: 1559–1562.
The 1559 edition is in Latin, the 1562 edition in Greek. *Language(s)*: Latin (probable) Greek (perhaps). Appraised at 8d in 1577.

131.25 Questiones Cultmanni
Leonhard Culmann. Probably *Disputationes seu argumentationes theologicae.*

Nuremberg: (different houses), 1544–1551.
Language(s): Latin. Appraised at 3d in 1577.

131.26   Themostenes contra Leptinum
Demosthenes. *Adversus Leptinem.* Continent: date indeterminable.
Language(s): Greek Latin (perhaps). Appraised at 4d in 1577.

131.27   Ramus
Pierre de La Ramée. Unidentified. Continent: date indeterminable.
Language(s): Latin. Appraised at 8d in 1577.

131.28   Sintaxis Pactolli
Unidentified. Continent (probable): date indeterminable.
Probably not an STC book. *Language(s)*: Latin (probable). Appraised at 4d
in 1577.

131.29   Ovidius de fastis
Publius Ovidius Naso. *Fasti.* Continent: date indeterminable.
STC 18947.5 and non-STC. *Language(s)*: Latin. Appraised at 4d in 1577.

131.30   Osorius contra Haddonem
Jeronimo Osorio da Fonseca, *Bishop. In Gualterum Haddonum magistrum
libellorum supplicum libri tres.* Continent: 1567–1576.
Language(s): Latin. Appraised at 10d in 1577.

131.31:1–2   ii paper bokes
Unidentified. Provenances unknown: dates indeterminable.
Manuscripts. *Language(s)*: Unknown. Appraised at 8d in 1577.

131.32   psalms in Frenche
[*Bible–O.T.–Psalms*]. Continent: date indeterminable.
Language(s): French. Appraised at 4d in 1577.

131.33   pars Livii
Titus Livius. [*Historiae Romanae decades* (part)]. Continent: date indeter-
minable.
Language(s): Latin. Appraised at 8d in 1577. *Current location*: Durham
Cathedral. We are grateful to Mrs. M.L. Ford for bringing the signature of
Stanley in the Durham volume to our attention.

131.34   Philosophia Ciceronis in 2bus
Marcus Tullius Cicero. [*Selected works–Philosophica*]. Continent: date inde-
terminable.
Language(s): Latin. Appraised at 22d in 1577.

131.35 Epistole Ciceronis
Marcus Tullius Cicero. Perhaps [*Selected works–Epistolae*]. Continent: date indeterminable.
Conceivably the *Epistolae ad familiares*. *Language(s)*: Latin. Appraised at 22d in 1577.

131.36 Rethorica Ciceronis
Marcus Tullius Cicero. [*Selected works–Rhetorica*]. Continent: date indeterminable.
The attributed *Rhetorica ad Herennium* is possible. *Language(s)*: Latin. Appraised at 12d in 1577.

131.37 Fabricius de re poetie
Georgius Fabricius. *De re poetica*. Continent: 1556–1575.
Language(s): Latin. Appraised at 3d in 1577.

131.38 Corvinus in Epist
Antonius Corvinus. [*Epistles (liturgical): commentary and text*]. (*Bible–N.T.*). Continent: 1538.
Four editions in 1538, published in four different cities. *Language(s)*: Latin. Appraised at 3d in 1577.

131.39 Palingenius
Marcellus Palingenius (Pietro Angelo Manzolli [Stellatus]). *Zodiacus vitae*. Britain or Continent: date indeterminable.
STC 19138.5 and non-STC. *Language(s)*: Latin. Appraised at 4d in 1577.

131.40 Officia Ciceronis
Marcus Tullius Cicero. *De officiis*. Continent: date indeterminable.
Conceivably a collection, perhaps *Works*, which frequently led with *De officiis*, or even one of the Latin-English editions that had appeared by the date of this inventory. *Language(s)*: Latin. Appraised at 4d in 1577.

Thomas Bolt. Scholar (student): Inventory. 1578

MARC L. SCHWARZ

Thomas Bolt (Belt, Bolte) of Staffordshire matriculated from University College on 10 January 1575 at the age of eighteen. The inventory of his books listed below was made on 16 May 1578 from among the goods he "left behynd hym in hys chamber . . . at hys departure." The reason for Bolt's departure is not given, and nothing more is known of him, including when he died.

The inventory reveals a scholar's expected acquaintance with the classics, both Greek and Roman, as well with the works of Renaissance luminaries like Valla and Erasmus. For the most part, the collection is a standard scholar's library of literature, theology, philosophy, rhetoric, and history. Although the collection gives no evidence of Bolt's being acquainted with Hebrew and only possibly with Greek, the French and Italian grammars reveal him to have been a student of those two modern languages. Indeed, his copy of an English version of *Il cortegiano* and perhaps an English version of *Galateo* conceivably could have been used for practice in translation. A slightly larger number of English works appear in Bolt's library than is usually found in Oxford scholars' book-lists, including items by Thomas Wilson and Geoffrey Fenton. He shows an interest in contemporary affairs with a work on Elizabeth I's coronation and a copy of George Buchanan's diatribe against Mary, Queen of Scots, which, perhaps, more personally defines Bolt's copy of Calvin's cathechism found in the list. Gillian Lewis (1986, 248) notes that Bolt's collection of inventoried instruments reflects an interest in science ("mortar and pestle, three gold weights, scissors, a small brass pan") that is also seen in books by Mizauld and by Cardano.

Oxford University Archives, Bodleian Library: Hyp.B.10.

§

Lewis, Gillian. 1986. "The Faculty of Medicine," in *The Collegiate University*, ed., James McConica. Volume 3 of *The History of the University of Oxford*, gen. ed., T.H. Aston. Oxford: Oxford Univ. Press, pp. 213–56.

§

132.1	osorius de gloria
132.2	osorii historia
132.3	Ciceronis opera 7 voluminibus
132.4	Hierony: Cardanus de subtilitate
132.5	Aristotelis Organum
132.6	Aristotelis ethica
132.7	Aristotelis Physica
132.8	Toleti Logica
132.9	Valerii maximi historia
132.10	Johannes Sturmius in partitiones Ciceronis
132.11	Trapezuntius rhetorica
132.12	Erasmi Apophthegma
132.13	Articella nuperrime impressa
132.14	Faber in ethica Aristotelis
132.15	Thomas Lynacrus de structura sermonis latini
132.16	Textoris officina
132.17	questionista in Scotum
132.18	Hortus vocabulorum
132.19	Lawren' Vallae de elegantiis
132.20	Nizolius
132.21	Lovaniensis in organon
132.22	Scotus in metaphysica
132.23	Tractatus diversorum doctorum
132.24	venetus in Dioscoridem
132.25	Sambuci Emblemata
132.26	Georgius Aemilius
132.27	horatius
132.28	virgilius
132.29	ovidius de fastis
132.30	palingenius
132.31	marcailis [marcialis] epigrammata
132.32	Terentius
132.33	Ciceronis epithete
132.34	Ovidius de fastis
132.35	Ovidii metamorphosis
132.36	Lucretius
132.37	Antonii mizaldi medicina
132.38	Anto: mizaldi de arcanis naturae

132.39	Baptiste de miraculis rerum
132.40	Caelis sec: in partiti: Ciceronis
132.41	Lytletones Tenures
132.42	Omphalius de imitatione
132.43	Salustius
132.44	Copia verborum
132.45	Erythraeus de eluctione
132.46	copia Erasmi alia
132.47	colloqu: Erasmi
132.48	Omphalius de elocutione
132.49	Justinus
132.50	homerus poeta
132.51	Aphthonius
132.52	Rodolphus de inventione
132.53	Titlemanni Dialectica
132.54	Agrippa de vanitate scientiarum
132.55	Angelus Politianus
132.56	despoterii Grammatica
132.57	Libri de Agricultura
132.58	Longleii orationes duae
132.59	Wilson logick
132.60	phrases manuntii
132.61	Sex Linguae
132.62	Ciceronis sententiae
132.63	Alcabasius
132.64	philip' melanchth' grammatic'
132.65	philip' melanchton in ethica
132.66	The quenes passage
132.67	Mantuanus
132.68	Epistolae selectae ciceronis
132.69	A prognosicon for ever
132.70	De maria scotorum Regina
132.71	Ovidius translated
132.72	Valerii dialectica
132.73	Henerus de pestilentia
132.74	cathechismus Calvini
132.75	Persius cum commento
132.76	epistolae carali
132.77	de pace ecclesiae
132.78	An Italian Grammar
132.79	A french grammer
132.80	Galataeo
132.81	Bartholomeus Georgofitius [?]
132.82:1–5	iiiii paper bokes
132.83	Testamentum Latinum

132.84   fenton Golden epistles
132.85   the courtier in english
132.86:A Lycostheni similia
132.86:B [See 132.86:A]

§

132.1 osorius de gloria
Jeronimo Osorio da Fonseca, *Bishop*. *De gloria*. Continent: date indetermin-able.

Conceivably Osorio's frequently published *Selected works* with this title lead-ing. Only one solo edition of *De gloria* was published (Florence, 1552). *Lan-guage(s)*: Latin. Appraised at 7d in 1578.

132.2 osorii historia
Jeronimo Osorio da Fonseca, *Bishop*. *De rebus Emmanuelis regis Lusitaniae*. Continent: 1571–1576.
Language(s): Latin. Appraised at 9d in 1578.

132.3 Ciceronis opera 7 voluminibus
Marcus Tullius Cicero. [*Works*]. Continent: date indeterminable.
A note at the end of the inventory indicates that this item has been lent to an unidentified Mr. King. *Language(s)*: Latin. Appraised at 10s in 1578.

132.4 Hierony: Cardanus de subtilitate
Girolamo Cardano. *De subtilitate*. Continent: 1550–1560.
Language(s): Latin. Appraised at 3s in 1578.

132.5 Aristotelis Organum
Aristotle. *Organon*. Continent: date indeterminable.
Language(s): Greek (perhaps) Latin (perhaps). Appraised at 12d in 1578.

132.6 Aristotelis ethica
Aristotle. *Ethica*. Britain or Continent: date indeterminable.
STC 752 and non-STC. *Language(s)*: Greek (perhaps) Latin (perhaps). Ap-praised at 8d in 1578.

132.7 Aristotelis Physica
Aristotle. *Physica*. Continent: date indeterminable.
Language(s): Greek (perhaps) Latin (perhaps). Appraised at 16d in 1578.

132.8 Toleti Logica
Franciscus Toletus, *Cardinal*. [*Aristotle–Selected works–Logica: commentary*].
Continent: date indeterminable.

According to a note at the end of the inventory, lent out to an unidentified Mr. King. *Language(s)*: Latin. Appraised at 20d in 1578.

132.9 Valerii maximi historia

Valerius Maximus. *Facta et dicta memorabilia*. Continent: date indeterminable.
Language(s): Latin. Appraised at 6d in 1578.

132.10 Johannes Sturmius in partitiones Ciceronis

Joannes Sturmius. *In partitiones oratorias Ciceronis dialogi*. Continent: date indeterminable.
Language(s): Latin. Appraised at 8d in 1578.

132.11 Trapezuntius rhetorica

Georgius Trapezuntius. [*Rhetorica*]. Continent: date indeterminable.
Language(s): Latin. Appraised at 8d in 1578.

132.12 Erasmi Apophthegma

Desiderius Erasmus. *Apophthegmata*. Continent: date indeterminable.
There is no reason to assume the English translation that had appeared by the date of this inventory. *Language(s)*: Latin. Appraised at 8d in 1578.

132.13 Articella nuperrime impressa

Articella. Continent: date indeterminable.
With this title, probably one of the editions from Lyon (1515–1534). *Language(s)*: Latin. Appraised at 6d in 1578.

132.14 Faber in ethica Aristotelis

Jacobus Faber, *Stapulensis*. [*Aristotle–Ethica: commentary*]. Continent: date indeterminable.
Language(s): Latin. Appraised at 8d in 1578.

132.15 Thomas Lynacrus de structura sermonis latini

Thomas Linacre. *De emendenta structura Latini sermonis libri sex*. Britain or Continent: 1524–1560.
STC 15634 and non-STC. *Language(s)*: Latin. Appraised at 8d in 1578.

132.16 Textoris officina

Joannes Ravisius (Textor). [*Officina*]. Continent: date indeterminable.
Language(s): Latin. Appraised at 2s in 1578.

132.17 questionista in Scotum

Unidentified. Continent: date indeterminable.
Perhaps one of a number of works, usually on Aristotle or Peter Lombard, entitled *Questiones . . . ad mentem Scotus*. *Language(s)*: Latin. Appraised at 8d in 1578.

132.18 Hortus vocabulorum
Hortus vocabulorum. Britain or Continent: 1500–1532.
STC 13829 *et seq.* Usually attributed to Galfridus, *Anglicus*. *Language(s)*:
English Latin. Appraised at 4d in 1578.

132.19 Lawren' Vallae de elegantiis
Laurentius Valla. *Elegantiae*. Continent: date indeterminable.
Language(s): Latin. Appraised at 6d in 1578.

132.20 Nizolius
Marius Nizolius. Probably [*Observationes*]. Continent: date indeterminable.
Language(s): Latin. Appraised at 5s in 1578.

132.21 Lovaniensis in organon
Commentaria in Isagogen Porphyrii et in omnes libros Aristotelis de dialectica.
(*Louvain University*). Louvain: Probably Servatius Sassenus, 1535–1568.
See BCI 2:505. Sassenus published the 1535 and 1568 editions; biblio-
graphical sources do not name the publisher of the 1547 and 1553 editions.
Language(s): Latin Greek (perhaps). Appraised at 2s 5d in 1578.

132.22 Scotus in metaphysica
John Duns, *Scotus*. [*Aristotle–Metaphysica: commentary*]. Venice: (different
houses), 1497–1520.
Language(s): Latin. Appraised at 10d in 1578.

132.23 Tractatus diversorum doctorum
[*Tractatus solemnis multum praedicabilis*]. Continent: date indeterminable.
At least one of the many editions, mostly incunabula, carries in the long
title . . . *ex diversis sacrorum doctorum scripturis. Language(s)*: Latin. Appraised
at 12d in 1578.

132.24 venetus in Dioscoridem
Dioscorides. *Joannis Baptistae Egnatii Veneti in Dioscoridem ab Hermolao
Barbaro tralatum annotamenta.* Translated by Hermolaus Barbarus; edited by
Joannes Baptista Egnatius. Venice: Aloisius et Franciscus Barbari et Joannes
Bartholomeus Astensis in Gregorium officina, 1516.
The first part of the long title is given to show the book's connection with
the manuscript entry. The volume includes the *De medica materia*. NLM6 no.
1140. *Language(s)*: Latin. Appraised at 10d in 1578.

132.25 Sambuci Emblemata
Joannes Sambucus. *Emblemata*. Antwerp: Christopher Plantin, 1564–
1576.
Language(s): Latin. Appraised at 8d in 1578.

132.26   Georgius Aemilius
Unidentified. Continent: date indeterminable.
Language(s): Latin. Appraised at 2d in 1578.

132.27   horatius
Quintus Horatius Flaccus. Probably [*Works*]. Britain or Continent: date indeterminable.
STC 13784 and non-STC. *Language(s)*: Latin. Appraised at 6d in 1578.

132.28   virgilius
Publius Virgilius Maro. Probably [*Works*]. Britain or Continent: date indeterminable.
STC 24787 *et seq.* and non-STC. *Language(s)*: Latin. Appraised at 4d in 1578.

132.29   ovidius de fastis
Publius Ovidius Naso. *Fasti*. Britain or Continent: date indeterminable.
STC 18947.5 and non-STC. Another copy at 132.34. *Language(s)*: Latin. Appraised at 2d in 1578.

132.30   palingenius
Marcellus Palingenius (Pietro Angelo Manzolli [Stellatus]). *Zodiacus vitae*. Britain or Continent: date indeterminable.
STC 19138.5 *et seq.* and non-STC. *Language(s)*: Latin. Appraised at 2d in 1578.

132.31   marcailis [marcialis] epigrammata
Epigrammata. Continent: date indeterminable.
Language(s): Latin. Appraised at 5d in 1578.

132.32   Terentius
Publius Terentius, *Afer*. [*Works*]. Britain or Continent: date indeterminable.
STC 23885 *et seq.* and non-STC. *Language(s)*: Latin. Appraised at 3d in 1578.

132.33   Ciceronis epithete
Pedro Juan Nuñez. *Epithetha M.T. Ciceronis*. Continent: 1570–1571.
Language(s): Latin. Appraised at 4d in 1578.

132.34   Ovidius de fastis
Publius Ovidius Naso. *Fasti*. Britain or Continent: date indeterminable.
STC 18947.5 and non-STC. Another copy at 132.29. *Language(s)*: Latin. Appraised at 3d in 1578.

132.35 Ovidii metamorphosis
Publius Ovidius Naso. *Metamorphoses.* Continent: date indeterminable. *Language(s)*: Latin. Appraised at 6d in 1578.

132.36 Lucretius
Titus Lucretius Carus. *De rerum natura.* Continent: date indeterminable. *Language(s)*: Latin. Appraised at 6d in 1578.

132.37 Antonii mizaldi medicina
Antoine Mizauld. Unidentified. Continent: date indeterminable.
This could be any of Mizauld's works on medicine. *Language(s)*: Latin. Appraised at 7d in 1578.

132.38 Anto: mizaldi de arcanis naturae
Antoine Mizauld. *De arcanis naturae.* Continent: date indeterminable.
The only extant edition found was published in 1558 by Jacques Kerver in Paris (see Adams M1496), but it carries on the title page "Editio tertia." Perhaps the smaller *Memorabilium aliquot naturae arcanorum sylvula* (1554, also published by Kerver) was considered an earlier edition, but there may also have been two, now lost, earlier editions with this title. *Language(s)*: Latin. Appraised at 6d in 1578.

132.39 Baptiste de miraculis rerum
Giovanni Battista della Porta. *Magia naturalis.* Continent: date indeterminable.
The manuscript entry is the work's subtitle. *Language(s)*: Latin. Appraised at 8d in 1578.

132.40 Caelis sec: in partiti: Ciceronis
Caelius Secundus Curio. [*Cicero–De partitione oratoria: commentary* (and other works)]. Continent: 1556–1567.
Joannes Oporinus was involved with both editions. *Language(s)*: Latin. Appraised at 8d in 1578.

132.41 Lytletones Tenures
Sir Thomas Littleton. [*Tenures*]. Britain or Continent: date indeterminable.
STC 15719 *et seq.* One early edition was printed in Rouen; the rest were issued from London. *Language(s)*: English or Law/French. Appraised at 2d in 1578.

132.42 Omphalius de imitatione
Jacobus Omphalius. *De elocutionis imitatione ac apparatu.* Continent: date indeterminable.
Another copy at 132.48. *Language(s)*: Latin. Appraised at 6d in 1578.

132.43 Salustius
Caius Sallustius Crispus. Unidentified. Place unknown: stationer unknown, date indeterminable.
STC/non-STC unknown. If *Works*, then STC 21622.2–21622.6 are possibilities. *Language(s)*: Latin. Appraised at 6d in 1578.

132.44 Copia verborum
Desiderius Erasmus. *De duplici copia verborum ac rerum*. Britain or Continent: date indeterminable.
STC 10471.4 *et seq.* and non-STC. Another copy at 132.46. *Language(s)*: Latin. Appraised at 3d in 1578.

132.45 Erythraeus de eluctione
Valentinus Erythraeus. *De elocutione*. Strassburg: excudebat J. Rihelius, 1567.
Language(s): Latin. Appraised at 6d in 1578.

132.46 copia Erasmi alia
Desiderius Erasmus. *De duplici copia verborum ac rerum*. Britain or Continent: date indeterminable.
STC 10471.4 *et seq.* and non-STC. Another copy at 132.44. *Language(s)*: Latin. Appraised at 2d in 1578.

132.47 colloqu: Erasmi
Desiderius Erasmus. *Colloquia*. Britain or Continent: date indeterminable.
STC 10450.6 *et seq.* and non-STC. *Language(s)*: Latin. Appraised at 3d in 1578.

132.48 Omphalius de elocutione
Jacobus Omphalius. *De elocutionis imitatione ac apparatu*. Continent: date indeterminable.
Another copy at 132.42. *Language(s)*: Latin. Appraised at 8d in 1578.

132.49 Justinus
Trogus Pompeius and Justinus, *the Historian*. [*Epitomae in Trogi Pompeii historias*]. Britain or Continent: date indeterminable.
STC 24287 *et seq.* and non-STC. *Language(s)*: Latin. Appraised at 4d in 1578.

132.50 homerus poeta
Homer. Probably [*Works*]. Continent: date indeterminable.
Language(s): Latin (probable) Greek (perhaps). Appraised at 8d in 1578.

132.51 Aphthonius
Aphthonius, *Sophista*. *Progymnasmata*. Britain or Continent: date indeterminable.

STC 699 *et seq.* and non-STC. *Language(s)*: Latin. Appraised at 4d in 1578.

132.52 Rodolphus de inventione
Rodolphus Agricola. *De inventione dialectica*. Continent: date indeterminable.
Language(s): Latin. Appraised at 4d in 1578.

132.53 Titlemanni Dialectica
Franz Titelmann. [*Dialectica*]. Continent: date indeterminable.
Language(s): Latin. Appraised at 6d in 1578.

132.54 Agrippa de vanitate scientiarum
Henricus Cornelius Agrippa. *De incertitudine et vanitate scientiarum*. Continent: date indeterminable.
Language(s): Latin. Appraised at 4d in 1578.

132.55 Angelus Politianus
Angelus Politianus (Angelo Ambrogini). Unidentified. Continent: date indeterminable.
Language(s): Latin. Appraised at 6d in 1578.

132.56 despoterii Grammatica
Jean Despautère. [*Grammatica*]. Continent: date indeterminable.
Language(s): Latin. Appraised at 7d in 1578.

132.57 Libri de Agricultura
Probably *De re rustica*. Continent: date indeterminable.
Language(s): Latin. Appraised at 6d in 1578.

132.58 Longleii orationes duae
Christophorus Longolius. *Orationes duae pro defensione sua*. Continent: 1524–1539.
At least five editions of this collection were published, making it much more likely than the earlier (1520), single issue of a different collection, *Orationes dua; una de laudibus divi Ludovici et Francorum* (Brunet 3:1153). *Language(s)*: Latin. Appraised at 6d in 1578.

132.59 Wilson logick
Thomas Wilson, *Secretary of State. The rule of reason, conteinyng the arte of logique*. London: (different houses), 1551–1567.
STC 25809 *et seq. Language(s)*: English. Appraised at 8d in 1578.

132.60 phrases manuntii
Aldo Manuzio, *the Younger. Purae, elegantes et copiosae latinae linguae phrases*.

Britain or Continent: date indeterminable.

STC 17278.8 and non-STC. The 1573 London edition includes an English translation. *Language(s)*: Latin English (perhaps). Appraised at 3d in 1578.

132.61 Sex Linguae

Unidentified. Place unknown: stationer unknown, date indeterminable.

STC/non-STC status unknown. At this valuation, more likely something like a hexaglot Lord's Prayer than a dictionary. See Adams L1490. *Language(s)*: Latin. Appraised at 1d in 1578.

132.62 Ciceronis sententiae

Marcus Tullius Cicero. [*Selections*]. Britain or Continent: date indeterminable.

STC 5138.3 and non-STC. The 1575 edition published in England contained selections from Demosthenes and Terence as well. *Language(s)*: Latin. Appraised at 6d in 1578.

132.63 Alcabasius

Alchabitius. Unidentified. Continent: date indeterminable.

Language(s): Latin. Appraised at 4d in 1578.

132.64 philip' melanchth' grammatic'

Philipp Melanchthon. *Grammatica latina*. Continent: date indeterminable. There is no reason to suspect his *Grammatica graeca* in this library. Struck out and not appraised. *Language(s)*: Latin.

132.65 philip' melanchton in ethica

Philipp Melanchthon. [*Aristotle–Ethica: commentary*]. Continent: date indeterminable.

Language(s): Latin. Appraised at 3d in 1578.

132.66 The quenes passage

Richard Mulcaster (attributed). *The quenes majesties passage through the citie of London to westminster the daye before her coronacion*. London: R. Tottill, 1559.

STC 7589.5 *et seq*. This item is struck out of the inventory and not appraised. *Language(s)*: English.

132.67 Mantuanus

Baptista Spagnuoli (Mantuanus). Unidentified. Place unknown: stationer unknown, date indeterminable.

STC/non-STC status unknown. This entry was struck out and not appraised. *Language(s)*: Latin.

132.68 Epistolae selectae ciceronis
Marcus Tullius Cicero. [*Selected works–Epistolae*]. Continent: date indeterminable.
Language(s): Latin. Appraised at 6d in 1578.

132.69 A prognosicon for ever
Erra Pater. *Pronostycacyon for ever, of mayster Erra Pater*. London: R. Wyer, 1540 (probable)–1562 (probable).
STC 439.3 *et seq.* Struck out and not appraised. *Language(s)*: English.

132.70 De maria scotorum Regina
George Buchanan. *De Maria Scotorum regina, . . . plena, et tragica planè historia*. London: [J. Day], 1571 (probable).
STC 3978. Published anonymously. *Language(s)*: English. Appraised at 1d in 1578.

132.71 Ovidius translated
Publius Ovidius Naso. Unidentified. London: (stationer unknown), date indeterminable.
Unidentifiable in the STC. The only English translations of Ovid by the date of this inventory were published in London. This item was struck out of the inventory and not appraised. *Language(s)*: English.

132.72 Valerii dialectica
Cornelius Valerius. *Tabulae totius dialectices*. Continent: date indeterminable.
This entry was struck out and not appraised. *Language(s)*: Latin.

132.73 Henerus de pestilentia
Joannes Henerus. *De tristissimo pestilentiae malo commentarius*. Paris: apud Catherinum Barbé viduam Jacobi Gazelli, 1551.
Language(s): Latin. Appraised at 1d in 1578.

132.74 cathechismus Calvini
Jean Calvin. [*Cathechism*]. Britain or Continent: date indeterminable.
STC 4375 *et seq.* and non-STC. *Language(s)*: Latin (probable). Appraised at 1d in 1578.

132.75 Persius cum commento
Aulus Persius Flaccus. [*Works*]. Continent: date indeterminable.
Language(s): Latin. Appraised at 1d in 1578.

132.76 epistolae carali
Carolus Maneken. *Formulae epistolarum*. Continent: date indeterminable.
This entry was struck out and not appraised. *Language(s)*: Latin.

132.77   de pace ecclesiae

Perhaps Matthias Richter (Matthaeus Judex). *De vera pace ecclesiae, et de seditione duplici ecclesiastica, et politica, libelli duo.* Rostock (perhaps): (stationer unknown), 1566.

This entry is crossed out and not appraised. *Language(s)*: Latin.

132.78   An Italian Grammar

Probably William Thomas. *Principal rules of the Italian grammer, with a dictionarie.* London: (different houses), 1550–1567.

STC 24020 *et seq. Language(s)*: English Italian. Appraised at 4d in 1578.

132.79   A french grammer

Unidentified [grammar]. Place unknown: stationer unknown, date indeterminable.

STC/non-STC status unknown. See STC 7377 *et seq.* and the collection of French grammars following STC 11375. STC 24865 *et seq.* are less likely possibilities because of their early dates of publication. *Language(s)*: French English (probable). Appraised at 6d in 1578.

132.80   Galataeo

Giovanni della Casa. *Galateo.* Translated by Robert Peterson. London: [H. Middleton] for R. Newbery, 1576.

STC 4738. Conceivably an Italian edition since Bolt had an Italian grammar (see 132.78). *Language(s)*: English (probable) Italian (perhaps). Appraised at 2d in 1578.

132.81   Bartholomeus Georgofitius [?]

Bartholomaeus Georgievits. Unidentified. Place unknown: stationer unknown, date indeterminable.

STC/non-STC status unknown. The English translation of Georgievits's *De Turcarum moribus epitome* (STC 11746) is a likely possibility, but the original Latin versions of his works on Turkish history and geography are also possible. Not appraised. *Language(s)*: English (perhaps) Latin (perhaps).

132.82:1–5   iiiii paper bokes

Unidentified. Provenances unknown: dates indeterminable.

Manuscripts. Perhaps notebooks. Not appraised. *Language(s)*: Unknown.

132.83   Testamentum Latinum

[*Bible–N.T.*]. Britain or Continent: date indeterminable.

STC 2799 *et seq.* and non-STC. *Language(s)*: Latin. Appraised at 20d in 1578.

132.84   fenton Golden epistles

Sir Geoffrey Fenton. *Golden epistles, contayning varietie of discourse gathered as well out of the remaynder of Gueuaraes workes, as other authors, Latine, French, and Italian.* London: H. Middleton for R. Newbery, 1575–1577.

STC 10794 *et seq.* Often bound with *The familiar epistles* of Antonius de Guevera, *Bishop* (STC 12432), and at this valuation, probably so appearing here. *Language(s)*: English. Appraised at 2s 6d in 1578.

132.85 the courtier in english

Baldassare Castiglione, *Count. The courtyer.* Translated by Sir Thomas Hoby. London: (different houses), 1561–1577.

STC 4778 *et seq.* This entry was crossed out with a note that Bolt had "Borowed yt" from "Sir Dew," probably Henry Dewe, who had matriculated at University College with Bolt on 10 January 1575 (*Alumni Oxonienses*, 1:399). Not appraised. *Language(s)*: English.

132.86:A   Lycostheni similia

Conrad Lycosthenes (Conrad Wolffhart). *Similium loci communes.* Basle: per E. Episcopium et Nicolai fr. haeredes, 1575 (composite publication).

Language(s): Latin. Appraised [a composite volume] at 4d in 1578.

132.86:B   [See 132.86:A]

Theodor Zwinger. *Similitudinem methodo.* [Composite publication].

Language(s): Latin. Appraised [a composite volume] at 4d in 1578.

John Glover. Scholar (M.A.): Probate Inventory. 1578

KATY HOOPER

John Glover was admitted as a student to Christ Church, Oxford, in 1564, taking his M.A. in 1568. In 1574 he was elected to the vacant post of medical fellow in St. John's College, Oxford, but, as an outsider to the college, the legality of his election was disputed and referred successively to the Bishop of Winchester and the College Visitors before his estate as fellow of the college was finally confirmed in 1577. He is recorded as a senior proctor of the University in 1577, and bursar of St. John's in 1578, but died in July 1578, aged 35 (*Alumni Oxonienses*, 2:572, and Stevenson and Salter 1939, 200, 346). It is not clear whether Glover was a practicing physician, since none of the standard biographical sources indicates that he held either a license or a medical degree. The nature of his library, with its emphasis upon practical medicine, would certainly suggest that he did practice, as do the terms of the medical fellowship at St. John's. The college statutes exempted the medical fellow from taking holy orders "so long as he was attending the public medical lectures or was engaged in practice after attaining the degree of M.D." (Stevenson and Salter 1939, 149). The Catalogus Sociorum entries for Glover's immediate successors to the fellowship, Roger Kibblethwaite and Ralph Hutchinson, describe each as "Medicus," and Hutchinson was appointed medical fellow in succession to Kibblethwaite when the latter "renounced all his rights in a physician's place in the College" (Stevenson and Salter 1939, 342–43). If Glover did indeed practice, his appointment would have been timely, since within weeks of the confirmation of his fellowship, "The Black Assizes" struck Oxford with an outbreak of the plague; six hundred are reckoned to have died in the months of July and August 1577. The letters of Sir William Cordell, visitor of the college, refer to the plague's effect on St. John's from July to September 1577 (quoted in Stevenson and Salter 1939, 484–86). McConica (468), citing more recent studies, identifies the epidemic that struck Oxford that year as typhus. Whatever the actual disease, Glover's collection includes appropriate medical works at 133.195, Gulielmus Magistry, *De pestis saevitia* (1572), and at 133.187, Jacques Peletier, *De peste compendium* (1560s or 1570s). Whether he acquired those books in response to the visitation of the contagion in 1577 is, of course, impossible to say. Glover himself was dead a year later; Ralph Hutchinson was one of those responsible for Glover's memorial brass in the college chapel, on which he is described as "Medicinae studioso" (Wood 1786, 1:565).

At the time of his death, Glover had a library of nearly three hundred titles, remarkable for its breadth and depth. Medicine predominates, accounting for nearly three-fifths of the titles, but of the remainder well over a third is literary, with history and philosophy also well represented, and a smattering of titles from a wide variety of other branches of knowledge. This wide range has occasionally made it impossible to distinguish medical from non-medical titles (see 133.172), but overall the inventory's compilers have provided sufficient, accurate information, particularly in respect of size: 133.1–133.22 are grouped together as folio editions, 133.23–133.61 as quarto editions, 133.62–133.204 and 133.273–133.279 as octavo editions, with 133.205–133.272 identified as sextodecimo editions. Such detailed description permits the positive identification, down to the exact edition, of more than one-third of the titles; many of the remainder can be identified within a narrow date range. It is clear, therefore, that Glover was chiefly a buyer of new books, owning thirty-five titles definitely printed in the 1570s, and another fifty or so likely to have been, but virtually nothing printed before the 1530s. Although Latin naturally predominates, one-eighth of the library consists of English books (from vernacular medical texts to the tragedy *Gorboduc*), with half or less of that number in Greek, and a handful in French or Italian.

The medical section of Glover's library is impressive in its coverage of the subject. There are twenty-three editions of works by Galen, thirteen of which are sextodecimo editions. Almost half of these are certainly the "students' editions" with which "the Lyonnese publisher Rouille . . . swamped the market from 1546 onwards" (Durling, 242). It is in keeping with the nature of the collection that the classics of the medical curriculum are present in Renaissance translation, alongside the "new medicine" of the sixteenth century, for example, Fernel and Fallopius, and the vernacular works of Securis, Record, Elyot, and Baker.

I would like to include grateful thanks to Robert Fehrenbach for giving "a local habitation and a name" to those entries whose identities eluded me.

Oxford University Archives, Bodleian Library: Hyp.B.13.

§

Stevenson, W.H. and H.E. Salter. 1939. *The Early History of St. John's College,*

Oxford. Oxford: For the Oxford Historical Society at the Clarendon Press.

Wood, Anthony à. 1786. *The History and Antiquities of the Colleges and Halls in the University of Oxford*. Edited by John Gutch. 2 Vols. Oxford: Clarendon Press.

§

133.1	In commentarii Gwintheri de utraque medecena
133.2	Mathei Paris historia
133.3	Syntaxes medicae Wickeri
133.4	Delineatio Anatomiae per Geminum anglice
133.5	Julius Alexandrinus de sanitate tuenda
133.6	Aristoteles de historia animalium
133.7	epitome Galeni
133.8	Cardanus in Hippocratis Prognostica
133.9	dixonarium gallicarum et latinum
133.10	Johannis Baptistae Montani opera
133.11	quaestiones Johannis canonici in Phisica
133.12	opera Petri Penae et Matthei de Lobel, medicorum
133.13	Practica Alexandri Yatros
133.14	Canones Johannis Mesuae
133.15	Galenus de temperamentis
133.16	Galenus de natura hominis
133.17	Phernelius de abditis rerum causis
133.18	historia rerum gallicarum
133.19	Vasseus in corporis anatomen
133.20	Onomasticon medicinae
133.21	Volcherus de ossibus
133.22	Chirurgica Consilia Montani
133.23	Petri Andrei medici compendium
133.24	Ethica Aristotelis
133.25:1	Gabriel Falloppius de aquis et fossibilis et de simplicibus medicamentis
133.25:2	[See 133.25:1]
133.26	Jacobus Grevinus de venenis
133.27	Aphorismi Hippocratis
133.28	Weckeri Antidotarium Speciale
133.29	Eiusdem Antidotarium generale
133.30	Hippocratis de genitura etc
133.31	dialogus Iacobi Curionis
133.32	Symon Simonis de vera nobilitate
133.33	Peripatetica Patricii

133.34	Gwinterii Anatomica Institutio
133.35	Gynecaeorum de puerperorum effectibus
133.36	catalogus medicorum
133.37	consilia medica Mariae Venusti
133.38	Ferdinandus Mena de methodo febrium
133.39	tabulae Partitionum Sturmii
133.40	Glariani Geographia
133.41	Demosthenis et Aeschinis epistolae graecae
133.42	chronica herbarum
133.43	praeceptiones Gruchii dialecticae
133.44	Demosthenis ad Leptinem oratio graeca
133.45	Cosmographia Appiani
133.46	Jason de arcenda sterilitate
133.47	The Virtues of the Bathes
133.48	A Mirrour of Magistrates
133.49	Virgill his Aeneidos in Englishe
133.50	A Discourse of St. Peter's traveile
133.51	Aschame his Schole of Shootinge
133.52	comaedia Aristophanis de pace
133.53	A Larum to Englande by Captaine Riche
133.54	Gabuchinius de comitiali morbo
133.55	Erasthus de occultis pharmacorum potestatibus
133.56	certaine of Demosthenes' orations in englishe
133.57	Examen Catapotiorum
133.58	Ovide his Metamorphosis in englishe
133.59	opera Poli Cratici
133.60	Saluste in Englishe
133.61	Cardanus comforte
133.62	opera Actuarii medici
133.63	Caelius Aurelianus de occultis morbis
133.64	Fernelius de methodo medendi
133.65	Phuccius de institutione medecine
133.66	Realdus Columbus de re anatomica
133.67	Galenus de sanitate tuenda
133.68	Johannes Mesua de re medica
133.69	Hyppocratis Aphorismi
133.70	Galenus de humoribus
133.71	Medicorum quaedam monumenta
133.72	Albertus de formatione hominis
133.73	Compendiolum Curationis Scientiae
133.74	Johannes Baptista de re medica
133.75	Flores Poetarum
133.76	Hippocrates de hominis aetate
133.77	Pictor de compositione et usu medicinae
133.78	Lemnius de complexionibus

133.79	Schola Salernitana
133.80	epitome operum Valesci Tarantae
133.81	Tagauceus Ambianus de chirurgia
133.82	******* [Arnoldus?] de morbis curandis
133.83	Gatinarius de cognitione aegritudinum
133.84	Novum testamentum Gallice
133.85	Phritschius de meteoris
133.86	Senicae tragediae
133.87	Chekus de pronuntiatione graeca
133.88	Gaudentius Merula de rebus memorabilibus
133.89	Historia de Gentibus Septentrionalibus
133.90	Sebastianus Focius de naturali philosophia
133.91	epitome Adagiorum
133.92	Noctes Atticae Auli Gellii
133.93	Manutius de legibus romanis
133.94	Humfredus de s***tate
133.95	opera Thomae Mori Angli
133.96	Osorius de justitia
133.97	Osorius de gloria
133.98	Osorius de regis institutione
133.99	Osorius in Haddonum
133.100	Osorius de rebus gestis Emanuelis
133.101	Epistolae Ciceronis ad Atticum
133.102	epistolae Aschami
133.103	philosophia Ciceronis in duobus voluminibus
133.104	Familiares epistolae Ciceronis
133.105	Orationes Ciceronis tribus voluminibus
133.106	Fragmenta Ciceronis
133.107	Ciceronis rhetorica
133.108	Partitiones Curionis
133.109	Rondoletius de methodo curandi
133.110	Cornelius Agrippa de occulta philosophia
133.111	An Italian grammer
133.112	De arthritide Assertio
133.113	De Aromatum Historia
133.114	epistola Monlucii ad Polonos
133.115	Arceus de curandis vulneribus
133.116	Thaddeus Dunus de re medica
133.117	Gordonius de aetate hominis
133.118	Adverbiorum connubium
133.119	Lavaterus de spectris
133.120	Galenus de succo
133.121	Introductio Apotelesmetica
133.122	Fragmentum Britannicum
133.123	Joachimus de natura et differentiis colorum

133.124 Stanhufius de meteoris
133.125 Menezius de natura hominis
133.126 Chitreus de lectione historiarum
133.127 Quintus Curtius in Englishe
133.128 Syntaxis Linguae Graecae
133.129 Oribatius in Aporismos Hippocratis
133.130 Compendium Arithmeticae
133.131 Emillius macer de viribus herbarum
133.132 Monchiasenus de veritate Christi
133.133 Euricii Botanologicon
133.134 Argenterius de medicis consultationibus
133.135 Viaticum Morborum
133.136 The Treasure of Healthe
133.137 Bartholomeus in Sphaeram
133.138 Nicholaus Leonicus de morbo gallico
133.139 epistole Manerdi
133.140 Agrippa de occulta philosophia
133.141 epistolae Thaddaei Duni
133.142 Regimen Iter Agentium
133.143 Enchyridion de simplicibus pharmacibus
133.144 Joubertus de medicina practica
133.145 Boussuetus de arte medendi
133.146 Nycandri Alexi pharmaca
133.147 Bartholomaeus de naturali philosophia
133.148 Brudeus de ratione victus
133.149 Carvinus de missione sanguinis
133.150 Jacobus Praefecti de natura vini
133.151 Paulus Adgineta de simplicibus
133.152 R*bertus Dodoneus de radicum historia
133.153 de historia frumentorum
133.154 Hyppocrates de flatibus
133.155 Litterae quaedam italicae
133.156 a Frenche grammer
133.157 Garseus de erigndis figuris caeli
133.158 Valverdus de tuenda sanitate
133.159 Cornacis Enchyridion de medica consultatione
133.160 Middendorpius de academiis
133.161 Munster his epitome in englishe
133.162 Franciscus Ruise de gemmis
133.163 Aristoteles de anima
133.164 Wyerus de ira
133.165 The Proprietie of Herbes
133.166 Trincavellus de reactione
133.167 de arte conficiendae aquavitae, Savanorola
133.168 Machiavell de principe

133.169   Or*** de verbo Ch***i
133.170   The Wellspringe of Sciences
133.171   Viperanus de scribenda historia
133.172   A Riche Storehouse
133.173   de morbo gallico curando
133.174   The Interpretation of Dreames
133.175   The Debate betweene pride and lowlinesse
133.176   Tullie's Offices in Englishe
133.177   Aristoteles de natura
133.178   A Warninge to beware the Salter of Fowler
133.179   the earle of Surrie's songes and sonnettes
133.180   Turberveiles songes and sonnettes
133.181   The Flowers of Philosophie
133.182   Regimen Sanitatis
133.183   epitome Hippocratis de arte medendi
133.184   Arsanes' orationes
133.185   Cabellii Astrolabium
133.186   Canones Astronomici
133.187   Pelitarius de peste
133.188   Mercurius de divisione vocabulorum astronomiae
133.189   Progymnasmata graecae grammatices
133.190   the tragedie of Gorbaducke
133.191   An Introduction into Arithmeticke
133.192   The line of liberalitie
133.193   Recordes urinall of phisicke
133.194   The sighte of Urines
133.195   Guilielmus Magister de pestis saevitia
133.196   Sententiae Plauti
133.197   Bunelli epistolae
133.198   Petrus Ramus logicke in englishe
133.199   Troas scenice in englishe
133.200   The castle of healthe
133.201   The Detection of enormitie in phisicke
133.202   The composition of the oil Magistrale
133.203   The Paralelis
133.204   The Praise of Phisicke
133.205   Thesaurus Sanitatis
133.206   Aesopi fabulae graecolatinae
133.207   Cominaeus de gestis Ludovici regis Gallii
133.208   epistolae Manutii
133.209   Comediae Plauti
133.210   testamentum latinum
133.211   Centuriae Amati Lucitani, 5 et 6 libri
133.212   commentarii Brachelii in Technen Galeni
133.213   Dispensatorium Pharmacorum

133.214	Balthasur in Italian
133.215	Tullies epistles in french and lattin
133.216	Centuriae Amati 3 et 4ti
133.217	Alnoldus de conservanda valetudine
133.218	Caelum Philosophorum
133.219	Centuriae Amati 1a et 2a
133.220	Phuccius de ratione curandi
133.221	Faventinus de morbis medendis
133.222	Ovidii Amores
133.223	Fontanonus de morborum internorum curatione
133.224	Sylvius de medicamentis componendis
133.225	Bottallus de medici et aegroti munere
133.226	Dioschorides de materia medica
133.227	Balthasur de Curtesan
133.228	Cornelius Celsus de re medica
133.229	Musae Brasavolae, Examen Simplicium
133.230	Phuccius de re medica
133.231	Pergaminus de differentiis febrium
133.232	Galenus de facile parabilibus
133.233	Phicinus de vita
133.234	Galenus de ossibus
133.235	Galenus de compositione medicamentorum
133.236	eiusdem anatomica
133.237	idem de locorum affectorum notitia
133.238	idem de morborum et symptomatum differentiis
133.239	idem de ratione curandi
133.240	idem de Hippocratis et Platonis dogmatibus
133.241	idem de compositione pharmacorum
133.242	eiusdem ars medica
133.243	idem de alimentorum facultatibus
133.244	idem de usu partium
133.245	Hippocratis epidemia
133.246	medicorum introductiones
133.247	Patricius de regno
133.248	Galenus de simplicibus medicamentis
133.249	Hyppocratis Aphorismi
133.250	Salustius
133.251	Vitae Plutarchi
133.252	Pallingenius
133.253	Cordi Dispensatorium
133.254	Les Treasaures des Amadis
133.255	Sambusi emblemata
133.256	Galenus de naturalibus facultatibus
133.257	Galenus de chrysibus
133.258	de ebriosorum generibus

133.259   Herodiani historiae
133.260   de moribus Turcarum
133.261   Medicina Practica
133.262   Bertosii Methodus Medendi
133.263   de tempore purgandi
133.264   Pharmacapolorum officina
133.265   Formulae Remediorum
133.266   Praesagia Hippocratis
133.267   Galeni Ars Medecinalis
133.268   Methodus in Aphorismos Hippocratis
133.269   de lumbricis
133.270   orationes Muretae
133.271   The Regiment of Life
133.272   Historia Planetarum
133.273   Bodinus de methodo historiarum in 8°
133.274   Isaac Judaeus de dietis in 8°
133.275   Practica Petri Bayri in 8°
133.276   Cardanus de methodo medendi in 8°
133.277   Observationes Anatomicae Fallopii in 8°
133.278   Placatomus de valetudine tuenda in 8°
133.279   Victor de compositione medicamentum in 8°

§

133.1 In commentarii Gwintheri de utraque medecena
Joannes Guinterius (Andernacus). *De medicina commentarii duo*. Basle: ex officina Henricpetrina, 1571.
Language(s): Latin. Appraised at 10s in 1578.

133.2 Mathei Paris historia
Matthaeus Paris. *Historia major*. Edited by Matthew Parker, *Archbishop*. London: ap. R. Wolfium, 1571.
STC 19209 *et seq. Language(s)*: Latin. Appraised at 4s in 1578.

133.3 Syntaxes medicae Wickeri
Hanss Jacob Wecker. [*Medicinae utriusque syntaxes*]. Basle: (different houses), 1562–1576.
Language(s): Latin. Appraised at 3s 3d in 1578.

133.4 Delineatio Anatomiae per Geminum anglice
Thomas Geminus. *Compendiosa totius anatomie delineatio*. Translated by Nicholas Udall. London: (different houses) for T. Geminus, 1553–1559.
STC 11715.5 *et seq.* The illustrations are copied from Vesalius's *Fabrica*, 1543. *Language(s)*: English. Appraised at 4s in 1578.

133.5 Julius Alexandrinus de sanitate tuenda

Julius Alexandrinus. *Salubrium sive de sanitate tuenda*. Cologne: apud Gervinum Calenium, et haeredes Quentelios, 1575.
Language(s): Latin. Appraised at 2s 8d in 1578.

133.6 Aristoteles de historia animalium

Aristotle. *Historia animalium*. Continent: date indeterminable.
Language(s): Latin. Appraised at 16d in 1578.

133.7 epitome Galeni

Galen. [*Works–Epitome*]. Edited by Andres de Laguna. Continent: 1551–1571.

Editions of some of Galen's individual works were published, but the only epitome to appear in folio was of the complete works, edited by de Laguna. *Language(s)*: Latin. Appraised at 4s in 1578.

133.8 Cardanus in Hippocratis Prognostica

Girolamo Cardano. *In Hippocratis Prognostica* [and other works]. Basle: ex officina Henricpetrina, 1568.

Includes the Latin text of the *Prognostica* and *De septimestri partu*. *Language(s)*: Latin. Appraised at 18d in 1578.

133.9 dixonarium gallicarum et latinum

Unidentified [dictionary]. Continent: date indeterminable.

Robert Estienne's *Dictionariolum puerorum* should be considered a possibility. *Language(s)*: French Latin. Appraised at 20d in 1578.

133.10 Johannis Baptistae Montani opera

Joannes Baptista Montanus. Probably [*Consultationes medicinales*]. Continent: 1554–1572.

The only collection of Montanus's published in folio at this date. Some editions carry the word *opera* on the title page. *Language(s)*: Latin. Appraised at 2s 6d in 1578.

133.11 quaestiones Johannis canonici in Phisica

Joannes, *Canonicus*. [*Aristotle–Physica: commentary*]. Britain or Continent: 1475–1520.

STC 14621 and non-STC. Shaaber C104–111. *Language(s)*: Latin. Appraised at 16d in 1578.

133.12 opera Petri Penae et Matthei de Lobel, medicorum

Petrus Peña and Matthias de L'Obel. *Stirpium adversaria nova, perfacilis vestigatio*. Britain or Continent: 1570–1576.

STC 19595 *et seq*. The 1576 Antwerp edition is listed in the STC along with the first edition published in London. An edition was issued in 1576 as part two of L'Obel's *Plantarum seu stirpium historia. Language(s)*: Latin. Appraised at 3s 4d in 1578.

133.13 Practica Alexandri Yatros
Alexander, *Trallianus. Practica.* Venice: cum diligentia impressa heredum Octaviani Scoti ac soc., 1522.
Language(s): Latin. Appraised at 6d in 1578.

133.14 Canones Johannis Mesuae
Joannes Mesue (Yahya Ibn Masawaih). [*Works*]. Continent: date indeterminable.
Language(s): Latin. Appraised at 16d in 1578.

133.15 Galenus de temperamentis
Galen. *De temperamentis.* Continent: date indeterminable.
Durling 114 (in the "Analytical Index"), listing no separately published folio edition. The text appears in Galen's collected works and as the first work in several Paris editions of Thomas Linacre's translations of this work and Galen's *De inaequali intemperie* together. *Language(s)*: Latin (probable) Greek (perhaps). Appraised at 4d in 1578.

133.16 Galenus de natura hominis
Galen. [*Hippocrates–De natura hominis: commentary*]. Translated by Joannes Guinterius (Andernacus). Paris: Christian Wechel, 1537–1540.
Durling 156 (in the "Analytical Index"). Earlier and later editions appeared in smaller formats or with other works, but these are the only folio editions. *Language(s)*: Latin. Appraised at 4d in 1578.

133.17 Phernelius de abditis rerum causis
Joannes Fernelius. *De abditis rerum causis.* Continent: 1548–1577.
Language(s): Latin. Appraised at 12d in 1578.

133.18 historia rerum gallicarum
Unidentified. Continent (probable): date indeterminable.
Probably not an STC book. Possibilities include Comines, Sleidanus, and Gaguin. *Language(s)*: Latin. Appraised at 6d in 1578.

133.19 Vasseus in corporis anatomen
Lodoicus Vassaeus. *In anatomen corporis humani tabulae quatuor.* Paris: (different houses), 1540–1553.
Language(s): Latin. Appraised at 8d in 1578.

133.20 Onomasticon medicinae
Otto Brunfels. *Onomasticon medicinae.* Strassburg: apud Joannem Schottum, 1534–1543.

Language(s): Latin. Appraised at 2s 4d in 1578.

133.21 Volcherus de ossibus

Volcherus Coiter. *De ossibus et cartilaginibus humani corporis tabulae.*
Bologna: apud Joannem Rossium, 1566.
Language(s): Latin. Appraised at 5d in 1578.

133.22 Chirurgica Consilia Montani

Joannes Baptista Montanus. *Chirurgica consilia.* Nuremberg: in officina
J. Montani et U. Newberi, 1559.
Published as the third volume of the *Consilia medica omnia. Language(s)*:
Latin. Appraised at 4d in 1578.

133.23 Petri Andrei medici compendium

Pietro Andrea Mattioli. [*Compendium de plantis*]. Venice: in officina Valgri-
siana, 1571.
Other editions in print at this time were in duodecimo. *Language(s)*: Latin.
Appraised at 4s in 1578.

133.24 Ethica Aristotelis

Aristotle. *Ethica.* Britain or Continent: date indeterminable.
STC 752 and non-STC. *Language(s)*: Latin (probable) Greek (perhaps). Appraised at 12d in 1578.

133.25:1 Gabriel Falloppius de aquis et fossibilis et de simplicibus
medicamentis

Gabriel Fallopius. *De medicatis aquis atque de fossilibus.* Venice: (different
houses), 1564–1569.
Language(s): Latin. Appraised with one other at 4s in 1578.

133.25:2 [See 133.25:1]

Gabriel Fallopius. *De simplicibus medicamentis purgantibus.* Venice: ad
insigne stellae Jordani Ziletti, 1565.
The colophon gives 1566. *Language(s)*: Latin. Appraised with one other at
4s in 1578.

133.26 Jacobus Grevinus de venenis

Jacques Grévin. *De venenis libri duo.* Translated by Hieremias Martius. Antwerp: ex officina Christophori Plantini, 1571.
Language(s): Latin. Appraised at 18d in 1578.

133.27 Aphorismi Hippocratis

Hippocrates. *Aphorismi.* Continent: date indeterminable.
The verse adaptation at STC 13520 (1567) is in octavo. *Language(s)*: Latin.
Appraised at 5d in 1578.

133.28   Weckeri Antidotarium Speciale
Hanss Jacob Wecker. *Antidotarium speciale*. Basle: per Eusebium Episcopium et Nicolai fratris haered., 1574–1577.
Language(s): Latin. Appraised at 2s 6d in 1578.

133.29   Eiusdem Antidotarium generale
Hanss Jacob Wecker. *Antidotarium generale*. Basle: per Eusebium Episcopium, et Nicolai fr. haeredes, 1576.
Struck out. *Language(s)*: Latin. Appraised at 7d in 1578.

133.30   Hippocratis de genitura etc
Hippocrates. *De genitura. De natura pueri*. Translated by Joannes Gorraeus.
Paris: ex officina Michaëlis Vascosani, 1545.
Language(s): Latin. Appraised at 3d in 1578.

133.31   dialogus Iacobi Curionis
Jacobus Curio. *Inscriptus Hermotini nomine dialogus*. Basle: apud Petrum Pernam, 1570.
Language(s): Latin. Appraised at 5d in 1578.

133.32   Symon Simonis de vera nobilitate
Simon Simonius. *De vera nobilitate*. Leipzig: Joannes Rhamba excude., 1572.
Language(s): Latin. Appraised at 4d in 1578.

133.33   Peripatetica Patricii
Francesco Patrizi, *Philosophical Writer*. *Discussiones peripateticae*. Venice: apud Dominicum de Franciscis, 1571.
Language(s): Latin. Appraised at 12d in 1578.

133.34   Gwinterii Anatomica Institutio
Joannes Guinterius (Andernacus). *Institutiones anatomicae*. Basle: in officina Roberti Winter, 1539.
The only quarto edition. *Language(s)*: Latin. Appraised at 5d in 1578.

133.35   Gynecaeorum de puerperorum effectibus
Gynaeciorum libri. Edited by Caspar Wolf. Basle: per Thomam Guarinum, 1566.
Language(s): Latin. Appraised at 12d in 1578.

133.36   catalogus medicorum
Otto Brunfels. *Catalogus illustrium medicorum, sive de primis medicinae scriptoribus*. Strassburg: apud Joannem Schottum, 1530.
Language(s): Latin. Appraised at 2d in 1578.

133.37 consilia medica Mariae Venusti
Antonio Maria Venusti. *Consilia medica*. Venice: apud Franciscum Zilettum, 1571.
Language(s): Latin. Appraised at 6d in 1578.

133.38 Ferdinandus Mena de methodo febrium
Ferdinandus de Mena, *Physician*. *Methodus febrium omnium*. Antwerp: ex officina Christophori Plantini, 1568.
Language(s): Latin. Appraised at 6d in 1578.

133.39 tabulae Partitionum Sturmii
Valentinus Erythraeus. [*Tabulae in Ciceronem et Sturmium*]. Continent: date indeterminable.
The *Partitionum dialecticarum libri quatuor* would be a possibility except that it seems to have appeared in folio, not quarto as indicated here. *Language(s)*: Latin. Appraised at 5d in 1578.

133.40 Glariani Geographia
Henricus Loritus Glareanus. *De geographia*. Continent: 1527–1551.
Language(s): Latin. Appraised at 1d in 1578.

133.41 Demosthenis et Aeschinis epistolae graecae
Aeschines and Demosthenes. [*Selected works–Epistolae*]. Paris: (different houses), 1550–1557.
The 1550 edition is in Greek and Latin. *Language(s)*: Greek Latin (perhaps). Appraised at 1d in 1578.

133.42 chronica herbarum
Nicolaus Winckler. *Chronica herbarum*. Augsburg: in officina typographica Michaëlis Mangeri, 1571.
Language(s): Latin. Appraised at 5d in 1578.

133.43 praeceptiones Gruchii dialecticae
Nicolaus Gruchius. *Praeceptiones dialecticae*. Paris: (stationer unknown), 1555–1558.
Language(s): Latin. Appraised at 2d in 1578.

133.44 Demosthenis ad Leptinem oratio graeca
Demosthenes. *Adversus Leptinem*. Continent: 1526–1559.
Language(s): Greek. Appraised at 2d in 1578.

133.45 Cosmographia Appiani
Peter Apian. *Cosmographia*. Continent: 1524–1574.
Language(s): Latin. Appraised at 8d in 1578.

133.46 Jason de arcenda sterilitate

Jason Pratensis. *Liber de arcenda sterilitate et progignendis liberis*. Antwerp: apud Michaelem Hillenium in Rapo, 1531.
Language(s): Latin. Appraised at 2d in 1578.

133.47 The Virtues of the Bathes

Unidentified. Britain: date indeterminable.

Unidentifiable in the STC. The second part of Turner's *Herball* is on the baths, but it was published in folio (see STC 24366–24367); John Jones's two books on the baths are in quarto, but neither title is verbally similar to the manuscript entry (see STC 14724a.3 and 14724a.7). *Language(s)*: English. Appraised at 3d in 1578.

133.48 A Mirrour of Magistrates

William Baldwin and others. *A myrroure for magistrates*. London: Thomas Marshe, 1559–1578.

STC 1247 *et seq.* First issued in 1554 under a different title; see STC 1246. The less well-known, "first parte" addition by John Higgins, *Poet*, brought out in 1574 (STC 13443), is not likely to have been entered as above. *Language(s)*: English. Appraised at 3d in 1578.

133.49 Virgill his Aeneidos in Englishe

Publius Virgilius Maro. *Aeneid*. London: (different houses), 1557–1573.

STC 24798 *et seq.* The 1573 edition (STC 24801) is the only complete *Aeneid* in English in the date range in quarto. *Language(s)*: English. Appraised at 12d in 1578.

133.50 A Discourse of St. Peter's traveile

Unidentified. Britain: date indeterminable.

Unidentifiable in the STC. Christopher Carlile's *A discourse. Wherein is plainly proved that Peter was never in Rome* (STC 4655) should be considered a possibility. *Language(s)*: English. Appraised at 3d in 1578.

133.51 Aschame his Schole of Shootinge

Roger Ascham. *Toxophilus, the schole of shootinge conteyned in two bookes*. London: (different houses), 1545–1571.

STC 837 *et seq. Language(s)*: English. Appraised at 3d in 1578.

133.52 comaedia Aristophanis de pace

Aristophanes. *Pax*. Louvain: ex officina S. Sasseni, 1547.
Language(s): Greek. Appraised at 1d in 1578.

133.53 A Larum to Englande by Captaine Riche

Barnaby Rich. *Allarme to England, foreshewing what perilles are procured, where the people live without regarde of martiall lawe*. London: C. Barker, 1578.

STC 20978 *et seq.* Two editions in 1578, the second printed by Henry Middleton for Barker. *Language(s)*: English. Appraised at 3d in 1578.

133.54 Gabuchinius de comitiali morbo
Hieronymus Gabucinus. *De comitiali morbo*. Venice: [Aldine Press], 1561. *Language(s)*: Latin. Appraised at 7d in 1578.

133.55 Erasthus de occultis pharmacorum potestatibus
Thomas Erastus. *De occultis pharmacorum potestatibus. De medicamentorum purgantium facultate*. Basle: per Petrum Pernam, 1574. *Language(s)*: Latin. Appraised at 6d in 1578.

133.56 certaine of Demosthenes' orations in englishe
Demosthenes. *The three orations of Demosthenes ... in favour of the Olynthians, with fower orations against king Philip most nedefull to be redde in these daungerous dayes*. Translated by Thomas Wilson, *Secretary of State*. London: H. Denham, 1570.
STC 6578. *Language(s)*: English. Appraised at 5d in 1578.

133.57 Examen Catapotiorum
Antonio Musa Brasavola. *Examen omnium catapotiorum*. Basle: ex officina Frobeniana (per Hieronymum Frobenium et Nicolaum Episcopium), 1543.
The only quarto edition listed by Durling. *Language(s)*: Latin. Appraised at 3d in 1578.

133.58 Ovide his Metamorphosis in englishe
Publius Ovidius Naso. *Metamorphoses*. Translated by Arthur Golding. London: William Seres, 1565–1575.
STC 18955 *et seq.* Whether complete (STC 18956–18957) or part (STC 18955) cannot be determined. *Language(s)*: English. Appraised at 10d in 1578.

133.59 opera Poli Cratici
John, *of Salisbury, Bishop of Chartres. Policraticus de nugis curialium*. Paris: venale apud (opera et expensa) Bertholdum Rembolt et Joannem Parvum, 1513.
Language(s): Latin. Appraised at 6d in 1578.

133.60 Saluste in Englishe
Caius Sallustius Crispus. *The historye of Jugurth*. Translated by Alexander Barclay. London: J. Waley, 1557.
STC 10752. The second part of a two-volume publication, the first part of which is Constantius Felicius's *The conspiracie of Catiline*, here, apparently, absent. *Language(s)*: English. Appraised at 14d in 1578.

133.61 Cardanus comforte

Girolamo Cardano. *Cardanus comforte translated into Englishe*. Translated by Thomas Bedingfield. London: T. Marshe, 1573–1576.

STC 4607 *et seq. Language(s)*: English. Appraised at 3d in 1578.

133.62 opera Actuarii medici

Joannes Actuarius. [*Works*]. Continent: 1556.

At least three editions appeared in 1556, two in Paris, one in Lyon. *Language(s)*: Latin. Appraised at 16d in 1578.

133.63 Caelius Aurelianus de occultis morbis

Caelius Aurelianus. *De acutis morbis lib. III. De diurnis lib. V.* Lyon: apud Guliel. Rouillium, 1566–1569.

The word *acutis* is written above *occultis*, which is not crossed out. *Language(s)*: Latin. Appraised at 3d in 1578.

133.64 Fernelius de methodo medendi

Joannes Fernelius. *Therapeutices universalis seu medendi rationis libri septem.* Continent: 1569–1574.

Language(s): Latin. Appraised at 7d in 1578.

133.65 Phuccius de institutione medecine

Leonard Fuchs. *Institutiones medicinae.* Continent: 1555–1572.

Language(s): Latin. Appraised at 6d in 1578.

133.66 Realdus Columbus de re anatomica

Realdus Columbus. *De re anatomica.* Paris: (different houses), 1562–1572.

Language(s): Latin. Appraised at 8d in 1578.

133.67 Galenus de sanitate tuenda

Galen. *De sanitate tuenda.* Continent: 1526–1549.

Durling 103 (in the "Analytical Index"). *Language(s)*: Latin (probable) Greek (perhaps). Appraised at 4d in 1578.

133.68 Johannes Mesua de re medica

Joannes Mesue (Yahya Ibn Masawaih). *De re medica.* Translated by Jacques Dubois (Jacobus Sylvius). Continent: 1548–1566.

Earlier editions are in a folio format. *Language(s)*: Latin. Appraised at 6d in 1578.

133.69 Hyppocratis Aphorismi

Hippocrates. *Aphorismi.* Continent: date indeterminable.

Language(s): Latin Greek (perhaps). Appraised at 6d in 1578.

133.70 Galenus de humoribus

Galen (spurious). *De humoribus.* Continent: 1556–1558.

Durling 54 (in the "Analytical Index"). *Language(s)*: Latin (probable) Greek (perhaps). Appraised at 4d in 1578.

133.71 Medicorum quaedam monumenta
Probably *Ars de dosibus medicinarum, et alia praestantissimorum medicorum monumenta*. Padua: apud Gratiosum Perchacinum, 1564.
Six tracts. *Language(s)*: Latin. Appraised at 8d in 1578.

133.72 Albertus de formatione hominis
Albertus Magnus. *Libellus de formatione hominis in utero*. Antwerp: ex off. vid. Martini Caesaris, 1538.
Language(s): Latin. Appraised at 3d in 1578.

133.73 Compendiolum Curationis Scientiae
Hieronymus Montuus. *Compendiolum curatricis scientiae*. Lyon: apud Joan. Tornaesium et Guliel. Gazeium, 1556.
Language(s): Latin. Appraised at 4d in 1578.

133.74 Johannes Baptista de re medica
Unidentified. Continent (probable): date indeterminable.
Almost certainly not an STC book. Nothing of Joannes Baptista Montanus's can be identified with the manuscript entry. The *Rei medicae studio in stipendia sex* of Joannes Baptista Donatus exists in a 1590 edition, identified as the third, and in a 1591 edition, but no earlier edition can be found. A pre-1578 edition, no longer extant, must be considered a possibility since at least one of Donatus's works was published in 1566. *Language(s)*: Latin. Appraised at 8d in 1578.

133.75 Flores Poetarum
Flores poetarum. Continent: date indeterminable.
An anthology with editions dating from 1480. *Language(s)*: Latin. Appraised at 4d in 1578.

133.76 Hippocrates de hominis aetate
Hippocrates. *De hominis aetate* [and other works]. Geneva: apud Crispinum, 1571.
No solo edition of this work can be found. *Language(s)*: Greek Latin. Appraised at 8d in 1578.

133.77 Pictor de compositione et usu medicinae
Georg Pictorius. *Medicinae tam simplices quam compositae* [and other works]. Basle: [per Henricum Petri], 1560.
Language(s): Latin. Appraised at 5d in 1578.

133.78 Lemnius de complexionibus
Levinus Lemnius. *De habitu et constitucione corporis.* Antwerp: apud Guliel-
mum Simonem, 1561.
Language(s): Latin. Appraised at 7d in 1578.

133.79 Schola Salernitana
[*Regimen sanitatis Salernitatum*]. *Salerno.* Britain or Continent: date indeterminable.
STC 21600 *et seq.* and non-STC. Earlier editions cited in the STC are all in
quarto. The STC editions are in both Latin and English. Another copy at
133.182. *Language(s)*: Latin English (perhaps). Appraised at 10d in 1578.

133.80 epitome operum Valesci Tarantae
Valescus de Taranta. *Epitome operis utilis morbis curandis.* Compiled by
Guido Desiderius. Lyon: apud Joan. Tornaesium et Gulielmum Gazeium,
1560.
Language(s): Latin. Appraised at 10d in 1578.

133.81 Tagauceus Ambianus de chirurgia
Joannes Tagaultius. *De chirurgica institutione.* Continent: 1544–1567.
The *editio princeps* (1543) is a folio edition. Tagaultius was of Amiens. *Lan-
guage(s)*: Latin. Appraised at 10d in 1578.

133.82 ***** [Arnoldus?] de morbis curandis**
Probably Arnaldus, *de Villa Nova.* [*Regulae universales curationis morborum*].
Continent: date indeterminable.
Commentary by Georg Pictorius. Struck out and nearly illegible. *Lan-
guage(s)*: Latin. Appraised at 12d in 1578.

133.83 Gatinarius de cognitione aegritudinum
Marco Gatinaria. Probably [*De curis aegritudinum*]. Continent: date indeter-
minable.
Language(s): Latin. Appraised at 10d in 1578.

133.84 Novum testamentum Gallice
[*Bible–N.T.*]. Britain or Continent: date indeterminable.
STC 2957.6 *et seq.* and non-STC. *Language(s)*: French. Appraised at 12d in
1578.

133.85 Phritschius de meteoris
Marcus Fritsche. [*De meteoris*]. Nuremberg: in officina Joannis Montani et
Ulrici Neuberi, 1555–1563.
Language(s): Latin. Appraised at 8d in 1578.

133.86 Senicae tragediae
Lucius Annaeus Seneca. *Tragoediae*. Continent: date indeterminable.
Language(s): Latin. Appraised at 5d in 1578.

133.87 Chekus de pronuntiatione graeca
Sir John Cheke. *De pronuntiatione graecae*. Basle: per N. Episcopium juniorem, 1555.
Language(s): Latin. Appraised at 7d in 1578.

133.88 Gaudentius Merula de rebus memorabilibus
Gaudentius Merula. *Memorabilia*. Continent: 1550–1556.
Language(s): Latin. Appraised at 8d in 1578.

133.89 Historia de Gentibus Septentrionalibus
Olaus Magnus. *Historia de gentibus septentrionalibus*. Continent: date indeterminable.
Could be the epitome. *Language(s)*: Latin. Appraised at 8d in 1578.

133.90 Sebastianus Focius de naturali philosophia
Sebastiano Fox Morzillo. *De naturae philosophia, seu de Platonis et Aristotelis consensione*. Continent: 1554–1560.
The 1554 and 1560 editions are in octavo, coinciding with the manuscript entry. NUC lists a 1551 edition, without indication of format; it cannot be found elsewhere. *Language(s)*: Latin. Appraised at 8d in 1578.

133.91 epitome Adagiorum
Desiderius Erasmus. [*Adagia–Epitome*]. Continent: date indeterminable.
Language(s): Latin. Appraised at 6d in 1578.

133.92 Noctes Atticae Auli Gellii
Aulus Gellius. *Noctes Atticae*. Continent: date indeterminable.
Language(s): Latin. Appraised at 6d in 1578.

133.93 Manutius de legibus romanis
Paolo Manuzio. *Antiquitatum Romanarum liber de legibus*. Continent: 1557–1570.
Language(s): Latin. Appraised at 6d in 1578.

133.94 Humfredus de s***tate
Unidentified. Place unknown: stationer unknown, date indeterminable.
STC/non-STC status unknown. Something of Laurence Humphrey?
The *De tuenda sanitate* of Hugo Fridaevallis, published in octavo, the format of this item, is a very remote possibility. *Language(s)*: Latin. Appraised at 5d in 1578.

133.95   opera Thomae Mori Angli
Sir Thomas More. *Lucubrationes.* Basle: apud Episcopium F. [Nicolaus Episcopius, *Junior*], 1563.
All specifically entitled *opera* are folio editions. *Language(s)*: Latin. Appraised at 10d in 1578.

133.96   Osorius de justitia
Jeronimo Osorio da Fonseca, *Bishop. De justitia.* Continent: 1564–1574. *Language(s)*: Latin. Appraised at 10d in 1578.

133.97   Osorius de gloria
Jeronimo Osorio da Fonseca, *Bishop.* [*Selected works*]. Continent: date indeterminable.
The only solo edition is a 1552 quarto. Osorio's popular collection, frequently referred to by its lead title, *De gloria*, appeared in a number of octavo editions, the size of this item. *Language(s)*: Latin. Appraised at 10d in 1578.

133.98   Osorius de regis institutione
Jeronimo Osorio da Fonseca, *Bishop. De regis institutione et disciplina.* Cologne: apud haered. Arnoldi Birckmanni, 1572–1574.
An earlier 1571 edition is in quarto. *Language(s)*: Latin. Appraised at 12d in 1578.

133.99   Osorius in Haddonum
Jeronimo Osorio da Fonseca, *Bishop. In Gualterum Haddonum magistrum libellorum supplicum libri tres.* Continent: 1567–1574.
Language(s): Latin. Appraised at 10d in 1578.

133.100   Osorius de rebus gestis Emanuelis
Jeronimo Osorio da Fonseca, *Bishop. De rebus Emmanuelis regis Lusitaniae.* Cologne: apud haered. Arnoldi Birckmanni, 1574–1576.
Also published in folio in 1571. *Language(s)*: Latin. Appraised at 20d in 1578.

133.101   Epistolae Ciceronis ad Atticum
Marcus Tullius Cicero. *Epistolae ad Atticum.* Continent: date indeterminable.
The *Epistolae ad Atticum* is the leading title in numerous collections of Cicero's letters. *Language(s)*: Latin. Appraised at 8d in 1578.

133.102   epistolae Aschami
Roger Ascham. *Familiarium epistolarum libri tres.* Edited by Edward Grant. London: Henry Middleton for Francis Coldock, 1576–1578.
STC 826 *et seq. Language(s)*: Latin. Appraised at 5d in 1578.

133.103 philosophia Ciceronis in duobus voluminibus
Marcus Tullius Cicero. [*Selected works–Philosophica*]. Continent: date indeterminable.
Language(s): Latin. Appraised at 14d in 1578.

133.104 Familiares epistolae Ciceronis
Marcus Tullius Cicero. *Epistolae ad familiares*. Britain or Continent: date indeterminable.
STC 5295 *et seq.* and non-STC. *Language(s)*: Latin. Appraised at 4d in 1578.

133.105 Orationes Ciceronis tribus voluminibus
Marcus Tullius Cicero. [*Selected works–Orations*]. Continent: date indeterminable.
Language(s): Latin. Appraised at 2s in 1578.

133.106 Fragmenta Ciceronis
Marcus Tullius Cicero. [*Selections–Fragmenta*]. Continent: date indeterminable.
Language(s): Latin. Appraised at 6d in 1578.

133.107 Ciceronis rhetorica
Marcus Tullius Cicero. [*Selected works–Rhetorica*]. Continent: date indeterminable.
Language(s): Latin. Appraised at 6d in 1578.

133.108 Partitiones Curionis
Caelius Secundus Curio. [*Cicero–De partitione oratoria: commentary* (and other works)]. Continent: 1556–1567.
Joannes Oporinus was involved in printing both the Basle and the Frankfurt editions. *Language(s)*: Latin. Appraised at 3d in 1578.

133.109 Rondoletius de methodo curandi
Guillaume Rondelet. *Methodus curandorum omnium morborum*. Continent: c.1570–1576.
The first date is supplied by Wellcome; Adams gives it as 1563 and NLM6 as c.1567. *Language(s)*: Latin. Appraised at 2s in 1578.

133.110 Cornelius Agrippa de occulta philosophia
Henricus Cornelius Agrippa. *De occulta philosophia*. Continent: 1531–1567.
There is another entry for an octavo edition of this text at 133.140, appraised at the much lower sum of 2*d*. *Language(s)*: Latin. Appraised at 16d in 1578.

133.111   An Italian grammer
Probably Scipio Lentulo. *An Italian grammer written in Latin and turned in Englishe*. Translated by Henry Granthan. London: Thomas Vautrollier, 1575. STC 15469. A Continental publication must be considered a possibility. *Language(s)*: English Italian. Appraised at 8d in 1578.

133.112   De arthritide Assertio
Toussaint Ducret. *De arthritide vera assertio, eiusque curandae methodus adversus Paracelsistas*. Lyon: apud Bartholomaeum Vincentium, 1575. *Language(s)*: Latin. Appraised at 6d in 1578.

133.113   De Aromatum Historia
Garcia de Orta. *Aromatum et simplicium aliquot medicamentorum apud Indos nascentium historia*. Antwerp: Christopher Plantin, 1567–1574. *Language(s)*: Latin. Appraised at 4d in 1578.

133.114   epistola Monlucii ad Polonos
Jean de Montluc, *Bishop. Epistola de Andium Duce in regnum Polonicorum*. Lusignan: excud. Ivo Durerius, 1573–1574. *Language(s)*: Latin. Appraised at 4d in 1578.

133.115   Arceus de curandis vulneribus
Franciscus Arcaeus. *De recta curandorum vulnerum ratione* [and other works]. Edited by Benito Arias Montano. Antwerp: ex officina Christopheri Plantini, 1574. *Language(s)*: Latin. Appraised at 4d in 1578.

133.116   Thaddeus Dunus de re medica
Thaddeus Dunus. Probably *Miscellaneorum de re medica*. Continent: date indeterminable.
This work is extant only as a composite publication with Dunus's *Epistolae medicinales* in a 1592 edition, but PLRE 104 (1573) includes an entry *dunius de arte medica* (PLRE 104.61). See 133.141. *Language(s)*: Latin. Appraised at 4d in 1578.

133.117   Gordonius de aetate hominis
Bernardus de Gordonio. Probably *Tractatus de conservatione vitae humanae*. Leipzig: imprimebat Joannes Rhamba, curante Ernest Vogelin, 1570.
Contains only *De regiminie sanitatis*, the last of the four medical treatises appearing in *De conservatione vitae humanae*, which appears complete only in his *Practica*. *Language(s)*: Latin. Appraised at 3d in 1578.

133.118   Adverbiorum connubium
Hubertus Sussanaeus. *Connubium adverbiorum Ciceronianorum*. Continent: 1548–1576.

Language(s): Latin. Appraised at 2d in 1578.

133.119   Lavaterus de spectris
Ludwig Lavater. *De spectris*. Geneva: (different houses), 1570–1575.
Language(s): Latin. Appraised at 4d in 1578.

133.120   Galenus de succo
Galen. *De succedaneis*. Paris: Gulielmus Morelius, 1557?
Durling 111 (in the "Analytical Index"). Not separately published.
Assumed here to have been separated from a collection of various works of
Galen issued in octavo, the only octavo edition in which *De succedaneis* is
found. *Language(s)*: Greek (probable). Appraised at 1d in 1578.

133.121   Introductio Apotelesmetica
Joannes ab Indagine. [*Chiromantia*]. Continent: date indeterminable.
Language(s): Latin. Appraised at 2d in 1578.

133.122   Fragmentum Britannicum
Humphrey Llwyd. *Commentarioli Britannicae descriptionis fragmentum*.
Cologne: apud Joannem Birckmannum, 1572.
Language(s): Latin. Appraised at 2d in 1578.

133.123   Joachimus de natura et differentiis colorum
Joachim Cureus. *Libellus physicus*. Wittenberg: (different houses), 1567–
1572.
    The long title includes ... *continens doctrina de natura, et differentis colorum,*
Language(s): Latin. Appraised at 4d in 1578.

133.124   Stanhufius de meteoris
Michael Stanhufius. *De meteoris*. Wittenberg: (stationer unknown), 1562–
1578.
Language(s): Latin. Appraised at 4d in 1578.

133.125   Menezius de natura hominis
Perhaps Meletius, *Monk. De natura structuraque hominis opus* [and other
works]. Venice: ex officina Gryphii, sumptibus Francisci Camotii et sociorum,
1552.
    This edition, the only one found in the standard sources, is in quarto, un-
like the manuscript entry, which is listed as octavo. That, with the entry,
Menezius, makes this identification speculative. *Language(s)*: Latin. Appraised
at 3d in 1578.

133.126   Chitreus de lectione historiarum
David Chytraeus. *De lectione historiarum*. Continent: 1563–1565.
Language(s): Latin. Appraised at 4d in 1578.

133.127   Quintus Curtius in Englishe
Quintus Curtius Rufus. *The historie of Quintus Curcius, contayning the actes of the greate Alexander*. Translated by John Brende. London: in aed. R. Tottell, 1570.
STC 6144. *Language(s)*: English. Appraised at 10d in 1578.

133.128   Syntaxis Linguae Graecae
Unidentified. Continent (probable): date indeterminable.
Probably not an STC book. Joannes Varrenius and Joannes Posselius each wrote a *Syntaxis linguae graecae* published in octavo. There are probably others. *Language(s)*: Greek Latin. Appraised at 4d in 1578.

133.129   Oribatius in Aporismos Hippocratis
Oribasius. [*Hippocrates–Aphorismi: commentary and text*]. Edited by Joannes Guinterius (Andernacus). Continent: 1533–1535.
Language(s): Latin. Appraised at 3d in 1578.

133.130   Compendium Arithmeticae
Unidentified. Continent (probable): date indeterminable.
Probably not an STC book. Johann Fischer (Joannes Piscator) and Joannes Scheubelius are two possible authors. *Language(s)*: Latin. Appraised at 3d in 1578.

133.131   Emillius macer de viribus herbarum
Odo, *Magdunensis*. *De viribus herbarum*. Continent: date indeterminable.
Formerly attributed to Aemelius Macer, *Floridus*. *Language(s)*: Latin. Appraised at 5d in 1578.

133.132   Monchiasenus de veritate Christi
Antoine de Mouchy (Demochares). *De veritate Christi, nec non corporis et sanguinis eius in missae sacrificio*. Continent: 1570–1573.
The author was also known as Antonius Monchiacenus. *Language(s)*: Latin. Appraised at 4d in 1578.

133.133   Euricii Botanologicon
Euricius Cordus. *Botanologicon*. Cologne: apud Joannem Gymnicum, 1534.
There was a Paris 1551 duodecimo edition that could have been mistaken for an octavo. *Language(s)*: Latin. Appraised at 2d in 1578.

133.134   Argenterius de medicis consultationibus
Joannes Argenterius. *De consultationibus medicis*. Continent: 1551–1552.
Language(s): Latin. Appraised at 2d in 1578.

133.135 Viaticum Morborum
Jacobus Hollerius. [*De omnium morborum curatione*]. Edited by Caspar Wolf.
Continent: date indeterminable.
Language(s): Latin. Appraised at 3d in 1578.

133.136 The Treasure of Healthe
John XXI, *Pope* (Petrus, *Hispanus*). *The treasury of healthe conteynyng many profitable medycines gathered by Petrus Hispanus*. Translated by Humphrey Lloyd. London: (different houses), 1550?–c.1570.
STC 14651.5 *et seq. Language(s)*: English. Appraised at 5d in 1578.

133.137 Bartholomeus in Sphaeram
Bartholomaeus Mercator. *Breves in sphaeram meditatiunculae*. Cologne: apud haeredes Arnoldi Birckmanni, 1563.
Language(s): Latin. Appraised at 2d in 1578.

133.138 Nicholaus Leonicus de morbo gallico
Liber de morbo gallico. Venice: per Joannem Patavinum et Venturinum de Rufinellis, 1535.
This anthology leads with Nicolaus Leonicenus's work. All solo editions of his *De morbo gallico* are in quarto. Nicolaus Leonicus, *Thomaeus* did not write a *De morbo gallico*. *Language(s)*: Latin. Appraised at 4d in 1578.

133.139 epistole Manerdi
Joannes Manardus. [*Epistolae medicinales*]. Continent: date indeterminable.
The collection, *Epistolae medicinales diversorum authorum*, with Manardus named first, was published in folio in all editions. This item is in the octavo section of Glover's library. *Language(s)*: Latin. Appraised at 3d in 1578.

133.140 Agrippa de occulta philosophia
Henricus Cornelius Agrippa. *De occulta philosophia*. Continent: 1531–1567.
Another copy at 133.110. *Language(s)*: Latin. Appraised at 2d in 1578.

133.141 epistolae Thaddaei Duni
Thaddeus Dunus. Perhaps *Epistolae medicinales* [and other works]. Continent: date indeterminable.
This work is extant only in a 1592 edition, but see 133.116. Conceivably, a 1555 anthology of medical treatises (. . . *disputationum per epistolas* . . .) with Dunus's name leading is intended. *Language(s)*: Latin. Appraised at 2d in 1578.

133.142 Regimen Iter Agentium
Gulielmus Gratarolus. [*De regimen iter agentium*]. Continent: 1561–1571.
Language(s): Latin. Appraised at 2d in 1578.

133.143 Enchyridion de simplicibus pharmacibus

Unidentified. Continent (probable): date indeterminable.

Almost certainly not an STC book. One of the sixteenth-century compilations of pharmacological works; for example, those by Nicolaus Leonicenus or Symphorien Champier. Probably not Paulus, *Aegineta*'s *Pharmaca simplicia* since it appears at 133.151. *Language(s)*: Latin. Appraised at 3d in 1578.

133.144 Joubertus de medicina practica

Laurent Joubert (Valentinus). *Medicinae practicae priores libri tres.* Continent: date indeterminable.

Language(s): Latin. Appraised at 4d in 1578.

133.145 Boussuetus de arte medendi

François Boussuet. *De arte medendi.* Lyon: apud Mathiam Bonhomme, 1557.

Struck out. *Language(s)*: Latin.

133.146 Nycandri Alexi pharmaca

Nicander, *Colophonius. Alexipharmaca.* Translated by Joannes Gorraeus. Paris: apud Vascosanum, 1549.

Only solo edition of *Alexipharmaca*, which was usually published with Nicander's *Theriaca. Language(s)*: Greek Latin. Appraised at 1½d in 1578.

133.147 Bartholomaeus de naturali philosophia

Perhaps Bartholomaeus Cocles. *Chiromantia et Physiomania.* Continent: 1533–1555.

Cocles is described on some title pages of this widely published work as "naturalis philosophiae et medicinae doctor." Earlier editions were published in folio. *Language(s)*: Latin. Appraised at 3d in 1578.

133.148 Brudeus de ratione victus

Brudus, *Lusitanus. Liber de ratione victus in singulis febribus secundum Hippocratem.* Venice: (different houses), 1544–1549.

Language(s): Latin. Appraised at 6d in 1578.

133.149 Carvinus de missione sanguinis

Joannes Carvinus. *De sanguine dialogi VII.* Lyon: apud haered. Seb. Gryphii, 1562.

Language(s): Latin. Appraised at 3d in 1578.

133.150 Jacobus Praefecti de natura vini

Jacobus Praefectus. *De diversorum vini generum natura.* Venice: ex officina J. Ziletti, 1559.

Language(s): Latin. Appraised at 2d in 1578.

133.151   Paulus Adgineta de simplicibus
Paulus, *Aegineta. Pharmaca simplicia*. Translated by Otto Brunfels. Continent: 1531–1532.
Language(s): Latin. Appraised at 3d in 1578.

133.152   R*bertus Dodoneus de radicum historia
Rembert Dodoens. *Purgantium aliarumque eo facientium, tum et radicum, convolvulorum ac deleteriarum herbarum historiae libri IIII*. Continent: 1572–1574.
Language(s): Latin. Appraised at 10d in 1578.

133.153   de historia frumentorum
Rembert Dodoens. *Historia frumentorum, leguminum, palustrium et aquatilium herbarum*. Antwerp: ex officina Christophi Plantini, 1566–1569.
Other titles, including *De stirpium historia*, remain possibilities. *Language(s)*: Latin. Appraised at 8d in 1578.

133.154   Hyppocrates de flatibus
Hippocrates. *De flatibus*. Paris: apud Martinum Juvenem, 1557.
A 1525 Paris edition in sextodecimo could, conceivably, have been mistaken for an octavo. *Language(s)*: Latin. Appraised at 4d in 1578.

133.155   Litterae quaedam italicae
Unidentified. Continent: date indeterminable.
See Adams L557 for more than a score of possibilities. *Language(s)*: Italian Latin. Appraised at 8d in 1578.

133.156   a Frenche grammer
Unidentified. Place unknown: stationer unknown, date indeterminable.
STC/non-STC status unknown. Works published in England that might be so described include STC 1852 and STC 11376. STC 24865 *et seq.* are not in octavo. *Language(s)*: French English (probable). Appraised at 6d in 1578.

133.157   Garseus de erigndis figuris caeli
Joannes Garcaeus. *Tractatus brevis de erigendis figuris coeli*. Wittenberg: (different houses), 1556–1578.
Language(s): Latin. Appraised at 6d in 1578.

133.158   Valverdus de tuenda sanitate
Juan Valverde de Amusco. *De animi et corporis sanitate tuenda libellus*. Continent: 1552–1553.
Language(s): Latin. Appraised at 2d in 1578.

133.159   Cornacis Enchyridion de medica consultatione
Matthias Cornax. *Medicae consultationis apud aegrotos enchiridion*. Basle: per

Joannem Oporinum, 1564.
Language(s): Latin. Appraised at 3d in 1578.

133.160   Middendorpius de academiis
Jacob Middendorp. [*De celebrioribus universi terrarum orbis academiis*].
Cologne: (different houses), 1567–1572.
Language(s): Latin. Appraised at 4d in 1578.

133.161   Munster his epitome in englishe
Sebastian Muenster. *A briefe collection and compendious extract of straunge
and memorable thinges, gathered oute of the Cosmographye of S. Muenster.* London:
T. Marshe, 1572–1576.
STC 18242 *et seq. Language(s)*: English. Appraised at 2d in 1578.

133.162   Franciscus Ruise de gemmis
Franciscus Rueus. *De gemmis aliquot libri II.* Continent: 1547–1565.
The octavo editions were published in Paris and in Zürich. *Language(s)*:
Latin. Appraised at 2d in 1578.

133.163   Aristoteles de anima
Aristotle. *De anima.* Continent: date indeterminable.
Language(s): Latin (probable) Greek (perhaps). Appraised at 3d in 1578.

133.164   Wyerus de ira
Johann Wier. *De ira morbo eiusdem curatione philosophica, medica et theolo-
gica.* Basle: ex officina Oporiniana, 1577.
Language(s): Latin. Appraised at 3s 3d in 1578.

133.165   The Proprietie of Herbes
A boke of the propertyes of herbes. London: (different houses), c.1537–
c.1567.
STC 13175.4 *et seq.* Attributed to Odo, *Magdunensis* and formerly to Aemilius Macer, *Floridus. Language(s)*: English. Appraised at 1½d in 1578.

133.166   Trincavellus de reactione
Victor Trincavelius. *Quaestio de reactione juxta doctrinam Aristotelis et
Averrois.* Padua: G. Perchacinus, 1556.
Marked with an "x" in the margin. Above the entry is written: "Mr Allin
his booke"; beside the valuation is written: "Vacat." *Language(s)*: Latin. Ap-
praised at 3d in 1578.

133.167   de arte conficiendae aquavitae, Savanorola
Giovanni Michele Savonarola. *Libellus singularis de arte conficiendi aquam
vitae simplicem et compositam.* Hagenau: Valentin Kobian, 1532.
Language(s): Latin. Appraised at 1½d in 1578.

133.168   Machiavell de principe
Niccolò Macchiavelli. *De principe*. Translated by Sylvester Telius. Basle: apud Petrum Pernam, 1560.
Language(s): Latin. Appraised at 3d in 1578.

133.169   Or*** de verbo Ch***i
Unidentified. Continent (probable): date indeterminable.
Probably not an STC book. *Language(s)*: Latin. Appraised at 2d in 1578.

133.170   The Wellspringe of Sciences
Humphrey Baker. *The well sprynge of sciences*. London: (different houses), 1562–1576.
STC 1209.5 *et seq. Language(s)*: English. Appraised at 4d in 1578.

133.171   Viperanus de scribenda historia
Giovanni Antonio Viperano. *De historia scribenda liber*. Antwerp: ex officina Christopheri Plantini, 1569.
Language(s): Latin. Appraised at 1d in 1578.

133.172   A Riche Storehouse
Unidentified. Britain: date indeterminable.
Unidentifiable in the STC. In the context of Glover's library, this could be either a medical or a literary work; for example, for the former, STC 13905 (Caspar Hueber) and, for the latter, STC 23408 (Joannes Sturmius). *Language(s)*: English. Appraised at 1d in 1578.

133.173   de morbo gallico curando
Unidentified. *De morbo gallico*. Place unknown: stationer unknown, date indeterminable.
STC/non-STC status unknown. Several possibilities, including another copy of the anthology at 133.138 as well as Ulrich von Hutten's work published both on the Continent and in England where it appeared in an English translation with the Latin title above (see STC 14024 *et seq.*). *Language(s)*: Latin English (perhaps). Appraised at 5d in 1578.

133.174   The Interpretation of Dreames
Thomas Hill, *Londoner*. Unidentified. London: (different houses), 1571–1576.
Unidentifiable in the STC. Either STC 13497.5–13498 or STC 13498.5, both of which contain the phrase in the titles. *Language(s)*: English. Appraised at 2d in 1578.

133.175   The Debate betweene pride and lowlinesse
Francis Thynne (attributed). *The debate betweene pride and lowlines, pleaded to an issue in assise*. London: J. Charlwood for R. Newbery, 1577?

STC 24061. According to STC, the attribution to Thynne is erroneous. *Language(s)*: English. Appraised at 1d in 1578.

133.176   Tullie's Offices in Englishe
Marcus Tullius Cicero. [*De officiis*]. London: (different houses), 1534–1574.
STC 5278 *et seq.* Some editions were diglot. *Language(s)*: English Latin (perhaps). Appraised at 4d in 1578.

133.177   Aristoteles de natura
Aristotle. *Physicorum libri*. Translated by Joachim Perion. Lyon: Guliel. Rouillium, 1567.
De natura, seu de rerum principiis leads. Cranz no. 108.519. *Language(s)*: Latin. Appraised at 3d in 1578.

133.178   A Warninge to beware the Salter of Fowler
Thomas Sampson. *A warning to take heede of Fowlers psalter*. London: T. Vautrollier for G. Bishoppe, 1578.
STC 21685. The *Fowler* reference is to STC 14563.3, a psalter issued by the Dutch publisher Joannes Fowler in 1575. *Language(s)*: English. Appraised at 1d in 1578.

133.179   the earle of Surrie's songes and sonnettes
Henry Howard, *Earl of Surrey*. *Songes and sonettes*. London: Richard Tottell, 1559–1574.
STC 13863.5 *et seq. Language(s)*: English. Appraised at 2d in 1578.

133.180   Turberveiles songes and sonnettes
George Turberville. *Epitaphes, epigrams, songs and sonets*. London: Henry Denham, 1567–1570.
STC 24326 *et seq. Language(s)*: English. Appraised at 3d in 1578.

133.181   The Flowers of Philosophie
Sir Hugh Platt. *The floures of philosophie, with the pleasures of poetrie annexed to them*. London: H. Bynneman and F. Coldocke, 1572.
STC 19990.5. *Language(s)*: English. Appraised at 1d in 1578.

133.182   Regimen Sanitatis
[*Regimen sanitatis Salernitatum*]. *Salerno*. Britain or Continent: date indeterminable.
STC 21600 *et seq.* and non-STC. Another copy at 133.79. *Language(s)*: Latin English (perhaps). Appraised at 2d in 1578.

133.183   epitome Hippocratis de arte medendi
Hippocrates. Perhaps *Ex libris de nova, et prisca arte medendi, deque diebus*

decretoriis epithomae. Rome: impressum per Hieronymum de Cartulariis, 1545.
Language(s): Latin. Appraised at 1d in 1578.

133.184 Arsanes' orationes

Thomas Norton. *Orations.* London: J. Daye, 1560?–1573?
STC 785 *et seq.* Most sources, including DNB, give Norton as author, constructing the orations from historical sources. STC lists it under Arsanes. *Language(s)*: English. Appraised at 1d in 1578.

133.185 Cabellii Astrolabium

Jakob Koebel. *Astrolabii declaratio.* Continent: 1545–1552.
Language(s): Latin. Appraised at 1½d in 1578.

133.186 Canones Astronomici

Perhaps Joannes de Aguilera. *Canones astrolabii universales.* Salamanca: (stationer unknown), 1556.
The 1556 is the only edition in *Aureliensis* and is described as the second; no first edition has been found in the standard sources. *Language(s)*: Latin. Appraised at 1½d in 1578.

133.187 Pelitarius de peste

Jacques Peletier. *De peste compendium.* Basle: per Joannem Oporinum, no date.
NLM6 and BL supply 1560? as date; Wellcome gives 1570? *Language(s)*: Latin. Appraised at ½d in 1578.

133.188 Mercurius de divisione vocabulorum astronomiae

Joannes Mercurius, *Morsshemius. Divisio vocabuli astronomiae juxta methodum dialecticam.* Heidelberg: excudebat Joannes Eberbach, 1548.
Language(s): Latin. Appraised at 1d in 1578.

133.189 Progymnasmata graecae grammatices

Perhaps Matthaeus Dresser. *Gymnasmatum litteraturae graecae.* Leipzig: imprim. Andreas Schneider, typis Voegelianis, 1574.
Language(s): Greek Latin. Appraised at 1d in 1578.

133.190 the tragedie of Gorbaducke

Thomas Norton and Thomas Sackville, *Earl of Dorset. The tragedie of Gorboduc, whereof three actes were wrytten by T. Nortone, and the two laste by T. Sackvyle.* London: (different houses), 1565–1570?
STC 18684 *et seq. Language(s)*: English. Appraised at 1d in 1578.

133.191 An Introduction into Arithmeticke

Unidentified. Britain: date indeterminable.

Unidentifiable in the STC. *Language(s)*: English. Appraised at 1½d in 1578.

133.192   The line of liberalitie
Nicholas Haward. *The line of liberalitie dulie directinge the wel bestowing of benefites*. London: T. Marsh, 1569.
STC 12939. A translation of the first three books of Seneca's *De beneficiis*. *Language(s)*: English. Appraised at 2d in 1578.

133.193   Recordes urinall of phisicke
Robert Record. *The urinal of physick*. London: R. Wolfe, 1547–1567.
STC 20816 *et seq*. *Language(s)*: English. Appraised at 2d in 1578.

133.194   The sighte of Urines
Here begynneth the seynge of uryns. London: (different houses), 1540?–1575?
STC 22153b *et seq*. NLM6 and Wellcome give the supplied date of the earlier edition as 1530? Two earlier editions were published in quarto. *Language(s)*: English. Appraised at 1d in 1578.

133.195   Guilielmus Magister de pestis saevitia
Gulielmus Magistry. *Isagoge therapeutica de pestis saevitia, eiusque curatione, et praeventione*. Frankfurt am Main: haeredes C. Egen[olph], 1572.
Language(s): Latin. Appraised at 1d in 1578.

133.196   Sententiae Plauti
Titus Maccius Plautus. [*Selections–Sententiae*]. Continent: date indeterminable.
Language(s): Latin. Appraised at 1d in 1578.

133.197   Bunelli epistolae
Pierre Bunel. [*Epistolae*]. Continent: 1551–1568.
The 1551 Paris edition contains letters by Manutius. *Language(s)*: Latin. Appraised at 1½d in 1578.

133.198   Petrus Ramus logicke in englishe
Pierre de La Ramée. *The logike of . . . P. Ramus*. Translated by R. Makilmenaeus. London: Thomas Vautrollier, 1574.
STC 15246. *Language(s)*: English. Appraised at 1d in 1578.

133.199   Troas scenice in englishe
Lucius Annaeus Seneca. *Troas*. Translated by Jasper Heywood. London: (different houses), 1559–1562?
STC 22227 *et seq*. *Language(s)*: English. Appraised at 1d in 1578.

133.200   The castle of healthe
Sir Thomas Elyot. *The castell of helthe, gathered, oute of the chyefe authors of phisyke.* London: (different houses), c.1537–1576.
STC 7642.5 *et seq. Language(s)*: English. Appraised at 4d in 1578.

133.201   The Detection of enormitie in phisicke
John Securis. *A detection and querimonie of the daily enormities committed in physick.* London: in aedibus T. Marshi, 1566.
STC 22143. *Language(s)*: English. Appraised at 1d in 1578.

133.202   The composition of the oil Magistrale
George Baker. *The composition or making of the oil called oleum magistrale.* London: J. Alde, 1574.
STC 1209. Included is a work by Galen translated by Baker. *Language(s)*: English. Appraised at ½d in 1578.

133.203   The Paralelis
Unidentified. Britain (probable): date indeterminable.
Unidentifiable in the STC. In a group of medical works, but it could be on mathematics. *Language(s)*: English (probable). Appraised at ½d in 1578.

133.204   The Praise of Phisicke
Desiderius Erasmus. *Declamatio in laudem nobilissimae artis medicinae. A declamacion in the prayse and commendation of phisyke, newly tr. out of Latyn.* London: R. Redman, 1537?
STC 10473.5. The translator is not given. *Language(s)*: English. Appraised at 1d in 1578.

133.205   Thesaurus Sanitatis
Jean Liebault. *Thesaurus sanitatis paratu facilis. Selectus ex variis authoribus.* Paris: apud Jacobum Du Puys, 1577.
Language(s): Latin. Appraised at 9d in 1578.

133.206   Aesopi fabulae graecolatinae
Aesop. *Fabulae.* Continent: date indeterminable.
Language(s): Greek Latin. Appraised at 7d in 1578.

133.207   Cominaeus de gestis Ludovici regis Gallii
Philippe de Comines. [*Memoires*]. Continent: date indeterminable.
Language(s): Latin. Appraised at 8d in 1578.

133.208   epistolae Manutii
Paolo Manuzio. [*Epistolae*]. Continent: date indeterminable.
The 1573 London edition was issued in octavo. *Language(s)*: Latin. Appraised at 6d in 1578.

133.209   Comediae Plauti
Titus Maccius Plautus. *Comoediae.* Continent: date indeterminable.
Struck out. *Language(s)*: Latin. Appraised at 16d in 1578.

133.210   testamentum latinum
[*Bible–N.T.*]. Britain or Continent: date indeterminable.
STC 2800 *et seq.* and non-STC. *Language(s)*: Latin. Appraised at 5d in
1578.

133.211   Centuriae Amati Lucitani, 5 et 6 libri
Amatus, *Lusitanus, pseudonym. Curationum medicinialium centuriae duae,
quinta et sexta.* Lyon: apud Gulielmum Rouillium, 1576.
An octavo edition was published in Venice in 1560. See also 133.216 and
133.219. *Language(s)*: Latin. Appraised at 7d in 1578.

133.212   commentarii Brachelii in Technen Galeni
Hieremias Triverius (Brachelius). *In Technen* [*Ars medica*] *Galeni commentarii.* Lyon: apud Godefridum et Marcellum Beringos, 1547.
Language(s): Latin. Appraised at 4d in 1578.

133.213   Dispensatorium Pharmacorum
Unidentified. Continent (probable): date indeterminable.
Almost certainly not an STC book. See 133.253 (Valerius Cordus) and
133.264 (Guillaume Rondelet) for two possibilities. *Language(s)*: Latin. Appraised at 5d in 1578.

133.214   Balthasur in Italian
Baldassare Castiglione, *Count. Il cortegiano.* Continent: date indeterminable.
Language(s): Italian. Appraised at 7d in 1578.

133.215   Tullies epistles in french and lattin
Marcus Tullius Cicero. [*Selected works–Epistolae*]. Continent: date indeterminable.
Struck out. *Language(s)*: French Latin. Appraised at 16d in 1578.

133.216   Centuriae Amati 3 et 4ti
Amatus, *Lusitanus, pseudonym. Curationum medicinialium centuriae duae,
tertia et quarta.* Lyon: (different houses), 1556–1565.
See also 133.211 and 133.219. *Language(s)*: Latin. Appraised at 7d in
1578.

133.217   Alnoldus de conservanda valetudine
[*Regimen sanitatis Salernitatum*]. *Salerno.* Continent: date indeterminable.
The commentary was wrongly attributed to Arnaldus, *de Villa Nova.* The

form of the title approximated in the manuscript entry appeared mainly in later editions. *Language(s)*: Latin. Appraised at 6d in 1578.

133.218 Caelum Philosophorum

Philippus Ulstadius. *Coelum philosophorum*. Continent: date indeterminable.
Language(s): Latin. Appraised at 6d in 1578.

133.219 Centuriae Amati 1a et 2a

Amatus, *Lusitanus, pseudonym*. *Curationum medicinialium centuriae duae, prima et secunda*. Paris: apud Sebastianum Nivellium, 1554.
See also 133.211 and 133.216. *Language(s)*: Latin. Appraised at 8d in 1578.

133.220 Phuccius de ratione curandi

Leonard Fuchs. *De medendi methodo*. Continent: date indeterminable.
Struck out. *Language(s)*: Latin. Appraised at 9d in 1578.

133.221 Faventinus de morbis medendis

Leonellus de Victoriis (*Faventinus*). *Practica medicinalis*. Continent: date indeterminable.
The long title of several editions continues ... *de medendis morbis*. *Language(s)*: Latin. Appraised at 8d in 1578.

133.222 Ovidii Amores

Publius Ovidius Naso. *Amores*. Continent: date indeterminable.
Language(s): Latin. Appraised at 6d in 1578.

133.223 Fontanonus de morborum internorum curatione

Denys Fontanon. *De morborum internorum curatione*. Paris: apud Antonium de Harsy, 1574.
The only sextodecimo edition found. *Language(s)*: Latin. Appraised at 7d in 1578.

133.224 Sylvius de medicamentis componendis

Jacques Dubois (Jacobus Sylvius). *Methodus medicamenta componendi*. Lyon: Guillaume Rouille, 1549–1556.
Only two sextodecimo editions have been found. Rouille collaborated with other stationers on the 1549 edition. *Language(s)*: Latin. Appraised at 8d in 1578.

133.225 Bottallus de medici et aegroti munere

Leonardo Botallo. *Commentarioli duo, alter de medici, alter de aegroti munere* [and other works]. Lyon: apud Antonium Gryphium, 1565.
Language(s): Latin. Appraised at 8d in 1578.

133.226   Dioschorides de materia medica
Dioscorides. *De medica materia*. Continent: date indeterminable.
Language(s): Latin Greek (perhaps). Appraised at 6d in 1578.

133.227   Balthasur de Curtesan
Baldassare Castiglione, *Count. Le curtesin*. Translated by Jacobus Colinaeus. Paris: N. du Chemin, 1545.
   The only French version in sextodecimo. *Language(s)*: French. Appraised
at 7d in 1578.

133.228   Cornelius Celsus de re medica
Aulus Cornelius Celsus. *De re medica*. Continent: date indeterminable.
Language(s): Latin. Appraised at 7d in 1578.

133.229   Musae Brasavolae, Examen Simplicium
Antonio Musa Brasavola. *Examen omnium simplicium medicamentorum*.
Lyon: apud Joannem Frellonium, 1556.
   The 1556 edition is the only sextodecimo among the eight editions listed
in *Aureliensis*, which gives as the printer, Antonius Frellonius, who is not
found elsewhere. BL gives Jean Frellon, the known Lyon stationer. *Language(s)*: Latin. Appraised at 7d in 1578.

133.230   Phuccius de re medica
Leonard Fuchs. *De componendorum medicamentorum ratione*. Continent: date
indeterminable.
   Struck out, with *componendis medicinis* inserted above, also struck out. *Language(s)*: Latin. Appraised at 3d in 1578.

133.231   Pergaminus de differentiis febrium
Galen. *De differentiis febrium*. Continent: date indeterminable.
Language(s): Latin. Appraised at 3d in 1578.

133.232   Galenus de facile parabilibus
Galen. *De remediis parabilibus liber*. Translated by Joannes Guinterius (Andernacus); edited by Jacobus Hollerius. Paris: in officina J. Gazelli, 1543.
   The only sextodecimo edition. *Language(s)*: Latin. Appraised at 5d in
1578.

133.233   Phicinus de vita
Marsilio Ficino. [*De triplici vita*]. Continent: date indeterminable.
Language(s): Latin. Appraised at 4d in 1578.

133.234   Galenus de ossibus
Galen. *De ossibus ad tyrones*. Continent: 1538–1549.
   The only sextodecimo editions listed in Durling. The 1538 edition was

published in Venice, the 1549 in Lyon by Guillaume Rouille, many of whose editions are found in Glover's collection. The appraisal is trimmed away. *Language(s)*: Latin.

133.235   Galenus de compositione medicamentorum
Galen. *De compositione medicamentorum per genera.* Lyon: apud Gulielmum Rouillium, 1549.
See also 133.241. *Language(s)*: Latin. Appraised at 7d in 1578.

133.236   eiusdem anatomica
Galen. *De anatomicis administrationibus.* Translated by Joannes Guinterius, *Andernacus.* Lyon: apud G. Rouillium; excudebat Philibertus Rolletius, 1551.
Language(s): Latin. Appraised at 5d in 1578.

133.237   idem de locorum affectorum notitia
Galen. *De locis affectis.* Continent: date indeterminable.
Language(s): Latin. Appraised at 4d in 1578.

133.238   idem de morborum et symptomatum differentiis
Galen. *De morborum et symptomatum differentiis et causis libri sex.* Continent: date indeterminable.
Language(s): Latin. Appraised at 4d in 1578.

133.239   idem de ratione curandi
Galen. *De curandi ratione per venae sectionem.* Continent: date indeterminable.
Language(s): Latin. Appraised at 5d in 1578.

133.240   idem de Hippocratis et Platonis dogmatibus
Galen. *De Hippocratis et Platonis decretis libri ix.* Lyon: apud Paulum Mirallietum, excudebat Nicolaus Baccaneus, 1550.
Language(s): Latin. Appraised at 10d in 1578.

133.241   idem de compositione pharmacorum
Galen. *De compositione medicamentorum secundum locos.* Translated by Janus Cornarius. Continent: 1539–1561.
Durling lists three sextodecimo editions; the 1549 and 1561 were published in Lyon by Guillaume Rouille in Lyon, a number of whose books are found in Glover's collection. See also 133.235. *Language(s)*: Latin. Appraised at 10d in 1578.

133.242   eiusdem ars medica
Galen. *Ars medica.* Continent: date indeterminable.
See also 133.267. Durling 8 (in the "Analytical Index"). *Language(s)*: Latin. Appraised at 8d in 1578.

133.243 idem de alimentorum facultatibus

Galen. *De alimentorum facultatibus libri tres. De attenuante victus ratione.*
Translated by Martinus Gregorius. Lyon: Guillaume Rouille, 1547–1570.

The sole Latin single edition of this title, published in Paris in 1530, is a quarto, and therefore an unlikely match for this title. Three of the five editions represented in the date range contain additional works. Durling 13 (in the "Analytical Index"). *Language(s)*: Latin. Appraised at 11d in 1578.

133.244 idem de usu partium

Galen. *De usu partium.* Translated by Nicolaus, *Rheginus.* Lyon: Guillaume Rouille, 1550.

The only edition in sextodecimo. Durling 122 (in the "Analytical Index"). *Language(s)*: Latin. Appraised at 10d in 1578.

133.245 Hippocratis epidemia

Hippocrates. *Epidemia.* Continent: date indeterminable.
Language(s): Latin. Appraised at 12d in 1578.

133.246 medicorum introductiones

Otto Brunfels. *Neotericorum aliquot medicorum in medicinam practicam introductiones.* Strassburg: per Joannem Albertum, 1533.
Language(s): Latin. Appraised at 4d in 1578.

133.247 Patricius de regno

Francesco Patrizi, *Bishop. De regno et regis institutione.* Paris: apud J. de Bordeaux, 1578.
Language(s): Latin. Appraised at 4d in 1578.

133.248 Galenus de simplicibus medicamentis

Galen. *De simplicium medicamentorum facultatibus* [and other works]. Lyon: Guillaume Rouille, 1547–1561.

No solo edition of the *De simplicium* is in sextodecimo. Durling 108 (in the "Analytical Index"). *Language(s)*: Latin. Appraised at 8d in 1578.

133.249 Hyppocratis Aphorismi

Hippocrates. *Aphorismi.* Continent: date indeterminable.
Language(s): Latin Greek (perhaps). Appraised at 4d in 1578.

133.250 Salustius

Caius Sallustius Crispus. Unidentified. Continent: date indeterminable.
Few editions of Sallust were issued in sextodecimo; none in England. *Language(s)*: Latin. Appraised at 8d in 1578.

133.251 Vitae Plutarchi

Plutarch. *Vitae parallelae.* Continent: date indeterminable.
Language(s): Latin (probable) Greek (perhaps). Appraised at 8d in 1578.

133.252 Pallingenius
Marcellus Palingenius (Pietro Angelo Manzolli [Stellatus]). *Zodiacus vitae.* Britain or Continent: date indeterminable.

STC 19140 and non-STC. The one sextodecimo edition issued in England was published in 1574. *Language(s)*: Latin. Appraised at 8d in 1578.

133.253 Cordi Dispensatorium
Valerius Cordus. [*Dispensatorium*]. Continent: date indeterminable. *Language(s)*: Latin. Appraised at 4d in 1578.

133.254 Les Treasaures des Amadis
Amadis, *de Gaule. Le tresor des livres.* Continent: date indeterminable. *Language(s)*: French. Appraised at 4d in 1578.

133.255 Sambusi emblemata
Joannes Sambucus. *Emblemata.* Antwerp: Christopher Plantin, 1569–1576.

The third edition was published in 1569, the fourth in 1576, both in sextodecimo. *Language(s)*: Latin. Appraised at 5d in 1578.

133.256 Galenus de naturalibus facultatibus
Galen. *De naturalibus facultatibus.* Lyon: Guillaume Rouille, 1548–1561.

Four sextodecimo editions. Durling 72 (in the "Analytical Index"). *Language(s)*: Latin. Appraised at 3d in 1578.

133.257 Galenus de chrysibus
Galen. *De crisibus.* Lyon: Guillaume Rouille, 1549–1558.

Two sextodecimo editions only. Durling 33 (in the "Analytical Index"). *Language(s)*: Latin. Appraised at 4d in 1578.

133.258 de ebriosorum generibus
De generibus ebriosorum. Compiled by Jacob Hartlieb. Continent: date indeterminable.

The only sextodecimo edition found was published in 1515, but there were many small-sized editions issued that might have been mistakenly identified as sextodecimo. *Language(s)*: Latin. Appraised at 2d in 1578.

133.259 Herodiani historiae
Herodian. [*Historiae*]. Continent: date indeterminable. *Language(s)*: Latin. Appraised at 2d in 1578.

133.260 de moribus Turcarum
Bartholomaeus Georgievits. *De Turcarum moribus epitome.* Lyon: Jean de Tournes, 1553–1578. *Language(s)*: Latin. Appraised at 2d in 1578.

133.261   Medicina Practica
Unidentified. Continent (probable): date indeterminable.
Almost certainly not an STC book. *Language(s)*: Latin. Appraised at 3d in
1578.

133.262   Bertosii Methodus Medendi
Alphonsus Bertotius. *Methodus curativa generalis et compendiaria*. Lyon:
apud Gabrielem Coterium, 1558.
Language(s): Latin. Appraised at 4d in 1578.

133.263   de tempore purgandi
Nobile Socio. *De temporibus et modis purgandi in morbis*. Lyon: (different
houses), 1555–1577.
Language(s): Latin. Appraised at 5d in 1578.

133.264   Pharmacapolorum officina
Guillaume Rondelet. *Dispensatorium seu pharmacopolarum officina*. Cologne:
apud Joannem Byrckmannum, 1565.
   This sole edition was published in duodecimo rather than sextodecimo.
Language(s): Latin. Appraised at 4d in 1578.

133.265   Formulae Remediorum
Petrus Gorraeus. *Formulae remediorum*. Continent: 1555–1572.
   Four sextodecimo editions, variously published in Lyon and Paris. *Language(s)*: Latin. Appraised at 2d in 1578.

133.266   Praesagia Hippocratis
Hippocrates. [*Prognostica*]. Continent: date indeterminable.
Language(s): Latin Greek (perhaps). Appraised at 1d in 1578.

133.267   Galeni Ars Medecinalis
Galen. *Ars medica*. Continent: date indeterminable.
See also 133.242. *Language(s)*: Latin. Appraised at 2d in 1578.

133.268   Methodus in Aphorismos Hippocratis
Perhaps Benedictus Bustamante Paz. *Methodus in septem aphorismorum
libris*. Venice: apud Aldi filios, 1550.
   The sole extant edition is in quarto, not sextodecimo as the compiler indicates. A different work, perhaps an edition of the *Aphorismi* itself, may, then, have been intended. *Language(s)*: Latin. Appraised at 3d in 1578.

133.269   de lumbricis
Hieronymus Gabucinus. *De lumbricis alvum occupantibus commentarius*.
Lyon: Guillaume Rouille, 1549.
Language(s): Latin. Appraised at 4d in 1578.

133.270 orationes Muretae
Marcus Antonius Muretus. [*Selected works–Orations*]. Continent: date inde-terminable.
Language(s): Latin. Appraised at 5d in 1578.

133.271 The Regiment of Life
Jehan Goeurot. *The regiment of lyfe*. Translated by Thomas Phaer. London: (different houses), 1544–1567.
STC 11967 *et seq*. English editions were published with Phaer's *The book of children* and Phaer's translation of Nicholas de Houssemaine's *Régime contre la peste* (*Treatise of the pestilence*). *Language(s)*: English. Appraised at 4d in 1578.

133.272 Historia Planetarum
Probably Antoine Du Pinet. *Historia plantarum*. Lyon: (different houses), 1561–1567.
BN gives the sizes as sextodecimo as the compiler lists it; other sources give both octavo and duodecimo. *Historia plantarum et vires*, twice appearing in 1541 in octavo, is a less likely possibility. *Language(s)*: Latin. Appraised at 8d in 1578.

133.273 Bodinus de methodo historiarum in 8°
Jean Bodin, *Bishop*. *Methodus ad facilem historiarum cognitionem*. Basle: ex Petri Pernae off., 1576.
This edition contains other works. *Language(s)*: Latin. Appraised at 7d in 1578.

133.274 Isaac Judaeus de dietis in 8°
Isaac Ben Solomon Israeli (Isaac Judaeus). *De diaetis universalibus et parti-cularibus*. Basle: ex officina Sixti Henricpetri, 1570.
Language(s): Latin. Appraised at 9d in 1578.

133.275 Practica Petri Bayri in 8°
Pietro Bairo. *De medendis humani corporis malis enchiridion*. Edited by Theodore Zwinger. Continent: 1560–1578.
Language(s): Latin. Appraised at 8d in 1578.

133.276 Cardanus de methodo medendi in 8°
Girolamo Cardano. *De methodo medendi*. Paris: in aedibus Rouillii, 1565.
An NUC entry gives a Paris 1563 edition not found elsewhere. *Language(s)*: Latin. Appraised at 6d in 1578.

133.277 Observationes Anatomicae Fallopii in 8°
Gabriel Fallopius. *Observationes anatomicae*. Continent: 1561–1566.
Language(s): Latin. Appraised at 6d in 1578.

133.278 Placatomus de valetudine tuenda in 8°

Helius Eobanus, *Hessus*. [*De tuenda bona valetudine*]. Continent: 1556–1571.

With commentary by Joannes Placotomas. *Language(s)*: Latin. Appraised at 8d in 1578.

133.279 Victor de compositione medicamentum in 8°

Victor Trincavelius. *De compositione et usu medicamentorum*. Basle: [ex officina Petrus Perna], 1570–1571.

Language(s): Latin. Appraised at 5d in 1578.

John Hornsley. Scholar (M.A.):
Probate Inventory. 1578

SANDRA BURR and E. S. LEEDHAM-GREEN

John Hornsley is listed as a demy of Magdalen College from 1567, having apparently come up at about the age of eleven. (He was sixteen years old at an unknown date in 1572.) He matriculated on 8 October 1571 aged fifteen or sixteen, and in the following year was elected a fellow of the college. He graduated B.A. on 1 April 1573, and was the college praelector in Greek in 1574, 1575, and 1576 before proceeding M.A. on 11 June 1577 (Bloxam 1873, 4:166).

His was no affluent life-style. In addition to his books, valued at four pounds, eight shillings, and ten pence, he owned only two coffers, a feather-bed and pillow, a flockbed and bolster, three coverlets "good and bad," two pairs of sheets, one handkerchief, one habit, one old mockado gown, three pairs of old hose, an old doublet and jerkin, a pair of jersey stockings, and ten quires of paper, all valued together at three pounds, sixteen shillings. Administration of his estate was granted to his sister, Elizabeth West, on 13 August 1578 (Bloxam 1873, 4:166).

His books reveal eclectic tastes, the largest group consisting of classical literature, supported by numerous grammatical and rhetorical texts, as might be expected of a Greek lecturer, but history and theology are very close rivals. Law (134.40 and 134.80) and medicine (134.31) are both represented, as is cosmography (134.18 and 134.65). He also owned a work by Ramón Lull (134.69) and a commentary on Lull's *Ars brevis* by Cornelius Agrippa (134.73). Two Hebrew grammars mark at least intentions in that direction, while English is represented by a translation of Cicero's *Tusculan Questions* (134.29) and Castiglione's *Courtyer*.

Oxford University Archives. Bodleian Library: Hyp.B.14.

§

Bloxam, J.R. 1873. *A Register of the Presidents, Fellows, Demies ... of St. Mary Magdalen College in the University of Oxford.* Vol. 4. Oxford: James Parker and Co.

§

134.1	Dictionarium Cooperi
134.2	Harmonia Calvini 8°
134.3	Plinii historia
134.4	Justinus historicus pri Dore
134.5	Novum testamentum Bezae 8° gre lat
134.6	Lexicon grecum crespini 4to
134.7	Courtyer 8°
134.8	Philippus Beroaldus in quest: Tuscul: 4°
134.9	Liber papiratius in folio
134.10	Artes rami in folio
134.11	Opuscula Calvini in 8°
134.12	Illiades homeri in 8°
134.13	Graca [Grammatica] antesignani 8°
134.14	Titus Livius imperfect 3 bus
134.15	Vita plutarchi in 3bus pri
134.16	Lambinus in Pollitica arlis [aristotelis]
134.17	Sebastiani Corradi questura 8°
134.18:A	Pomponius mela cum Sonii [Solini] 2bus
134.18:B	[See 134.18:A]
134.19	Methodus Bodini in 8°
134.20	Melanchton in Aethica 8°
134.21	Hemingius De lege natura 8°
134.22	Dialectica titelmanni 8°
134.23	Scotus in porphirium
134.24	Dialectica rodolphi 8°
134.25	Nomologia omphali cum ceteris
134.26	Sermones Bullingeri 1a pars Sermones Bullingeri 3a pars
134.27	Orat Ciceronis 2a pars pri
134.28	Graca [Grammatica] R. in 8°
134.29	Questiones Ciceronis anglice
134.30	Organum arls gre 8°
134.31	Galeni aliquot per Gunterum 4to
134.32	Biblia hieronimi 8°
134.33	Graca [Grammatica] theodori gazae 8°
134.34	Quintus Curtius in 8°
134.35	Tragediae senecae 8°

134.36	Epistolas pauli grecae
134.37	Horatius in 8° roberti
134.38	Graca [Grammatica] Crusii in 8°
134.39	Graca [Grammatica] hebraica Campensis 8°
134.40	Institutiones Justiniani gr
134.41	Comineus pri
134.42	Appianus alexandrinus pri
134.43	Quintilianus in 8°
134.44	Quest disp [disputate] de magistris in phisicam
134.45	Ammianus Marcellinus pars
134.46	Institutiones Calvini folio
134.47	Aristoteles de mundo 8°
134.48	Ethica arls [aristotelis] in 4to inter
134.49	Hiperius de ratione studii theologice 8°
134.50	Copia verborum
134.51	fabulae Aesopi grecae
134.52	Dialectica Cesarii in 8°
134.53	Illiades Homeri grece
134.54	Aulus gellius in 8°
134.55	Comentaria Caesaris 8°
134.56	Demosthenis olinthiacae 8°
134.57	Ovidii opuscula 8°
134.58	Diodorus Siculus pri
134.59	Propheti Minores hebraice roberti stephani
134.60	Demosthenis philippica gre lat
134.61:1	2 Salustius in 8°
134.61:2	[See 134.61:1]
134.62	Catechismus Calvini gre lat
134.63	Justinus historicus in 8°
134.64	Topica Theologica hiperii 8°
134.65	Pomponius mela sine tabulis
134.66	Vita Juwelli in 4to
134.67	Odisea Homeri gre 8°
134.68	Odisea Homeri lat 8°
134.69	Opuscula Lulii in 4to
134.70	Orationes Longolii 4to
134.71	Aristotelis ethica grecae
134.72	Rami Dialectica 8°
134.73	Agrippa in artem Lullii 8°
134.74	Graca [Grammatica] chevalleri 4to
134.75	Epistole Ciceronis 8°
134.76	Omphalius de elocutione 8°
134.77	Calepinus in folio
134.78	Rhetorica hermoginis grece
134.79	Observationes Nizolii folio

134.80   Liteltone
134.81   Calimachus grec 4to
134.82   Nonnius marcellinus Folio
134.83   Manutus in epistolas ad Brutum
134.84   Novum testamentum grec roberti
134.85:1–27   27 Smale bookes
134.86   Demosthenes de falsa Legatione grec
134.87   Graca [Grammatica] hebraica Avenarii 8°
134.88   Aeschines gre
134.89   Demosthens de Corona 8°

§

134.1 Dictionarium Cooperi

Thomas Cooper, *Bishop*. *Thesaurus linguae Romanae et Britannicae*. London: (different houses), 1565–1578.

STC 5686 *et seq*. *Language(s)*: Latin. Appraised at 2s in 1578.

134.2 Harmonia Calvini 8°

Jean Calvin. *Harmonia ex tribus evangelistis composita, Matthaeo, Marco, et Luca*. Geneva: excudebat N. Barbirius et T. Courteau, 1563.

Language(s): Latin. Appraised at 3s 4d in 1578.

134.3 Plinii historia

Pliny, *the Elder*. *Historia naturalis*. Continent: date indeterminable.

Language(s): Latin. Appraised at 1s 6d in 1578.

134.4 Justinus historicus pri Dore

Trogus Pompeius and Justinus, *the Historian*. [*Epitomae in Trogi Pompeii historias* (part one)]. Britain or Continent: date indeterminable.

STC 24287 *et seq*. and non-STC. The *Dore* in the manuscript may represent a legatee. Another copy at 134.63. *Language(s)*: Latin. Appraised at 1s 8d in 1578.

134.5 Novum testamentum Bezae 8° gre lat

[*Bible–N.T.*]. Translated and edited by Théodore de Bèze. Geneva: Henricus Stephanus and Ulrich Fugger, 1565–1567.

The so-called minor editions of Bèze. *Language(s)*: Greek Latin. Appraised at 2s in 1578.

134.6 Lexicon grecum crespini 4to

Jean Crespin. *Lexicon graecolatinum*. Continent: 1566–1568.

Language(s): Greek Latin. Appraised at 3s 4d in 1578.

134.7 Courtyer 8°
Baldassare Castiglione, *Count. The courtyer of count Baldessar Castilio.*
Translated by Sir Thomas Hoby. London: H. Denham, 1577.
STC 4779. If an English version, as the manuscript entry indicates, the
1577 edition, quarto in eights, may have been mistaken for an octavo. *Language(s)*: English. Appraised at 1s in 1578.

134.8 Philippus Beroaldus in quest: Tuscul: 4°
Marcus Tullius Cicero. *Quaestiones Tusculanae.* Edited by Philippus Beroaldus, *the Elder.* Continent: date indeterminable.
Although Beroaldus's *Commentarii questionum Tusculanarum,* published in
quarto in 1509 (Paris), is possible, other editions of the *Quaestiones Tusculanae*
with commentary by Beroaldus and others could be intended. *Language(s)*:
Latin. Appraised at 2s 4d in 1578.

134.9 Liber papiratius in folio
Unidentified. Provenance unknown: date indeterminable.
Manuscript. Perhaps a ledger, an account book, or some other personal
manuscript. *Language(s)*: Unknown. Appraised at 1s 8d in 1578.

134.10 Artes rami in folio
Pierre de La Ramée. Unidentified. Basle: (different houses), date indeterminable.
Either the *Professio regia, hoc est, septem artes liberales in regia cathedra, per
ipsum Parisiis propositae* (1576) or the *Scholae in liberales artes* (1569). Editions
of both were published in Basle. See Ong nos. 651 and 695 (Adams R115 and
R123). *Language(s)*: Latin. Appraised at 1s 6d in 1578.

134.11 Opuscula Calvini in 8°
Jean Calvin. *Opuscula. De animae immortalitate.* Edited by Nicolas Des
Gallars (Nicolaus Salicetus). Geneva (probable): excudebat Nicolaus Barbirius,
et Thomas Courteau, 1563.
The only "opuscula" of Calvin's in octavo. *Language(s)*: Latin. Appraised at
1[s] 4d in 1578.

134.12 Illiades homeri in 8°
Homer. *Iliad.* Continent: date indeterminable.
For another more expensive copy in Greek, see 134.53. *Language(s)*: Latin
Greek (perhaps). Appraised at 4d in 1578.

134.13 Graca [Grammatica] antesignani 8°
Nicolaus Clenardus and Petrus Antesignanus. *Institutiones ac meditationes in
graecam linguam, cum scholiis et praxi P. Antesignani.* Continent: date indeterminable.

A school version of Clenardus's grammar, with exercises. *Language(s)*: Greek Latin. Appraised at 1s 4d in 1578.

134.14   Titus Livius imperfect 3 bus

Titus Livius. [*Historiae Romanae decades* (part)]. Continent: date indeterminable.
Language(s): Latin. Appraised at 3s 6d in 1578.

134.15   Vita plutarchi in 3bus pri

Plutarch. *Vitae parallelae* (part). Continent: date indeterminable.
Language(s): Latin (probable) Greek (perhaps). Appraised at 3s in 1578.

134.16   Lambinus in Pollitica arlis [aristotelis]

Aristotle. *Politica*. Translated by Dionysius Lambinus. Paris: apud J. Benenatum, 1567.
The only edition of Lambinus's translation published by the date of this inventory. *Language(s)*: Latin. Appraised at 1s 4d in 1578.

134.17   Sebastiani Corradi questura 8°

Sebastian Corradus. [*Quaestura*]. Continent: 1537–1556.
Language(s): Latin. Appraised at [1]s 10d in 1578.

134.18:A   Pomponius mela cum Sonii [Solini] 2bus

Pomponius Mela. *De situ orbis*. Continent: date indeterminable (composite publication).
Another copy of Mela alone at 134.65. *Language(s)*: Latin. Appraised [a composite volume] at 1s 8d in 1578.

134.18:B   [See 134.18:A]

Caius Julius Solinus. *Polyhistor*. [Composite publication].
Language(s): Latin. Appraised [a composite volume] at 1s 8d in 1578.

134.19   Methodus Bodini in 8°

Jean Bodin, *Bishop*. *Methodus historica*. Basle: ex Petri Pernae officina, 1576.
This edition contains Bodin's *Methodus ad facilem historiarum cognitionem* as well as other works. *Language(s)*: Latin. Appraised at 1s 4d in 1578.

134.20   Melanchton in Aethica 8°

Philipp Melanchthon. [*Aristotle–Ethica: commentary*]. Continent: date indeterminable.
Language(s): Latin. Appraised at 1s 6d in 1578.

134.21   Hemingius De lege natura 8°

Niels Hemmingsen. *De lege naturae apodictica methodus*. Wittenberg:

(different houses), 1562–1577.
Language(s): Latin. Appraised at [1]s 8d in 1578.

134.22 Dialectica titelmanni 8°
Franz Titelmann. [*Dialectica*]. Continent: date indeterminable.
Language(s): Latin. Appraised at [1]s 8d in 1578.

134.23 Scotus in porphirium
John Duns, *Scotus. Quaestiones super Universalibus Porphyrii ac libris Praedicamentorum et Perihermeneias Aristotelis.* Continent: date indeterminable.
Language(s): Latin. Appraised at [1]s 8d in 1578.

134.24 Dialectica rodolphi 8°
Probably Caspar Rhodolphus. [*Dialectica*]. Continent: date indeterminable.
Rodolphus Agricola's *De inventione dialectica* is another possibility.
Language(s): Latin. Appraised at 1s in 1578.

134.25 Nomologia omphali cum ceteris
Jacobus Omphalius. *Nomologia.* Continent: date indeterminable.
Language(s): Latin. Appraised at [1]s 8d in 1578.

134.26 Sermones Bullingeri 1a pars Sermones Bullingeri 3a pars
Heinrich Bullinger. *Sermonum decades* (part). Zürich: in officina Christopheri Froschoueri, 1552–1577.
More likely the first and third volumes of one of the three-volume editions than the first and third *Decades. Language(s)*: Latin. Appraised at 2s [1]d in 1578.

134.27 Orat Ciceronis 2a pars pri
Marcus Tullius Cicero. [*Selected works–Orations* (part)]. Continent: date indeterminable.
Language(s): Latin. Appraised at [1]s 8d in 1578.

134.28 Graca [Grammatica] R. in 8°
Perhaps William Lily. *Institutio compendiaria totius grammaticae.* Britain or Continent: 1557–1574.
STC 15610.8 *et seq.* The entry's *R.* is taken as the standard abbreviation for "Rex," making the entry *Grammatica Regia*, by which name Lily's grammar was known. See PLRE 62.10 and 92.115. The date range is for the octavo editions. *Language(s)*: Latin. Appraised at [1]s 6d in 1578.

134.29 Questiones Ciceronis anglice
Marcus Tullius Cicero. *Those fyve questions, which Marke Tullye Cicero, disputed in his manor of Tusculanum.* Translated by John Dolman. London:

T. Marshe, 1561.
STC 5317. *Language(s)*: English. Appraised at [1]s 8d in 1578.

134.30 Organum arls gre 8°
Aristotle. *Organon*. Continent: date indeterminable.
Language(s): Greek. Appraised at 1s in 1578.

134.31 Galeni aliquot per Gunterum 4to
Galen. *Aliquot libelli ... partim recogniti, partim nunc primum versi*. Edited and translated by Joannes Guinterius (Andernacus). Basle: in officina Frobeniana per Hieronymum Frobenium et Joannem Hervagium, 1529.
Language(s): Latin. Appraised at [1]s 6d in 1578.

134.32 Biblia hieronimi 8°
The Bible. Continent: date indeterminable.
The sole Vulgate version published in England before the date of this inventory, STC 2055 (1535), is in quarto. *Language(s)*: Latin. Appraised at 1s 4d in 1578.

134.33 Graca [Grammatica] theodori gazae 8°
Theodorus, *Gaza*. [*Institutiones grammaticae*]. Continent: date indeterminable.
Language(s): Greek Latin. Appraised at 2d in 1578.

134.34 Quintus Curtius in 8°
Quintus Curtius Rufus. *De rebus gestis Alexandri Magni*. Continent: date indeterminable.
Language(s): Latin. Appraised at 8d in 1578.

134.35 Tragediae senecae 8°
Lucius Annaeus Seneca. *Tragoediae*. Continent: date indeterminable.
Language(s): Latin. Appraised at 8d in 1578.

134.36 Epistolas pauli grecae
[*Bible–N.T.–Epistles–Paul*]. Continent: date indeterminable.
Language(s): Greek. Appraised at 6d in 1578.

134.37 Horatius in 8° roberti
Quintus Horatius Flaccus. [*Works*]. Continent: Robertus Stephanus, 1544–1549.
The 1544 edition is found in Adams (H887) and BL, while Brunet cites both the 1544 and 1549 editions. No other Stephanus octavo editions have been found, though others may exist. Another, less likely possibility is R. Stephanus's 1541 octavo edition of Horace's *Epistolae*. *Language(s)*: Latin. Appraised at 8d in 1578.

134.38 Graca [Grammatica] Crusii in 8°

Martin Crusius. Unidentified. Basle: Joannes Oporinus, date indeterminable.

His *Grammatica graeca, cum latina congruens, Grammatica latina, cum graeca congruens*, and *Puerilis in lingua graeca institutio* could all have been entered as *grammatica*. By the date of this inventory, all three had been published by Oporinus only. *Language(s)*: Greek Latin. Appraised at 1s 6d in 1578.

134.39 Graca [Grammatica] hebraica Campensis 8°

Joannes Campensis. [*Grammatica hebraica*]. Continent: date indeterminable.
Language(s): Hebrew Latin. Appraised at 6d in 1578.

134.40 Institutiones Justiniani gr

Justinian I. *Institutiones*. (*Corpus juris civilis*). Continent: date indeterminable.
Language(s): Greek. Appraised at 1s 6d in 1578.

134.41 Comineus pri

Philippe de Comines. [*Memoires*]. Translated by Joannes Philippson, *Sleidanus*. Continent: date indeterminable.
Language(s): Latin. Appraised at 6d in 1578.

134.42 Appianus alexandrinus pri

Appian, *of Alexandria*. [*Historia Romana*]. Continent: date indeterminable.
Language(s): Latin. Appraised at 1s in 1578.

134.43 Quintilianus in 8°

Marcus Fabius Quintilianus. Unidentified. Continent: date indeterminable.
Institutiones oratoriae more likely than the *Declamationes*, but the complete works might be intended. *Language(s)*: Latin. Appraised at 8d in 1578.

134.44 Quest disp [disputate] de magistris in phisicam

Joannes de Magistris. [*Aristotle–Selected works–Philosophia naturalis: commentary*]. Continent: date indeterminable.
Language(s): Latin. Appraised at 4d in 1578.

134.45 Ammianus Marcellinus pars

Ammianus Marcellinus. [*Res gestae* (part)]. Continent: date indeterminable.
Language(s): Latin. Appraised at 1s in 1578.

134.46 Institutiones Calvini folio

Jean Calvin. *Institutio Christianae religionis*. Continent: 1539–1572.

The one Latin edition published in England by the date of this inventory was issued in octavo. *Language(s)*: Latin. Appraised at 2s in 1578.

134.47 Aristoteles de mundo 8°
Aristotle (spurious). *De mundo*. Continent: date indeterminable. Appraisal torn away. *Language(s)*: Latin.

134.48 Ethica arls [aristotelis] in 4to inter
Aristotle. *Ethica*. Britain or Continent: date indeterminable.
STC 752 and non-STC. The *inter* in the manuscript entry may have been a false start of "interprete . . ." (translator) by the compiler. *Language(s)*: Latin. Appraised at 1s in 1578.

134.49 Hiperius de ratione studii theologice 8°
Andreas Gerardus, *Hyperius. De theologo, sive De ratione studii theologici*. Continent: 1556–1572.
Language(s): Latin. Appraised at 1s in 1578.

134.50 Copia verborum
Probably Desiderius Erasmus. *De duplici copia verborum ac rerum*. Britain or Continent: date indeterminable.
STC 10471.4 and non-STC. The most likely of the several works that carry this title. *Language(s)*: Latin. Appraised at 4d in 1578.

134.51 fabulae Aesopi grecae
Aesop. *Fabulae*. Continent: date indeterminable.
Language(s): Greek Latin (perhaps). Appraised at 6d in 1578.

134.52 Dialectica Cesarii in 8°
Joannes Caesarius, *Juliacensis. Dialectica*. Continent: date indeterminable.
Many editions include Joannes Murmellius's commentary on Aristotle's *Categoriae*. *Language(s)*: Latin. Appraised at 1s in 1578.

134.53 Illiades Homeri grece
Homer. *Iliad*. Continent: date indeterminable.
For a less expensive copy, see 134.12. *Language(s)*: Greek. Appraised at 8d in 1578.

134.54 Aulus gellius in 8°
Aulus Gellius. Probably *Noctes Atticae*. Continent: date indeterminable.
Language(s): Latin. Appraised at 8d in 1578.

134.55 Comentaria Caesaris 8°
Caius Julius Caesar. *Commentarii*. Continent: date indeterminable.
Language(s): Latin. Appraised at 10d in 1578.

134.56 Demosthenis olinthiacae 8°
Demosthenes. *Olynthiacae orationes tres.* Continent: date indeterminable.
Language(s): Latin. Appraised at 6d in 1578.

134.57 Ovidii opuscula 8°
Publius Ovidius Naso. [*Selected works*]. Britain or Continent: date indeterminable.
STC 18926.1 *et seq.* and non-STC. *Language(s)*: Latin. Appraised at 4d in 1578.

134.58 Diodorus Siculus pri
Diodorus, *Siculus. Bibliotheca historia.* Continent: date indeterminable.
Language(s): Latin (probable) Greek (perhaps). Appraised at 1s in 1578.

134.59 Propheti Minores hebraice roberti stephani
[*Bible–O.T.–Minor Prophets*]. Continent: Robertus Stephanus, 1539–1556.
Only the 1539 edition contains all twelve books. See DM, nos. 5089 and 5097. *Language(s)*: Hebrew. Appraised at 6d in 1578.

134.60 Demosthenis philippica gre lat
Demosthenes. *Philippicae orationes.* Continent: date indeterminable.
Language(s): Greek Latin. Appraised at 4d in 1578.

134.61:1 2 Salustius in 8°
Caius Sallustius Crispus. Unidentified. Place unknown: stationer unknown, date indeterminable.
STC/non-STC status unknown. If *Works*, three Latin editions were published in England by the date of this inventory. *Language(s)*: Latin. Appraised with one other at 4d in 1578.

134.61:2 [See 134.61:1]
Caius Sallustius Crispus. Unidentified. Place unknown: stationer unknown, date indeterminable.
STC/non-STC status unknown. See notes to 134.61:1. *Language(s)*: Latin. Appraised with one other at 4d in 1578.

134.62 Catechismus Calvini gre lat
Jean Calvin. [*Catechism*]. Geneva: Henricus Stephanus, 1563–1575.
Language(s): Greek Latin. Appraised at 8d in 1578.

134.63 Justinus historicus in 8°
Trogus Pompeius and Justinus, *the Historian.* [*Epitomae in Trogi Pompeii historias*]. Britain or Continent: date indeterminable.
STC 24287 *et seq.* and non-STC. Another copy at 134.4 *Language(s)*: Latin. Appraised at 6d in 1578.

134.64 Topica Theologica hiperii 8°

Andreas Gerardus, *Hyperius. Topica theologica*. Continent: 1565–1573. *Language(s)*: Latin. Appraised at 6d in 1578.

134.65 Pomponius mela sine tabulis

Pomponius Mela. *De situ orbis*. Continent: date indeterminable. A composite copy with Solinus at 134.18. *Language(s)*: Latin. Appraised at 4d in 1578.

134.66 Vita Juwelli in 4to

Laurence Humphrey. *Joannis Juelli Angli, episcopi Sarisburiensis vita et mors, eiusque; verae doctrinae defensio*. London: apud J. Dayum, 1573. STC 13963. *Language(s)*: Latin. Appraised at 1s 4d in 1578.

134.67 Odisea Homeri gre 8°

Homer. *Odyssey*. Continent: date indeterminable. For a less expensive copy in Latin, see 134.68. *Language(s)*: Greek. Appraised at 1s in 1578.

134.68 Odisea Homeri lat 8°

Homer. *Odyssey*. Continent: date indeterminable. For another, more expensive copy in Greek, see 134.67. *Language(s)*: Latin. Appraised at 4d in 1578.

134.69 Opuscula Lulii in 4to

Ramón Lull. Probably *De alchimi opuscula*. Nuremberg: apud Johan Petreium, 1546. The 1518 *Opusculum Raymundinum de auditu* ... (Wellcome no. 3901 and NLM6 no. 2875) is octavo. *Language(s)*: Latin. Appraised at 10d in 1578.

134.70 Orationes Longolii 4to

Christophorus Longolius. *Orationes duae pro defensione sua*. Continent: date indeterminable. *Language(s)*: Latin. Appraised at 10d in 1578.

134.71 Aristotelis ethica grecae

Aristotle. *Ethica*. Continent: date indeterminable. *Language(s)*: Greek. Appraised at 6d in 1578.

134.72 Rami Dialectica 8°

Pierre de La Ramée. [*Dialectica*]. Britain or Continent: date indeterminable. STC 15241.7 *et seq.* and non-STC. *Language(s)*: Latin. Appraised at 1d in 1578.

134.73 Agrippa in artem Lullii 8°

Henricus Cornelius Agrippa. *In artem brevem Raymundi Lullii.* Continent: 1531–1568.

Language(s): Latin. Appraised at 6d in 1578.

134.74 Graca [Grammatica] chevalleri 4to

Antonius Rodolphus Cevallerius. *Rudimenta hebraicae linguae.* Continent: 1567–1574.

Two quarto editions by the date of this inventory, the earliest from Geneva, the second from Wittenberg. *Language(s)*: Hebrew. Appraised at 1s in 1578.

134.75 Epistole Ciceronis 8°

Marcus Tullius Cicero. [*Selected works–Epistolae*]. Continent: date indeterminable.

If the *Epistolae ad familiares*, STC 5295 *et seq.* would be possibilities. *Language(s)*: Latin. Appraised at 6d in 1578.

134.76 Omphalius de elocutione 8°

Jacobus Omphalius. *De elocutionis imitatione ac apparatu.* Continent: date indeterminable.

Language(s): Latin. Appraised at [1]s 4d in 1578.

134.77 Calepinus in folio

Ambrogio Calepino. *Dictionarium.* Continent: date indeterminable.

Several vernacular languages are possible. *Language(s)*: Greek Latin. Appraised at 4d in 1578.

134.78 Rhetorica hermoginis grece

Hermogenes. [*Rhetorica*]. Continent: date indeterminable.

Either his popular *Ars rhetorica*, alone or with other texts, or some other collection of his rhetorical texts. Other authors might be included as well. *Language(s)*: Greek. Appraised at 6d in 1578.

134.79 Observationes Nizolii folio

Marius Nizolius. [*Observationes*]. Continent: date indeterminable.

Language(s): Latin. Appraised at 4s in 1578.

134.80 Liteltone

Sir Thomas Littleton. [*Tenures*]. Britain or Continent: date indeterminable.

STC 15719 *et seq.* One edition (STC 15721) was printed in Rouen in 1490 in folio, but a later, smaller edition is likely to be represented here. *Language(s)*: English or Law/French. Appraised at 6d in 1578.

134.81   Calimachus grec 4to
Callimachus. Probably [*Hymni*]. Continent: date indeterminable.
Language(s): Greek. Appraised at 10d in 1578.

134.82   Nonnius marcellinus Folio
Nonius Marcellus. Perhaps [*De compendiosa doctrina*]. Continent: date indeterminable.
Language(s): Latin. Appraised at 6d in 1578.

134.83   Manutus in epistolas ad Brutum
Paolo Manuzio. [*Cicero–Selected works–Epistolae: commentary*]. Venice: (different houses), date indeterminable.
Which edition of Paolo's commentary—with or without Cicero's text—cannot be determined, and, therefore, neither can the date range. Place of publication, however, would be the same for all. *Language(s)*: Latin. Appraised at 1s in 1578.

134.84   Novum testamentum grec roberti
[*Bible–N.T.*]. Continent: Robertus Stephanus, date indeterminable.
Stephanus, *the Elder* is more likely than *the Younger*, but the latter is possible and, therefore, the date range is best left unspecified. *Language(s)*: Greek. Appraised at 10d in 1578.

134.85:1–27   27 Smale bookes
Unidentified. Places unknown: stationers unknown, dates indeterminable.
STC/non-STC status unknown. *Language(s)*: Unknown. Appraised as a group at 2s 6d in 1578.

134.86   Demosthenes de falsa Legatione grec
Demosthenes. *De falsa legatione*. Continent: date indeterminable.
Language(s): Greek. Appraised at 6d in 1578.

134.87   Graca [Grammatica] hebraica Avenarii 8°
Johann Habermann (Joannes Avenarius). [*Grammatica hebraica*]. Continent: date indeterminable.
Language(s): Hebrew Latin. Appraised at 1s 2d in 1578.

134.88   Aeschines gre
Aeschines. Probably *Epistolae*. Continent: 1536–1578.
If Aeschines alone, as in the manuscript entry, then the *Epistolae*; the compiler could, however, have simply neglected to enter *et Demosthenes*. The appraisal is probably too low for a large collection with Aeschines leading. *Language(s)*: Greek. Appraised at 4d in 1578.

134.89   Demosthens de Corona 8°
Demosthenes. *De corona*. Geneva: apud Joannem Le Preux, 1545–1550.
Language(s): Greek Latin. Appraised at 6d in 1578.

Thomas Pope. Scholar (M.A.):
Probate Inventory. 1578

RUDOLPH P. ALMASY

Thomas Pope, of Gloucester Hall, was granted the B.A. degree from St. Mary Hall on 9 December 1572, and he received the M.A. degree on 23 June 1576. Not quite two years later, on 2 April 1578, he made his will (*Alumni Oxonienses*, 3:1181); he died shortly thereafter since an inventory of his possessions was made on 5 April 1578. It is tempting, given the reputation of Gloucester Hall for recusancy, to suspect a relationship between this Thomas Pope and Sir Thomas Pope (1507?–1559), the founder of Trinity College, Oxford, the only Oxford college founded during the reign of Mary. The elder Pope was a member of Mary's Privy Council and had been sufficiently committed a Catholic to withdraw from public life in the reign of Edward VI (see DNB). He died without issue, but had at least one brother whose son this Thomas Pope might have been.

The great majority of Pope's books reflect the standard studies for the M.A. degree, with some remnants from the B.A. course and an indication that in his subsequent theological studies he had embarked on learning Hebrew. These are books of a serious student, who had paid serious attention to those parts of the M.A. course that had a bearing on mathematics, astronomy, and cosmography; five of the identifiable books in his library are either copies of or commentaries on Aristotle's *Physica*. To these ends he had acquired "certayne tooles or other instruments" and a globe. His extracurricular interests are represented by the "cyturne and a olde lute" also listed in his inventory.

Oxford University Archives, Bodleian Library: Hyp.B.17.

§

135.1   Ephimerides Stadii
135.2   Leonitius de eclipsibus
135.3   Alfonsi tabulae astronomicae
135.4   Munsteri hebraicum dixtionarium
135.5   Donatus in Ethica
135.6   Biblium [Bibliorum] veterum impressio
135.7   Biblium Stelsii
135.8   Quintiliani Declamationes
135.9   Phisica Aristoteles
135.10:A   Humphridus de nobilitate
135.10:B   [See 135.10:A]
135.11   Ochini dialogi
135.12   Stoflerinus de usu astrolabii
135.13   Toletus in Phisica
135.14   Ethica Aristotelis grece et latine
135.15   Haddoni opera
135.16   Luciani dialogi deorum
135.17   Scheggius in Aristotelis Phisica
135.18   Theodorus in lib. de anima [animalibus]
135.19   Jovius de principibus Mediolani
135.20   P. Venetus de anima
135.21   Prophetiae Hieremiae hebraice
135.22   the Pathewaie
135.23   Aulicus latine
135.24   Grammatica greca Ceporini
135.25   Bricot in Phisica
135.26   Arithmetica et Geometria Rami
135.27   Genesis hebraice
135.28   Phisica Aristotelis grece
135.29   Dariotus, Astronomia
135.30   Cathecismus Nowella latine
135.31   Grammatica greca Cleonardi
135.32   Aristotelis Organum
135.33   Arithmetica Gemmae Phrisii
135.34   Testamentum latinum
135.35   Galenus de simplicibus medicamentis
135.36   Rhetorica Tulli
135.37   Orationes Tulli in tribus voluminibus
135.38   Psalmi hebraice
135.39   Ovidii Metamorphosis anglice
135.40:1–70 about thre scoore and x bookes

§

135.1 Ephimerides Stadii
Joannes Stadius. *Ephemerides*. Cologne: [probably] Heirs of Arnold Birckman, 1554?–1570.
The printer is not identified in the 1560 edition, but all other editions were issued by Birckman's heirs. *Language(s)*: Latin. Appraised at 7s in 1578.

135.2 Leonitius de eclipsibus
Perhaps Cyprianus von Leowitz. *Eclipsium omnium ab anno Domini 1554 usque in annum Domini 1606 descriptio*. Augsburg: Philippus Ulhardus excud., 1556.
Language(s): Latin. Appraised at 3s in 1578.

135.3 Alfonsi tabulae astronomicae
Alfonso X, *King of Castile*. *Astronomicae tabulae*. Continent: date indeterminable.
Language(s): Latin. Appraised at 8d in 1578.

135.4 Munsteri hebraicum dixtionarium
Sebastian Muenster. *Dictionarium hebraicum*. Basle: (different houses), 1523–1564.
Language(s): Hebrew Latin. Appraised at 14d in 1578.

135.5 Donatus in Ethica
Donatus Acciaiolus. [*Aristotle–Ethica: commentary*]. Continent: date indeterminable.
Language(s): Latin. Appraised at 20d in 1578.

135.6 Biblium [Bibliorum] veterum impressio
The Bible. Continent (probable): date indeterminable.
Probably not an STC book, but see STC 2055. The single 1535 edition of the Vulgate printed in England is, given the particular description of the entry, not nearly as likely as one of the scores of early Continental editions. *Language(s)*: Latin. Appraised at 20d in 1578.

135.7 Biblium Stelsii
The Bible. Antwerp: Joannes Steelsius, date indeterminable.
Steelsius printed at least five editions of the Bible from 1537 on, perhaps more. *Language(s)*: Latin. Appraised at 2s 6d in 1578.

135.8 Quintiliani Declamationes
Marcus Fabius Quintilianus. *Declamationes*. Continent: date indeterminable.
Language(s): Latin. Appraised at 18d in 1578.

135.9 Phisica Aristoteles
Aristotle. *Physica*. Continent: date indeterminable.

See 135.28 for a Greek edition. *Language(s)*: Latin. Appraised at 20d in 1578.

135.10:A Humphridus de nobilitate
Laurence Humphrey. *Optimates, sive de nobilitate*. Basle: Joannes Oporinus, 1560 (composite publication).
Published with the following. *Language(s)*: Latin. Appraised [a composite volume] at 10d in 1578.

135.10:B [See 135.10:A]
Philo, *Judaeus*. *De nobilitate*. [Composite publication].
Language(s): Latin. Appraised [a composite volume] at 10d in 1578.

135.11 Ochini dialogi
Bernardino Ochino. *Dialogi*. Britain or Continent: date indeterminable.
Ochino's dialogues were published in various combinations and sometimes individually. It is impossible to know what the present volume contained. *Language(s)*: Latin. Appraised at 6d in 1578.

135.12 Stoflerinus de usu astrolabii
Joannes Stoeffler. *Elucidatio fabricae ususque astrolabii*. Continent: date indeterminable.
The compiler had first written "Stobeus" (Joannes Stobaeus?) before altering the entry to *Stoflerinus*. *Language(s)*: Latin. Appraised at 12d in 1578.

135.13 Toletus in Phisica
Franciscus Toletus, *Cardinal*. [*Aristotle–Physica: commentary*]. Continent: 1574–1578.
Language(s): Latin. Appraised at 2s in 1578.

135.14 Ethica Aristotelis grece et latine
Aristotle. *Ethica*. Continent: date indeterminable.
Language(s): Greek Latin. Appraised at 10d in 1578.

135.15 Haddoni opera
Walter Haddon. *Lucubrationes passim collectae, et editae*. Edited by Thomas Hatcher. London: apud G. Seresium, 1567.
STC 12596. *Language(s)*: Latin. Appraised at 12d in 1578.

135.16 Luciani dialogi deorum
Lucian, *of Samosata*. *Deorum dialogi*. Continent: date indeterminable.
STC 16891. *Language(s)*: Latin Greek (perhaps). Appraised at 4d in 1578.

135.17 Scheggius in Aristotelis Phisica
Jacob Schegk, *the Elder*. *In octo Physicorum, sive de auditione physica libros*

Aristotelis, commentaria. Basle: per Joannem Hervagium, 1546.

Schegk's commentary on the *De anima* is included in this volume. See next item. Adams S638. *Language(s)*: Latin. Appraised at 2s 6d in 1578.

135.18 Theodorus in lib. de anima [animalibus]
Aristotle. Probably *Historia animalium*. Translated by Theodorus, *Gaza*. Continent: date indeterminable.

Sometimes given the title *De animalibus historia*. No edition of Aristotle's *De anima* is connected with any Theodorus. *Language(s)*: Latin. Appraised at 4d in 1578.

135.19 Jovius de principibus Mediolani
Paolo Giovio, *Bishop*. *Vitae duodecim vicecomitum Mediolani principum*. Paris: ex officina Robert. Stephani, 1549.

Language(s): Latin. Appraised at 6d in 1578.

135.20 P. Venetus de anima
Paulus, *Venetus* (Paulus Nicolettus). [*Aristotle–De anima: commentary*]. Continent: 1481–1524.

Language(s): Latin. Appraised at 2s in 1578.

135.21 Prophetiae Hieremiae hebraice
[*Bible–O.T.–Jeremiah*]. Continent: date indeterminable.

Perhaps from one of the multi-volume sets of the Hebrew Old Testament printed by Robertus Stephanus in the 1540s. See Adams B1221–1222 and B1224. See 135.27 and 135.38. *Language(s)*: Hebrew. Appraised at 14d in 1578.

135.22 the Pathewaie
Perhaps Robert Record. *The pathway to knowledg, containing the first principles of geometrie*. London: (different houses), 1551–1572.

STC 20812. Of the five "Pathways" published by this date, the next most likely candidate is STC 24462–24464, William Tyndale's *A pathway to the holy scriptures*. *Language(s)*: English. Appraised at 12d in 1578.

135.23 Aulicus latine
Baldassare Castiglione, *Count. De curiali sive aulico libri quatuor ex Italico sermone in Latinum conversi*. Translated by Bartholomew Clerke. London: (different houses), 1571–1577.

STC 4782 *et seq*. The 1577 translation of *Il cortegiano* by R. Ricius, printed in Strassburg, is not considered a likely possibility, especially given the popularity of Clerke's translation. *Language(s)*: Latin. Appraised at 10d in 1578.

135.24 Grammatica greca Ceporini
Jacobus Ceporinus. *Compendium grammaticae graecae*. Continent: date inde-

terminable.
Language(s): Latin. Appraised at 4d in 1578.

135.25 Bricot in Phisica
Thomas Bricot. [*Aristotle–Physica: commentary*]. Continent: date indeterminable.
Language(s): Latin. Appraised at 10d in 1578.

135.26 Arithmetica et Geometria Rami
Pierre de La Ramée. *Arithmeticae libri duo: geometriae septem et viginti.* Basle: per Eusebium Episcopium et Nicolai fratris haeredes, 1569.
Ong no. 691. *Language(s)*: Latin. Appraised at 16d in 1578.

135.27 Genesis hebraice
[*Bible–O.T.–Genesis*]. Continent: date indeterminable.
See 135.21, the note there, and 135.38. *Language(s)*: Hebrew. Appraised at 10d in 1578.

135.28 Phisica Aristotelis grece
Aristotle. *Physica*. Continent: date indeterminable.
Language(s): Greek. Appraised at 8d in 1578.

135.29 Dariotus, Astronomia
Claude Dariot. *Ad astrorum judicia facilis introductio* [and other works]. Lyon: apud Mauricium Roy, et Ludovicum Pesnot, 1557.
Language(s): Latin. Appraised at 12d in 1578.

135.30 Cathecismus Nowella latine
Alexander Nowell. *Catechismus*. London: (different houses), 1570–1577. STC 18701 *et seq. Language(s)*: Latin. Appraised at 6d in 1578.

135.31 Grammatica greca Cleonardi
Nicolaus Clenardus. [*Institutiones linguae graecae*]. Continent: date indeterminable.
Language(s): Greek Latin. Appraised at 10d in 1578.

135.32 Aristotelis Organum
Aristotle. *Organon*. Continent: date indeterminable.
Language(s): Latin Greek (probable). Appraised at 6d in 1578.

135.33 Arithmetica Gemmae Phrisii
Reiner Gemma, *Frisius. Arithmeticae practicae methodus facilis*. Continent: date indeterminable.
Language(s): Latin. Appraised at 4d in 1578.

135.34 Testamentum latinum
[*Bible–N.T.*]. Britain or Continent: date indeterminable.
STC 2799 and non-STC. *Language(s)*: Latin. Appraised at 12d in 1578.

135.35 Galenus de simplicibus medicamentis
Galen. *De simplicium medicamentorum facultatibus.* Continent: 1530–1543.
Perhaps *Selected works* with this title leading. *Language(s)*: Latin. Appraised at 8d in 1578.

135.36 Rhetorica Tulli
Marcus Tullius Cicero. Probably [*Selected works–Rhetorica*]. Continent: date indeterminable.
Conceivably the *Rhetorica ad Herennium*, widely published alone. *Language(s)*: Latin. Appraised at 10d in 1578.

135.37 Orationes Tulli in tribus voluminibus
Marcus Tullius Cicero. [*Selected works–Orations*]. Continent: date indeterminable.
Language(s): Latin. Appraised at 2s in 1578.

135.38 Psalmi hebraice
[*Bible–O.T.–Psalms*]. Continent: date indeterminable.
See 135.21, the note there, and 135.27. *Language(s)*: Hebrew. Appraised at 4d in 1578.

135.39 Ovidii Metamorphosis anglice
Publius Ovidius Naso. *Metamorphosis.* Translated by Arthur Golding. London: W. Seres, 1565–1575.
STC 18955 *et seq. Language(s)*: English. Appraised at 16d in 1578.

135.40:1–70 about thre scoore and x bookes
Unidentified. Places unknown: stationers unknown, dates indeterminable.
STC/non-STC status unknown. *Language(s)*: Unknown. Appraised as a group at 15s in 1578.

Alan Scott. Cleric, Scholar (M.A.): Probate Inventory. 1578

GRADY A. SMITH

Virtually the whole of Alan Scott's working life, from his student days onward, was spent at the Queen's College. Proceeding Bachelor of Arts on 5 July 1554, and Master of Arts on 6 July 1556, he became a fellow of the college in 1559 and senior fellow two years later. In 1565 he was elected its twenty-second provost (Magrath 1921, 1:195).

Prior to his tenure as provost, the office had fallen upon difficult times. Thomas Francis obtained the office "by royal influence. . . . He had none of the statutable qualifications" (Magrath 1921, 1:186). After two years he resigned, his place being filled in 1563 by the election of Lancelot Shaw. In his turn Shaw vacated the post two years later while being investigated for peculation and public drunkenness (Magrath 1921, 1:186–88). Scott then succeeded and remained in the office for ten years, returning stability and respect to it. During his incumbency he was appointed vicar of Edenhall, Cumberland, and rector of Bletchingdon, Oxfordshire. His will was probated at Oxford on 27 July 1578.

Nearly half of the titles in the probate inventory are theological works; there is a scattering of works in political philosophy (most notably a Latin copy of Macchiavelli's *The Prince*), medicine, history, and geography to lend some variety. The single entry, "thirty-three odd books" will unfortunately ensure an abiding uncertainty concerning the full range of Scott's interests.

The inventory exists in two manuscripts: the original (A) and a fair copy (B). Manuscript A has been adopted as the copy-text except where manuscript B clearly presents a preferred reading. Significant variants are noted in the annotations.

Oxford University Archives, Bodleian Library: Hyp.B.18.

§

Magrath, John Richard. 1921. *The Queen's College*. 2 vols. Oxford: the Clarendon Press.

§

136.1	biblitheca
136.2	Sermones pomerii
136.3	Barnardi
136.4	Thomas quani sancti paule
136.5	bede history
136.6	the offolack
136.7	coloniensis
136.8	pigiuss
136.9	greostum unperfitt
136.10	the first volume of origin
136.11	demostines
136.12	arthore joane ganario
136.13	marcus antonius
136.14	postilla poligrana
136.15	homillia placentinus
136.16	marcus orellius
136.17	swillius articulorum
136.18	bridgment of histories
136.19	sanctorum catholicam
136.20	scoferus epistils
136.21	Erasmus parrafferis
136.22	hessius confutac**
136.23	de sigismundo
136.24	in creridion hemmingii
136.25	evangelica
136.26	the castell of helthe
136.27	hiperius comminplaces
136.28	homilia in evangellia
136.29	peter lumbarde Sentences
136.30	de conscribendis epistolis
136.31	Hosius confutacion
136.32	machivin de principe
136.33	De libero arbitero
136.34	appinans cosmografi
136.35	hiperius de Sacra Scriptura
136.36	ii partes of levi

136.37   a pece of St barnard
136.38:1–33   xxxiii odd bookes
136.39   irineus
136.40   pollidorus
136.41   the rule of the worlde
136.42   lenardus colman
136.43   ageus
136.44   juels appologi

§

136.1 biblitheca
Unidentified. Place unknown: stationer unknown, date indeterminable.

STC/non-STC status unknown. Various possibilities, including the *Biblio-theca historia* of Diodorus, *Siculus*, the *Bibliotheca sancta* of Sixtus, *Senensis*, and even Elyot's dictionary, the *Bibliotheca Eliotae*. Manuscript B reads *Biblica*. *Language(s)*: Latin. Appraised at 6s 8d in 1578.

136.2 Sermones pomerii
Pelbartus, *de Themeswar*. [*Sermones Pomerii*]. Continent: date indetermin-able.

STC/non-STC status unknown. Manuscript B reads *Pomereri*. *Language(s)*: Latin. Appraised at 12d in 1578.

136.3 Barnardi
Bernard, *Saint*. Unidentified. Continent: date indeterminable.

Language(s): Latin. Appraised at 12d in 1578.

136.4 Thomas quani sancti paule
Thomas Aquinas, *Saint*. [*Epistles–Paul: commentary*]. Continent: date inde-terminable.

Language(s): Latin. Appraised at 12d in 1578.

136.5 bede history
Beda, *the Venerable*. *The history of the church of Englande*. Translated by T. Stapleton. Antwerp: J. Laet, 1565.

STC 1778. *Language(s)*: English. Appraised at 2s in 1578.

136.6 the offolack
Theophylact, *Archbishop of Achrida*. Unidentified. Continent: date indeter-minable.

Language(s): Latin. Appraised at 2s in 1578.

136.7 coloniensis
Unidentified. Continent: date indeterminable.

Probably either the *Canones* of the 1536 Council of Cologne, the *Decreta* of the 1549 Council, a publication of the Cologne diocese, or a work of Cologne University. *Language(s)*: Latin. Appraised at 12d in 1578.

136.8 pigiuss

Albertus Pighius. Unidentified. Continent: date indeterminable. *Language(s)*: Latin. Appraised at 12d in 1578.

136.9 greostum unperfitt

Perhaps John, *Chrysostom, Saint*. Unidentified. Place unknown: stationer unknown, date indeterminable.

STC/non-STC status unknown. If Chrysostom, Greek is unlikely since there is no other item in Scott's library collection identified as Greek. *Language(s)*: Latin (probable). Appraised at 2s 6d in 1578.

136.10 the first volume of origin

Origen. [*Works* (part)]. Continent: date indeterminable. *Language(s)*: Latin. Appraised at 2s 6d in 1578.

136.11 demostines

Demosthenes. Unidentified. Place unknown: stationer unknown, date indeterminable.

STC/non-STC status unknown. A word preceding *demostines* is struck out. *Language(s)*: Latin (probable). Appraised at 8d in 1578.

136.12 arthore joane ganario

Unidentified. Continent (probable): date indeterminable.

Probably not an STC book. Giovanni Battista Guarini is a possibility. *Language(s)*: Latin (probable). Appraised at 8d in 1578.

136.13 marcus antonius

Probably Stephen Gardiner, *Bishop* (Marcus Antonius Constantius, *pseudonym*). *Confutatio cavillationum quibus eucharistiae sacramentum ab impiis Capernaitis impeti solis*. Continent: 1552–1554.

Perhaps, however, a work by Marcus Antonius Sabellicus (Coccius). *Language(s)*: Latin. Appraised at 6d in 1578.

136.14 postilla poligrana

Franciscus Polygranus. *Postillae sive enarrationes in evangelia*. Cologne: apud haeredes Arnoldi Birckmanni, 1557–1570. *Language(s)*: Latin. Appraised at 14d in 1578.

136.15 homillia placentinus

Unidentified [sermons]. Continent (probable): date indeterminable.

Probably not an STC book. Manuscript B reads *Placentius*. No Placentinus or Placentius can be identified with *homillia*. *Language(s)*: Latin (probable). Appraised at 16d in 1578.

136.16 marcus orellius
Marcus Aurelius Antoninus. [*De vita sua*]. Continent: date indeterminable.

The popular fictional biography, *The golden boke of Marcus Aurelius* by Antonio Guevara, is a less likely possibility for this library. *Language(s)*: Latin. Appraised at 6d in 1578.

136.17 swillius articulorum
Ulrich Zwingli. *Opus articulorum sive conclusionum*. Translated by Leo Juda. Zürich: excud. Christophorus Froschouerus, 1535?

A nearly illegible insertion would alter *swillius* to either *suigllius* or *swhinglius*. Manuscript B provides an unhelpful *swollius*. *Language(s)*: Latin. Appraised at 8d in 1578.

136.18 bridgment of histories
Trogus Pompeius and Justinus, *the Historian. Thabridgment of the histories of Trogus Pompeius*. Translated by Arthur Golding. London: T. Marsh, 1564–1578.

STC 24290 *et seq*. *Language(s)*: English. Appraised at 6d in 1578.

136.19 sanctorum catholicam
Unidentified. Continent (probable): date indeterminable.

Probably not an STC book. Manuscript B reads *storum catholicam*. *Language(s)*: Latin. Appraised at 6d in 1578.

136.20 scoferus epistils
Unidentified. Place unknown: stationer unknown, date indeterminable.

STC/non-STC status unknown. Manuscript B reads *Scoferus epostils*. Perhaps letters, perhaps a commentary on the Epistles of the New Testament. If the latter, Jakob Schoepper's commentary on the liturgical Gospels and Epistles is a possibility. Arsatius Schofer seems not to have written on the Epistles, only the Gospels (see Adams S693). *Language(s)*: Unknown. Appraised at 12d in 1578.

136.21 Erasmus parrafferis
Desiderius Erasmus. Unidentified. (*Bible–N.T.*). Continent: date indeterminable.

At this valuation only a part of paraphrases of the New Testament, but which part cannot be known. His *Paraphrasis in Elegantias Vallae* is a remote possibility. Manuscript B gives *perrafferis* as the last word. *Language(s)*: Latin. Appraised at 6d in 1578.

136.22 hessius confutac**
Unidentified. Continent (probable): date indeterminable.
Probably not an STC book. The *confutac*** may have been lined through.
Whether this is another copy of Hozyusz's confutation of Brentz, one of which
appears at 136.31, a different work of Hozyusz's, or something of Helius
Eobanus, *Hessus*'s cannot be determined. *Language(s)*: Latin. Appraised at 6d
in 1578.

136.23 de sigismundo
Unidentified. Continent (probable): date indeterminable.
Probably not an STC book. If the entry is descriptive of a title or subject,
possibilities include Jodocus Ludovicus Decius, *Contenta: de vetustatibus polo-*
norum, 1521 (liber II: *De sigismundi regis temporibus*), and Johann Eck, *Ad invic-*
tissimum poloniae regem sigismundum, 1526. *Language(s)*: Latin. Appraised at 6d
in 1578.

136.24 in creridion hemmingii
Niels Hemmingsen. *Enchiridion theologicum*. Britain or Continent: 1557–
1577.
STC 13056.5 and non-STC. Manuscript B gives *Hemigie* for the last word.
Language(s): Latin. Appraised at 8d in 1578.

136.25 evangelica
Unidentified. Place unknown: stationer unknown, date indeterminable.
STC/non-STC status unknown. A commentary on the Gospels is an obvi-
ous possibility, but so also are other works, including the *De evangelica prae-*
paratione of Eusebius, *Pamphili, Bishop*. *Language(s)*: Latin (probable). Appraised at 4d in 1578.

136.26 the castell of helthe
Sir Thomas Elyot. *The castell of helthe*. London: (different houses), 1537?–
1576.
STC 7642.5 *et seq*. *Language(s)*: English. Appraised at 2d in 1578.

136.27 hiperius comminplaces
Andreas Gerardus, *Hyperius*. Probably [*Methodus theologiae sive loci*
communes]. Basle: Joannes Oporinus, 1567–1574.
Although an English entry, the first English edition of any commonplaces
of Gerardus was published in 1581, three years after the date of this inventory. See also 136.35. *Language(s)*: Latin. Appraised at 16d in 1578.

136.28 homilia in evangellia
Unidentified [sermons]. Place unknown: stationer unknown, date indeterminable.
STC/non-STC status unknown. *Language(s)*: Latin. Appraised at 6d in
1578.

136.29 peter lumbarde Sentences
Peter Lombard. *Sententiarum libri IIII*. Continent: date indeterminable. *Language(s)*: Latin. Appraised at 16d in 1578.

136.30 de conscribendis epistolis
Probably Desiderius Erasmus. *De conscribendis epistolis*. Britain or Continent: 1521–1573.

STC 10496 and non-STC. Works with this or similar titles were written not only by Erasmus but also by Georgius Macropedius, Christoph Hegendorff, and others. Nevertheless, the numerous editions published from 1521 make it probable that this is Erasmus's work. Dates from VHe. *Language(s)*: Latin. Appraised at 4d in 1578.

136.31 Hosius confutacion
Stanislaus Hozyusz, *Cardinal. Confutatio prolegomenon Brentii*. Continent: 1558–1571.

Manuscript A reads "Hosiais." See 136.22. *Language(s)*: Latin. Appraised at 14d in 1578.

136.32 machivin de principe
Niccolò Macchiavelli. *De principe*. Translated by Sylvester Telius. Basle: apud Petrum Pernam, 1560.

Language(s): Latin. Appraised at 6d in 1578.

136.33 De libero arbitero
Unidentified. *De libero arbitrio*. Continent (probable): date indeterminable.

Probably not an STC book. Augustine, Erasmus, Laurentius Valla, and Calistus Placentinus all wrote works with this title. The word *libero* replaces a lined-through *beblo*. *Language(s)*: Latin. Appraised at 3d in 1578.

136.34 appinans cosmografi
Peter Apian. *Cosmographia*. Continent: 1524–1574. *Language(s)*: Latin. Appraised at 4d in 1578.

136.35 hiperius de Sacra Scriptura
Andreas Gerardus, *Hyperius. De sacrae scripturae lectione*. Basle: Joannes Oporinus, 1563–1569.

See also 136.27. *Language(s)*: Latin. Appraised at 4d in 1578.

136.36 ii partes of levi
Unidentified. Continent (probable): date indeterminable.

Probably not an STC book. Perhaps something of Lemnius Levinus, but nothing of his was published in parts. It could represent separated sections of a book, but the valuation is inconsistent with detached pieces. Also, the entry could refer to one of several Jewish authors, such as Elias, *Levita* and Joannes Isaac, *Levita*, but the collection gives no evidence that Scott read Hebrew. *Language(s)*: Unknown. Appraised at 2s 6d in 1578.

136.37 a pece of St barnard
Bernard, *Saint*. Unidentified. Place unknown: stationer unknown, date indeterminable.

STC/non-STC status unknown. At the valuation, likely part of *Works*. *Language(s)*: Latin. Appraised at 2s in 1578.

136.38:1–33 xxxiii odd bookes
Unidentified. Places unknown: stationers unknown, dates indeterminable.

STC/non-STC status unknown. Manuscript B reads *old* for *odd*. *Language(s)*: Unknown. Appraised as a group at 2s in 1578.

136.39 irineus
Irenaeus, *Saint*. [*Adversus haereses*]. Continent: 1526–1576. *Language(s)*: Latin. Appraised at 14d in 1578.

136.40 pollidorus
Polydorus Vergilius. Unidentified. Place unknown: stationer unknown, date indeterminable.

STC/non-STC status unknown. *Language(s)*: Latin. Appraised at 12d in 1578.

136.41 the rule of the worlde
Pierre Boaistuau. *Theatrum mundi, the theatre or rule of the world, wherein may be sene the course of everye mans life, as touching miserie and felicity.* Translated by John Alday. London: (different houses) for T. Hacket, 1566?–1574.

STC 3168 *et seq.* A Latin translation appeared in 1576, but the entry would be unusual for either a Latin or the original French version. *Language(s)*: English. Appraised at 8d in 1578.

136.42 lenardus colman
Leonhard Culmann. Unidentified. Continent: date indeterminable. *Language(s)*: Latin. Appraised at 6d in 1578.

136.43 ageus
Unidentified. Place unknown: stationer unknown, date indeterminable.

STC/non-STC status unknown. Likely a work on Haggai. James Pilkington's English commentary (STC 19926) is one possibility, and Johann Eck's *Super Aggaeo commentarius* is another. Given the careless hand of the compiler, the entry could possibly represent Aegidius. *Language(s)*: Latin (probable) English (perhaps). Appraised at 10d in 1578.

136.44   juels appologi

John Jewel, *Bishop. An apologie or aunswer in defence of the Church of England.* London: R. Wolfe, 1562–1564.

STC 14590 *et seq.* and non-STC. *Language(s)*: English. Appraised at 4d in 1578.

John Lewis. Manciple, Merchant (white-baker): Probate Inventory. 1579

W. P. GRIFFITH

Unlike most Oxford book owners in this series, John Lewis (Lewes, Lewys) was not an academic but rather a leading college official who took his privileged status within the university from his role as manciple of University College. (Details are taken from BRUO2, 355, except where stated.) Lewis was also an important figure in the city of Oxford. He was a freeman or hanaster, having been elected to that status by virtue of his membership in the baker's guild in 1538 (Turner 1880, 178), and he was a major employer of apprentice labor (Elrington 1979, 4:118, 164). By 1568 Lewis was resident in the city's southeast ward and thus was close by the college he served (Turner 1880, 321–22).

In the history of Oxford, Lewis is noted for his opposition to the monopoly of milling rights possessed by the city millers at the Castle mills and to their abuse of that monopoly by the imposition of unduly heavy tolls or levies in kind on the meal that was ground there (Rogers 1891, 283–95). In 1546, probably as a result of having gone to the Court of Requests, Lewis won from the city the right to be compensated by the millers for being misused and the freedom to mill as he willed at the Castle mills (Rogers 1891, 293; Turner 1880, 179–80). Soon after, but whether because of the same issue is unclear, he was ordered by the city council to be imprisoned for perjury (Turner 1880, 180). Lewis was still obliged to employ the town mills for grinding, but twenty years later, in 1568–1569, he again challenged the monopoly, asserting his right to be totally free of the city millers. Perhaps because of his seniority and prominence, the city, in return for a fine of £14, licensed him for life to grind at least part of his corn elsewhere (Turner 1880, 326–27; Elrington 1979, 4:328).

Lewis does not seem to have been a very active participant in the city's government—in 1547 he commuted for the office of chamberlain—but he did act as a master of the city mills in 1562, supervising the conduct of the millers, which may again have aroused his hostility to their monopoly (Turner 1880, 186 and 300). By then, Lewis was well established in his post of manciple of University College, having been appointed to the office in 1556 (Hammer 1986, 79). His duties would have involved ensuring the ready supply of provisions, furnishings, and equipment to provide a comfortable life for the entire college society. His inventory, therefore, is fascinating for the lists of kitchen and domestic equipment, furniture, and bedding in his possession, located at different parts of the college. As a baker he would have had a major voice in the college's food purchasing policy. Moreover, as a wealthy citizen Lewis acted, as the inventory reveals, as a line of credit to several colleges, including his own, as well as to senior academics and townsmen (Hammer 1974, 251–55). No doubt college members gave him various items as cautions or pledges in return for money. Stuff such as student clothing features in the inventory, and unredeemed pledges probably make up much of his collection of books.

Strictly speaking, there are two inventories of books. The majority, which Lewis had at the college, were appraised and proved along with all the other items on 4 August 1579 and exhibited on 8 August. Another set of books was listed, but not valued, at Lewis's own house in Oxford. The date given for the year of the latter inventory, 19 August 1569, is taken to be a scribal error. The books contained in the second inventory seem, on the whole, to be of an earlier date than those in the first. Indeed, they may be the ones referred to in the first list as "Certeyne old unperfect bookes" (137.54) valued *en bloc* at 6s 8d.

Both sets of books have a theological bent to them, the second set especially so, and have been described by N.R. Ker (470n) as "a strongly catholic collection." Hammer (1974, 251–55; see also Elrington 1979, 3:21) has gone so far as to suggest that, through his library, Lewis was associated with "reactionary papist elements" at University College, but there is no evidence to confirm this. We do not know whether Lewis was at all academically inclined, certainly not to the degree of actively collecting and studying such books. If they were exchanged for credit with him it is possible that they were gathered together early on in his career as manciple, during the Marian years or perhaps in the early 1560s as the Elizabethan settlement was made operative at the university and as many of these works became unfashionable or redundant. Emden (BRUO2, 725–26) has implied that the books are a distinct, whole library and that they may represent the collection of Lewis's namesake, John Lewis, fellow of All Souls' in 1537, which the baker might have inherited (BRUO2, 355). However Lewis amassed his books, they are typical of the material that might have been read by arts and theology graduates whose academic interests were formed during the second quarter of the sixteenth century.

The fifty-three titles in the first inventory are almost equally divided between books suitable for the unreconstructed divinity course and books appropriate for the arts course. The theological works include some by the early saints and church fathers, notably Jerome, works about the priestly order, and late medieval devotional books and spiritual commentaries. The arts volumes indicate a great emphasis on Aristotle and his late-medieval interpreters, including rare editions by, for example, Odonis (137.44) and Bricot (137.37 and 137.42), but Latin authors were also numerous, and the humanist influence is apparent in the works by Faber (137.29, 137.30, 137.35, and 137.38) and Erasmus (137.47). Continental editions, predictably, predominate in the first list—where Elyot's *Dictionary* (137.3) and Lyndewode's *Constitutiones* (137.20) are among the exceptions—as well as in the second with its exclusively theological, scholastic, and patristic character.

Oxford University Archives, Bodleian Library: Hyp.B.15.
Transcribed in BRUO2, pp. 725–26.

§

Elrington, C.R., ed. 1979. *Victoria History of the County of Oxford.* Vol. 4 of *The Victoria History of the Counties of England.* Oxford: Oxford Univ. Press for the University of London Institute of Historical Research.

Hammer, Carl I., Jr. 1974. "Some Social and Institutional Aspects of Town-Gown Relations in late Medieval and Tudor Oxford." D.Phil. thesis, University of Toronto.

——. 1986. "Oxford Town and Oxford University," in *The Collegiate University,* ed., James McConica. Volume 3 of *The History of the University of Oxford,* gen. ed., T.H. Aston. Oxford: Oxford Univ. Press, pp. 69–116.

Rogers, J.E. Thorold, ed. 1891. *Oxford City Documents: Financial and Judicial 12681665.* Oxford: Oxford Historical Society.

Turner, W.H. 1880. *Selections from the Records of the City of Oxford [1509–83].* Oxford: James Parker.

§

137.1	Biblia sacra in folio
137.2	Biblia sacra
137.3	Eliotes dictionarie
137.4	Eckii homilliarii in 2 volumes
137.5	Ireneus
137.6	Hieronomus super prophetas

137.7	Hieronimi epistolae
137.8	Pomerii sermones in 3 volumes
137.9	Index in Opera Hieronimi
137.10	Dionysius Ariopagita
137.11	damascenus
137.12	Scotus super sententias in 2 volums
137.13	Thomas Aquimas [sic] in 2m [secundum] sententiarum
137.14	Hieronimus in two volumes
137.15	concordantiae bibliae
137.16	Claudius Guilaudus in omnes epist pauli
137.17	Polianthia hist:
137.18	M. Anthonius de Eucharistia
137.19	Liber magnus de trinitate
137.20	Linwoodes constitutions
137.21	distructorium vitiorum
137.22	Rationale divinorum officiorum
137.23	Mariale de laudibus virginis
137.24	Johannes maior in 1m [primum] sententiarum
137.25	Artopeus in evang
137.26	Johannes Canonicus in physica Arist:
137.27	Petrus Barthous super bibliam sacram
137.28	Andreas in Metaphis: Arist:
137.29	Stapulensis in phisica Arist:
137.30	Jacobus faber stap:
137.31	Averrois in phisica Arist:
137.32	Burleus in dialecticam Arist:
137.33	Euclid Geometria
137.34	Venetus in phis: Arist:
137.35	Clictovius in phis: Arist:
137.36	Senec: traged:
137.37	Bricot super dialec:
137.38	Stapulensis de sphera
137.39	Lucanus cum comment
137.40	mantuanus cum comment
137.41	Albertus de saxona super lib: Arist: de caelo
137.42	Bricot in phis: Arist:
137.43	Scotus in metaph: Arist:
137.44	Odo in Ethic: arist:
137.45	Johannes Raulin in sermones in 2 vol
137.46	Epist: Plinii in 2 vol
137.47	Erasmus in Epist: Pauli
137.48	Virgilius cum comment: Serbii
137.49	Polydorus de inventoribus rerum
137.50	Terentius
137.51	Egidius Romanus de anima

137.52   Tulii officia
137.53   Grammat: Greca Cleonardi
137.54 multiple   Certeyne old unperfect bookes
137.55   Sermones Sancti Francisci
137.56   Omilia aecleani
137.57   opus beate marie
137.58   opus Sancti Thomae
137.59   op [opera] petrus berterius
137.60   Expositio beati gregorii super Ezekielem
137.61   Summa que catholica nominatur
137.62   Sermones aurei de Sanctis fratris benedicti
137.63   Psalterii expositio per petri orientalis
137.64   Quadragesimale de legibus
137.65   manipulus curatorum
137.66   Sermones petri fratris
137.67   A boke begynnyng Quicunque mellificatis
137.68   Sermones pomerii
137.69   Casus papales episcopales et abbitiales
137.70   doctrinale fratris Johannis Rawlyns
137.71   Stella clericorum
137.72   Sermones Jacobi de lenda
137.73   opus barardi [barnardi]
137.74   destructorium viciorum
137.75   postilla qwillermi super epistolas et evangelia
137.76   Sermones michaelis hungarii
137.77   liber quadraginta omiliarum gregorii pape
137.78   bonaventure

§

137.1 Biblia sacra in folio

The Bible. Continent: date indeterminable.

This is the only entry to which the list compiler ascribes a format, so it is impossible to determine whether he was accurate. Folio editions were in print from 1527. *Language(s)*: Latin. Appraised at 4s in 1579.

137.2 Biblia sacra

The Bible. Britain or Continent: date indeterminable.
STC 2055 and non-STC. *Language(s)*: Latin. Appraised at 12d in 1579.

137.3 Eliotes dictionarie

Sir Thomas Elyot. *The dictionary of syr Thomas Eliot*. London: Thomas Berthelet, 1538–1563.

STC 7659 *et seq. Language(s)*: English Latin. Appraised at 5s in 1579.

137.4 Eckii homilliarii in 2 volumes

Joannes Eckius. [*Homiliae*]. Continent: 1533–1579.

A two-volume edition appeared in Paris in 1549 (Jacques Dupuys), but the entry could represent two volumes of a three- or four-volume set, or three or four volumes bound as two. See 137.56. *Language(s)*: Latin. Appraised at 2s in 1579.

137.5 Ireneus

Irenaeus, *Saint*. Probably [*Adversus haereses*]. Continent: date indeterminable.

The only substantial work in print during the period associated with Irenaeus. *Language(s)*: Latin. Appraised at 16d in 1579.

137.6 Hieronomus super prophetas

Jerome, *Saint*. Unidentified. Continent: date indeterminable.

There were various editions of Jerome on individual prophets, but no full collection of all the prophets, minor and major; there were, however, at least two editions of his commentaries on various minor prophets. *Language(s)*: Latin. Appraised at 2s in 1579.

137.7 Hieronimi epistolae

Jerome, *Saint*. *Epistolae*. Continent: date indeterminable.

Language(s): Latin. Appraised at 12d in 1579.

137.8 Pomerii sermones in 3 volumes

Pelbartus, *de Themeswar*. [*Sermones Pomerii*]. Continent: date indeterminable.

See 137.68. *Language(s)*: Latin. Appraised at 18d in 1579.

137.9 Index in Opera Hieronimi

Jerome, *Saint*. [*Works* (part): *index*]. Continent: date indeterminable.

An index to Jerome, compiled by Joannes Oecolampadius, was published by Froben in Basle in 1520; this could, however, be the *Index*, which comprised the tenth volume of the *Works* published in Rome, 1570–1576. *Language(s)*: Latin. Appraised at 6d in 1579.

137.10 Dionysius Ariopagita

Dionysius *Areopagita*. Probably [*Works*]. Continent: date indeterminable.

Language(s): Latin (probable) Greek (perhaps). Appraised at 10d in 1579.

137.11 damascenus

John, *of Damascus, Saint*. Unidentified. Continent: date indeterminable.

Note that a work of Damascenus, *of Thessalonica*, appeared in 1561. *Language(s)*: Latin. Appraised at 10d in 1579.

137.12 Scotus super sententias in 2 volums
John Duns, *Scotus*. [*Sentences: commentary*]. Continent: date indeterminable. Either commentaries on two of the four books or, conceivably, four volumes bound as two. *Language(s)*: Latin. Appraised at 12d in 1579.

137.13 Thomas Aquimas [sic] in 2m [secundum] sententiarum
Thomas Aquinas, *Saint*. [*Sentences II: commentary*]. Continent: date indeterminable.
Language(s): Latin. Appraised at 10d in 1579.

137.14 Hieronimus in two volumes
Jerome, *Saint*. Perhaps [*Works*]. Continent: date indeterminable.
No two-volume edition of the *Works* can be found, however, and conceivably some selection is referred to here. There were two-volume editions of the *Epistolae*. *Language(s)*: Latin. Appraised at 2s 6d in 1579.

137.15 concordantiae bibliae
Unidentified [Biblical concordance]. Continent: date indeterminable.
There was an English concordance published in 1550 (STC 17300); Walter Lynne's work (STC 17117–17118) could also be described as a Biblical concordance. *Language(s)*: Latin. Appraised at 12d in 1579.

137.16 Claudius Guilaudus in omnes epist pauli
Claudius Guilliaudus. [*Epistles–Paul: commentary and text*]. (*Bible–N.T.*). Continent: 1542–1552.
Language(s): Latin. Appraised at 10d in 1579.

137.17 Polianthia hist:
Unidentified. Continent (probable): date indeterminable.
Almost certainly not an STC book. Probably the popular encyclopedic *Polyanthea* of Dominicus Nannus, but the anonymous *Polyanthea opus auctoritatibus scripturarum* (1536) is just possible, and perhaps also Nicolaus Reusner's *Polyanthea seu paradisus poeticus* (1578). *Language(s)*: Latin. Appraised at 18d in 1579.

137.18 M. Anthonius de Eucharistia
Stephen Gardiner, *Bishop* (Marcus Antonius Constantius, *pseudonym*). *Confutatio cavillationum quibus eucharistiae sacramentum ab impiis Capernaitis impeti solet*. Continent: 1552–1554.
Shaaber G13–14, with the 1522 date at G13 an error. *Language(s)*: Latin. Appraised at 12d in 1579.

137.19 Liber magnus de trinitate
Probably Augustine, *Saint*. Probably *De Trinitate*. Continent: date indeterminable.
Several folio editions of *De Trinitate* had appeared by the date of this inven-

ventory. *Language(s)*: Latin. Appraised at 12d in 1579.

137.20   Linwoodes constitutions
William Lyndewode, *Bishop. Constitutiones provinciales.* Britain or Continent: 1483–1557.
STC 17102 *et seq. Language(s)*: Latin. Appraised at 2s in 1579.

137.21   distructorium vitiorum
Alexander, *Anglus* (Alexander Carpenter). *Destructorium viciorum.* Continent: 1480–1521.
See Shaaber A217–227. An often-printed fifteenth-century critique of the Roman Church and clergy of which Alexander, *Anglus* is considered the compiler. See 137.74. *Language(s)*: Latin. Appraised at 8d in 1579.

137.22   Rationale divinorum officiorum
Gulielmus Durandus I, *Bishop of Mende. Rationale divinorum officiorum.* Continent: date indeterminable.
Language(s): Latin. Appraised at 6d in 1579.

137.23   Mariale de laudibus virginis
Bernardino de Busti. *Mariale.* Continent: date indeterminable.
Language(s): Latin. Appraised at 6d in 1579.

137.24   Johannes maior in 1m [primum] sententiarum
Joannes Major. [*Sentences I: commentary*]. Paris: (different houses), 1510–1530.
Language(s): Latin. Appraised at 2d in 1579.

137.25   Artopeus in evang
Petrus Artopoeus (Peter Becker). Unidentified. Continent: date indeterminable.
Either his *Evangelicae conciones Dominicarum totius anni* (1537–1550) or his *Postilla Evangeliarum ac epistolarum Dominicarum, et praecipuarum festarum totius anni* (1550). *Language(s)*: Latin. Appraised at 6d in 1579.

137.26   Johannes Canonicus in physica Arist:
Joannes, *Canonicus.* [*Aristotle–Physica: commentary*]. Britain or Continent: 1475–1520.
STC 14621 and non-STC. *Language(s)*: Latin. Appraised at 12d in 1579.

137.27   Petrus Barthous super bibliam sacram
Petrus Berthorius. *Liber Bibliae moralis.* Continent: date indeterminable.
See 137.59. *Language(s)*: Latin. Appraised at 6d in 1579.

137.28 Andreas in Metaphis: Arist:
Antonius Andreae. [*Aristotle–Metaphysica: commentary*]. Britain or Continent: 1471–1523.
STC 581 and non-STC. *Language(s)*: Latin. Appraised at 8d in 1579.

137.29 Stapulensis in phisica Arist:
Jacobus Faber, *Stapulensis*. [*Aristotle–Physica: commentary and paraphrase*]. Continent: 1492–1540.
See also 137.35. *Language(s)*: Latin. Appraised at 10d in 1579.

137.30 Jacobus faber stap:
Jacobus Faber, *Stapulensis*. Unidentified. Continent: date indeterminable.
In the context of this list this is probably another Aristotle commentary. *Language(s)*: Latin. Appraised at 8d in 1579.

137.31 Averrois in phisica Arist:
Averroes. [*Aristotle–Physica: commentary*]. Continent: date indeterminable. *Language(s)*: Latin. Appraised at 12d in 1579.

137.32 Burleus in dialecticam Arist:
Walter Burley. [*Aristotle–Selected works–Logica: commentary*]. Britain or Continent: date indeterminable.
STC 4122 and non-STC. See Shaaber B875–881. *Language(s)*: Latin. Appraised at 8d in 1579.

137.33 Euclid Geometria
Euclid. *Elementa*. Continent: date indeterminable.
The 1570 translation of Sir Henry Billingsley (STC 10560) would probably not be so listed. *Language(s)*: Latin. Appraised at 10d in 1579.

137.34 Venetus in phis: Arist:
Paulus, *Venetus* (Paulus Nicolettus). Probably *Expositio super VIII libros Physicorum necno super commento Averrois*. Venice: Gregorius de Gregoriis, 1499.
See Goff P217. Conceivably one of the several compilations of his commentary on Aristotle's natural philosophy featuring the *Physica*. *Language(s)*: Latin. Appraised at 6d in 1579.

137.35 Clictovius in phis: Arist:
Jacobus Faber, *Stapulensis* and Jodocus Clichtoveus. [*Aristotle–Physica: commentary and paraphrase*]. Continent: 1510–1522.
Date range from VHc. See also 137.29. *Language(s)*: Latin. Appraised at 8d in 1579.

137.36 Senec: traged:
Lucius Annaeus Seneca. *Tragoediae*. Continent: date indeterminable.
Perhaps, from the valuation, a selection rather than the complete corpus of

the tragedies. *Language(s)*: Latin. Appraised at 4d in 1579.

137.37 Bricot super dialec:
Thomas Bricot. Unidentified. Continent: date indeterminable.
This could be either his *Quaestiones logicales* or the *Textus abbreviatus totius logices Aristotelis*. See 137.42. *Language(s)*: Latin. Appraised at 6d in 1579.

137.38 Stapulensis de sphera
John Holywood (Joannes Sacrobosco). *Sphaera mundi*. Edited by Jacobus Faber, *Stapulensis*. Continent: date indeterminable.
Language(s): Latin. Appraised at 6d in 1579.

137.39 Lucanus cum comment
Marcus Annaeus Lucanus. *Pharsalia*. Continent: date indeterminable.
Commentators on the text included Omniboni, Sulpitius, P. Beroaldus, and Jodocus Badius, *Ascensius*. *Language(s)*: Latin. Appraised at 6d in 1579.

137.40 mantuanus cum comment
Baptista Spagnuoli (Mantuanus). Unidentified. Place unknown: stationer unknown, date indeterminable.
STC/non-STC status unknown. *Language(s)*: Latin. Appraised at 4d in 1579.

137.41 Albertus de saxona super lib: Arist: de caelo
Albertus, *de Saxonia*. [*Aristotle–De caelo: commentary*]. Continent: date indeterminable.
Language(s): Latin. Appraised at 4d in 1579.

137.42 Bricot in phis: Arist:
Thomas Bricot. [*Aristotle–Physica: commentary*]. Continent: date indeterminable.
See 137.37. *Language(s)*: Latin. Appraised at 6d in 1579.

137.43 Scotus in metaph: Arist:
John Duns, *Scotus*. [*Aristotle–Metaphysica: commentary*]. Continent: 1497–1520.
Language(s): Latin. Appraised at 4d in 1579.

137.44 Odo in Ethic: arist:
Geraldus Odonis. [*Aristotle–Ethica: commentary*]. Continent: 1482–1500.
Language(s): Latin. Appraised at 4d in 1579.

137.45 Johannes Raulin in sermones in 2 vol
Joannes Raulin. [*Sermones*]. Continent: date indeterminable.
Perhaps the *Opus sermonum quadragesimalium super epistolas et evangelia quadrigesimalia*, of which the Paris edition of 1518 was in two volumes, or the

Sermones de festivitatibus sanctorum totius anni, of which the Paris 1530 edition was also in two volumes. *Language(s)*: Latin. Appraised at 16d in 1579.

137.46 Epist: Plinii in 2 vol
Pliny, *the Younger. Epistolae*. Continent: date indeterminable.
The 1521 edition of Robertus Stephanus was in two parts. *Language(s)*: Latin. Appraised at 6d in 1579.

137.47 Erasmus in Epist: Pauli
Desiderius Erasmus. [*Epistles–Paul: paraphrase*]. (*Bible–N.T.*). Continent: date indeterminable.
This could be an edition of a collection or of individual Epistles. *Language(s)*: Latin. Appraised at 6d in 1579.

137.48 Virgilius cum comment: Serbii
Publius Virgilius Maro. Probably [*Works*]. With commentary by Servius Maurus Honoratus. Continent: date indeterminable.
Some editions of Virgil contained Servius's commentary exclusively, while other editions included other commentators along with Servius. No STC edition includes Servius's commentary. *Language(s)*: Latin. Appraised at 10d in 1579.

137.49 Polydorus de inventoribus rerum
Polydorus Vergilius. *De inventoribus rerum*. Continent: date indeterminable.
Language(s): Latin. Appraised at 4d in 1579.

137.50 Terentius
Publius Terentius, *Afer*. Probably [*Works*]. Britain or Continent: date indeterminable.
STC 23885 *et seq.* and non-STC. *Language(s)*: Latin. Appraised at 2d in 1579.

137.51 Egidius Romanus de anima
Aegidius Columna, *Romanus*. [*Aristotle–De anima: commentary*]. Continent: 1491–1501.
Language(s): Latin. Appraised at 4d in 1579.

137.52 Tulii officia
Marcus Tullius Cicero. *De officiis*. Britain or Continent: date indeterminable.
STC 5265.7 *et seq.* and non-STC. *Language(s)*: Latin. Appraised at 2d in 1579.

137.53 Grammat: Greca Cleonardi
Nicolaus Clenardus. Probably [*Institutiones linguae graecae*]. Continent: 1530–1576.

A less likely possibility is Clenardus's *Meditationes Graecanicae in artem grammaticam* published jointly with the *Institutiones* in 1557 and separately in 1572. *Language(s)*: Greek Latin. Appraised at 2d in 1579.

137.54 multiple Certeyne old unperfect bookes
Unidentified. Places unknown: stationers unknown, dates indeterminable. STC/non-STC status unknown. It is just possible that this entry may refer to the supplementary inventory of Lewis's books kept at his Oxford house and listed in 137.55 following. *Language(s)*: Unknown. Appraised as a group at 6s 8d in 1579.

137.55 Sermones Sancti Francisci
Unidentified. Continent (probable): date indeterminable.
Almost certainly not an STC book. 137.55 *et seq.* appear in a supplementary inventory of books kept at Lewis's house; he is identified as a white-baker, with no mention of his being a manciple. The inventory is dated 1569 and is surely an error for "1579," meaning that the list was compiled about a week after the inventory containing 137.1–54 was exhibited at the Vice-Chancellor's court. Several entries in this supplementary list replicate entries in the first fifty-four items, which fact may argue that this second inventory duplicates rather than supplements much of what precedes. This first entry, however, does not duplicate any item in the first inventory; indeed no title compatible with 137.55 has been found. One possibility is that it was one of the several editions of the *Fioretti* of St. Francis of Assisi, another that it was a misreading of the title page of Franciscus de Mayro's *Sermones de laudibus sanctorum*. Not appraised. *Language(s)*: Latin.

137.56 Omilia aecleani
Unidentified. Place unknown: stationer unknown, date indeterminable. STC/non-STC status unknown. Not appraised. Johann Eck might be suggested by the entry. See 137.4. *Language(s)*: Latin.

137.57 opus beate marie
Unidentified. Place unknown: stationer unknown, date indeterminable. STC/non-STC status unknown. A great many books about, or devoted to, the Blessed Virgin Mary were produced in the late fifteenth and early sixteenth centuries, of which *Opus insigne de laudibus beate marie virginis* is among the likeliest. More remote possibilities are works by Petrus, *de Vincentia* or Adam, *de Saint-Victor*, as well as STC 17539 *et seq.* See 137.23. Not appraised. *Language(s)*: Latin.

137.58 opus Sancti Thomae
Thomas Aquinas, *Saint*. Unidentified. Continent: date indeterminable. The likeliest work is probably the *Summa*, of which the *Opus praeclaram*

quarti scripti forms the first two parts. Not appraised. *Language(s)*: Latin.

137.59 op [opera] petrus berterius
Petrus Berthorius. Perhaps *Liber Bibliae moralis*. Continent: date indeterminable.
This seems the likeliest work since it was the most frequently published. See 137.27. The *Dictionarium seu repertorium morale* (1517–1522) is also a possibility. The *Opera* seems not to have been printed until 1609. Not appraised. *Language(s)*: Latin.

137.60 Expositio beati gregorii super Ezekielem
Gregory I, *Saint, Pope*. [*Ezechiel: commentary*]. Continent: date indeterminable.
Not appraised. *Language(s)*: Latin.

137.61 Summa que catholica nominatur
Joannes Balbus (*de Janua*). *Catholicon*. Continent: 1460–1520.
Not appraised. *Language(s)*: Latin.

137.62 Sermones aurei de Sanctis fratris benedicti
Perhaps Petrus Hieremias, *Saint* (Panormitanus). [*Sermones*]. Continent: date indeterminable.
BN notes a composite volume of sermons by Hieremias that carries on the verso of the title page: "Frater Benedictus Britannicus ... Fratri Thome Calsano ..." and on the colophon: "Sermones aurei excellentissimi doctoris Petri Hieremie." Not appraised. *Language(s)*: Latin.

137.63 Psalterii expositio per petri orientalis
Petrus, *de Herentals*. [*Psalms: commentary*]. Continent: date indeterminable.
Not appraised. *Language(s)*: Latin.

137.64 Quadragesimale de legibus
Leonardus, *de Utino* (Leonardus Matthaei). *Sermones quadragesimales de legibus*. Continent: 1473–1501.
Not appraised. *Language(s)*: Latin.

137.65 manipulus curatorum
Guido, *de Monte Rocherii*. *Manipulus curatorum*. Continent: date indeterminable.
STC 12470 *et seq.* and non-STC. Not appraised. *Language(s)*: Latin.

137.66 Sermones petri fratris
Unidentified [sermons]. Continent (probable): date indeterminable.

Almost certainly not an STC book. Possibilities include: the *Sermo fratris Petri, ordinis minorum procuratoris* (Rome: Eucharius Silber, n.d.) and, less likely, *Divi Petri Chrysologi ... Sermones nunc primum in vulgus editi*, edited by Agapitus Vincentius (Bologna: Giovanni Battista di Phaelli, 1534). Not appraised. *Language(s)*: Latin.

137.67   A boke begynnyng Quicunque mellificatis

Anonymous. *Sermones sensati*. Gouda: per Gerardum Leeu, 1482.

The sermon *Quicunque mellificantis apis* has been traced only to the above work. Not appraised. *Language(s)*: Latin.

137.68   Sermones pomerii

Pelbartus, *de Themeswar*. [*Sermones Pomerii*]. Continent: date indeterminable.

See 137.8. Not appraised. *Language(s)*: Latin.

137.69   Casus papales episcopales et abbitiales

Casus papales, episcopales et abbatiales. (*Papal cases*). Continent: 1475 (probable)–1515.

Not appraised. *Language(s)*: Latin.

137.70   doctrinale fratris Johannis Rawlyns

Joannes Raulin. *Doctrinale mortis*. Continent: 1518–1531.

Not appraised. *Language(s)*: Latin.

137.71   Stella clericorum

Stella clericorum. Britain or Continent: date indeterminable.

STC 23242.5 *et seq.* and non-STC. Not appraised. *Language(s)*: Latin.

137.72   Sermones Jacobi de lenda

Jacobus, *de Lenda*. [*Sermones*]. Paris: (different houses), 1499–1501.

Not appraised. *Language(s)*: Latin.

137.73   opus barardi [barnardi]

Bernard, *Saint*. Unidentified. Continent: date indeterminable.

Possibilities include the *Opus preclarissimum Epistolarum* (two editions in 1494) and the *Opus preclarum suos complectens sermones de tempore* (two editions in 1513). Not appraised. *Language(s)*: Latin.

137.74   destructorium viciorum

Alexander, *Anglus* (Alexander Carpenter). *Destructorium viciorum*. Continent: 1480–1521.

See 137.21. Not appraised. *Language(s)*: Latin.

137.75   postilla qwillermi super epistolas et evangelia
Gulielmus, *Parisiensis, Professor*. [*Gospels and Epistles (liturgical): commentary and text*]. (*Bible–N.T.*). Britain or Continent: date indeterminable.
STC 12513 and non-STC. Not appraised. *Language(s)*: Latin.

137.76   Sermones michaelis hungarii
Michael, *de Ungaria*. [*Sermones*]. Britain or Continent: date indeterminable.
STC 17853 and non-STC. Which collection cannot be determined, but his *Sermones praedicabiles*, printed in London with the title *Evagatorium modus predicandi sermones xiii*, was his most frequently published collection. Not appraised. *Language(s)*: Latin.

137.77   liber quadraginta omiliarum gregorii pape
Gregory I, *Saint, Pope*. [*Homeliae super Evangeliis*]. Continent: date indeterminable.
Not appraised. *Language(s)*: Latin.

137.78   bonaventure
Bonaventura, *Saint*. Unidentified. Place unknown: stationer unknown, date indeterminable.
STC/non-STC status unknown. An English translation is unlikely in this collection. Not appraised. *Language(s)*: Latin.

Books of Sir Edward Dering, First Baronet, of Kent

A SUPPLEMENT TO PLRE 4

R. J. FEHRENBACH and LAETITIA YEANDLE

The seven books listed below are from a leaf of the Dering manuscript catalogue at the Folger Shakespeare Library (V.b.297) not included in PLRE 4 (Volume 1, pp. 137–269). They are from the single remaining leaf of "Classis 2" of Dering's catalogue, a classis which consists of folio volumes. See Volume 1, p. 142 for explanations of Dering's arrangement and his scheme for numbering his volumes.

§

4.632	****4 5.6.7. *****Martini Lutheri opera omnia Tom:7. witeberg' 1557 1558 1562 1574 1580 1582 1583
4.633	* 1. *******pi [Philippi] melanthonis disputationes. witeberg' 1582
4.634	* 8 Dan: F**tley [Featley] D.D: his clavis mystica in 70. sermons Lond': 1636
4.635	* 9.10.11.12.13.14.15 Eccleasiastica Historia per centuriatores magdeburgenses. ad Annum Basileae 1564 1574 Autorum nomina 1.2.3.4.5.6. Matthias Flacius Illyricus. 1.2.3.4.5.6.7. Johes' Wigandus. 1.2.3.4. matthaeus Judex. 1.2. Basilius Faber. 5.6.7. Andreas Corvinus. 6.7. Thom: Holthuter
4.636	* 16 Johis' merceri: commentarius in lib. Job. Genevae 1573
4.637	2 17 Johis' merceri commentarius in Proverbia Ecclsiasten' cantica. Genevae 1573
4.638	In Esayam Commentarius Francisci, Forerii ulysseponensis dominicani Venetiis 1563

§

4.632 ***4 5.6.7. *****Martini Lutheri opera omnia Tom:7. witeber' 1557 1558 1562 1574 1580 1582 1583

Martin Luther. [*Works*]. Wittenberg: (different houses), 1557–1583. *Language(s)*: Latin.

4.633 * 1. *******pi [Philippi] melanthonis disputationes. witeberg' 1582

Philipp Melanchthon. *Disputationes theologicae*. Wittenberg: typis Zachariae Lehmani, 1582.

The *Disputationes theologicae* frequently appears in sets of Luther's works, usually in volume one. With a volume of the Wittenberg 1582 edition of Luther's *opera* (published by Zacharias Lehmann) in the preceding entry, it is reasonable to assume that this Melanchthon item may also have been part of that edition, here separated. That connection with the larger set may also explain Dering's otherwise odd recording of "0-0-0" as the book's cost. *Language(s)*: Latin.

4.634 * 8 Dan: F**tley [Featley] D.D: his clavis mystica in 70. sermons Lond': 1636

Daniel Featley. *Clavis mystica: a key opening divers texts of scripture; in seventy sermons*. London: R.Y[oung] for N. Bourne, 1636.

STC 10730. The word *his* in the entry is struck through. *Language(s)*: English. Cost 11s in an unspecified year.

4.635 * 9.10.11.12.13.14.15 Eccleasiastica Historia per centuriatores magdeburgenses. ad Annum Basileae 1564 1574 Autorum nomina 1.2.3.4.5.6. Matthias Flacius Illyricus. 1.2.3.4. 5.6.7. Johes' Wigandus. 1.2.3.4. matthaeus Judex. 1.2. Basilius Faber. 5.6.7. Andreas Corvinus. 6.7. Thom: Holthuter

Matthias Flacius, *Illyricus* (editor). *Ecclesiastica historia*. (*Magdeburg centuriators*). Basle: (different houses), 1564–1574.

Joannes Oporinus had the primary stationer's role in the publication of the many volumes. *Language(s)*: Latin. Cost £3 10s in an unspecified year.

4.636 * 16 Johis' merceri: commentarius in lib. Job. Genevae 1573

Joannes Mercerus, *Professor of Hebrew at Paris*. *Commentarii in librum Job*. Geneva: excudebat Eustathius Vignon, 1573. *Language(s)*: Latin.

4.637 2 17 Johis' merceri commentarius in Proverbia Ecclsiasten' cantica. Genevae 1573

Joannes Mercerus, *Professor of Hebrew at Paris*. *Commentarii in Salomonis Proverbia, Ecclesiasten, Canticum canticorum*. Geneva: excudebat Eustathius Vignon, 1573. *Language(s)*: Latin.

**4.638 In Esayam Commentarius Francisci, Forerii ulysseponensis domini-
cani Venetiis 1563**

Iesaiae prophetae vetus et nova ex Hebraico versio. (*Bible–O.T.*). Translated and
edited, with commentary, by Francisco Foreiro. Venice: ex officina J. Zileti,
1563.

Struck through. *Language(s)*: Latin.

PLRE Cumulative Catalogue

In the following lists, *entry* refers to a single entry made by a compiler of a manuscript book-list; *record* refers to a single record created from an *entry* by an editor. An *entry* may contain more than one *record*; conversely, a *record* may constitute only part of an *entry*. A *record* always represents at least one book but may represent more, including a volume set.

I. PLRE Database Totals

Book-lists: 167; Entries: 7,971; Records: 8,283
Number of Books Represented: More than 9,313
(Ninety-nine records of the 8,283 records specify two or more unidentified books for a determinable total of 1,129 books, adding a net 1,030 books to the record total. In addition, forty-seven records contain an indeterminable number of books, identified in the database as *multiple*. Also, one book may possibly be traced to two owners of collections included in the PLRE database [see PLRE 52.14:1–2 and PLRE 57.3], and another may have been listed twice in one owner's list, once when purchased and later in his probate inventory [PLRE Ad5.5 and PLRE Ad5.21].)

II. Book-list Indices

A. Arrangement and Size of Each PLRE Unit

Volume 1: PLRE 1–4	1,394 records (seven records in Volume 5)
Volume 2: PLRE 5–66	1,151 records
Volume 3: PLRE 67–86	1,365 records
Volume 4: PLRE 87–112	1,673 records
Volume 5: PLRE 113–137	1,815 records
APND Lists: PLRE Ad1–Ad30	885 records

B. Owners of Book-lists Arranged by Owners' Names

Owner and book-list information below is ordered in the following manner:

Name, degree(s). (Born–died) PLRE number. Profession. Social status. *Date* [of book-list, actual or *terminus ad quem*]: 1631. *Type* [of book-list]: inventory (probate). *Entries*: 25; *Records*: 29.

Allen, Richard, B.A. (c.1547–1569) PLRE 79. Scholar. Professional. *Date:* 1569. *Type:* inventory (probate). *Entries:* 97; *Records:* 98.

Allen, Thomas, B.A. (?–1561) PLRE 69. Scholar. Professional. *Date:* 1561. *Type:* inventory (probate). *Entries:* 34; *Records:* 35.

Anlaby (Aulaby), Edmund, M.A., B.Th. (?–1559) PLRE Ad5. Scholar. Professional. *Date:* 1533, 1559. *Type:* bookseller's accounts, inventory (probate). *Entries:* 28; *Records:* 33.

Atkins, Henry, M.A. (?–1560) PLRE 113. Scholar. Professional. *Date:* 1560. *Type:* inventory (probate). *Entries:* 16; *Records:* 16.

Atkinson, John, M.A. (?–1570) PLRE 83. Scholar. Professional. *Date:* 1570. *Type:* inventory (probate). *Entries:* 25; *Records:* 25.

Austin (given name unknown). (?–?) PLRE 98. Scholar (probable). Professional (probable). *Date:* 1572. *Type:* inventory. *Entries:* 20; *Records:* 20.

Badger, John, M.A. (?–1577) PLRE 115. Scholar. Professional. *Date:* 1577. *Type:* inventory (probate). *Entries:* 78; *Records:* 79.

Balborough, William, D.U.L. (?–1514) PLRE 29. Scholar. Professional. *Date:* 1514. *Type:* inventory (probate). *Entries:* 25; *Records:* 29.

Balyn, John, B.A. (?–1513) PLRE 25. Scholar. Professional. *Date:* 1513. *Type:* inventory (probate). *Entries:* 18; *Records:* 18.

Barwyck, Stephen. (?–1547) PLRE Ad29. Butler, Scholar (probable) (student, probable). Retainer, Professional (probable). *Date:* 1547. *Type:* inventory (probate). *Entries:* 35; *Records:* 36.

Batchelor, Robert. (1506–?) PLRE Ad6. Cleric (chaplain), Scholar. Professional. *Date:* 1533. *Type:* bookseller's accounts. *Entries:* 8; *Records:* 10.

Battbrantes, William. (?–1572) PLRE 99. Scholar (student, probable). Professional. *Date:* 1572. *Type:* inventory (probate). *Entries:* 35; *Records:* 35.

Beaumont, Edward, B.A. (1531–1552) PLRE 64. Scholar. Professional. *Date:* 1552. *Type:* inventory (probate). *Entries:* 117; *Records:* 118.

Beddow, John, M.A. (?–c.1577) PLRE 91. Scholar (schoolmaster). Professional. *Dates:* 1571 and 1577. *Type:* inventories. *Entries:* 40; *Records:* 41.

Bidnell, William, M.A. (?–1512) PLRE 23. Scholar. Professional. *Date:* 1512. *Type:* inventory (probate). *Entries:* 9; *Records:* 9.

Bill, Thomas, M.A. (?–1552) PLRE Ad7. Physician, Scholar. Professional. *Date:* 1532. *Type:* bookseller's accounts. *Entries:* 4; *Records:* 4.

Bisley (given name unknown), M.A. (perhaps), B.Th. (perhaps). (?–1543?) PLRE 60. Scholar. Professional. *Date:* 1543. *Type:* inventory (probate). *Entries:* 122; *Records:* 134.

Blomefield, Miles. (1525–1603) PLRE Ad2. Physician, Alchemist. Professional. *Date:* reconstruction. *Type:* reconstruction. *Entries:* 24; *Records:* 25.

Bolt, Thomas. (1557–?) PLRE 132. Scholar (student). Professional. *Date:* 1578. *Type:* inventory. *Entries:* 86; *Records:* 87.

Bonenfant, Thomas, M.A. (?–?) PLRE Ad8. Scholar. Professional. *Date:* 1533. *Type:* bookseller's accounts. *Entries:* 17; *Records:* 18.

Bowerman, John, M.A., B.C.L. (?–1507) PLRE 5. Scholar. Professional. *Date:* 1507. *Type:* will. *Entries:* 3; *Records:* 4.

Bradford, Ralph, M.A. (c.1502?) PLRE Ad9. Scholar. Professional. *Date:* c.1527. *Type:* bookseller's accounts. *Entries:* 13; *Records:* 14.

Brewer, John, M.A. (?–1535) PLRE Ad10. Scholar. Professional. *Date:* 1533. *Type:* bookseller's accounts. *Entries:* 4; *Records:* 4.

Bromsby, John, B.Th. (?–?) PLRE Ad11. Scholar. Professional. *Date:* 1531. *Type:* bookseller's accounts. *Entries:* 4; *Records:* 5.

Brown, William, M.A. (?–1558) PLRE 67. Scholar. Professional. *Date:* 1558. *Type:* inventory (probate). *Entries:* 223; *Records:* 242.

Bryan, Robert, D.Cn.L. (?–1508) PLRE 11. Scholar. Professional. *Date:* 1508. *Type:* inventory (probate). *Entries:* 19; *Records:* 19.

Buckingham, Edward, B.Cn.L. (?–1568) PLRE Ad12. Scholar. Professional. *Date:* 1533. *Type:* bookseller's accounts. *Entries:* 3; *Records:* 3.

Burton, Edmund, M.A. (?–1529) PLRE 43. Scholar. Professional. *Date:* 1529. *Type:* inventory (probate). *Entries:* 42; *Records:* 46.

Bury, John, B.A. (probable). (?–1567) PLRE 74. Scholar. Professional. *Date:* 1567. *Type:* inventory (probate). *Entries:* 19; *Records:* 19.

Carpenter, Thomas, M.A. (?–1577) PLRE 116. Scholar. Professional. *Date:* 1577. *Type:* inventory (probate). *Entries:* 83; *Records:* 84.

Carter, John, B.C.L. (?–1509) PLRE 17. Scholar. Professional. *Date:* 1509. *Type:* inventory (probate). *Entries:* 3; *Records:* 5.

Cartwright, Thomas, M.A. (?–1532) PLRE 50. Scholar. Professional. *Date:* 1532. *Type:* inventory (probate) and will. *Entries:* 8; *Records:* 11.

Cauthorn, John, B.A. (?–?) PLRE Ad13. Scholar. Professional. *Date:* 1531. *Type:* bookseller's accounts. *Entries:* 12; *Records:* 12.

Chantry, William, B.A. (?–1507) PLRE 6. Scholar. Professional. *Date:* 1507. *Type:* will. *Entries:* 2; *Records:* 3.

Charnock, Roger, M.A. (1549–?) PLRE 117. Scholar. Professional. *Date:* 1577. *Type:* inventory. *Entries:* 80; *Records:* 83.

Chastelain, George. (?–1513) PLRE 26. Stationer. Middle class. *Date:* 1513. *Type:* inventory (probate). *Entries:* 1; *Records:* 1.

Cheke, Agnes. (?–1549) PLRE Ad30. Merchant (vintner). Middle class, Privileged person. *Date:* 1549. *Type:* inventory (probate) *Entries:* 3; *Records:* 4.

Chogan, William. (?–1537) PLRE 56. Scholar (student). Professional. *Date:* 1537. *Type:* will. *Entries:* 1; *Records:* 1.

Cliff, Richard, M.A. (?–1566) PLRE 73. Cleric (chaplain), Scholar. Professional. *Date:* 1566. *Type:* inventory (probate) and will. *Entries:* 261; *Records:* 261.

Cliffley (given name unknown). (?–?) PLRE 118. Cleric (probable). Professional (probable). *Date:* 1577. *Type:* inventory. *Entries:* 22; *Records:* 22.

Coles, John, B.Th. (?–1529) PLRE 44. Scholar. Professional. *Date:* 1529. *Type:* inventory (probate). *Entries:* 5; *Records:* 5.

Collins, Robert. (?–?) PLRE 24. Scholar (student). Professional. *Date:* 1512. *Type:* receipt. *Entries:* 8; *Records:* 8.

Conner, John, B.Th. (c.1490–1569) PLRE 80. Cleric, Scholar. Professional. *Date:* 1569. *Type:* inventory (probate). *Entries:* 46; *Records:* 48.

Cox, Richard, D.Th. (1500–1581) PLRE 1. Cleric (bishop). Gentry. *Date:* 1581. *Type:* inventory. *Entries:* 196; *Records:* 208.

Dalaber, Anthony. (?–1562) PLRE 45. Scholar (student). Professional. *Date:* 1529. *Type:* inventory. *Entries:* 8; *Records:* 8.

Davy, William (perhaps), B.Cn.L. (?–1546) PLRE Ad14. Scholar. Professional. *Date:* 1533. *Type:* bookseller's accounts. *Entries:* 9; *Records:* 9.

Dawson, William, M.A. (?–1577) PLRE 119. Scholar. Professional. *Date:* 1577. *Type:* inventory (probate). *Entries:* 37; *Records:* 37.

Day, Thomas, B.C.L. (?–1570) PLRE 84. Cleric, Scholar. Professional. *Date:* 1570. *Type:* inventory (probate). *Entries:* 137; *Records:* 149.

Dayrell, William, B.A. (?–1577) PLRE 120. Scholar. Professional. *Date:* 1577. *Type:* inventory (probate). *Entries:* 30; *Records:* 30.

Deegen, Peter. (?–1527) PLRE 37. Scholar (student). Professional. *Date:* 1527. *Type:* will. *Entries:* 5; *Records:* 5.

Derbyshire, William. (?–1551) PLRE 61. Scholar (student). Professional. *Date:* 1551. *Type:* inventory (probate). *Entries:* 11; *Records:* 23.

Dering, Sir Edward. (1598–1644) PLRE 4. Member of Parliament. Gentry. *Date:* 1628 and c.1642. *Type:* account book, catalogue, and reconstruction. *Entries:* 638; *Records:* 683. (See Volume 1 and Volume 5.)

Dewer, William, M.A. (probable). (?–1514) PLRE 30. Scholar. Professional. *Date:* 1514. *Type:* inventory (probate). *Entries:* 6; *Records:* 10.

Dewhurst, Giles, M.A. (?–1577) PLRE 121. Scholar. Professional. *Date:* 1577. *Type:* inventory (probate). *Entries:* 45; *Records:* 45.

Dickinson, Thomas (probable), B.A. (?–1558) PLRE Ad15. Scholar. Professional. *Date:* 1533. *Type:* bookseller's accounts. *Entries:* 7; *Records:* 9.

Digby, George and Simon. (?–?) PLRE 81. Scholars (students). Professional. *Date:* 1569. *Type:* inventory. *Entries:* 47; *Records:* 48.

Digby, Simon. (see George Digby).

Dunnet, John. (?–1570) PLRE 85. Scholar (student). Professional. *Date:* 1570. *Type:* inventory (probate). *Entries:* 37; *Records:* 37.

Dyllam, Walter. (?–?) PLRE 106. Scholar (student). Professional. *Date:* 1575. *Type:* inventory. *Entries:* 1; *Records:* 3.

Faringdon, Tristram. (?–1577) PLRE 122. Scholar (student). Professional. *Date:* 1577. *Type:* inventory (probate). *Entries:* 17; *Records:* 18.

Ferne, Richard, M.A. (?–1577) PLRE 123. Scholar. Professional. *Date:* 1577. *Type:* inventory (probate). *Entries:* 51; *Records:* 51.

Foster, Thomas. (?–1577) PLRE 124. Unknown. Privileged person (probable). *Date:* 1577. *Type:* inventory (probate). *Entries:* 9; *Records:* 9.

Froster, Roger. (?–1514) PLRE 31. Scholar (student). Professional. *Date:* 1514. *Type:* inventory (probate). *Entries:* 1; *Records:* 1.

Gilbert, John. (?–?) PLRE Ad16. Scholar (student). Professional. *Date:* 1528. *Type:* bookseller's accounts. *Entries:* 2; *Records:* 2.

Gilbert, Nicholas. (see Hilbert, Nicholas).

Glover, John, M.A. (?–1578) PLRE 133. Scholar. Professional. *Date:* 1578. *Type:* inventory (probate). *Entries:* 279; *Records:* 280.

Gofton, William, B.C.L. (?–1507) PLRE 7. Scholar. Professional. *Date:* 1507. *Type:* inventory (probate). *Entries:* 11; *Records:* 12.

Goldsmith, Francis. (?–?) PLRE Ad17. Scholar (student) (probable). Professional (probable). *Date:* 1533. *Type:* bookseller's accounts. *Entries:* 1; *Records:* 1.

Grant, Philip. (?–1560) PLRE 114. Scholar (student). Professional. *Date:* 1560. *Type:* inventory (probate). *Entries:* 26; *Records:* 26.

Gray, John. (?–1577) PLRE 125. Scholar (student). Professional. *Date:* 1577. *Type:* inventory (probate). *Entries:* 18; *Records:* 18.

Griffin, Roger, B.A. (?–1510) PLRE 19. Scholar. Professional. *Date:* 1510. *Type:* inventory (probate). *Entries:* 2; *Records:* 2.

Griffith, Thomas, M.A., B.M. (perhaps). (?–1562) PLRE 70. Scholar, Physician (perhaps). Professional. *Date:* 1562. *Type:* inventory (probate). *Entries:* 92; *Records:* 97.

Gryce, William, D.Th. (?–1528) PLRE 41. Scholar. Professional. *Date:* 1528. *Type:* inventory (probate). *Entries:* 15; *Records:* 15.

Hamlyn, William, M.A. (?–1534) PLRE 51. Scholar. Professional. *Date:* 1534. *Type:* inventory (probate). *Entries:* 10; *Records:* 15.

Hart, Robert, M.A. (?–1571) PLRE 92. Scholar. Professional. *Date:* 1571. *Type:* inventory (probate). *Entries:* 135; *Records:* 137.

Hartburn, John, M.A. (?–1513) PLRE 27. Scholar. Professional. *Date:* 1513. *Type:* inventory (probate). *Entries:* 2; *Records:* 4.

Harwood, Thomas, B.A., D.M. (?–?) PLRE Ad18. Scholar. Professional. *Date:* 1530. *Type:* bookseller's accounts. *Entries:* 14; *Records:* 14.

Hawarden, Robert, M.A. (?–1527) PLRE 38. Scholar. Professional. *Date:* 1527. *Type:* inventory (probate). *Entries:* 6; *Records:* 6.

Heywood, John, B.A. (?–1514) PLRE 32. Scholar. Professional. *Date:* 1514. *Type:* inventory (probate). *Entries:* 13; *Records:* 14.

Hilbert, John. (see Gilbert, John).

Hilbert, Nicholas. (c.1509–1561) PLRE Ad19. Scholar (student). Professional. *Date:* 1528. *Type:* bookseller's accounts. *Entries:* 1; *Records:* 1.

Hodges, Thomas, B.A. (?–1539) PLRE 58. Scholar. Professional. *Date:* 1539. *Type:* inventory (probate). *Entries:* 28; *Records:* 33.

Hogan, Matthias. (?–1508) PLRE 12. Scholar (student). Professional. *Date:* 1508. *Type:* inventory (probate). *Entries:* 2; *Records:* 2.

Hooper, Robert, M.A. (?–c.1571) PLRE 93. Scholar. Professional. *Date:* 1571. *Type:* inventory (probate). *Entries:* 77; *Records:* 77.

Hoppe, Edward, M.A. (?–1538) PLRE 57. Scholar. Professional. *Date:* 1538. *Type:* will. *Entries:* 17; *Records:* 19.

Hornby, Nicholas, B.A., M.A. (perhaps). (?–?) PLRE Ad20. Scholar. Professional. *Date:* c.1532. *Type:* bookseller's accounts. *Entries:* 4; *Records:* 4.

Hornsley, John. (?–1578) PLRE 134. Scholar. Professional. *Date:* 1578. *Type:* inventory (probate). *Entries:* 89; *Records:* 91.

Horsley, Thomas. (?–?) PLRE Ad21. Scholar. Professional. *Date:* 1533. *Type:* bookseller's accounts. *Entries:* 4; *Records:* 4.

Horsman, Leonard, M.A. (?–1551) PLRE Ad22. Scholar. Professional. *Date:* 1531. *Type:* bookseller's account. *Entries:* 24; *Records:* 25.

Horsman, Ralph. (?–?) PLRE Ad23. Scholar (student). Professional. *Date:* 1531. *Type:* bookseller's accounts. *Entries:* 2; *Records:* 2.

Hunt, Robert, D.C.L., D.Th. (c.1499–1536) PLRE 53. Scholar. Professional. *Date:* 1536. *Type:* inventory (probate). *Entries:* 2; *Records:* 5.

Hurde, William. (?–1551) PLRE 62. Scholar (student). Professional. *Date:* 1551. *Type:* inventory (probate). *Entries:* 20; *Records:* 21.

Hutchinson, Henry, B.A. (1550–1573) PLRE 103. Scholar. Professional. *Date:* 1573. *Type:* inventory (probate). *Entries:* 99; *Records:* 99.

Jackson, Lionel, M.A. (?–1514) PLRE 33. Scholar. Professional. *Date:* 1514. *Type:* inventory (probate) and will. *Entries:* 32; *Records:* 33.

Jewel, John, D.Th. (1522–1571) PLRE Ad1. Cleric (bishop). Professional. *Date:* reconstruction. *Type:* reconstruction. *Entries:* 74; *Records:* 74.

Johnson, James. (?–1568) PLRE 77. Cleric (chaplain). Professional. *Date:* 1568. *Type:* inventory (probate). *Entries:* 4; *Records:* 4.

Johnson, Philip, B.Th. (?–1576) PLRE 110. Scholar. Professional. *Date:* 1576. *Type:* inventory (probate). *Entries:* 270; *Records:* 274.

Jones, Lewis, B.A. (?–1571) PLRE 94. Scholar. Professional. *Date:* 1571. *Type:* inventory (probate). *Entries:* 41; *Records:* 41.

Jones, Robert. (?–1567) PLRE 75. Sexton. Professional. *Date:* 1567. *Type:* inventory (probate). *Entries:* 23; *Records:* 27.

Kettelby, William, M.A. (?–c.1572) PLRE 104. Scholar. Professional. *Date:* 1573. *Type:* inventory (probate). *Entries:* 93; *Records:* 96.

Kitley, John, M.A. (?–1531) PLRE 49. Scholar. Professional. *Date:* 1531. *Type:* inventory (probate). *Entries:* 1; *Records:* 2.

Kitson, John, M.A. (?–1536) PLRE 54. Scholar. Professional. *Date:* 1536. *Type:* will. *Entries:* 1; *Records:* 1.

Kyffen, John, B.Cn.L. (?–1514) PLRE 34. Scholar. Professional. *Date:* 1514. *Type:* inventory (probate). *Entries:* 22; *Records:* 24.

Lacy, Dunstan, M.A. (?–1534) PLRE 52. Scholar. Professional. *Date:* 1534. *Type:* will. *Entries:* 27; *Records:* 29.

Lanham, Richard, B.A. (?–?) PLRE 105. Scholar. Professional. *Date:* 1573. *Type:* inventory. *Entries:* 4; *Records:* 4.

Lewis, John. (?–1579) PLRE 137. Manciple, Merchant (white-baker). Middle class, Privileged person. *Date:* 1579. *Type:* inventory (probate). *Entries:* 78; *Records:* 78.

Lilbourn, William, M.A. (?–1514) PLRE 35. Scholar. Professional. *Date:* 1514. *Type:* inventory (probate). *Entries:* 9; *Records:* 10.

Lisle (given name unknown). (?–?) PLRE 86. Scholar (student). Professional. *Date:* 1570. *Type:* inventory. *Entries:* 11; *Records:* 11.

Llewellyn, David ap. (?–?) PLRE Ad24. Cleric (friar). Professional. *Date:* 1533. *Type:* bookseller's accounts. *Entries:* 7; *Records:* 7.

Lombard, Nicholas, M.A. (?–1575) PLRE 107. Scholar. Professional. *Date:* 1575. *Type:* inventory (probate) and will. *Entries:* 131; *Records:* 132.

Ludby, Richard. (?–1567) PLRE 76. Cleric. Professional. *Date:* 1567. *Type:* inventory (probate). *Entries:* 25; *Records:* 25.

Lye, Richard. (?–1575) PLRE 108. Manciple. Professional, Privileged person. *Date:* 1575. *Type:* inventory (probate). *Entries:* 94; *Records:* 95.

Marshall, John, M.A. (?–1577) PLRE 126. Scholar. Professional. *Date:* 1577. *Type:* inventory (probate). *Entries:* 30; *Records:* 30.

Mason, Roger, B.Cn.L. (?–1513) PLRE 28. Scholar. Professional. *Date:* 1513. *Type:* inventory (probate). *Entries:* 1; *Records:* 1.

Maudesley, Thomas, B.A. (?–1571) PLRE 95. Scholar (student). Professional. *Date:* 1571. *Type:* inventory (probate). *Entries:* 17; *Records:* 17.

Merven, George, B.A. (?–1529) PLRE 46. Scholar. Professional. *Date:* 1529. *Type:* inventory (probate). *Entries:* 5; *Records:* 5.

Mitchell, John. (?–1572) PLRE 100. Servant. Retainer, Privileged person. *Date:* 1572. *Type:* inventory (probate). *Entries:* 11; *Records:* 11.

Morcote, John, M.A. (?–1508) PLRE 13. Scholar. Professional. *Date:* 1508. *Type:* inventory (probate). *Entries:* 75; *Records:* 80.

Morgan, Thomas. (?–?) PLRE 87. Scholar (student). Professional. *Date:* 1570. *Type:* inventory. *Entries:* 4; *Records:* 4.

Mychegood, Robert. (?–1508) PLRE 14. Cleric (probable). Professional (probable). *Date:* 1509. *Type:* inventory (probate). *Entries:* 8; *Records:* 8.

Napper, William, B.A. (c.1544–1569) PLRE 82. Scholar. Professional. *Date:* 1569. *Type:* inventory (probate). *Entries:* 118; *Records:* 118.

Neale, Thomas. (1553–1572) PLRE 101. Scholar (student). Professional. *Date:* 1572. *Type:* inventory (probate). *Entries:* 6; *Records:* 6.

Pannell, William, M.A. (?–1537) PLRE Ad25. Scholar. Professional. *Date:* 1533. *Type:* bookseller's accounts. *Entries:* 14; *Records:* 15.

Pantry, John, M.A., D.Th. (?–1541) PLRE 59. Scholar. Professional. *Date:* 1541. *Type:* will and reconstruction. *Entries:* 3; *Records:* 3.

Peerpoynt, William. (?–?) PLRE Ad26. Scholar (student). Professional. *Date:* 1531. *Type:* bookseller's accounts. *Entries:* 6; *Records:* 6.

Petcher, Robert, M.A. (?–1507) PLRE 8. Scholar. Professional. *Date:* 1507. *Type:* will. *Entries:* 1; *Records:* 2.

Pope, Thomas, B.A. (?–1578) PLRE 135. Scholar. Professional. *Date:* 1578. *Type:* inventory (probate). *Entries:* 40; *Records:* 41.

Powell, James, M.A. (?–1575) PLRE 109. Scholar. Professional. *Date:* 1575. *Type:* inventory (probate). *Entries:* 42; *Records:* 42.

Price, John, B.Cn.L., B.C.L. (?–1554) PLRE 66. Scholar. Professional. *Date:* 1554. *Type:* inventory (probate). *Entries:* 17; *Records:* 25.

Purfrey, Anthony, B.C.L. (?–1527) PLRE 39. Scholar. Professional. *Date:* 1527. *Type:* inventory (probate). *Entries:* 7; *Records:* 7.

Purviar, Robert, M.A. (?–1536) PLRE 55. Scholar. Professional. *Date:* 1536. *Type:* will and reconstruction. *Entries:* 7; *Records:* 7.

Quarrendon, Thomas, B.C.L. (?–c.1507) PLRE 9. Scholar. Professional. *Date:* 1507. *Type:* inventory (probate). *Entries:* 14; *Records:* 15.

Rawson, Nicholas, B.Th. (?–1511) PLRE 20. Scholar. Professional. *Date:* 1511. *Type:* inventory (probate). *Entries:* 6; *Records:* 6.

Reynolds, James, M.A. (?–1577) PLRE 127. Scholar. Professional. *Date:* 1577. *Type:* inventory (probate). *Entries:* 229; *Records:* 231.

Reynolds, Jerome, M.A., B.M. (perhaps). (?–1571) PLRE 96. Scholar, Physician. Professional. *Date:* 1571. *Type:* inventory (probate). *Entries:* 108; *Records:* 108.

Reynolds, John, M.A. (?–1571) PLRE 97. Scholar. Professional. *Date:* 1571. *Type:* inventory (probate). *Entries:* 59; *Records:* 59.

Ringstead, Henry. (?–1561) PLRE Ad27. Appraiser. Privileged person. *Date:* 1533. *Type:* bookseller's acounts. *Entries:* 1; *Records:* 1.

Robinson, John. (?–1508) PLRE 15. Manciple. Professional, Privileged person. *Date:* 1508. *Type:* inventory (probate). *Entries:* 2; *Records:* 2.

Robinson, John, M.A. (?–1511) PLRE 21. Scholar. Professional. *Date:* 1511. *Type:* inventory (probate). *Entries:* 6; *Records:* 6.

Rothley, John, B.Cn.L., B.C.L. (?–1511) PLRE 22. Scholar. Professional. *Date:* 1507. *Type:* inventory. *Entries:* 23; *Records:* 24.

Roxburgh, John, M.A. (?–1509) PLRE 18. Scholar. Professional. *Date:* 1509. *Type:* inventory (probate). *Entries:* 1; *Records:* 1.

Scott, Alan, M.A. (?–1578) PLRE 136. Cleric, Scholar. Professional. *Date:* 1578. *Type:* inventory (probate). *Entries:* 44; *Records:* 44.

Seacole, Richard, B.A. (1550–1577) PLRE 128. Scholar. Professional. *Date:* 1577. *Type:* inventory (probate). *Entries:* 123; *Records:* 125.

Shoesmith, John. (?–1568) PLRE 78. Profession unknown. Privileged person (probable). *Date:* 1568. *Type:* inventory (probate). *Entries:* 11; *Records:* 11.

Sibthorpe, Henry. (?–c.1664) (and Lady Anne Southwell) PLRE Ad3. Soldier, Statesman. Gentry. *Date:* c.1640, c.1650. *Type:* inventory. *Entries:* 110; *Records:* 110.

Simons, Thomas, M.A., B.M. (?–1553) PLRE 65. Scholar. Professional. *Date:* 1553. *Type:* inventory (probate). *Entries:* 131; *Records:* 143.

Simpson, John, M.A. (?–1577) PLRE 129. Scholar. Professional. *Date:* 1577. *Type:* inventory (probate). *Entries:* 130; *Records:* 130.

Singleton, Robert, M.A. (?–1577) PLRE 130. Scholar. Professional. *Date:* 1577. *Type:* inventory (probate). *Entries:* 119; *Records:* 120.

Slatter, Richard, M.A. (?–?) PLRE 111. Scholar. Professional. *Date:* 1576. *Type:* inventory. *Entries:* 12; *Records:* 12.

Smallwood, William, M.A. (?–?) PLRE 102. Scholar. Professional. *Date:* 1572. *Type:* inventory. *Entries:* 17; *Records:* 17.

Southwell, Lady Anne. (?–1636) (see Henry Sibthorpe).

Stanhope, Sir Edward, D.U.L. (c.1546–1608) PLRE 2. Lawyer. Nobility. *Date:* c.1612. *Type:* will and reconstruction. *Entries:* 161; *Records:* 207.

Stanley, Thomas, B.A. (?–1577) PLRE 131. Scholar. Professional. *Date:* 1577. *Type:* inventory (probate). *Entries:* 40; *Records:* 40.

Stocker, William, M.A. (?–?) PLRE 88. Scholar. Professional. *Date:* c.1570. *Type:* inventory. *Entries:* 23; *Records:* 23.

Stonely, Richard. (c.1520–1600) PLRE Ad4. Court official (Teller of the Exchequer). Gentry. *Date:* 1597. *Type:* inventory against debt. *Entries:* 412; *Records:* 418.

Sykes, Nicholas. (?–1562) PLRE 71. Butler. Retainer, Privileged person. *Date:* 1562. *Type:* inventory (probate). *Entries:* 42; *Records:* 42.

Talley, Abbot of. (?–?) PLRE 42. Cleric (monk). Professional. *Date:* 1528. *Type:* inventory. *Entries:* 2; *Records:* 3.

Tatham, John, M.A. (?–1576) PLRE 112. Scholar. Professional. *Date:* 1576. *Type:* inventory (probate). *Entries:* 222; *Records:* 222.

Thixtell, John, B.Th. (?–1541) PLRE Ad28. Scholar. Professional. *Date:* 1528. *Type:* bookseller's accounts. *Entries:* 14; *Records:* 15.

Thomson, Thomas, M.A. (?–1514) PLRE 36. Scholar. Professional. *Date:* 1514. *Type:* will. *Entries:* 14; *Records:* 17.

Thomson, William, M.A. (?–1507) PLRE 10. Scholar. Professional. *Date:* 1507. *Type:* inventory (probate). *Entries:* 30; *Records:* 30.

Thornbury, Thomas. (?–1570) PLRE 89. Scholar (student, perhaps). Professional. *Date:* 1570. *Type:* inventory (probate). *Entries:* 5; *Records:* 5.

Tichborne (given name unknown), B.C.L. (probable). (?–?) PLRE 90. Scholar. Professional. *Date:* 1570. *Type:* inventory. *Entries:* 93; *Records:* 93.

Tolley, David, M.A., B.M. (c.1506–1558) PLRE 68. Physician. Professional. *Date:* 1558. *Type:* inventory (probate). *Entries:* 50; *Records:* 50.

Townrow, Henry, B.A. (?–1565) PLRE 72. Scholar. Professional. *Date:* 1565. *Type:* inventory (probate). *Entries:* 18; *Records:* 18.

Townshend, Sir Roger. (1596–1636) PLRE 3. Member of Parliament. Gentry. *Date:* c.1625. *Type:* inventory. *Entries:* 286; *Records:* 296.

Upton, William, M.A., B.Th. (perhaps). (?–1527) PLRE 40. Scholar. Professional. *Date:* 1527. *Type:* will. *Entries:* 1; *Records:* 1.

Wicking, John. (?–1551) PLRE 63. Almsman. Retainer. *Date:* 1551. *Type:* inventory (probate) and will. *Entries:* 1; *Records:* 1.

Wood, Richard, M.A. (?–1508) PLRE 16. Scholar. Professional. *Date:* 1508. *Type:* inventory (probate). *Entries:* 13; *Records:* 13.

Woodruff, William, M.A. (?–?) PLRE 47. Scholar. Professional. *Date:* 1529. *Type:* inventory. *Entries:* 35; *Records:* 35.

Yardley, William, B.Cn.L., B.C.L. (?–1530) PLRE 48. Scholar. Professional. *Date:* 1530. *Type:* inventory (probate). *Entries:* 11; *Records:* 11.

C. Owners of Book-lists According to PLRE Number

1. LISTS IN PLRE VOLUMES

PLRE 1: Cox, Richard, D.Th.
PLRE 2: Stanhope, Sir Edward, D.U.L.
PLRE 3: Townshend, Sir Roger
PLRE 4: Dering, Sir Edward
PLRE 5: Bowerman, John, M.A., B.C.L.
PLRE 6: Chantry, William, B.A.
PLRE 7: Gofton, William, B.C.L.
PLRE 8: Petcher, Robert, M.A.
PLRE 9: Quarrendon, Thomas, B.C.L.
PLRE 10: Thomson, William, M.A.
PLRE 11: Bryan, Robert, D.Cn.L.
PLRE 12: Hogan, Matthias
PLRE 13: Morcote, John, M.A.
PLRE 14: Mychegood, Robert
PLRE 15: Robinson, John
PLRE 16: Wood, Richard, M.A.
PLRE 17: Carter, John, B.C.L.
PLRE 18: Roxburgh, John, M.A.
PLRE 19: Griffin, Roger, B.A.
PLRE 20: Rawson, Nicholas, B.Th.
PLRE 21: Robinson, John, M.A.
PLRE 22: Rothley, John, B.Cn.L., B.C.L.
PLRE 23: Bidnell, William, M.A.
PLRE 24: Collins, Robert
PLRE 25: Balyn, John, B.A.
PLRE 26: Chastelain, George
PLRE 27: Hartburn, John, M.A.
PLRE 28: Mason, Roger, B.Cn.L.
PLRE 29: Balborough, William, D.U.L.
PLRE 30: Dewer, William, M.A. (probable)
PLRE 31: Froster, Roger
PLRE 32: Heywood, John, B.A.
PLRE 33: Jackson, Lionel, M.A.
PLRE 34: Kyffen, John, B.Cn.L.

PLRE 35: Lilbourn, William, M.A.
PLRE 36: Thomson, Thomas, M.A.
PLRE 37: Deegen, Peter
PLRE 38: Hawarden, Robert, M.A.
PLRE 39: Purfrey, Anthony, B.C.L.
PLRE 40: Upton, William, M.A., B.Th. (perhaps)
PLRE 41: Gryce, William, D.Th.
PLRE 42: Talley, Abbot of
PLRE 43: Burton, Edmund, M.A.
PLRE 44: Coles, John, B.Th.
PLRE 45: Dalaber, Anthony
PLRE 46: Merven, George, B.A.
PLRE 47: Woodruff, William, M.A.
PLRE 48: Yardley, William, B.Cn.L., B.C.L.
PLRE 49: Kitley, John, M.A.
PLRE 50: Cartwright, Thomas, M.A.
PLRE 51: Hamlyn, William, M.A.
PLRE 52: Lacy, Dunstan, M.A.
PLRE 53: Hunt, Robert, D.C.L., D.Th.
PLRE 54: Kitson, John, M.A.
PLRE 55: Purviar, Robert, M.A.
PLRE 56: Chogan, William
PLRE 57: Hoppe, Edward, M.A.
PLRE 58: Hodges, Thomas, B.A.
PLRE 59: Pantry, John, M.A., D.Th.
PLRE 60: Bisley, M.A. (perhaps), B.Th. (perhaps)
PLRE 61: Derbyshire, William
PLRE 62: Hurde, William
PLRE 63: Wicking, John
PLRE 64: Beaumont, Edward, B.A.
PLRE 65: Simons, Thomas, M.A., B.M.
PLRE 66: Price, John, B.Cn.L., B.C.L.
PLRE 67: Brown, William, M.A.
PLRE 68: Tolley, David, M.A., B.M.
PLRE 69: Allen, Thomas, B.A.
PLRE 70: Griffith, Thomas, M.A., B.M. (perhaps)
PLRE 71: Sykes, Nicholas
PLRE 72: Townrow, Henry, B.A.
PLRE 73: Cliff, Richard, M.A.
PLRE 74: Bury, John, B.A. (probable)
PLRE 75: Jones, Robert
PLRE 76: Ludby, Richard
PLRE 77: Johnson, James
PLRE 78: Shoesmith, John
PLRE 79: Allen, Richard, B.A.
PLRE 80: Conner, John, B.Th.
PLRE 81: Digby, George and Simon
PLRE 82: Napper, William, B.A.

PLRE 83: Atkinson, John, M.A.
PLRE 84: Day, Thomas, B.C.L.
PLRE 85: Dunnet, John
PLRE 86: Lisle
PLRE 87: Morgan, Thomas
PLRE 88: Stocker, William, M.A.
PLRE 89: Thornbury, Thomas
PLRE 90: Tichborne, B.C.L. (probable)
PLRE 91: Beddow, John, M.A.
PLRE 92: Hart, Robert, M.A.
PLRE 93: Hooper, Robert, M.A.
PLRE 94: Jones, Lewis, B.A.
PLRE 95: Maudesley, Thomas, B.A.
PLRE 96: Reynolds, Jerome, B.A., B.M. (perhaps)
PLRE 97: Reynolds, John, M.A.
PLRE 98: Austin
PLRE 99: Battbrantes, William
PLRE 100: Mitchell, John
PLRE 101: Neale, Thomas
PLRE 102: Smallwood, Thomas, M.A.
PLRE 103: Hutchinson, Henry, B.A.
PLRE 104: Kettelby, William, M.A.
PLRE 105: Lanham, Richard, B.A.
PLRE 106: Dyllam, Walter
PLRE 107: Lombard, Nicholas, M.A.
PLRE 108: Lye, Richard
PLRE 109: Powell, James, M.A.
PLRE 110: Johnson, Philip, B.Th.
PLRE 111: Slatter, Richard, M.A.
PLRE 112: Tatham, John, M.A.
PLRE 113: Atkins, Henry, M.A.
PLRE 114: Grant, Philip
PLRE 115: Badger, John, M.A.
PLRE 116: Carpenter, Thomas, M.A.
PLRE 117: Charnock, Roger, M.A.
PLRE 118: Cliffley
PLRE 119: Dawson, William, M.A.
PLRE 120: Dayrell, William, B.A.
PLRE 121: Dewhurst, Giles, M.A.
PLRE 122: Faringdon, Tristram
PLRE 123: Ferne, Richard, M.A.
PLRE 124: Foster, Thomas
PLRE 125: Gray, John
PLRE 126: Marshall, John, M.A.
PLRE 127: Reynolds, James, M.A.
PLRE 128: Seacole, Richard, B.A.
PLRE 129: Simpson, John, M.A.
PLRE 130: Singleton, Robert, M.A.

PLRE 131: Stanley, Thomas, B.A.
PLRE 132: Bolt, Thomas
PLRE 133: Glover, John, M.A.
PLRE 134: Hornsley, John, M.A.
PLRE 135: Pope, Thomas, M.A.
PLRE 136: Scott, Alan, M.A.
PLRE 137: Lewis, John

2. APND LISTS

[The source of each book-list follows the name of the owner. In the case of groups of lists from one source, the reference may precede the group.]

PLRE Ad1: Jewel, John, Bishop, D.Th.
  (Neil Ker, "The Library of John Jewel." *Bodleian Library Record* [1977] 9:256–65.)
PLRE Ad2: Blomefield, Miles.
  (Donald Baker and J. L. Murphy, "The Books of Myles Blomefylde." *The Library*, 5th ser. [1976] 31:374–85; John C. Coldewey, "Myles Blomefylde's Library: Another Book." *English Language Notes* [1977] 14:249–50.)
PLRE Ad3: Sibthorpe, Captain Henry (and Lady Anne Southwell).
  (Sister Jean Carmel Cavanaugh, S. L., "The Library of Lady Southwell and Captain Sibthorpe." *Studies in Bibliography* [1967] 20:243–54).
PLRE Ad4: Stonely, Richard.
  (Leslie Hotson, "The Library of Elizabeth's Embezzling Teller." *Studies in Bibliography* [1949] 2:49–61).

APND lists PLRE Ad5–Ad28 are taken from: Elisabeth Leedham-Green, D. E. Rhodes, and F. H. Stubbings. *Garrett Godfrey's Accounts c. 1527–1533*. Cambridge Bibliographical Society, Monograph no. 12. Cambridge: Cambridge University Library, 1992. [*Note:* Degrees assigned are senior degrees that had been earned when books were purchased.]

PLRE Ad5: Anlaby (Aulaby), Edmund (some entries drawn from BCI 1:244–45), M.A. (1533), B.Th. (1559)
PLRE Ad6: Batchelor, Robert
PLRE Ad7: Bill, Thomas, M.A.
PLRE Ad8: Bonenfant, Thomas, M.A.
PLRE Ad9: Bradford, Ralph, M.A.
PLRE Ad10: Brewer, John, M.A.
PLRE Ad11: Bromsby, John, B.Th.
PLRE Ad12: Buckingham, Edward, B.Cn.L.
PLRE Ad13: Cauthorn, John, B.A.
PLRE Ad14: Davy, William (perhaps), B.A.
PLRE Ad15: Dickinson, Thomas (probable), B.A.
PLRE Ad16: Gilbert, John
PLRE Ad17: Goldsmith, Francis

PLRE Ad18: Harwood, Thomas, B.A., D.M.
PLRE Ad19: Hilbert, Nicholas
PLRE Ad20: Hornby, Nicholas, M.A.
PLRE Ad21: Horsley, Thomas
PLRE Ad22: Horsman, Leonard, M.A.
PLRE Ad23: Horsman, Ralph
PLRE Ad24: Llewellyn, David ap
PLRE Ad25: Pannell, William, M.A.
PLRE Ad26: Peerpoynt, William
PLRE Ad27: Ringstead, Henry
PLRE Ad28: Thixtell, John, B.Th.
PLRE Ad29: Barwyck, Stephen (BCI 1:93–94)
PLRE Ad30: Cheke, Agnes (BCI 1:101–2)

D. Dates of Book-lists (actual or *terminus ad quem*), with PLRE Number

1507:	PLRE 5, 6, 7, 8, 9, 10, 22
1508:	PLRE 11, 12, 13, 15, 16
1509:	PLRE 14, 17, 18
1510:	PLRE 19
1511:	PLRE 20, 21
1512:	PLRE 23, 24
1513:	PLRE 25, 26, 27, 28
1514:	PLRE 29, 30, 31, 32, 33, 34, 35, 36
1527:	PLRE 37, 38, 39
c.1527:	PLRE Ad9
1528:	PLRE 40, 41, 42, Ad19, Ad28
1529:	PLRE 43, 44, 45, 46, 47
1530:	PLRE 48, Ad18
1531:	PLRE 49, Ad11, Ad13, Ad22, Ad23, Ad26
1532:	PLRE 50, Ad7
c.1532:	PLRE Ad20
1533:	PLRE Ad5 (part), Ad6, Ad8, Ad10, Ad12, Ad14, Ad15, Ad16, Ad17, Ad21, Ad24, Ad25, Ad27
1534:	PLRE 51, 52
1536:	PLRE 53, 54, 55
1537:	PLRE 56
1538:	PLRE 57
1539:	PLRE 58
1541:	PLRE 59
1543:	PLRE 60
1547:	PLRE Ad29
1549:	PLRE Ad30
1551:	PLRE 61, 62, 63
1552:	PLRE 64
1553:	PLRE 65
1554:	PLRE 66

1558:	PLRE 67, 68
1559:	PLRE Ad5 (part)
1560:	PLRE 113, 114
1561:	PLRE 69
1562:	PLRE 70, 71
1565:	PLRE 72
1566:	PLRE 73
1567:	PLRE 74, 75, 76
1568:	PLRE 77, 78
1569:	PLRE 79, 80, 81, 82, 90 (part)
1570:	PLRE 83, 84, 85, 86, 87, 88, 89, 90
1571:	PLRE 91, 92, 93, 94, 95, 96, 97
1572:	PLRE 98, 99, 100, 101, 102
1573:	PLRE 103, 104, 105
1575:	PLRE 106, 107, 108, 109
1576:	PLRE 110, 111, 112
1577:	PLRE 91 (part), 115, 116, 117, 118, 119, 120, 121, 122, 123, 124, 125, 126, 127, 128, 129, 130, 131
1578:	PLRE 132, 133, 134, 135, 136
1579:	PLRE 137
1581:	PLRE 1
1597:	PLRE Ad4
c.1612:	PLRE 2
c.1625:	PLRE 3
1628:	PLRE 4 (part)
c.1640:	PLRE Ad3 (part)
c.1642:	PLRE 4 (part)
c.1650:	PLRE Ad3 (part)
No date (reconstruction):	
	PLRE 2 (part), 4 (part), 55 (part), 59 (part), Ad1, Ad2

III. Summaries and Concordances

A. Manuscript Types

1. RECORD TOTALS FROM EACH MANUSCRIPT TYPE

Account book:	177
Bookseller's accounts:	188
Catalogue:	503
Inventory:	1,152
Inventory (against debt):	418
Inventory (probate):	5,377
Inventory (probate) and Will:	86
Memorial book (benefaction):	200
Receipt:	8
Will:	58
No manuscript (reconstruction):	112

2. NUMBER OF MANUSCRIPT TYPES PROVIDING BOOK-LISTS
(Some lists derive from more than one manuscript type.)

Account book:	1
Bookseller's accounts:	23
Catalogue:	1
Inventory:	20
Inventory (against debt):	1
Inventory (probate):	100
Inventory (probate) and Will:	7
Memorial book (benefaction):	1
Receipt:	1
Will:	16
No manuscript (reconstruction):	4

3. MANUSCRIPT TYPES ACCORDING TO PLRE NUMBERS
(Some lists derive from more than one manuscript type.)

Account book: PLRE 4 (part)

Bookseller's accounts: PLRE Ad5 (part), Ad6, Ad7, Ad8, Ad9, Ad10, Ad11, Ad12, Ad13, Ad14, Ad15, Ad16, Ad17, Ad18, Ad19, Ad20, Ad21, Ad22, Ad23, Ad24, Ad25, Ad26, Ad27, Ad28

Catalogue: PLRE 4 (part)

Inventory: PLRE 1, 3, 22, 42, 45, 47, 81, 86, 87, 88, 90, 91, 98, 102, 105, 106, 111, 117, 118, 132, Ad3

Inventory (against debt): PLRE Ad4

Inventory (probate): PLRE 7, 9, 10, 11, 12, 13 (part), 14, 15, 16, 17, 18, 19, 20, 21, 23, 25, 26, 27, 28, 29, 30 (part), 31, 32, 34, 35, 36 (part), 38, 39, 41, 43, 44, 46, 48, 49, 51, 53, 57 (part), 58, 60, 61, 62, 64 (part), 65, 66, 67, 68, 69, 70, 71, 72, 73 (part), 74, 75, 76, 77, 78, 79, 80, 82, 83, 84, 85, 89, 92, 93, 94, 95, 96, 97, 99, 100, 101, 103, 104, 107 (part), 108, 109, 110, 112, 113, 114, 115, 116, 119, 120, 121, 122, 123, 124, 125, 126, 127, 128, 129, 130, 131, 133, 134, 135, 136, 137, Ad5 (part), Ad30

Inventory (probate) and Will: PLRE 33 (part), 50, 52 (part), 57, 63, 64 (part), 107 (part)

Memorial book (benefaction): PLRE 2 (part)

Receipt: PLRE 24

Will: PLRE 5, 6, 8, 13 (part), 30 (part), 33 (part), 36 (part), 37, 40, 52 (part), 54, 55 (part), 56, 57 (part), 59 (part), 73 (part)

No manuscript (reconstruction): (See also Account book, Catalogue, Memorial book, and Will) PLRE 2 (part), 4 (part), 55 (part), 59 (part), Ad1, Ad2

B. Renaissance Locations of Book-lists

1. RECORD TOTALS FOR EACH LOCATION

Cambridgeshire, Cambridge:	464

Cambridgeshire, Downham: 187
Cambridgeshire, Fenstanton: 21
Kent, Surrenden: 680
London: 418
Middlesex, Acton: 110
Norfolk: 296
Northamptonshire, Brackley: 2
Oxfordshire, Oxford: 5,999
No Renaissance location (reconstruction):   112

2. PLRE NUMBERS OF LISTS IN EACH LOCATION

Cambridgeshire, Cambridge: PLRE 2, Ad5, Ad6, Ad7, Ad8, Ad9, Ad10, Ad11,
     Ad12, Ad13, Ad14, Ad15, Ad16, Ad17, Ad18, Ad19, Ad20, Ad21, Ad22,
     Ad23, Ad24, Ad25, Ad26, Ad27, Ad28, Ad29, Ad30
Cambridgeshire, Downham: PLRE 1 (part)
Cambridgeshire, Fenstanton: PLRE 1 (part)
Kent, Surrenden: PLRE 4
London: PLRE Ad4
Middlesex, Acton: PLRE Ad3
Norfolk: PLRE 3
Northamptonshire, Brackley: PLRE 91 (part)
Oxfordshire, Oxford: PLRE 5, 6, 7, 8, 9, 10, 11, 12, 13, 14, 15, 16, 17, 18, 19, 20,
     21, 22, 23, 24, 25, 26, 27, 28, 29, 30, 31, 32, 33, 34, 35, 36, 37, 38, 39, 40,
     41, 42, 43, 44, 45, 46, 47, 48, 49, 50, 51, 52, 53, 54, 55, 56, 57, 58, 59, 60,
     61, 62, 63, 64, 65, 66, 67, 68, 69, 70, 71, 72, 73, 74, 75, 76, 77, 78, 79, 80,
     81, 82, 83, 84, 85, 86, 87, 88, 89, 90, 91 (part), 92, 93, 94, 95, 96, 97, 98, 99,
     100, 101, 102, 103, 104, 105, 106, 107, 108, 109, 110, 111, 112, 113, 114,
     115, 116, 117, 118, 119, 120, 121, 122, 123, 124, 125, 126, 127, 128, 129,
     130, 131, 132, 133, 134, 135, 136, 137
No Renaissance location (reconstruction): PLRE 2 (part), 4 (part), 55 (part), 59
     (part), Ad1, Ad2

C. Professions of Owners

1. TOTALS OF PROFESSIONS REPRESENTED

Alchemist (see Physician)
Almsman: 1
Appraiser: 1
Butler: 2
Cleric: 1
Cleric (probable):   2
Cleric (bishop):   1
Cleric (chaplain):   3
Cleric (friar):   1
Cleric (monk):   1

Cleric, Scholar:	3
Court Official:	1
Lawyer:	1
Manciple:	3
Merchant (vintner):	1
Merchant (white-baker)	1
Member of Parliament:	2
Physician:	1
Physician, Alchemist:	1
Physician, Scholar:	2
Physician (perhaps), Scholar:	1
Scholar:	88
(see also Cleric, Physician, Schoolmaster)	
Scholar (student):	21
Schoolmaster, Scholar:	1
Servant:	1
Sexton:	1
Soldier, Statesman:	1
Statesman (see Soldier)	
Stationer:	1
Unknown:	2

2. NUMBER OF RECORDS LISTED FOR EACH PROFESSION

Alchemist (see Physician)	
Almsman:	1
Appraiser:	1
Butler:	78
Cleric:	25
Cleric (probable):	30
Cleric (bishop):	282
Cleric (chaplain):	275
Cleric (friar):	7
Cleric (monk):	3
Cleric, Scholar:	241
Court Official:	418
Lawyer:	207
Manciple:	175
Merchant (vintner):	4
Merchant (white-baker):	78
Member of Parliament:	979
Physician:	50
Physician, Alchemist:	25
Physician, Scholar:	112
Physician (perhaps), Scholar:	97
Scholar:	4,645
(see also Cleric, Physician, Schoolmaster)	
Scholar (student):	416

Schoolmaster, Scholar: 41
Servant: 11
Sexton: 27
Soldier, Statesman: 110
Statesman (see Soldier)
Stationer: 1
Unknown: 11

3. BOOK-LISTS BY PROFESSIONS, WITH PLRE NUMBERS

Alchemist (see Physician)
Almsman: PLRE 63
Appraiser: PLRE Ad27
Butler: PLRE 71, Ad29
Cleric: PLRE 76
Cleric (probable): PLRE 14
Cleric (bishop): PLRE 1, Ad1
Cleric (chaplain): PLRE 73, 77, Ad6
Cleric (friar): PLRE Ad24
Cleric (monk): PLRE 42
Cleric, Scholar: PLRE 80, 84, 136
Court Official: PLRE Ad4
Lawyer: PLRE 2
Manciple: PLRE 15, 108, 137
Member of Parliament: PLRE 3, 4
Merchant (vintner): PLRE Ad30
Merchant (white-baker): PLRE 137
Physician: PLRE 50
Physician, Alchemist: PLRE Ad2
Physician, Scholar: PLRE 96, Ad7
Physician (perhaps), Scholar: PLRE 70
Scholar (see also Cleric, Physician, Schoolmaster): PLRE 5, 6, 7, 8, 9, 10, 11, 13, 16, 17, 18, 19, 20, 21, 22, 23, 25, 27, 28, 29, 30, 32, 33, 34, 35, 36, 38, 39, 40, 41, 43, 44, 46, 47, 48, 49, 50, 51, 52, 53, 54, 55, 57, 58, 59, 60, 64, 65, 66, 67, 69, 72, 74, 79, 82, 83, 88, 90, 92, 93, 94, 97, 102, 103, 104, 105, 107, 109, 110, 111, 112, 113, 115, 116, 117, 118, 119, 120, 121, 122, 123, 125, 126, 127, 128, 129, 130, 131, 132, 133, 134, 135, Ad5, Ad8, Ad9, Ad10, Ad11, Ad12, Ad13, Ad14, Ad15, Ad18, Ad20, Ad21, Ad22, Ad23, Ad25, Ad28
Scholar (student): PLRE 12, 24, 31, 37, 45, 56, 61, 62, 83, 85, 86, 87, 89, 95, 98, 99, 101, 106, 114, Ad16, Ad17, Ad19, Ad26
Schoolmaster, Scholar: PLRE 91
Servant: PLRE 100
Sexton: PLRE 75
Soldier, Statesman: PLRE Ad3
Statesman (see Soldier)
Stationer: PLRE 26
Unknown: PLRE 78, 124

D. Social Status of Owners

1. TOTAL OF RECORDS IN PLRE DATABASE

Gentry:	1,715
Middle class:	83
Nobility:	207
Privileged person (with others):	200
Privileged person (probable):	20
Professional:	6,172
Professional (probable):	30
Retainer:	90

2. BOOK-LISTS BY SOCIAL STATUS, WITH PLRE NUMBERS

Gentry: PLRE 1, 3, 4, Ad3, Ad4
Middle class: PLRE 26, 137, Ad30
Nobility: PLRE 2
Privileged person (sometimes with others): PLRE 71, 100, 108, Ad27, Ad30
Privileged person (probable): PLRE 78, 124
Professional: PLRE 5, 6, 7, 8, 9, 10, 11, 12, 13, 15, 16, 17, 18, 19, 20, 21, 22, 23, 24, 25, 27, 28, 29, 30, 31, 32, 33, 34, 35, 36, 37, 38, 39, 40, 41, 42, 43, 44, 45, 46, 47, 48, 49, 50, 51, 52, 53, 54, 55, 56, 57, 58, 59, 60, 61, 62, 67, 68, 69, 70, 72, 73, 74, 75, 76, 77, 79, 80, 81, 82, 83, 84, 85, 86, 87, 88, 89, 90, 91, 92, 93, 94, 95, 96, 97, 98, 99, 101, 102, 103, 104, 105, 106, 107, 109, 110, 111, 112, 113, 114, 115, 116, 117, 118, 119, 120, 121, 122, 123, 125, 126, 127, 128, 129, 130, 131, 132, 133, 134, 135, 136, Ad1, Ad2, Ad5, Ad6, Ad7, Ad8, Ad9, Ad10, Ad11, Ad12, Ad13, Ad14, Ad15, Ad16, Ad17, Ad18, Ad19, Ad20, Ad21, Ad22, Ad23, Ad24, Ad25, Ad26, Ad28
Professional (probable): PLRE 14, 118
Retainer: PLRE 63, 71, 100, Ad29

APND Lists in Preparation (Selected)

Betts, John
   Source: Alain Wijffels, *Late Sixteenth-Century Lists of Law Books at Merton College.*
   Cambridge: LP Publications, 1992.

Bludder, Sir Thomas
   Source: John L. Lievsay and Richard B. Davis, "A Cavalier Library—1643."
   Studies in Bibliography (1954), 6:142–60.

Goodborne, John
   Source: R.G. Marsden, "A Virginian Minister's Library, 1635." *American Historical Review* (1906), 11:328–32.

Harding, Thomas
   Source: Christian Coppens, *Reading in Exile*. Cambridge: LP Publications, 1993.

Jonson, Ben
   Source: David McPherson, "Ben Jonson's Library and Marginalia: An Annotated Catalogue." *Studies in Philology* (1974), 71:23–106 [*Texts and Studies*].

Leech, John
   Source: Alain Wijffels, *Late Sixteenth-Century Lists of Law Books at Merton College.*
   Cambridge: LP Publications, 1992.

Shaw, Peter
   Source: David Pearson, "The Books of Peter Shaw in Trinity College, Cambridge." *Transactions of the Cambridge Bibliographical Society* (1986), 9:76–89.

Additions and Corrections

The following entries in Volumes 1–4 have been revised to include additions and corrections, both substantive and accidental, that have been made to the PLRE database since the publication of Volume 4. A correction to a Volume 4 index follows the revised entries.

1.42 Canones provinciales consilii Collonensis duo volumina
Canones concilii provincialis Coloniensis. (*Councils–Province of Cologne*). Continent: date indeterminable.
Language(s): Latin. Appraised at 5s in 1581.

1.103 expositio fidei Christianae per helvetium
Confessio et expositio simplex orthodoxae fidei [*Helveticae*]. (*Switzerland–Reformed Church*). Zürich: Christoph Froschouer, 1566–1568.
Language(s): Latin. Appraised at 1s in 1581.

1.152 de officio pii viri
Georgius Cassander. *De officio pii ac publicae tranquillitatis vere amantis viri*. Continent: 1561–1566.
Cassander was one of Cox's correspondents. *Language(s)*: Latin. Appraised at 6d in 1581.

1.186 Biblia Castalionis
The Bible. Translated by Sebastian Castalio. Basle: (different houses), 1551–1573.
The editions from 1551 to 1556 were produced either by or at the costs of Oporinus; the 1573 edition was by Petrus Perna. *Language(s)*: Latin.

3.8 Phalaridis Epistolae. in 4°.
Phalaris (spurious). *Epistolae*. Britain or Continent: date indeterminable.
STC 19827 and non-STC. The single English printing is a 1485 quarto. *Language(s)*: Latin Greek (probable).

3.171:1 2. A worke of the truenesse of xpian [Christian] Religion. in 4° (2. bookes)

Philippe de Mornay. *A woorke concerning the trewnesse of the christian religion.* Translated by Sir Philip Sidney and, later, by Arthur Golding. London: (different houses), 15871617.

STC 18149 *et seq.* The number 2. that appears in the left margin and in the parenthetically appended (*2. bookes*) may very well indicate two editions; Mornay's work went through four. The third edition (STC 18151, 1604) was edited by Thomas Wilcox, who dedicated one of his works to Ann, Lady Bacon, a title that may be represented by the preceding entry (3.170). *Language(s)*: English.

3.171:2 [See 3.171:1]

Philippe de Mornay. *A woorke concerning the trewnesse of the christian religion.* Translated by Sir Philip Sidney and, later, by Arthur Golding. London: (different houses), 15871617.

STC 18149 *et seq.* A second copy of 3.171:1. *Language(s)*: English.

3.211 Matthei laei Germani. in 4°.

Matthias Leius and Joannes Nicolaus Secundus. *Mathiae Lei Germani reginae pecuniae liber I.* London: [Eliot's Court Press], 1623.

STC 15439. *Language(s)*: English Latin.

10.15 sermones augustini

Augustine, *Saint*. [*Sermones*]. Continent: date indeterminable.

There are numerous collections, *ad heremitas, De vita clericorum*, and comprehensive. This, by its price, could be one of the larger editions, like Amerbach's, of 1494–1495. See also 10.16. *Language(s)*: Latin. Appraised at 5s 4d in 1507.

14.6 A prymar

Probably [*Liturgies–Latin Rite–Hours and Primers–Salisbury and Reformed*]. Britain or Continent: date indeterminable.

STC 15867 *et seq.* and non-STC. A use other than Sarum is possible. *Language(s)*: Latin. Appraised at 2d in 1509.

33.2 Sermones sancti Augustini

Augustine, *Saint*. [*Sermones*]. Continent: date indeterminable.

Perhaps *Sermones ad heremitas*. Bequeathed to an executor of Jackson's estate, "dno [dominus] Thome Cooke" (see BRUO2, 126 for two Thomas Cookes at Oxford in 1514). *Language(s)*: Latin. Appraised at 3s in 1514.

45.6 Vergilius sine commento

Publius Virgilius Maro. Probably [*Works*]. Britain or Continent: date indeterminable.

STC 24787 and non-STC. *Language(s)*: Latin.

57.6 Parva biblia

The Bible. Britain or Continent: date indeterminable.

STC 2055 and non-STC. Hoppe bequeathed to "Thomas Symondes my bibull with knoppes," with "gret" struck out before "my," which might identify the bequest as this, the smaller (*Parva*) of his Bibles. He also directed "a bibul to remayn in the election annually." See 57.16. *Language(s)*: Latin. Appraised at 16d in 1538.

58.8 sermones Augustini

Augustine, *Saint*. [*Sermones*]. Continent: date indeterminable.

Perhaps the popular *Sermones ad heremitas*, but the appraisal suggests the larger collection. *Language(s)*: Latin. Appraised at 2s in 1539.

58.27 septem psalmi Joannis Fisheri

John Fisher, *Saint and Cardinal*. Probably *This treatise concernynge the fruytfull saynges of Davyd in the seven penytencyall psalmes*. London: (different houses), 1508–1529.

STC 10902 *et seq*. No edition in Latin is known to exist; the Latin entry, however, appears elsewhere in PLRE lists (see PLRE 80.30). All but one of the seven editions before 1529 were printed by Wynkyn de Worde. *Language(s)*: English.

64.15 Euripidis tragedia grecolatina

Euripides. Probably [*Selected works*]. Continent: date indeterminable.

Several editions of the collected works have Greek and Latin title pages, but the first Greek-Latin edition was published in 1562, ten years after this inventory. Perhaps this is a Greek edition and a Latin edition bound together, but a Greek-Latin edition of the *Selected works* is more likely. See Adams E1042. *Language(s)*: Greek Latin. Appraised at 9d in 1552.

64.48 Eiusdem [i.e., Erasmi] apophthegmata

Desiderius Erasmus. *Apophthegmata*. Continent: date indeterminable.

The single edition of the *Apophthegmata* published in England by the date of this inventory is in English. *Language(s)*: Latin. Appraised at 18d in 1552.

65.51 Vasseus in anatomen corporis humani

Lodoicus Vassaeus. *In anatomen corporis humani tabulae quatuor*. Continent: 1540–1553.

Language(s): Latin. Appraised at 8d in 1553.

65.90 Ovidii Metamorphosis

Publius Ovidius Naso. *Metamorphoses*. Continent: date indeterminable.

Language(s): Latin. Appraised at 6d in 1553.

67.17 nonius marcellus

Nonius Marcellus. Probably [*De compendiosa doctrina*]. Continent: date indeterminable.

Language(s): Latin.

67.201 Novum testamentum in frenche

[*Bible–N.T.*]. Britain or Continent: date indeterminable.

STC 2957.6 *et seq*. and non-STC. *Language(s)*: French.

70.43 psalterium
[*Bible–O.T.–Psalms*]. Continent (probable): date indeterminable.
Probably not an STC book, but see STC 2354. *Language(s)*: Latin.
Appraised at 3d in 1562.

72.10 virgilii
Publius Virgilius Maro. Probably [*Works*]. Britain or Continent: date
indeterminable.
STC 24787 and non-STC. *Language(s)*: Latin. Appraised at 4d in 1565.

73.79 pars bibliae
The Bible (part). Britain or Continent: date indeterminable.
STC 2055 and non-STC. Taken to be either a volume of a multi-volume
edition or a damaged single-volume edition. *Language(s)*: Latin. Appraised at
12d in 1566.

73.112 dialec Aug
Probably Augustinus Hunnaeus. [*Aristotle–Organon: commentary*]. Conti-
nent: 1551–1566.
Language(s): Latin. Appraised at 2d in 1566.

73.132 bibli vulg edi
The Bible. Britain or Continent: date indeterminable.
STC 2055 and non-STC. St. Jerome's Vulgate. *Language(s)*: Latin. Ap-
praised at 2s 8d in 1566.

73.181 Caesar
Probably Caius Julius Caesar. *Commentarii*. Continent (probable): date
indeterminable.
Probably not an STC book, but see STC 4335. Because the entries are so
often truncated, an author other than a "*Caesar*" is possible, including
Joannes Caesarius, *Juliacensis* (logic) and Priscianus, *Caesariensis* (grammar),
both of whose writings would fit well in Cliff's collection. *Language(s)*: Latin
(probable). Appraised at 2d in 1566.

73.189 stur in part
Joannes Sturmius. Perhaps *In partitiones oratorias Ciceronis dialogi*.
Continent: 1539–1565.
Language(s): Latin. Appraised at 8d in 1566.

73.248 burle in dial
Walter Burley. [*Aristotle–Selected works–Logica: commentary*]. Britain or
Continent: date indeterminable.
STC 4122 and non-STC. *Language(s)*: Latin. Appraised at 12d in 1566.

73.256 Donatus in Aethi
Donatus Acciaiolus. [*Aristotle–Ethica: commentary*]. Continent: 1478–1566.
Language(s): Latin. Appraised at 2s 1d in 1566.

74.13 Marcellus Palengelius
Marcellus Palingenius (Pietro Angelo Manzolli [Stellatus]). *Zodiacus vitae.* Britain or Continent: 1531?–1566.
Probably not an STC book, but see STC 19148 *et seq. Language(s)*: Latin (probable) English (perhaps). Appraised at 4d in 1567.

76.3 Virgilius
Publius Virgilius Maro. Probably [*Works*]. Britain or Continent: date indeterminable.
STC 24787 and non-STC. *Language(s)*: Latin. Appraised at 4d in 1567.

80.30 fisherus in 7 psalmos penitentiales
John Fisher, *Saint and Cardinal. This treatise concernynge the fruytfull saynges of Davyd in the seven penytencyall psalmes.* London: (different houses), 1508–1555.
STC 10902 *et. seq.* No Latin version of this work is extant. The Latin entry, however, appears elsewhere in PLRE lists (see PLRE 58.27). *Language(s)*: English (perhaps). Appraised at 8d in 1569.

80.34 tria volumina biblie
The Bible (part). Britain or Continent: date indeterminable.
STC 2055 and non-STC. With the relatively low appraisal, the entry would suggest only part of The Bible. *Language(s)*: Latin. Appraised at 6d in 1569.

82.20 biblia latine
The Bible. Britain or Continent: date indeterminable.
STC 2055 and non-STC. *Language(s)*: Latin. Appraised at 2s 6d in 1569.

83.15 biblia
The Bible. Britain or Continent: date indeterminable.
STC 2055 and non-STC. *Language(s)*: Latin. Appraised at 6d in 1570.

84.41 Biblia in translatione hieronymi
The Bible. Britain or Continent: date indeterminable.
STC 2055 and non-STC. St. Jerome's Vulgate. *Language(s)*: Latin. Appraised at 13s 4d in 1570.

84.126 vergilius
Publius Virgilius Maro. Probably [*Works*]. Britain or Continent: date indeterminable.
STC 24787 *et seq.* and non-STC. *Language(s)*: Latin. Appraised at 6d in 1570.

85.29 Vergilius
Publius Virgilius Maro. Probably [*Works*]. Britain or Continent: date indeterminable.
STC 24787 *et seq.* and non-STC. *Language(s)*: Latin. Appraised at 6d in 1570.

86.8 Spsalter
[*Bible–O.T.–Psalms*]. Britain or Continent: date indeterminable.
STC 2354 and non-STC. A liturgical form may, however, be intended. *Language(s)*: English (perhaps) Latin (perhaps). Appraised at 1d in 1570.

93.1 a latayne bible
The Bible. Britain or Continent: date indeterminable.
STC 2055 and non-STC. *Language(s)*: Latin. Appraised at 12d in 1571.

95.11 Dialectica Hunei
Augustinus Hunnae. [*Aristotle–Organon: commentary*]. Continent: 1551–1570.
Language(s): Latin. Appraised at 8d in 1571.

96.56 Rabanus de sacramento eucharistie
Rabanus Maurus. *De sacramento eucharistae*. Cologne: apud Joannem Quentel, 1551.
Adams R4. *Language(s)*: Latin. Appraised at 12d in 1571.

104.37 epistole ovidii
Publius Ovidius Naso. *Heroides*. Continent: date indeterminable.
The less popular *De ponto* is a slim possibility. *Language(s)*: Latin. Appraised at 2d in 1573.

104.48 Epistole Celii 2i
Caelius Secundus Curio. *Selectarum epistolarum libri duo. Orationum liber unus*. Basle: per Joannem Oporinum, 1553.
Language(s): Latin. Appraised at 3d in 1573.

104.52 demostenes de falsa legacione
Demosthenes. *De falsa legatione*. Paris: venundatur Jodoco Badio, 1532.
See BN for what is apparently the only edition; confirmed by Philippe Renouard, *Bibliographie des impressions et des oeuvres de Josse Badius Ascensius* (Paris, 1908), 2:378, where it is erroneously listed under Demosthenes' *De senectute*. *Language(s)*: Greek Latin. Appraised at 4d in 1573.

104.61 dunius de arte medica
Thaddeus Dunus. Probably *Miscellaneorum de re medica*. Continent: date indeterminable.
This work is extant only as a composite publication with Dunus's *Epistolae medicinales* in a 1592 edition, but PLRE 133 (1578) includes an entry *Thaddeus Dunus de re medica* (PLRE 133.116). The rough copy of Kettleby's list reads *dunus* for *dunius*. *Language(s)*: Latin. Appraised at 6d in 1573.

107.52 Schola veneta
Unidentified. Probably from the *Academia Veneta*. Venice (probable): date indeterminable.
There was a great outpouring of books from the Academia Veneta in

1558–1560, including commentaries on the Bible and Aristotle, humanistic works of scholarship, and some original belles lettres. This volume may be the work on the *Topica* published by Paulus Manutius in 1559. See the next item. *Language(s)*: Latin. Appraised at 3s in 1575.

107.78 Velcurio
Joannes Velcurio. Unidentified. Continent: date indeterminable.
Velcurio wrote commentaries on Aristotle's *Physica* and Livy, as well as on Erasmus's *De duplici copia verborum ac rerum*, all published repeatedly during Lombard's lifetime. *Language(s)*: Latin. Appraised at 8d in 1575.

108.75 Apohthonius
Aphthonius, *Sophista. Progymnasmata*. Britain or Continent: date indeterminable.
STC 699 *et seq*. and non-STC. *Language(s)*: Latin. Appraised at 12d in 1575.

109.39 Epistolae Tullii
Marcus Tullius Cicero. [*Selected works–Epistolae*]. Continent (probable): date indeterminable.
Probably not an STC book, but see STC 5295. Among the many versions of Cicero's letters, the popularity of the *Epistolae ad familiares*, which includes the 1573 STC 5295, makes it a reasonable possibility. *Language(s)*: Latin. Appraised at 8d in 1575.

110.186 osorius de gloria
Jeronimo Osorio da Fonseca, *Bishop. De gloria*. Florence: apud Laurentium Torrentinum, 1552.
Conceivably Osorio's *Selected works* with *De gloria* leading. *Language(s)*: Latin. Appraised at 8d in 1576.

112.27 ocham in phisicam
Gulielmus, *de Occam*. [*Aristotle–Physica: commentary*]. Continent: 1494–1506. Shaaber O16–17. *Language(s)*: Latin. Appraised at 5d in 1576.

112.89 osorius de gloria
Jeronimo Osorio da Fonseca, *Bishop. De gloria*. Florence: apud Laurentium Torrentinum, 1552.
Conceivably Osorio's *Selected works* with *De gloria* leading. For other works by Osorio see 112.64 and 112.90. *Language(s)*: Latin. Appraised at 8d in 1576.

112.162 boemus
Joannes Boemus. [*Omnium gentium mores, leges et ritus*]. Continent (probable): date indeterminable.
Probably not an STC book, but see STC 3196.5 *et seq*. Possibly in the partial English translation of 1554 or that of 1555, but quite unlikely. *Language(s)*: Latin (probable) English (perhaps). Appraised at 4d in 1576.

112.170 Biblia Hieronimi
The Bible. Continent (probable): date indeterminable.
Probably not an STC book, but see STC 2055. St. Jerome's Vulgate. Not in
A version of inventory; inserted in B version, included in text of C. The
valuation suggests a particularly fine copy. *Language(s)*: Latin. Appraised at
3s 4d in 1576.

Volume 4 *Index I* (Authors and Works)
 For: Aristotle . . . *Parva naturalia*: 93.7; 94.2; 95.6; 97.56; 108.51; 109.4;
          111.11; 112.28; 112.29
 Read: Aristotle . . . *Parva naturalia*: 93.7; 97.56; *Physica*: 94.2; 95.6; 108.51;
          109.4; 111.11; 112.28; 112.29

ADDRESSES FOR REQUESTING DATA
OR FOR SENDING CORRECTIONS

R. J. Fehrenbach   E. S. Leedham-Green
Department of English   University Archives
College of William and Mary   University Library, West Road
Williamsburg, VA 23187–8795 USA   Cambridge CB3 9DR UK

Index I
Authors and Works

The words *perhaps* and *probable* indicate degrees of doubt about an identification. Names and titles appear in accordance with the methodology described in the introduction to this volume. A search of the database, available upon request, will provide more detailed information, including cross-referencing, than can be offered here.

Albertus, *de Saxonia. Aristotle–De caelo:*
commentary: 137.41

Alchabitius. *Unidentified:* 132.63

Alciati, Andrea. *Emblemata:* 130.110

Alexander, *Anglus. Destructorium vicio-*
rum: 137.21; 137.74

Alexander, *Trallianus. Practica:* 133.13

Alexandrinus, Julius. *Salubrium sive de*
sanitate tuenda: 133.5

Alexandro, Alexander ab. *Geniales dies:*
117.14; 127.80

Alfonso X, *King of Castile. Astronomicae*
tabulae: 135.3

Allen, Edmond. *catechism, A:* 123.39

Almain, Jacobus (probable). *Moralia*
(probable): 130.53

Althamer, Andreas. *Conciliatio locorum*
scripturae: 128.78; 130.94

Amadis, *de Gaule. tresor des livres, Le:*
133.254

Amasaeus, Romulus. *Orationes:* 127.53

Amatus, *Lusitanus, pseudonym. Curatio-*
num medicinialium centuriae duae,
prima et secunda: 133.219; *Curationum*
medicinialium centuriae duae, quinta et
sexta: 133.211; *Curationum medicini-*
alium centuriae duae, tertia et quarta:
133.216

Ammianus, Marcellinus. *Res gestae:*
127.148

Andreae, Antonius. *Aristotle–Metaphy-*
sica: commentary: 137.28

Anonymous. *Here begynneth the seynge of*
uryns: 133.194; *Sermones sensati:*
137.67; *Stella clericorum:* 137.71

Anthologia graeca (perhaps): 127.174

Aphthonius, *Sophista. Progymnasmata:*
126.15; 130.75; 132.51

Apian, Peter. *Cosmographia:* 133.45;
136.34

Appian, of Alexandria. *Historia Romana:*
127.4; 127.184; 134.42

Aquinas, Thomas, *Saint. Aristotle–Phy-*
sica: commentary: 121.7; *Aristotle–Po-*
litica: commentary: 129.112; *Epistles–*
Paul: commentary: 136.4; *Quaestiones:*
130.22; *Sentences II:* commentary:
137.13; *Unidentified:* 127.25; 137.58

Arboreus, Joannes. *Commentarii in qua-*
tuor Domini Evangelistas (perhaps):
121.5; *Theosophia:* 123.1

Arcaeus, Franciscus. *De recta curandorum*
vulnerum ratione [and other works]:
133.115

Aretius, Benedictus (probable). *Problem-*
ata theologica (probable): 128.72

Argenterius, Joannes. *De consultationibus*
medicis: 133.134

Aristophanes. *Pax:* 133.52; *Unidentified:*
128.4; *Works:* 121.12; 123.10; 127.119

Aristotle. *De anima:* 133.163; *De genera-*
tione et corruptione: 130.52; *Ethica:*
115.31;   116.11;   121.23;   123.25;
123.27;   126.29;   128.47;   129.89;
130.19; 130.36; 131.19; 132.6; 133.24;
134.48;   134.71;   135.14;   *Historia*
animalium: 116.6; 133.6; (probable):
135.18;   *Organon:*   118.21;   125.4;
126.10; 132.5; 134.30; 135.3; *Physica:*
116.25; 121.16; 130.59; 130.72; 131.7;
132.7; 133.177; 135.9; 135.28; *Politica:*
116.12;   127.52;   130.43;   130.68;
130.76;   134.16;   *Rhetorica:*   130.79;
Selected works–Logica: 116.20; 120.6;
130.18;   *Selected   works–Philosophia*
naturalis: 129.92; *Selections:* 127.208;
Topica: 129.93;   *Works*   (perhaps):
128.67

Aristotle (spurious). *De mundo:* 134.47;
Problemata: 115.50; 127.199; 127.207;
128.48; 129.107; 130.1

Arnaldus, *de Villa Nova* (probable).
Regulae universales curationis morborum
(probable): 133.82

Arrianus, Flavius. *Expeditio Alexandri:*
126.26

Ars de dosibus medicinarum, et alia prae-
stantissimorum medicorum monumenta
(probable): 133.71

Articella: 132.13

Artemidorus, *Daldianus. De somniorum*
interpretatione: 130.66

Artopoeus, Petrus. *Unidentified:* 137.25

Ascham, Roger. *Familiarium epistolarum*
libri tres: 120.27; 133.102; *Toxophilus,*
the schole of shootinge conteyned in two
bookes: 133.51

Asconius Pedianus, Quintus. *Cicero–*
Selected works–Orations: commentary:
129.78

Athanasius, *Saint. Unidentified:* 122.8;
Works: 127.26

133.84; 133.210; 134.5; 134.84;
135.34; 136.21; (part): 115.28
Acts: 117.18
Epistles: 131.15; 131.38
Epistles–Paul: 131.11; 134.36; 137.16;
137.47
Epistles–Ephesians: 119.11
Epistles–Peter I and II: 119.13
Epistles–Romans: 119.6
Gospels: 115.26; 121.5; 131.3
Gospels and Epistles: 137.75
Gospels and Epistles (liturgical): 128.56
Gospels–John: 116.62; 119.2
Gospels–Matthew: 116.55;   119.4;
127.31:2
Biblical   concordance   (unidentified):
117.9; 130.15; 137.15
Biel, Gabriel. *Sentences: commentary*:
128.76
Billick, Everhard. *Judicii Universitatis et
cleri Coloniensis, adversus calumnias
Philippi Melanthonis, Martini Buceri,
Oldendorpii, et eorum asseclarum defen-
sio*: 123.21
Bizzarus,   Petrus.   *Cyprium   bellum*:
127.163
Boaistuau, Pierre. *Theatrum mundi, the
theatre or rule of the world, wherein may
be sene the course of everye mans life, as
touching miserie and felicity*: 136.41
Boccaccio, Giovanni. *Here begynnethe the
boke calledde John bochas descrivinge the
falle of princis*: 127.41
Bodin, Jean, *Bishop*. *Methodus ad facilem
historiarum   cognitionem*:   127.164;
133.273; *Methodus historica*: 134.19
Boemus, Joannes. *Omnium gentium
mores, leges et ritus*: 116.9; 128.49
Boethius, Anicius M. T. S. *De consolatione philosophiae*: 117.71; 127.45;
(probable): 121.9; *De disciplina scholarium*: 129.62
Boethius, Anicius M. T. S. (probable).
De consolatione philosophiae (probable):
128.10
Boethius, Hector. *Scotorum historiae*:
117.63
Boke of the propertyes of herbes, A:
133.165
Bonaventura,   Saint.   *Unidentified*:
130.63; 137.78

Botallo, Leonardo. *Commentarioli duo,
alter de medici, alter de aegroti munere*
[and other works]: 133.225
Botallo, Leonardo (probable). *Unidentified*: 129.49
Botallo, Leonardo (perhaps). *Unidentified*: 129.23
Boussuet, François. *De arte medendi*:
133.145
Brandolinus, Aurelius. *De ratione scribendi*: 117.40; (perhaps): 129.120
Brasavola, Antonio Musa. *Examen omnium catapotiorum*: 133.57; *Examen
omnium simplicium medicamentorum*:
133.229; *Unidentified*: 129.19
Brentz, Johann, *the Elder*. *Gospels (liturgical): commentary*: 119.17
Bricot, Thomas. *Aristotle–Physica: commentary*: 127.23; 135.25; 137.42; *Aristotle–Unidentified: commentary*:
129.116; *Unidentified*: 137.37
Bridget, *Saint*. *Revelationes celestes*: 113.4
Broickwy a Konigstein, Antonius. *Concordantiae breviores ex sacris Bibliorum
libris*: 130.64
Brudus, *Lusitanus*. *Liber de ratione victus
in singulis febribus secundum Hippocratem*: 129.45; 133.148
Brunfels, Otto. *Catalogus illustrium
medicorum, sive de primis medicinae
scriptoribus*: 133.36; *Neotericorum aliquot medicorum in medicinam practicam
introductiones*: 133.246; *Onomasticon
medicinae*: 133.20
Brunfels, Otto (probable). *Pandectae
scripturarum* (probable): 115.34
Brunus, Conrad. *Opera tria: De legationibus libri quinque. De caeremoniis
libri sex. De imaginibus liber unus*:
127.42
Brusonius, Lucius Domitius. *Facetiarum
exemplorumque libri VII*: 128.94
Bucer, Martin. *Metaphrasis et enarratio in
epistolam ad Romanos*: 119.6
Buchanan, George. *De Maria Scotorum
regina, . . . plena, et tragica planè historia*: 132.70; *Psalms: paraphrase*:
116.29
Budaeus, Gulielmus. *Commentarii linguae graecae*: 128.69; *Unidentified*:
116.49

132.1; *De justitia*: 123.17; 133.96; *De nobilitate civili libri II. De nobilitate christiana libri III*: 115.67; *De rebus Emmanuelis regis Lusitaniae*: 132.2; 133.100; *De regis institutione et disciplina*: 133.98; *In Gualterum Haddonum magistrum libellorum supplicum libri tres*: 116.40; 130.51; 131.30; 133.99; *Selected works*: 116.39; 133.97; *Unidentified*: 131.21

Ovidius Naso, Publius. *Amores*: 133.222; *Fasti*: 123.49; 127.173; 131.29; 132.29; 132.34; *Heroides*: 117.76; 118.11; 127.131; *Metamorphoses*: 121.39; 127.177; 132.35; 133.58; 135.39; *Selected works*: 134.57; *Unidentified*: 132.71; *Works*: 130.96

Palingenius, Marcellus. *Zodiacus vitae*: 116.26; 117.77; 127.179; 131.39; 132.30; 133.252

Pantaleon, Heinrich. *Chronographia ecclesiae christianae*: 117.12

Paris, Matthaeus. *Historia major*: 133.2

Patrizi, Francesco, *Bishop. Compendiosa rerum memorandarum descriptio*: 127.195; *De institutione reipublicae libri novem*: 115.66; *De regno et regis institutione*: 133.247

Patrizi, Francesco, *Bishop* (probable). *Unidentified*: 116.68; 127.170

Patrizi, Francesco, *Philosophical Writer. Discussiones peripateticae*: 133.33

Paulus, *Aegineta. Pharmaca simplicia*: 133.151

Paulus, *Venetus. Aristotle–De anima: commentary*: 135.20; *Expositio super VIII libros Physicorum necno super commento Averrois* (probable): 137.34

Pelbartus, *de Themeswar. Sermones Pomerii*: 136.2; 137.8; 137.68

Peletier, Jacques. *De peste compendium*: 133.187

Peña, Petrus. *Stirpium adversaria nova, perfacilis vestigatio*: 129.9; 133.12

Pepin, Guillaume. *Sermones dominicales*: 114.9

Perez de Valentia, Jacobus, *Bishop. Unidentified*: 115.6

Perion, Joachim. *De dialectica* (probable): 115.16

Perottus, Nicolaus (probable). *Cornucopia*: 127.14; 130.9; (probable): 121.8

Persius Flaccus, Aulus. *Works*: 116.38:B; 130.8:B; 132.75

Peter Lombard. *Sententiarum libri IIII*: 136.29

Petrus, *de Herentals. Psalms: commentary*: 137.63

Peucer, Kaspar. *Elementa doctrinae de circulis coelestibus*: 128.43

Philippson, Joannes, *Sleidanus. De statu religionis et reipublicae, Carolo Quinto, Caesare, commentarii*: 115.13; *Unidentified*: 117.21

Philo, *Judaeus. De mundo*: 130.114; *De nobilitate*: 135.10:B; *In libros Mosis, de mundi opificio, historicos, de legibus*: 122.2

Philoponus, Joannes, *Grammaticus. Unidentified*: 122.5

Pico della Mirandola, Giovanni, *Count. Works*: 130.16

Pictorius, Georg. *Medicinae tam simplices quam compositae* [and other works]: 133.77

Pighius, Albertus. *Controversiarum praecipuarum in comitiis Ratisponensibus tractatarum, explicatio*: 130.49; *Unidentified*: 136.8

Pilotus, Joannes. *Gallicae linguae institutio*: 131.17

Pindar. *Works* (probable): 128.31

Pindar (perhaps). *Works* (perhaps): 130.23

Plato. *Gemmae, sive illustriores sententiae*: 128.25; 129.125

Platt, Sir Hugh. *floures of philosophie, with the pleasures of poetrie annexed to them, The*: 133.181

Plautus, Titus Maccius. *Comoediae*: 115.21; 117.20; 133.209; *Selections–Sententiae*: 133.196

Pliny, *the Elder. Historia naturalis*: 120.15; 128.68; 134.3

Pliny, *the Younger. Epistolae*: 137.46

Plutarch. *Moralia*: 120.13; 126.9; *Unidentified*: 127.32; *Vitae parallelae*: 128.51; 131.22; 133.251; (part): 134.15; *Vitae parallelae–Epitome*: 116.52; 127.194

Plutarch (spurious). *De fluviorum et*

of Fowlers psalter, A: 133.178

Sarcerius, Erasmus. *Loci communes:* 123.35; 128.12

Savonarola, Giovanni Michele. *Libellus singularis de arte conficiendi aquam vitae simplicem et compositam:* 133.167

Schegk, Jacob, *the Elder. Aristotle–Topica: commentary:* 131.4; *In octo Physicorum, sive de auditione physica libros Aristotelis, commentaria:* 135.17

Scheubelius, Joannes. *Compendium arithmeticae artis:* 127.101

Schindler, Valentin. *Institutionum hebraicarum libri V:* 131.16

Schopper, Jacob, *the Elder. Concionum:* 114.17

Schorus, Antonius. *Phrases linguae latinae:* 128.79; *Unidentified:* 129.77

Secundus, Joannes Nicolaus. *Works* (perhaps): 127.171

Securis, John. *detection and querimonie of the daily enormities committed in physick,* A: 133.201

Selneccer, Nicolaus. *In D. Petri apostoli epistolas carmen paraphrasticum et homiliae:* 119.13; *Pedagogia Christiana:* 119.14

Seneca, Lucius Annaeus. *Selections–Flores selecti:* 116.51; *Tragoediae:* 116.22; 121.32; 128.63; 130.90; 133.86; 134.35; 137.36; *Troas:* 133.199; *Works:* 127.122

Sermons (unidentified): 136.15; 136.28; 137.66

Seton, John. *Dialectica:* 120.10

Shepherds' Kalendar: 119.36

Sichardus, Joannes (editor). *Antidotum contra diversas omnium fere seculorum haereses:* 127.37

Siderocrates, Samuel. *Libellus geographicus:* 120.8

Sigonio, Carlo. *De vita, et rebus gestis P. Scipionis Aemiliani liber:* 129.105

Simonius, Simon. *De vera nobilitate:* 133.32; *Questionum dialectarum fragmentum:* 129.64

Smith, Richard, *Dean. De coelibatu sacerdotum liber unus. De votis monasticis liber alter:* 114.24

Socio, Nobile. *De temporibus et modis purgandi in morbis:* 129.106; 133.263

Solinus, Caius Julius. *Polyhistor:* 127.192; 134.18:B

Sophocles. *Works* (probable): 128.90

Spagnuoli, Baptista. *Unidentified:* 132.67; 137.40

Spangenberg, Johann. *Epistles (liturgical): commentary and text:* 131.15; *Margarita theologica:* 120.29

Spinello, Allessandro (probable). *Unidentified:* 127.120

Stadius, Joannes. *Ephemerides:* 135.1

Stanford, Sir William (probable). *plees del coron: divisees in plusiours titles, Les* (probable): 124.6

Stanhufius, Michael. *De meteoris:* 133.124

Stanyhurst, Richard. *Harmonia seu catena dialectica, in Porphyrianas institutiones:* 125.1

Stoeffler, Joannes. *Elucidatio fabricae ususque astrolabii:* 135.12

Strada, Jacobus de. *Epitome thesauri antiquitatum, hoc est, imperatorum romanorum icones:* 127.61

Strebaeus, Jacobus Lodovicus. *Cicero–De partitione oratoria: commentary and text:* 113.14; *Unidentified:* 117.52

Strigelius, Victorinus. *Bible–N.T.: commentary:* 130.29

Sturmius, Joannes. *Classicarum epistolarum, libri III* (perhaps): 128.59; *De imitatione oratoria:* 128.89; *De periodis:* 117.56; *Dialectica:* 115.54; 117.42; *In partitiones oratorias Ciceronis dialogi:* 127.110; 130.39; 132.10; *Unidentified:* 127.103

Suetonius Tranquillus, Caius. *De vita Caesarum:* 115.41; 127.167; 128.62; 130.56

Susius, Joannes Baptista, *Mirandulanus. Liber de sanguinis mittendi ratione:* 129.102

Sussanaeus, Hubertus. *Connubium adverbiorum Ciceronianorum:* 133.118

Switzerland—Reformed Church. *Confessio et expositio simplex orthodoxae fidei [Helveticae]:* 116.66

Sylvius, Franciscus, *of Amiens. In artem oratoriam progymnasmata:* 130.30

Synesius, *Bishop. Unidentified:* 116.74

Index II
Editors and Compilers

Index III
Translators

Alday, John: 136.41
Argyropoulos, Joannes: 130.17

Balamius, Ferdinandus: 129.52
Barbarus, Hermolaus: 115.27; 132.24
Barclay, Alexander: 115.12; 133.60
Bedingfield, Thomas: 133.61
Bèze, Théodore de: 117.13; 119.24; 123.31; 134.5
Bèze, Théodore de (probable): 128.53
Brende, John: 133.127
Brunfels, Otto: 133.151

Castalio, Sebastian: 115.49
Cheke, Sir John: 122.9
Clerke, Bartholomew: 129.73
Clerke, Bartholomew (probable): 135.23
Colinaeus, Jacobus: 133.227
Cornarius, Janus: 129.26; 133.241
Curtius, Jacobus (probable): 114.20

Dolman, John: 134.29
Dubois, Jacques (Jacobus Sylvius): 133.68

Eobanus, Helius, *Hessus*: 116.28; 123.42

Erasmus, Desiderius: 114.22

Filles, Robert: 119.31
Foreiro, Francisco: 4.638

Golding, Arthur: 119.10; 119.11; 133.58; 135.39; 136.18
Gorraeus, Joannes: 133.30
Granthan, Henry (probable): 133.111
Gregorius, Martinus: 133.243
Guinterius, Joannes (Andernacus): 133.232; 133.236; 134.31
Guinterius, Joannes (Andernacus) (probable): 133.16

Haller, Wolfgang: 129.58
Haloander, Gregorius: 114.21
Hellowes, Edward: 130.86
Heywood, Jasper: 133.199
Hoby, Sir Thomas: 123.20; 132.85; 134.7

James, Dane (dom): 113.9
Jerome, *Saint*: 114.23; 115.39; 123.18; 128.21; 130.3; 134.32
Juda, Leo: 136.17

Index IV
Stationers
(Publishers, Printers, Booksellers)

The stationers' names in the annotated book-lists are drawn either from imprints and colophons, which offer the names in a variety of forms, or from bibliographical sources, none of which consistently agrees with another on those forms. For indexing purposes and for searching the database, PLRE has, therefore, constructed a uniform stationers' names list. English stationers' names, with a few exceptions, are derived from the STC, Volume 3; the forms of Continental names derive from a number of sources, including the STC, but most especially Adams. Accordingly, the names below do not always duplicate forms that appear in the annotated book-lists.

Index V
Places of Publication

Antwerp: 127.158; 128.82; 129.34; 129.57; 129.109; 132.25; 133.26; 133.38; 133.46; 133.72; 133.78; 133.113; 133.115; 133.153; 133.171; 133.255; 135.7; 136.5

Augsburg: 133.42; 135.2

Basle: 4.635; 114.10; 115.17; 115.53; 115.64; 116.3; 116.56; 116.59; 117.31:A; 117.31:B; 119.4; 119.6; 119.7; 121.38; 123.7; 123.11; 123.14; 127.17; 127.37; 127.51; 127.60; 127.68; 127.89; 127.101; 127.104:A; 127.104:B; 127.132; 127.156; 127.163; 128.19; 128.73:A; 128.73:B; 128.110; 129.30; 129.31; 129.47; 129.64; 129.68; 129.75; 129.102; 130.33; 130.38; 130.69; 130.93; 131.12; 132.86:A; 132.86:B; 133.1; 133.3; 133.8; 133.28; 133.29; 133.31; 133.34; 133.35; 133.55; 133.57; 133.77; 133.87; 133.95; 133.159; 133.164; 133.168; 133.187; 133.273; 133.274; 133.279; 134.10; 134.19; 134.31; 134.38; 135.4; 135.10:A; 135.10:B; 135.17; 135.26; 136.27; 136.32; 136.35

Bologna: 117.70; 127.53; 129.105; 133.21

Britain: 123.28; 133.47; 133.50; 133.172; 133.191

Britain (probable): 115.5; 117.73; 124.5; 127.229:130; 133.203

Britain or Continent: 113.6; 114.13; 114.16; 115.1; 115.38; 115.39; 115.40; 115.44; 115.46; 115.57; 115.59; 116.2; 116.11; 116.26; 116.28; 116.30; 116.36; 116.41; 116.43; 117.13; 117.33; 117.40; 117.53; 117.58; 117.61; 117.62; 117.63; 117.64; 117.74; 117.75; 117.77; 118.1; 118.3; 118.10; 118.12; 119.3; 119.23; 119.24; 119.25; 120.1; 120.7; 120.23; 120.24; 120.29; 120.30; 121.9; 121.11; 121.17; 121.23; 121.28; 121.35; 121.37; 123.5; 123.15; 123.18; 123.22; 123.23; 123.31; 123.39; 123.42; 123.43; 123.45; 123.49; 125.2; 125.7; 125.8; 125.10; 125.12; 126.2; 126.12; 126.13; 126.15; 126.25; 127.5; 127.11; 127.19; 127.43; 127.49; 127.57; 127.81; 127.102; 127.111; 127.124;

127.125; 127.133; 127.135; 127.138;
127.173; 127.179; 127.189; 127.198;
127.202; 127.213; 128.7; 128.11;
128.21; 128.24; 128.29; 128.30;
128.32; 128.38; 128.47; 128.61;
128.70; 128.74; 128.80; 128.91;
128.111; 128.113; 128.118; 128.123;
129.5; 129.9; 129.74; 129.79; 129.87;
129.88; 129.89; 129.95; 129.97;
129.118; 129.119; 129.120; 129.121;
130.7; 130.11; 130.19; 130.27; 130.31;
130.50; 130.75; 130.101; 130.111;
130.118; 131.19; 131.39; 132.6;
132.15; 132.18; 132.27; 132.28;
132.29; 132.30; 132.32; 132.34;
132.41; 132.44; 132.46; 132.47;
132.49; 132.51; 132.60; 132.62;
132.74; 132.83; 133.11; 133.12;
133.24; 133.79; 133.84; 133.104;
133.182; 133.210; 133.252; 134.4;
134.28; 134.48; 134.50; 134.57;
134.63; 134.72; 134.80; 135.11;
135.34; 136.24; 136.30; 137.2; 137.20;
137.26; 137.28; 137.32; 137.50;
137.52; 137.71; 137.75; 137.76

Cologne: 115.24; 116.7; 127.29; 127.87;
127.97; 128.97; 133.5; 133.98;
133.100; 133.122; 133.133; 133.137;
133.160; 133.264; 135.1; 136.14
Continent:113.1; 113.4; 113.5; 113.8;
113.10; 113.11; 113.13; 113.14;
113.15; 113.16; 114.1; 114.2; 114.3;
114.4; 114.5; 114.8; 114.9; 114.11;
114.12; 114.14; 114.15; 114.19;
114.20; 114.21; 114.22; 114.23;
114.26; 115.2; 115.4; 115.8; 115.9;
115.14; 115.16; 115.19; 115.20;
115.21; 115.22; 115.23; 115.26;
115.27; 115.29; 115.31; 115.32;
115.33; 115.34; 115.35; 115.37;
115.41; 115.42; 115.43; 115.45;
115.47; 115.48; 115.49; 115.50;
115.54; 115.58; 115.61; 115.62;
115.63; 115.66; 115.67; 115.69;
115.70; 115.71; 115.72; 115.73;
115.74; 115.75; 115.76; 115.77; 116.4;
116.5; 116.6; 116.8; 116.10; 116.12;
116.13; 116.14; 116.15; 116.16;
116.17; 116.18; 116.19; 116.20;
116.21; 116.22; 116.23; 116.24;

116.25; 116.27; 116.29; 116.32;
116.33; 116.34; 116.37; 116.38:A;
116.38:B; 116.39; 116.42; 116.44;
116.45; 116.46; 116.47; 116.48;
116.49; 116.50; 116.51; 116.52;
116.53; 116.54; 116.55; 116.57;
116.58; 116.62; 116.67; 116.69;
116.71; 116.72; 116.73; 116.74;
116.75; 116.76; 116.77; 116.80;
116.81; 117.2; 117.3; 117.4:1; 117.4:2;
117.5; 117.7; 117.8:1; 117.8:2; 117.9;
117.10; 117.11; 117.12; 117.14;
117.15; 117.16; 117.17; 117.18;
117.19; 117.20; 117.21; 117.22;
117.24; 117.25; 117.26; 117.27;
117.28; 117.29; 117.30; 117.32;
117.34; 117.35; 117.36; 117.37;
117.39; 117.41; 117.42; 117.45;
117.49; 117.50; 117.52; 117.55;
117.59; 117.65; 117.66; 117.67;
117.68; 117.69; 117.71; 117.72;
117.76; 118.2; 118.5; 118.8:17; 118.9;
118.11; 118.14; 118.15; 118.17;
118.19; 118.20; 118.21; 119.1; 119.2;
119.5; 119.8; 119.15; 119.17; 119.21;
119.22; 119.27; 119.29; 119.30; 120.3;
120.4; 120.5; 120.6; 120.9; 120.12;
120.13; 120.14; 120.15; 120.16;
120.17; 120.19; 120.21; 120.25;
120.26; 120.28; 121.1; 121.2; 121.3;
121.4; 121.6; 121.7; 121.8; 121.10;
121.12; 121.13; 121.15; 121.16;
121.19; 121.20; 121.22; 121.24;
121.25; 121.26; 121.27; 121.29;
121.30; 121.32; 121.36; 121.39;
121.42; 121.44; 122.1; 122.3; 122.4;
122.5; 122.6; 122.8; 122.11; 122.12;
122.13; 122.14; 122.15; 122.16; 123.2;
123.3; 123.4; 123.6; 123.10; 123.16;
123.17; 123.19; 123.21; 123.24;
123.25; 123.26; 123.27; 123.29;
123.30; 123.33; 123.34; 123.35;
123.36; 123.37; 123.40; 123.41;
123.44; 123.46; 123.47; 123.48; 125.3;
125.4; 125.5; 125.9; 125.13; 125.14;
125.17; 126.4; 126.5; 126.6; 126.7;
126.8; 126.9; 126.10; 126.11; 126.14;
126.16; 126.18; 126.19; 126.21;
126.22; 126.23; 126.24; 126.26;
126.28; 126.29; 127.1; 127.3; 127.6;
127.7; 127.8; 127.9; 127.10; 127.12;

Rome: 133.183
Rostock (perhaps): 132.77

Salamanca: 133.186
Solingen: 130.67
Strassburg: 115.15; 117.56; 119.20;
    128.59; 129.38; 129.43; 129.50;
    130.62; 130.84; 130.116; 132.45;
    133.20; 133.36; 133.246

Tübingen: 120.8

Venice: 4.638; 117.51; 127.62; 127.99;
    129.44; 129.45; 131.20; 132.22;
    132.24; 133.13; 133.23; 133.25:1;
    133.25:2; 133.33; 133.37; 133.54;
    133.125; 133.138; 133.148; 133.150;
    133.268; 134.83; 137.34

Wittenberg: 4.632; 4.633; 119.32;
    123.12; 123.13; 128.22; 128.43;
    128.56; 130.100; 131.16; 133.123;
    133.124; 133.157; 134.21

Zürich: 116.66; 129.58; 134.26; 136.17

Index VI
Dates of Publication

Date ranges are not included. The abbreviation *c.* derives from the bibliographical source consulted. The word *probable* is a PLRE qualification.

1560:   133.77;   133.80;   133.168;
135.10:A; 135.10:B; 136.32
1561: 129.31; 133.54; 133.78; 134.29
1562: 119.6; 120.8; 128.39; 128.104;
133.149
1563: 4.638; 116.70; 119.32; 121.40;
128.97; 129.46; 133.95; 133.137;
134.2; 134.11
1564: 119.15; 127.53; 127.127; 129.30;
133.71; 133.159
1565: 121.18; 126.20; 129.38; 133.25:2;
133.225; 133.264; 133.276; 136.5
1566: 132.77; 133.21; 133.35; 133.201
1567: 117.70; 119.13; 127.158; 129.44;
129.67; 130.62; 130.116; 132.45;
133.177; 134.16; 135.15
1568: 116.7; 133.8; 133.38
1569:   127.87;   129.105;   133.171;
133.192; 135.26
1570: 125.1; 129.18; 129.39; 133.31;
133.56; 133.117; 133.127; 133.274
1571:   133.1;   133.2;   133.23;   133.26;
133.33; 133.37; 133.42; 133.76
1571 (probable): 115.10; 132.70

1572: 127.60; 128.56; 133.32; 133.122;
133.181; 133.195
1573: 4.636; 4.637; 129.64; 130.88;
134.66
1574: 117.44; 119.10; 119.18; 127.58;
128.2;   128.17;   128.109;   133.55;
133.115; 133.189; 133.198; 133.202;
133.223
1575:   117.31:A;   117.31:B;   123.12;
127.89;   127.104:A;   127.104:B;
128.73:A; 128.73:B; 130.46; 130.112;
131.16; 132.86:A; 132.86:B; 133.5;
133.111; 133.112
1575 (probable): 128.98
1576: 116.59; 119.34; 121.21; 130.42;
130.89;   132.80;   133.29;   133.211;
133.273; 134.19
1576 (probable): 120.27
1577: 118.4; 118.6; 119.11; 129.108;
130.107; 133.164; 133.205; 134.7
1577?: 133.175
1578: 133.53; 133.178; 133.247
1582: 4.633

1636: 4.634

R. J. Fehrenbach, Professor of English at the College of William and Mary, has specialized in English Renaissance studies since taking his Ph.D. in English and History. His publications include works on historical bibliography, particularly as related to the drama, and on Tudor popular literature and culture. He was chief editor of the computer-generated *A Concordance to the Plays, Poems, and Translations of Christopher Marlowe* (Cornell University Press, 1982).

◇

E. S. Leedham-Green, Deputy Keeper of the Archives and Fellow of Darwin College, Cambridge, holds the D.Phil., having specialized in the classical tradition in English literature, and is a Fellow of the Society of Antiquaries. She has published on archival history and on the history of the book, most notably as editor of *Books in Cambridge Inventories: Booklists from Vice-Chancellor's Court Probate Inventories in the Tudor and Stuart Periods* (Cambridge, 1986). She is General Editor of *Libri Pertinentes*, a bibliographical series relating to sixteenth- and seventeenth-century libraries.

ꟽRTS

ꟽedieval & Renaissance Texts & Studies
is the major publishing program of the
Arizona Center for Medieval and Renaissance Studies
at Arizona State University, Tempe, Arizona.

ꟽRTS emphasizes books that are needed —
texts, translations, and major research tools.

ꟽRTS aims to publish the highest quality scholarship
in attractive and durable format at modest cost.